BODIES AT WAR

BELINDA LINN RINCÓN

BODIES AT WAR

Genealogies of Militarism in Chicana Literature and Culture

THE UNIVERSITY OF ARIZONA PRESS
TUCSON

The University of Arizona Press
www.uapress.arizona.edu

Printed in the United States of America
22 21 20 19 18 17 6 5 4 3 2 1

ISBN-13: 978-0-8165-3585-9 (paper)

Cover design by Miriam Warren
Cover photo: *Tierra y Libertad, before the test shoot* (2012) by Nao Bustamente

Publication of this book is made possible in part by the proceeds of a permanent endowment created with the assistance of a Challenge Grant from the National Endowment for the Humanities, a federal agency.

Library of Congress Cataloging-in-Publication Data
Names: Rincón Belinda Linn, author.
Title: Bodies at war : genealogies of militarism in Chicana literature and culture / Belinda Linn Rincón.
Description: Tucson : : The University of Arizona Press, 2017. | Includes bibliographical references and index.
Identifiers: LCCN 2017010448 | ISBN 9780816535859 (pbk. : alk. paper)
Subjects: LCSH: Mexican American women—Social conditions. | Militarism—United States—History—20th century. | Militarism—United States—History—21st century. | Neoliberalism—United States—History—20th century. | Neoliberalism—United States—History—21st century.
Classification: LCC E184.S75 R56 2017 | DDC 305.48/86872073—dc23 LC record available at https://lccn.loc.gov/2017010448

♾ This paper meets the requirements of ANSI/NISO Z39.48-1992 (Permanence of Paper).

Para Rodrigo,
quien tiene todo mi corazón

For Stella and Lola,
my finest creations, my highest achievements, my deepest loves

CONTENTS

List of Illustrations *ix*
Acknowledgments *xi*

Introduction: Reading Chicana Literature in the Shadow of War 3

1 The Ethics of Chicana Grief and Grievance: Activist and Literary Responses to the U.S. War in Viet Nam 41

2 "Your Safety Net Is Yourself": Neoliberal Militarism in Elena Rodriguez's *Peacetime* 94

3 War, Time, Wound: Anti-Neoliberal Militarism in the Work of Graciela Limón and Lorna Dee Cervantes 120

4 Home/land Insecurities: Chicana/Latina Mothers and the Reproduction of National Security 159

Conclusion: Oneiric Futures 205

Notes *219*
Bibliography *267*
Index *289*

ILLUSTRATIONS

1. "Hispanic families instill important values," U.S. Marines advertisement, 2011 — 4
2. Cpl. Kristine Tejeda providing security in Iraq, 2013 — 29
3. *¡Fuera de Indochina!*, screen print by Rupert García, 1970 — 60
4. Page 1, antiwar pamphlet, *La batalla está aquí*, 1972 — 67
5. Page 5, antiwar pamphlet, *La batalla está aquí*, 1972 — 70
6. Page 4, antiwar pamphlet, *La batalla está aquí*, 1972 — 72
7. Screenshot of online flash game Border Patrol — 167
8. "Su entrenamiento empezó en casa," U.S. Marines advertisement, 2007 — 174
9. Illustrated page from bilingual children's book *Good Night Captain Mama*, 2013 — 181
10. *Resist U.S. Imperialism*, screen print by Favianna Rodriguez, 2007 — 213
11. "Test Shoot for *Tierra y Libertad*," by Nao Bustamante, 2012 — 216

ACKNOWLEDGMENTS

WHEN WORKSHOPPING OR PRESENTING SECTIONS of *Bodies at War*, I was often asked about what compelled me to write about war. Although I was always happy to respond—the question was, after all, a sign of interest in my work—I also regarded the query as the perfect example of the very presumptions about gender, war, and militarism that I had set out to examine in this book. For me, underlying the question is the notion that war is more properly a man's field of inquiry. I suspect that if I were writing about cookbooks, I would not be asked about my interest in the subject or my motives for writing. If I were a man, I probably would not be asked this question at all; my interest might be regarded as self-evident or presupposed. In *Bodies at War*, I analyze how our views on war and gender manifest and how Chicana cultural production and activism force us to examine our unstated assumptions.

The actual answer to the question is rooted in feminism, the mode of inquiry that I use to critique war and militarism. As part of generation X, I came of age in the nineties, when the first U.S. invasion of Iraq—the Persian Gulf War (1990–91)—reignited the perennial debate about women in combat. As a teen, I had already developed a feminist consciousness that rejected the arguments I heard about women's supposed physical and mental incapacities to handle combat. It was around that time that I considered joining the U.S. Army. Without fully understanding the geopolitical, economic, and imperial motivations behind the U.S. invasion, I was nonetheless entranced by the heightened wartime patriotism and nationalism that dominated the media. I further believed what recruitment advertising promised: that military training could help me break out of my shell. I would enter basic training as a shy, quiet schoolgirl and come out a confident, self-assured, and assertive woman. As a college-bound kid from a Chicano working-class family, I also knew that I needed a way to cover tuition costs. For these reasons, I briefly joined a program for high school students interested in enlisting in the California Army National Guard, where I learned how to silently approach an "enemy" from behind and how to rappel down rocks and other tall structures.

I also had a long-standing interest in my father's service during the U.S. war in Viet Nam. I remember seeing black-and-white pictures of him dressed in fatigues in the middle of a jungle. Another picture showed him standing next to his locker in the barracks as a young man, strong and full of life. I often wondered what his experience in war was like, a curiosity that eventually translated into my research on the military draft, Chicano casualty rates, and Chicana/o antiwar activism. That research helped me put a historical and political context to the photos and stories I had heard through the years. Fortunately, he returned from the war unharmed and eventually settled down with my mother. Despite the family military legacy, the promise of ontological transformation, tuition money, and the desire to prove that women were not "weak," I chose a different path. Yet, I honor the feminist impulses in my younger self, even as my understanding of feminism has evolved over the years. Although my teenage self subscribed to the more dominant, yet limited, form of liberal feminism that emphasized women's equality and advancement, I eventually came to understand that feminism is at its most visionary and ethical when it advocates not only for institutional inclusion and equality, but also for institutional and social transformation.

Not until graduate school did I have the chance to sit with my past and my could-have-been life and carefully examine the choices I had made. Several people guided my initial exploration into the topic and pushed me to think historically, theoretically, and creatively about Mexicanas, Chicanas, and war. Mary Pat Brady, Helena María Viramontes, Debra Castillo, and Raymond Craib gave me their time, expertise, and support, which made *Bodies at War*, the eventual iteration of my dissertation, possible. I also want to acknowledge how I have been blessed throughout the years with the continued support, advice, and friendship of Mary Pat and Helena—two intellectual pillars of Chicana studies.

In the years I spent writing and rewriting this book, many of the people who came in and out of my life each left an important imprint on me and this project. Gretchen Flesher Moon, Ken Nolley, Mike Chasar, and Frann Michel welcomed me to Willamette University and gave me my first sense of how academic departments can function as collegial and productive spaces. I also want to thank several colleagues who offered support and advice along my journey to the book's completion. Dionne Espinoza and Lorena Oropeza—two scholars whose work on Chicanas in the movement were early inspirations for this project—offered important advice. I thank Jeremy K. Saucier and Melissa T. Brown for being gracious enough to respond to my e-mails about how to obtain copyright permission from the U.S. military. My gratitude goes especially to Arlene Dávila and Sonia Saldívar-Hull, whose encouragement for my project came at a critical time and renewed my confidence in the book. I am further grateful for the many people who have kindly aided my efforts in seeking external funding to support this project. They include José Aranda, María Herrera-Sobek, Suzanne Oboler, Lisandro Pérez, Ben Olguín, Ramón Saldívar, Paula Moya, Yolanda Padilla, and Jorge Mariscal.

I have benefited from several readers who gave feedback and advice that helped me transform inchoate writing into a more refined argument. I want to acknowledge them here, beginning with Rodrigo Rodríguez, who is always the most careful reader of my work. I had the great fortune to participate in two extremely generative faculty writing fellowships sponsored by the City University of New York. I thank Shelly Eversley for her masterful and inspiring facilitation of the CUNY Faculty Fellowship Publication workshop and my generous coparticipants: Dongshin Chang, Gloria Fisk, Elyse Zucker, Hyo Kim, Tara Pauliny, and Richard Perez. I also benefited from an intellectually rejuvenating faculty fellowship at the Center for Place, Culture, and Politics led by David Harvey, Sujatha Fernandes, and Ruth Wilson Gilmore. I thank them and the following colleagues for pushing me to rethink some of my claims and to sharpen my focus: Noelia Díaz, Christina Heatherton, Jacob Lederman, Stephen McFarland, Keith Miyake, Preeti Sampat, Asaf Shamis, Tom Angotti, Libby Garland, Suha Kudsieh, Karen Miller, Irina Carlota Silber, Jarrett Martineau, and José Ribiero Jr. I was also fortunate to participate in the inaugural Young Scholars Symposium organized by the Institute for Latino Studies at the University of Notre Dame.

There, I enjoyed the warm hospitality and support of the program's directors, José Limón and Timothy Matovina. I also met great colleagues, who are doing exciting work to advance the field of Latina/o studies: Arlene Dávila, Priscilla Leiva, Jesse Mumm, Michael Rodríguez-Muñiz, Jonathan Rosa, Belkys Torres, Marisel Moreno, and Jason Ruiz. I am grateful to the Colloquium for Research in Latina/o Culture and Theory for allowing me to present a section of the book, particularly Bill Orchard and Laura Lomas for their intellectual engagement and for taking the time to give my draft a thorough reading. I thank Eddy Alvarez and R. Neville Choonoo for being such gracious hosts and inviting me to share my work at the State University of New York at Oneonta. A Ford Foundation Postdoctoral Fellowship made a significant part of this book possible by giving me time to reengage with my writing and research. I thank Jorge Mariscal for agreeing to serve as my Ford mentor and for laying the foundation for this book through his own scholarship and experience as a Chicano Viet Nam veteran.

I could not have successfully completed this book nor could I thrive as a teacher and scholar without an academic department—actually, two departments—supporting my work. My colleagues in the Latin American and Latina/o Studies Department at John Jay College of Criminal Justice, CUNY, offered critical advice and friendship and continue to inspire me with their own scholarship and scholar-activism: Lisandro Pérez, Suzanne Oboler, José Luis Morín, Luis Barrios, Brian Montes, Jodie Roure, John Gutiérrez, and Isabel Martínez. I also thank Christopher Aviles and Jacqueline Nieves for all their assistance and friendship. In the English Department, my second home, I owe special gratitude to Allison Pease and Richard Perez for being such stalwart allies throughout the years.

I am proud that *Bodies at War* will contribute to the University of Arizona Press's impressive literary and theoretical intervention in the field of Chicana/o and Latina/o studies. Working with Kristen Buckles, interim editor-in-chief, has been one of the highlights of this project. I thank Kristen for her enthusiasm for my work, her commitment to my success, and her patience in dealing with my missed deadlines. I also thank the members of the UAP staff, who perform the critical yet invisible labor necessary to publishing academic books, including Leigh McDonald and freelancer Melanie Mallon. I owe a special debt to the press's anonymous readers whose detailed responses and suggestions helped me polish some of the manuscript's rougher edges. While I could not address all their concerns, I value their insight and claim all remaining errors and oversights.

This book would not be complete without the images and artwork that inspired my analysis of Chicana literature and activism. I thank the artists and activists who generously allowed me to reprint their work in *Bodies at War* and for offering their insights and feedback: Nao Bustamante, Rupert García, Favianna Rodriguez, Graciela Tiscareño-Sato, and Lea Ybarra.

Finally, I thank my parents, Rosa and Sobel Rincón, and sister, Irene, for giving me the sturdy foundation of a home filled with love. My wonderful niece and nephews, Renee, Robert, and Ryan, eventually came along and added to its reservoir. My parents' humor, work ethic, sacrifices, and love shaped the person I have become. This book is a small token to them from an appreciative and loving daughter.

I struggle to write these last few lines because there really are no words to describe my profound gratitude for my husband, Rodrigo. There are no ways to count the many sacrifices he has made or to measure the impact of his unflagging faith in me. Like a delicate vein of gold embedded in coarse granite, his love, support, advice, and wisdom have been a constant resource that enabled me to write the words on the following pages. This book is dedicated to Rodrigo and to our Stella and Lola, who came into our world and made it beautiful, gave it meaning. I thank them for showing me where to find life-sustaining joy: in a baby's giggle, in a tiny hand's grasp around a finger, in a dimpled cheek. I hesitate to think about the future that awaits them, but I offer this book as my small contribution to making it better.

BODIES AT WAR

INTRODUCTION

Reading Chicana Literature in the Shadow of War

IN CELEBRATION OF HISPANIC HERITAGE MONTH, the U.S. Marine Corps disseminated its annual pro-Latina/o advertising campaign, entitled Family Values. One ad featured two Latinos and one Latina dressed in full military regalia, staring straight into the camera (figure 1). Below the resolute countenances and erect postures of the three service personnel, a caption heralds Hispanic families and the Marine Corps as twinned institutions that produce honorable, courageous, and committed citizens. For many, the image of Latinas/os in uniform is familiar. The Marine uniform is an emblem of pride, honor, and commitment to the nation and was symbolic of national inclusion for a generation of Mexican American men during and after World War II.[1] But the history of U.S. military invasion of Mexico is also ritually embroidered into the Marine uniform. According to the Marines' official website, "The scarlet stripe on the trouser leg is the 'blood stripe,' which was earned in 'the halls of Montezuma' during the Mexican War."[2] Thus, Mexican defeat in 1848 becomes part of institutional history and is embedded in the uniform worn by servicemen and women. Yet, the militarization of these Latina/o bodies is more than a matter of uniforms. Militarization is a social process that also induces an internal process, an ontological transformation that shapes values, beliefs, and practices. This is also how the Marines perceive militarization. "Honor, Courage, and Commitment" are at the "core" of the Marine body. The Latina and Latino bodies in the ad are thoroughly

FIGURE 1. "Hispanic families instill important values," U.S. Marines advertisement during Hispanic Heritage Month, 2011. The eagle, globe, and anchor emblem; term *Marines*; and slogan "The Few. The Proud" are trademarks of the U.S. Marine Corps. Courtesy of the Marine Corps Association and Foundation, http://www.mca-marines.org.

militarized—inside and out; their rigid, uniformed bodies manifest the physical comportment and properly internalized values that the Marines claim to foster and instill.

But what about the Latina in the background of the Family Values ad? What is her function in the project of empire and how are we supposed to read her body's uniformed presence? On the one hand, some might read her presence as a sign of gender and racial equality within a progressive and inclusive institution. If we momentarily put aside this feminist militarist claim of equality and read the Latina Marine's body as specifically Mexican American, we might then ask about the kind of narratives of Chicana femininity that are required to make images of Chicanas in uniform intelligible and appealing to potential recruits and their families. We might also seek to place her body within a larger borderlands history where war is the cause of historical wounding. In her poem "To Live in the Borderlands Means You," Gloria Anzaldúa reminds us that the mestiza embodies the site of violent conflict:

In the Borderlands
you are the battleground

where enemies are kin to each other;
you are at home, a stranger,
the border disputes have been settled
the volley of shots have shattered the truce
you are wounded, lost in action
dead, fighting back[3]

Borderlands/La Frontera (1987), the collection of essays and poetry from which Anzaldúa's poem is taken, makes clear that war is not only a metaphor of the borderlands, but also the reason for the border's existence in the first place. Through martial metaphor, the poem captures the confusion and contradiction that war creates. The work addresses a mestiza whose body remembers and is subsequently dismembered by previous histories of interstate violence. The violence is manifested in what Anzaldúa famously refers to as the "herida abierta," an open wound simultaneously reproduced on the mestiza body and on the land patrolled by "hunters in army-green uniforms" who "stalk and track" migrants and refugees along an intensely militarized border.[4] Anzaldúa contends that the U.S.-Mexican War left its mark on generations of borderland peoples: "*Con el destierro y el exilo fuimos desuñados, destroncados, destripados*—we were jerked out by the roots, truncated, disemboweled, dispossessed, and separated from our identity and our history."[5] In Anzaldúa's accounting, war leaves intimate traces of deracination experienced internally through the rending of bodily organs—a wound so deep as to be constitutive and irremediable. Thus, there is an epistemology of the wound. The body becomes both a "history and a map"—an embodied knowledge of historical conflict and gender oppression that shapes cultural identity.[6] In this sense, the Chicana-body-as-battleground provides a counterpoetics to the military uniform's official history of war and imperialism. The body underneath the uniform, the body that is literally vested in state power, becomes a site of agency and change, for, although wounded, the body fights back.

Chicana historian Antonia Castañeda argues that the marks left behind by martial histories leave border people sensitively attuned to the reiteration of war in manifold guises. The United States' recent and ongoing wars in the Middle East are familiar, if not uncanny, for inhabitants of the militarized U.S.-Mexico border, a region that has been repeatedly reshaped by warfare over the past five hundred years.[7] For people in the borderlands, "Las garras nuevas del imperialismo are anything but new."[8] Like old rags worn out by constant use, the repetition of imperialism's tropes appear to be new only to those who have the luxury of not living in militarized zones scarred by a violent past of territorial aggression and constant displacement. The Marine uniform—as an example of *las garras nuevas del imperialismo*—represents the violent borderlands history that Castañeda and Anzaldúa describe. It also calls attention to how the Chicana Marine's body is doubly inscribed by the "blood stripe" of Marine imperial attire and the borderland's history of conquest, which has given rise to today's militarized borders.

In the wake of unending U.S. military intervention abroad and collapsing domestic economies, scholars have turned their attention to neoliberalism and militarization, two ideological and material projects that are often treated as coincident, though not interdependent. *Bodies at War* examines neoliberal militarism, a term that signifies the complex ways in which neoliberalism and militarism interanimate each other as they naturalize dis/empowering notions of masculinity and femininity, alter democratic practices, and circumscribe the meaning of citizenship and national belonging. More than a set of economic policies, neoliberalism represents a political rationality that extends beyond the market and influences social practices and behaviors. Similarly, militarism has never been confined to just the battlefield or the barracks; rather, it pervades all aspects of society as it seeks cultural legitimacy. Taken together, both ideologies are coimplicated in shaping the changing social and political relations within the United States, a transformation that can be traced through an analysis of Chicana/o cultural production and activism.

Bodies at War examines the rise of neoliberal militarism from the early seventies to the present and its transformation of political, economic, and social relations. It charts neoliberal militarism's destructive impact on democratic practices, economic policies, notions of citizenship, race relations, and gender norms by focusing on how these changes affect the Chicana/o community. More specifically, I follow the multiple ways in which neoliberal militarism gets inscribed on Chicana bodies and how the body becomes a site from which to theorize the effects of war on the self, community, and nation. The process of bodily inscription—by discourse and state policies, by physical violation and trauma, by internalization, routinized behavior, and acquiescence—is often violent. From the end of the U.S. war in Viet Nam to the interminable war on terror, neoliberal militarism has relied on racialized and gendered bodies to function effectively and efficiently. I argue that the Chicana body is a critical index of neoliberal militarism's transformation of democracy, citizenship, and civic engagement as well as women's relationship to the state. Chicana authors and activists are critical of how the dominating narrative frames of war determine bodily precarity and how the state uses injured bodies to legitimate war. Their texts can help us construct alternative interpretive frames, expanding our affective responses to the bodily injury of others. I read Chicana literary, visual, and activist texts as a critical intervention that exposes the authorizing forces behind neoliberal militarism's discursive and material practices. What I am after is a way to understand how neoliberal militarism leaves its markings on Chicana bodies and what these inscriptions tell us about how states wage war, how we oppose or acquiesce to state violence, and how Chicana authors and activists can help us imagine alternatives to war.

War can take on various modes and scales ranging from a confined civil conflict to global multilateral warfare—all of which are defined by multiple levels of violence. Narrative often tames the chaos of violence by providing war with justifications, reasons, and the stuff from which national identities, patriotism, and militarized gender norms are constructed. Without literary narrative, war becomes what it is in fact: naked, discrete acts of violence. Literature is central to warfare because through the literary form, writers often portray war as a cohesive national narrative. Nationalist literature frequently buttresses official war narratives, becoming what Miriam Cooke calls the dominant or state "War Story" that "shapes reality as we would like it to be or as the government says it was."[9] Eventually, war becomes a "system of signs that we read without much effort because they have become so familiar to us."[10] To think of war as a "system of signs" is not meant to be a postmodernist detraction from the material reality of destruction and violence that war produces. Rather, I use it to emphasize how large-scale acts of devastation are made acceptable and comprehensible only with the aid of narrative framing. For Jean Bethke Elshtain, paraphrasing the work of Nancy Huston, narrative has a direct and recursive material impact as "war imitates war narrative imitating war."[11] If this is so, then literature becomes the first critical step in any antiwar ethic and praxis. Through literature, we can imagine how to write wars anew, and more importantly, we can begin to write war, in general, out of existence.

Chicanas' experiences of war and their critiques of patriarchal militarism are often neglected in studies of war, even though, as Cynthia Enloe points out, the "militarization of women has been necessary for the militarization of men."[12] Like Enloe, I am interested in seeing the militarization of women as more than a means to an end. Rather, my concern is to track how neoliberal militarism disciplines, regulates, and often destroys Chicana bodies and how these disciplined bodies are used to perpetuate the enduring gender constructs that enable warfare and its ideological underpinnings, constructs that include patriotic mothers and devoted sisters, feminized citizenries and feminist soldiers. Yet, by arguing that Chicana bodies are being militarized, I am not suggesting that Chicana bodies are blank or inert presocial surfaces awaiting inscription, for, as Judith Butler notes, there "is no reference to a pure body which is not at the same time a further formation of that body."[13] Rather, I read the physicality of Chicana bodies as "indissociable from the regulatory norms that govern their materialization and the signification of those material effects."[14] There is not only no prediscursive Chicana body, but also no such thing as "the Latina body," which, as Myra Mendible asserts, is "a convenient fiction—a historically contingent, mass-produced combination of myth, desire, location, marketing, and political expedience."[15] Instead of fostering reductive notions of passive or homogenous Latina embodiment, I draw on Mendible's claim that Latina bodies are "site[s] of knowledge production."[16] That is, Latina bodies inhabit "the interstices where lived reality and public fantasies converge" and where subjects negotiate competing discourses to become agents "in the constitution and decoding of our ethnic corporeality."[17] I would further add that Chicana writers use narrative to explore how bodies can function as incompliant, disobedient bodies that contest neoliberal militarism's corrective tactics. Chicana bodies become sources of communal and self-empowerment as Chicana authors write from a place of embodied experience to make political claims about and ethical challenges to war and militarism.

DEFINING NEOLIBERAL MILITARISM

Although pronounced in the post-9/11 context of the global war on terror, the relationship between neoliberalism and militarism actually began decades before the attacks on September 11, 2001, and can be traced to the end of the U.S. war in Viet Nam and the dominating influence of neoliberal economic policies. I provide a rough sketch of these origins to historicize neoliberal militarism in specific times and places and to point out its continuities and permutations from the seventies to the present. These decades represent significant periods for the rise of neoliberal militarism and for the Chicana antiwar activist and the Chicana soldier—two figures routinely overlooked in the fields of Latina/o and feminist studies.[18]

The tenets of neoliberal economic philosophy seem easy enough to enumerate: deregulation, privatization, free-market capitalism, and the decline of the welfare state. In this study, I am more interested in how these economic principles are translated into politics, or how neoliberalism functions as a mode of governance. My use of neoliberalism is informed by Aihwa Ong's description of neoliberal governmentality, a technology of governing that promotes the "government of free individuals who are then induced to self-manage according to market principles of discipline, efficiency, and competitiveness."[19] This is a form of governing that camouflages its own techniques of control and masquerades as nongoverning because it is premised on an unfettered individualism. People are free to make their own decisions without coercive pressures from the state, a condition that produces optimal consumer sovereignty and, proponents argue, optimal citizens. Ensuring freedom of choice requires the curtailment of state regulation and interference. Neoliberal governmentality's subject-making potential, however, is counterbalanced by its practices of subjection. Ong describes how neoliberalism uses "technologies of subjectivity," which prompt an individual's self-government, and "technologies of subjection," whereby entire populations are managed and controlled by governing regimes invested in optimizing resources and productivity.[20] Thus, neoliberalism operates within the multiscalar logic of biopolitics, which oscillates between "freedom" and regulation, as well as between individuals and populations. I show how the practices of disciplining "free" individual bodies and regulating populations for optimal well-being are at work in the figure of the volunteer soldier and through the biopolitics of military recruitment, in which the military targets poor and working-class youth of color to maintain national security. When paired with militarism, neoliberalism's market-driven principles of individualism, choice, and self-management produce conditions in which Latina/o communities have the freedom to choose among limited options that merely promise to improve their lives.

The notion of a neoliberal military is almost a contradiction in terms because the former term promotes individualism, and the latter requires the diminution of self. An ideology that privileges individual autonomy over collective attachment and obligation seems at odds with the military's ethos and organizational character. The military works to diminish individuality and autonomy in order to promote a central hierarchal command structure that minimizes individual choice and encourages esprit de corps, the spirit of a corporate unified body that eschews personal prerogatives for the sake of serving the state. Yet, the dissonance between the two ideologies only highlights neoliberalism's adaptive abilities and moments of mutability when it breaks with its traditional form to engender newer, more complex instantiations of power.[21] The marriage between neoliberalism and the U.S. military is such an instance where neoliberalism meshes with traditionally antithetical principles—patriotism, collective identity, personal sacrifice—to reproduce itself de novo.[22]

I define militarism as an ideology and discursive practice by which military institutions and discourses are imbricated into the social and cultural spaces of the home, family, workplace, schools, and so on. Militarism includes rituals of power, the circumscription of language, and the delimited practice of democratic citizenship. As an ideology that promotes an uncritical deference to the military and its role in society, militarism entails the belief that a hierarchical organization of society is preferable to democratic contestation and deliberation. As Michael Hardt and Antonio Negri make clear, "War always requires strict hierarchy and obedience and thus the partial or total suspension of democratic participation and exchange."[23] In other words, "Democracy does not belong to war." Instead, militarism's objective is to professionalize and naturalize violence in the name of national security. Its authoritarian organization scheme and its ethic of discipline and conformity make it, according to some supporters, the ideal model on which other institutions should be based. The military's efficiency is due largely to its emphasis on uniformity and de-emphasis on individualism—although the neoliberalization of military culture, as I explain momentarily, complicates this notion.

Militarism is so pervasive that we often fail to recognize how it shapes our own beliefs and assumptions about gender, violence, and state power. Enloe succinctly lists militarism's main tenets:

> (a) that armed force is the ultimate resolver of tensions; (b) that human nature is prone to conflict; (c) that having enemies is a natural condition; (d) that hierarchical relations produce effective action; (e) that a state without a military is naïve, scarcely modern, and barely legitimate; (f) that in times of crisis those who are feminine need armed protection; and (g) that in times of crisis any man who refuses to engage in armed violent action is jeopardizing his own status as a manly man.[24]

The values that Enloe attributes to militarism should be familiar to all of us, not necessarily because we endorse them, but because militarism is one of the most enduring and seductive ideologies around. We notice its machinations when it is explicitly on display in parades and other flag-waving events, but we should also think about how it silently permeates our everyday lives and our perceptions of how society should be ordered. As Slavoj Žižek reminds us, "An ideology is really 'holding us' only when we do not feel any opposition between it and reality—that is, when the ideology succeeds in determining the mode of our everyday experience of reality itself."[25] When and if we accept militarism's values as "natural" to human affairs, militarism succeeds in delegitimizing or negating other conceivable forms of sociality.

By focusing on Chicana embodiment, *Bodies at War* allows for a close examination of the kind of femininities that militarism (re)produces. One of the most important aspects of militarism is how it relies on normative *and* progressive constructions of femininity—a fact that often goes unobserved because masculinity tends to dominate gender analyses of war. In other words, while militarism is premised on gender norms that feminize defenselessness and masculinize protection, it also enables and relies on militarized forms of feminist agency. I use a feminist lens to advance a nuanced definition of neoliberal militarism that views it as an ideological and material form of violence against women deployed in the service of patriarchal state power and capital. I examine its preoccupation with femininities, sexualities, and women's bodies to expose its attempt to dominate women, delimit their autonomy, and degrade notions of the feminine. Yet, to say that neoliberal militarism is founded on the domination of women in a process that is often violently enacted is not to say that all men are violent. Like George Mariscal, I reject those studies of war "that mistakenly identify violent behavior as an essential quality of 'masculinity' or pretend to find its extreme forms within a particular ethnic group."[26] Violence is not inherent in men, nor is it an "essential quality" of masculinity. As Susan Jeffords argues in *The Remasculinization of America* (1989), any attempt to establish causality between war and gender "is itself symptomatic of the system that produces both."[27] The desire to wage war is not an urge located in biological man. Furthermore, war does not precede patriarchy; rather, it is "an eruption of systems already at work in patriarchal structures."[28] War perpetuates male dominance over women and the feminine, which can and often does include the feminization of other men. At no point does *Bodies at War* link war and violence to biological dispositions. To do so is not only grossly inaccurate, but also contradictory to my argument about militarism's norming practices and apparatuses. That is, to accept and participate in war and violence, men and women must be taught and trained through forms of indoctrination that are pervasive and persuasive but not incontestable.

As a distinctive ideology, militarism requires a continuous sociopolitical process, or the militarization of society, for its success.[29] It relies on social processes because it must condition society to ideologically accept the state's resort to violence and the toll paid in human lives and to legitimate the exorbitant public spending needed to maintain a highly technical military force.[30] Kathy Ferguson and Phyllis Turnbull see militarization as a "dynamic, contested process of constituting a particular kind of order, naturalizing and legitimating that order, while simultaneously undermining competing possibilities of order."[31] It relies on narratives of naturalization in which military institutions and discourses become embedded within quotidian life.[32] By claiming to ward off invasion or armed attack, proponents of militarization reassure the general public's sense of security, order, and peace. The Chicana antiwar activism and literature discussed here denaturalize the social processes of militarization by challenging militarism's comforting and pervasive narratives.

As a social process concerned with the reproduction of norms (the belief that war is an acceptable form of conflict resolution, that the abrogation of constitutional rights is necessary for national defense, etc.) and of normative behaviors (displaying patriotic support for war, buying toy soldiers and guns for children, etc.), militarization is relentless. It needs to be to continuously reaffirm its taken-for-grantedness. Yet, it is incredibly vulnerable, always on the verge of inefficacy, because normative production is an "iterable process" and thus is always "shadowed by its own failure."[33] In this sense, militarization not only relies on gender, but also is similar to how gender functions. One can repeat or refuse to repeat or differently repeat the normative injunctions of a prowar, promilitary culture. Chicana war literature expresses multiple reactions to militarization, showing how individuals can affirm or challenge the demands of militarization as well as the social consequences they face for doing so.

THE ASCENT OF THE NEOLIBERAL MILITARY

I locate the rise of the neoliberal military in the late sixties and early seventies, when the U.S. military experienced a fundamental challenge to its institutional identity as the debates over conscription went on in the waning years of the U.S. war in Viet Nam. At that point, a newly reelected Richard Nixon convened the Gates Commission, composed in part of leading economic scholars, including Milton Friedman and Walter Oi, to investigate the feasibility of an all-volunteer force (AVF). The commission's final report provides a glimpse into how neoliberalism's market-based logic gradually transformed traditional military practices, policies, and protocols. Friedman and Oi critiqued the draft for infringing on the neoliberal principles of free choice, opposition to government intervention, and market rationality in individual decision making. The eventual switch to an AVF led to new recruitment strategies, including competitive salaries, enlistment and resigning bonuses, and more comprehensive housing and medical benefits.

The military's reorientation to a volunteer force can only be understood within the context of the seventies, a tumultuous period economically and socially. The decade was marked by the devalued dollar, high unemployment and inflation, oil embargoes, capital flight, outsourcing, mechanization, tax revolts, and a global recession.[34] Ruth Wilson Gilmore argues that when the state shifted from fulfilling its "Keynesian job to produce equilibrium from profound imbalances" to securing private and corporate wealth, the result was a national surplus of finance capital, land, and labor.[35] These surpluses generated new crises for the state because "within any system of production, the idling, or surplusing, of productive capacities means that the society dependent on that production cannot reproduce itself as it had in the past."[36] Surplus human labor—resulting from capital flight, un/underemployment, and canceled state-run jobs programs—produced dire consequences for many sectors of the nation, particularly communities of color. Gilmore notes that prisons became California's solution to absorbing the varied surpluses produced by the state's abandonment of Keynesian policies. While the prison-industrial complex resolved California's self-generated surplus labor crisis, a different yet complementary government institution, the U.S. military, partly did the same nationwide, as Deborah Cowen and Amy Siciliano suggest: "National militaries . . . are means of managing the poor, and of warehousing reserve armies of labour."[37] As I show in chapter 1, plans for the absorption of surplused men and women from the working class are clearly spelled out in the Gates Commission report, as military planners and neoliberal architects based future projections of an AVF on the permanent availability of the economically marginalized. In fact, the ascent of the neoliberal military was simultaneous to the decline of the welfare state. With the rise of what Jennifer Mittelstadt calls the "military welfare state," it is no surprise that the elimination of the draft was initially successful in attracting personnel because of a struggling U.S. economy with high levels of youth unemployment.[38] Large portions of the enlistees were unemployed young black men and women of all races who may have been influenced by the women's movement "to regard the military as a channel for mobility."[39] David Segal suggests that, as a result of the military's new market orientation, the AVF from its inception "became increasingly dependent on the poor, the black, and, to a lesser extent, women." Elizabeth Hillman argues that "women rescued the all-volunteer force" from suffering a lack of personnel with the necessary education levels and test scores.[40]

The economic recession of 2007–2009 further helped military recruiters persuade economically vulnerable youth to enlist. Barbara Sutton and Julie Novkov explain how neoliberal policies have exacerbated unemployment, eviscerated funding for public education, and underfunded social programs, while military spending remained a budgetary priority.[41] These critical unmet social needs became "military recruiters' selling points" as recruiters touted the military's ability to compensate for the cut in social services. For Sutton and Novkov, the consequences are clear: neoliberalism militarizes civilians "by bolstering inequalities that push people into the military as a means of economic survival and social mobility." Under these conditions, choice becomes an illusion and voluntarism a myth as Chicanas and other people of color and the working class find themselves inveigled into military enlistment.

In more recent years, the U.S. military has also adopted a neoliberal approach to management through its increased reliance on civilian contractors, outsourcing, and privatization. To achieve cost-cutting measures, many branches of the military now privatize housing, utility services, military depots, the repair and maintenance of aircraft and equipment, and base upkeep, among other services.[42] While the state continues to allocate billions of dollars to defense spending, "a larger percentage of these funds will circulate in the private sector," so that "meals will be served, prisoners guarded, bases built, etc., but at a higher cost, and/or at lower wage and benefit levels, such that an impressive margin of profit can be extracted."[43] Although the state may seem to be absconding through policies of privatization, it would be a mistake to suggest that neoliberalism marks the decline of the state, especially given the alarming signs of an omnipotent security state. Characterized by invasive surveillance practices, unlawful detention, and the abuse of power in the name of protection, the security state is mobilized against an external enemy and internal threats posed by critics and dissenters. In its role as ultimate protector, the state requires compliance and obedience from citizens in return. For Iris Marion Young, the state operates within the "gendered logic of masculinist protection," in which "state officials adopt the stance of masculine protectors," thereby putting "the citizens and residents who depend on their strength and vigilance in the position of women and children under the charge of the male protector."[44] Yet, security under neoliberalism complicates the gender roles of masculinist protector and feminized citizenry. The outsourcing and downsizing logic of neoliberalism suggests that individuals are becoming increasingly responsible for their own security and protection.

THE GENDER OF TRANSNATIONAL NEOLIBERAL MILITARISM

Despite contradictions in the fundamental ideological tenets of neoliberalism and militarism, significant influences and dependencies draw both adversative positions together. Neoliberal policy requires the military to enforce free trade, guarantee open markets, and ensure debt repayment by borrower nations. From a neoliberalist perspective, one of the state's primary purposes is to establish and maintain institutional structures that use military force, if necessary, to protect private property rights and unfettered markets.[45] Thus, it is important to understand how neoliberal militarism foregrounds the interdependencies between capitalism, globalization, and militarism. Moreover, these processes—and their mutual reliance on racialized and gendered bodies—are predicated on the violence and exploitation of economically and politically marginalized people.

In chapter 3, I turn to Chicana Zapatista fiction to understand the transnational ties that implicate the United States in the rise of Mexican neoliberal militarism. In the eighties and nineties, the United States used its dominating influence in the International Monetary Fund and World Bank to construct loan programs that required neoliberal restructuring of debtor nation economies. During the nineties, the United States offered $10 billion to help Mexico stabilize itself in the face of economic crisis in exchange for its switch from import substitution and protectionism to privatization and foreign investment.[46] The infusion of U.S. aid went hand in hand with Mexican militarization. During the Carlos Salinas and George H. W. Bush administrations (1988–92), the

United States sold over $214 million in military equipment to bolster Mexico's army and police forces. Major arms deals continued into the nineties, which, according to John Ross, resulted in Mexico having the second largest military in Latin America.[47]

Salinas's embrace of neoliberalism in the form of the 1994 North American Free Trade Agreement (NAFTA) continued the neoliberalization of the Mexican economy and further undermined the chances for improving the lives and livelihoods of Indian communities. The Ejército Zapatista de Liberación Nacional (Zapatista Army of National Liberation), commonly referred to as the Zapatistas, recognized the threat that neoliberal reform posed to indigenous communities and understood that neoliberal globalization was a destructive force that threatened state sovereignties, democratic practices, and human rights. Through a series of communiqués and declarations, the Zapatistas theorized the evolution of capitalism into its current manifestation. For the Zapatistas, the rapacity of neoliberalism constituted an extreme form of violence akin to war and colonialism: "We Zapatistas say that neoliberal globalization is a war of conquest of the entire world, a world war, a war being waged by capitalism for global domination."[48] In this war, the exploited and marginalized groups are pitted against "the great capitalists who live in the countries which are powerful, like the United States." Because neoliberal globalization is organized according to the demands of the market, "those who do not produce nor buy nor sell modern merchandise get in their way," and like the Zapatistas and their community bases of Indian supporters, those who rebel are targeted for removal.

Saskia Sassen attributes the exploitation of women in developing countries to the diminishing employment opportunities for men, the demands of export industries, and the elimination or reduction of government programs due to austerity programs and debt servicing.[49] These processes have led to what Sassen calls the "feminization of survival," wherein "households and whole communities are increasingly dependent on women for their survival."[50] In Mexico, neoliberal policies that have resulted in poverty, unemployment, and migration are "the most important structural causes of the increase in violence against women."[51] In chapter 3, I turn to anti-neoliberal militarism in Graciela Limón's *Erased Faces* (2001) and Lorna Dee Cervantes's "Coffee" ([1998] 2006) as examples that engage with a long tradition of Chicana *transfronterista* solidarity narratives—a literary genre concerned with transnational and often panethnic affiliations, sympathies, and ideological alliances. In these texts, Limón and Cervantes narratively model the strategies for building transfronterista alliances to contest the violence of disposability and the feminization of survival instated by neoliberal militarism. Militarism functions best by isolating women from each other to perpetuate and secure the critical hierarchies of race and class that sustain dominant power structures. Enloe describes this process as "maneuvering," whereby military officials and their civilian counterparts discourage coalitions among mothers and wives of soldiers, military sex workers, and female soldiers: "The more distanced each group of women has felt from the other, the less likely any of them would be to notice how the political manipulations of gender affected them all. Thus the less likely any of them are to think about militarism."[52] Enloe's ultimate argument is that all women—whether or not they are directly connected to militaries—are capable of challenging militarism by forging alliances. Although geographic distance may foster isolation among women's movements around the world, Chicana Zapatista literature demonstrates how antimilitarist feminists must look beyond national borders to understand how their lives are connected to other women through neoliberal militarism.[53]

GENEALOGIES OF CHICANA WAR WRITING

In Jennifer James's study of African American war literature, she points out that the long history of U.S. military aggression and intervention has "affected every ethnic group existing within [U.S.] geographical boundaries (and most without)" to such an extent that "the literary history of any community within the United States must necessarily include war as text, subtext, and context."[54] Her assertion perfectly characterizes the formation of Chicana/o literature. Chicana fiction about various conflicts discussed in *Bodies at War*—the U.S. war in Viet Nam, the Zapatista uprising, and the global war on terror—provides a map of the changing nature of war and militarism and the culturally specific yet evolving articulations of capitalism, race, gender, sexuality, and citizenship within the Chicana/o imaginary. The body of literature discussed here is only the latest in a long line of Mexican American and Chicana literature about war, a tradition that extends back to 1858, with Juan Seguín's memoirs of the battle for Texas independence and María Amparo Ruiz de Burton's historical novels *Who Would Have Thought It?* (1872) and *The Squatter and the Don* (1885), which focus on the

Civil War and the U.S.-Mexico War of 1848, respectively. Whereas Ruiz de Burton narrated the decline of the elite landed gentry of the Californio class and their struggle to negotiate new postwar political, cultural, and racial realities in former Mexican territory, later writers would turn their attention to the social upheaval in Mexico that took place shortly after the turn of the twentieth century. As writers who were inspired by and often displaced because of the Mexican Revolution (1910–20), Josefina Niggli, Leonor Villegas de Magnón, Sara Estela Ramírez, and María Cristina Mena wrote poetry, plays, short stories, and memoirs, which were published or at least circulated within the United States, detailing Mexican women's experiences of war. As the twentieth century progressed, Mexican American authors continued to examine the impact of war on identity, citizenship, and culture, as writers like Américo Paredes described the experience of Mexican American soldiering during World War II, and Rolando Hinojosa recounted the Mexican American experience during the Korean War in his collection of stories known as the Klail City Death Trip Series. In the years following the U.S. war in Viet Nam, writers—many of whom were Viet Nam veterans themselves—interjected Chicano experiences into the U.S. canon of Viet Nam War literature, challenging its dominant perspective while adding to its critique of state policy. The Chicano movement's call for Third World solidarity in Latin America further inspired Helena María Viramontes, Demetria Martínez, Graciela Limón, Ana Castillo, and Alejandro Murguía to write about the Central American wars of the seventies and eighties and to reassert a literary tradition that links fiction and poetry with transnational social movements. During the nineties, José Zuniga and Elena Rodriguez challenged militarized masculinity in texts written from their perspective as former military personnel who served during and after the Persian Gulf War. Chicana/o authors have also contributed to what Ariana Vigil identifies as a third wave of Latina/o war writing, which largely presents a critique of U.S. colonialism and shifts the geographic parameters to focus on U.S. interventions in the Middle East.[55] Much of this body of war literature reflects a critical stance toward war and/or the military as well as toward the social value of service. In his study of Chicana/o writing on the U.S. war in Viet Nam, George Mariscal notes that the writing from this period reveals "a profound questioning of ethnocentrism, white supremacy, Cold War mythology, and traditional forms of masculinity."[56] He argues that the writers' socially marginalized positions gave them a "critical eye and a righteously indignant pen," which they used to expose fallacies of equality and the colonial legacy of U.S. militarism.

Ben Olguín's study of Latina/o life writing from the war on terror reveals that not all Latina/o war writing is oppositional or takes an antistatist position. He argues that this latest wave of writing, which includes autobiography, memoir, and what he calls "faux" *testimonios*, reveals how some Latina/o authors produce narratives that support "U.S. ultra-nationalist politics, messianic chauvinisms, alarmist discourses of internal and external threats, and an eroticized fetish of violence as purifying and transcendent."[57] Olguín traces a range of positions that are counterhegemonic, hegemonic, and even "proto-fascist."[58] His work suggests that as these Latin American immigrant and U.S.-born or raised Latina/o soldiers move from socially marginal positions to assimilated ones, many of them have embraced a neoimperialist perspective. While some authors maintain the "critical eye" that characterized earlier generations of Chicana/o war writers, Olguín insists that Latinas/os are not inherently opposed to racism, patriarchy, or state violence.

War literature, by definition, is a literature concerned with social and political rupture in societies undergoing fundamental change in the context of mobilization, deployment, invasion, and demobilization. Chicana/o studies scholars have paid increasing attention to the effects of war and militarism on Chicana/o communities and cultural production, realizing that without a comprehensive examination of Chicana/o war writing, we lose important analyses of how U.S. Latina/o writers reimagine social change, political protest, and cultural resistance, as well as how these same authors can reproduce "proto-fascist" and "neo-Orientalist" narratives that reaffirm wartime nationalism.[59] Indeed, as Theresa Delgadillo argues, for Latina/o authors, "it is increasingly impossible to write about Latino/a lives and to create Latino/a characters who are not in some way involved in, linked to, or touched by the horrors of war among national states or intra-national war."[60] A growing number of books and articles are beginning to examine the literary output and importance of Chicana/o war writing, providing much-needed analyses of the "criticality," to use Delgadillo's term, of Latina/o war writing. For example, Mariscal's foundational anthology of Chicana/o stories, poetry, and excerpted memoirs about the war in Viet Nam, *Aztlán and Viet Nam: Chicano and Chicana Experiences of the War* (1999), establishes the groundwork for thinking about how Chicanas/os are socialized for warfare. He explains how Chicana/o war stories reflect working-class experiences and how some writers use military service as a mode of assimilation, while others use it as the basis for critiques of U.S. imperialism. Mariscal's book cover features Malaquías Montoya's 1972 painting entitled *Vietnam*

Aztlán, which depicts male Chicano and Vietnamese faces in oppositional profile framed by the words for solidarity and victory in Spanish and Vietnamese. The two faces are visually conjoined to suggest the unification of both peoples and their parallel struggles for independence from U.S. imperialism. In his introduction, Mariscal describes how Chicana/o war writing of this period explored extranational affiliations with Vietnamese fighters and civilians and thus rejected the notion of ideological and national allegiance to the state. Jaime Javier Rodríguez's *The Literatures of the U.S.-Mexican War: Narrative, Time, and Identity* (2010) provides even earlier accounts of how Mexican American war writing about the U.S.-Mexico War of 1848 disrupted nationalist identity, revealing its mutability and exposing the social anxiety that results when idealizations of the nation are rendered as fictional. More recently, Ariana Vigil has demonstrated how Latina/o writers trouble the bonds of national membership and question the desirability, and even the feasibility, of nation-based identities. In *War Echoes: Gender and Militarization in U.S. Latina/o Cultural Production* (2014), Vigil analyzes Latina/o literature that focuses on military conflicts in Nicaragua, Guatemala, El Salvador, and Iraq, and she offers the term "glocal war narratives" as a theoretical and geographic analytic to examine how war shapes the relationships between national and extranational subjects and between national and domestic contexts.[61]

I draw on the insights offered in these studies and contribute to the shift within the field of Chicana/o studies toward the social, political, economic, and cultural effects of war and militarism on Chicana/o communities. *Bodies at War* challenges the gender and racial exclusivity of the war genre itself—a simple yet necessary intervention that produces literary and cultural narratives about the militarization of Chicana/o communities. To date there has not been one extended examination of Chicana/o war literature that focuses only on women's writing. The presumption may be that this genre does not exist or that its paucity does not merit monographic study. The brief and partial literary historiography I provide above, however, reveals a tradition of Chicana literature in which earlier authors introduce later Chicana writers to key figures and tropes that help distinguish a growing body of Chicana war writing. From antiwar poets and authors who write about the U.S. war in Viet Nam—María Herrera-Sobek, Gina Valdés, and Stella Pope Duarte—to writers of later wars, including Elena Rodriguez, Graciela Limón, Lorna Dee Cervantes, Graciela Tiscareño-Sato, and Virginia Grise, Chicana authors, playwrights, and poets have written astutely of the martial histories on which U.S. and Mexican nationalities are moored. These writers reveal the articulation of war and gender and their combinatory role in the militarization of mourning, the induction of women into state and subaltern militaries, and the socially constructed meaning of citizenship and patriotism. Thus, *Bodies at War* fills a significant gap within the field by focusing exclusively on women's writing and activism. This work is critical because, despite the increasing visibility of Latinas in the military and the growing body of Chicana war writing, no monographs are dedicated to examining these phenomena.

Excavating this corpus of writing requires what Michel Foucault refers to as genealogical methods of analysis, an attention to discarded and devalued experiences that, in this instance, would help us provide alternative forms of demilitarized knowledge and bodily epistemologies. A genealogical analysis is particularly necessary within the genre of war writing, where the author's gender often determines the legitimacy of his or her claims and perspective. For example, Viet Thanh Nguyen argues that for too long, the narratives of the U.S. war in Viet Nam have predominantly featured "melodramas of traumatized white manhood" in which the white male soldier, journalist, or politician represents the national experience.[62] George Mariscal further describes the tendency to grant epistemic authority to the male veteran but argues for the validation of multiple experiences of war: "No one can doubt that the physical and psychological contexts of a veteran's experience diverge radically from those of the nonveteran. The point, however, is not to privilege one experience over another, even as we concede that the 'something that happened' to the veteran will influence his later actions (and in the case of writers, his texts)."[63] While both Mariscal and Nguyen are referring specifically to literature of the U.S. war in Viet Nam, their claims about the dominance of the Euro-American male soldier and veteran perspective within the war literature genre still holds true. The epistemic privileging of the white male or male of color perspective transforms the female perspective into what Ileana Rodríguez calls, in a different context yet with apropos gendered terms, "pseudo- or bastard knowledge without patrimonial status or legitimacy."[64] By focusing on the "counterpoetics" of Chicana war writing and antiwar activism, we can simultaneously undo the tidy narratives of national homogeneity and wrest away the narrative control of war from the male soldier/veteran perspective.[65] The body itself becomes a locus of counterpoetics, where embodied experiences and epistemologies help us alter the bibliographies of war. A genealogy of Chicana war literature and activism helps to challenge dominant narratives and official martial histories, along with the manufactured truths of military recruitment advertising, in order to take part in dismantling militarism.

The second significant contribution that *Bodies at War* makes is its attention to war and militarism's political, discursive, and material effects on Chicana embodiment. The functions and formations of bodies are particularly prominent in this study of neoliberal militarism because what is war if not the injury or destruction of certain bodies for the alleged or earnest defense of other bodies? Despite Elaine Scarry's failure to recognize female soldiering, she argues that war can be reduced to its most basic truth: "Whether a boy announces that he is going off 'to die' for his country or going off 'to kill' for his country, he is saying that he is going off 'to alter body tissue' (either his own or another's) for his country."[66] Scarry's passage neatly summarizes how militarism, through narratives of patriotism and national service, produces the injuring and injurable bodies that make warfare possible. Militarism's injunctions are so powerful that they successfully convince at least some "boys" (and "girls") to voluntarily and violently "alter body tissue" through death or killing.

I enter a dialogue with Mariscal, Rodríguez, Vigil, and Olguín about how Chicana/o war writing challenges national identities, but I make the specific claim that such challenges are somatically inscribed and corporeally manifested, for I am also in conversation with scholars of Latina embodiment who demonstrate how race, ethnicity, class, gender, sexuality, nationality, and citizenship burden the densely overwritten bodies of Latinas.[67] For example, Myra Mendible describes how national identity "has historically involved the foregrounding of physical characteristics said to best represent 'Americanness' and register moral and intellectual fitness."[68] If the white female body has been historically privileged for its putative moral purity, heteronormative stability, and domesticity, then, as its symbolic foil, "the Latina body" represents the allure of exoticism, sexual availability, the feminized symbol of colonized peoples, and the cultural and demographic threat of an ever-encroaching Latin America. Isabel Molina-Guzmán goes even further by arguing that "feminine nonwhite bodies are central to the biological, cultural, and social reproduction of the nation and as such must be disciplined in the interest of maintaining governance."[69] This need for discipline is particularly pronounced for Latina bodies because they represent both sexual enticement and cultural threat to U.S. national self-conceptions. To impose some measure of symbolic control over Latina bodies, Molina-Guzmán argues, the corporate-owned media help settle fears of demographic threat and cultural plurality by promoting palatable images of racially ambiguous (though not black) Latinas who are acceptably feminine, heterosexual, and often ethnically homogenous. Thus, national identity "involve[s] an epistemology of the body: privileged body types function as connotative codes that structure a cultural order."[70] This helps explain the disjunctive image of the Latina uniformed body and the military's attempts to make it speak for the nation with varying degrees of success.

Olguín addresses how nationalism is literally incorporated into the bodies of patriots who affirm the sentiment behind the refrain commonly expressed by Mexican American veterans: "*Sangre Mexicana/Corazon Americano* (though our blood be Mexican, our heart is American)."[71] The refrain illustrates the way some Mexican Americans negotiate their bicultural status and reconcile their simultaneous ascription to two national identities. Olguín goes on to provide an expansive survey of Mexican American war writing, which features the "Mexican-American G.I.—or, *Government Issue*—body," a figure that often embodies conflicting hegemonic and counterhegemonic allegiances and ideological positions.[72] As compelling as this figure is, it is also important to understand how wartime nationalism operates outside the military barracks. Focusing solely on "government issue" bodies misses how other bodies function within the rubric of wartime nationalism. In times of war, women are subjected to a hypervigilance over their reproductive choices, sexual desires, physical mobility, grieving processes, family relationships, consumer practices, and affective investments in national identity and the state. Furthermore, female bodies are deemed ultravulnerable—sexually, physically, and morally—to justify their perceived need for military protection. *Bodies at War* attends to the literary and cultural representations of a wide spectrum of bodies, such as the Chicana/Latina maternal body and the symbolic plenitude it offers to national discourses.

Although I examine how Chicanas negotiate the demands and allures of wartime nationalism through the body, I also focus on how their bodies function under the regime of neoliberal militarism. When militarism combines with neoliberalism, a whole new set of attitudes and practices are produced and enacted on and through soldier and nonsoldier bodies. This ideological convergence results in an intensified process of depreciation, disposability, and disciplining of the body. If, as Marx theorized, capitalism enables the disarticulation of value from the laboring body in a process that transforms workers into variable capital, then under neoliberal militarism, that devaluation is not only exacerbated but also further used to justify the disposability of depreciated bodies. Moreover, because the neoliberal state no longer plays a prominent role in providing for the social reproduction of its citizens, and because it makes military defense its budgetary priority, women in particular experience the hardships of neoliberal militarism as policies of austerity, privatization, and disinvestment in social services shift the burdens of social reproduction onto the backs of individuals. In writing about the financial crisis of 2001 in Argentina, Barbara Sutton argues that the "economy is not something 'out there,' abstract, or with little relevance to the body, but a force shaping bodily experiences and consciousness."[73] She goes on to explain how the crisis of 2001 "produced bodies that were more fatigued, stressed, overworked, malnourished, and sick."[74] State disinvestment in social reproduction often means that basic daily needs go unmet as unemployment rises, public transportation systems fail, health care becomes unavailable, child care becomes unaffordable, and food becomes scarce. These deficiencies in the social safety net are experienced bodily as individuals endure the physical, emotional, and psychological toll of mere survival. Moreover, women often perform the unpaid labor that must make up for deficits in social support. Thus, women's bodies often endure the compounded physical effects of stress and fatigue that come with living under austerity.[75] The depreciation and slow attrition of the laboring body under neoliberalism point to how violence is enabled by the disarticulation of value from the body.

Bodies at War is concerned with how state and dominant narratives reproduce bodily injurability. Bodies injured from war are disturbingly utilitarian; they substantiate victory among belligerents (most atrociously through "body counts") and legitimate what Scarry refers to as the "unanchoredness of the exterior framing issues" of war.[76] By "unanchored" she means that war narratives are unsubstantiated; they are words on paper or the empty rhetoric of national leaders and are constantly open to reinterpretation and challenge. To assert its legitimacy, a war narrative requires the "anchored" experience of bodies in pain. The "reality-conferring" function of wounded bodies legitimizes the state narrative of war because "the sheer material factualness of the human body will be borrowed to lend that cultural construct the aura of 'realness' and 'certainty.'"[77] In this sense, bodies and war are interlocked in material and discursive ways. The injured and injurable body function as sites of interpretive struggle that enable the framing of war.

The physically vulnerable or disposable bodies of war are not arbitrarily or unintentionally chosen. Rather, the frames of war distinguish the relative value of bodies based on social norms, conventions, and practices that designate some individuals as protectable and others as expendable. The outcast bodies are defined by their precarity, which Butler describes as a "politically induced condition in which certain populations suffer from failing social and economic networks of support and become differentially exposed to injury, violence, and death."[78] In other words, not all bodies achieve the status of socially valued life—a failure of humanization that leaves those bodies open to violence.[79] As bodies that fall outside the narrative purview of worthiness and protection, they become the devalued, exploited, and battered casualties of warfare. The vulnerability of certain bodies becomes particularly acute during times of war when we see (or are prevented from seeing) state-legitimated violence and are called on to feel (or not to feel) a certain way toward the damaged bodies that populate our TV and computer screens. The Vietnamese victims of U.S. warfare are examples of precarious lives discussed in *Bodies at War*. While secretary of defense Robert McNamara relied on the metrics of body counts to verify U.S. progress in the war, Chicana antiwar activists and poets challenged the rhetorical erasure that such terms enact. The Chicana activism and literature discussed in chapter 1 call our attention to war's narrative and its material production of vulnerabilized, abjected bodies while highlighting how militarized Chicana/o bodies are often also abjected bodies.

Chicana war literature and antiwar activism depict and contest the depreciation and disposability of bodies under neoliberal militarism, but they also reveal how militarized individuals internalize and manifest the state's call for bodily sacrifice. Foucault's notion of "docile bodies" is perhaps a logical place to start a discussion of how the Chicana body is disciplined into a soldier body. Foucault describes the military as one of several institutions (the school, the hospital, and the prison are others) that exemplified the transformation in modern state power during the seventeenth and eighteenth centuries. The transformation was signaled by a new set of disciplinary methods that included a shift in institutional interest from bodies en masse to individual bodies.[80] Additionally, the focus was no longer only on the results of an individual's actions and their meanings, but also on the individual's "efficiency of movements" and on managing how individual bodies inhabit "time, space, movement."[81] As a process, discipline "defined how one may have a hold over others' bodies, not only so they may do what one wishes, but so that they may operate as one wishes, with the techniques, the speed, and the efficiency that one determines."[82] In Foucault's description, the regimented lives of recruits provide clear demonstrations of how bodies are disciplined through the "microphysics of power."[83] The process continues in the modern U.S. military, where through drills, psychological training, dehumanization, monotony, rote memorization, infantilization, feminization, humiliation, and patriotic indoctrination, among other tactics, the military produces a disciplined soldier body out of the unruly subjects who first enter basic training. The protagonist in Elena Rodriguez's *Peacetime*, discussed in chapter 2, experiences the process of military induction from a Chicana point of view as she endures seven weeks of army boot camp training. Using Rodriguez's semi-autobiographical novel and the experience of Mickiela Montoya, a Chicana army veteran of the Iraq War, I examine the meticulous and intimate process of military disciplining as the Chicana body becomes a site of intense regulation. Rodriguez and Montoya reveal how the Chicana soldier is formed through ideological and physical training within an institution that enables sexual violence against its members, particularly women. Moreover, I suggest that the normative culture and disciplining tactics that go into transforming the Chicana soldier body in boot camp are now evident in the larger social field, since neoliberal militarism has seeped out of the military base and into public schools, housing, U.S. consumerism, entertainment, toy manufacturing, border enforcement, academic disciplines, and public services, among other arenas.[84] Through examples of Chicana soldiering, we can glean the corporeal and ontological transformation of Chicana bodies in the military, a transformation that I argue is indicative of a fundamental reconfiguration of citizenship currently at work within neoliberal militarism's regime.

Bodies at War demonstrates how neoliberal militarism functions according to disciplinary and biopolitical logics of control and regulation. The state's investment in the individual bodies of Chicanas/os is part of its larger interest in the Latina/o population as a whole. Analyzing military recruitment advertising in chapter 4 is my entry into the mechanics of how the military, as an arm of the state, constructs an identifiable Latina/o demographic to enable more invasive processes of militarizing Latina/o communities. Foucault has described the state's regulatory interest in managing the population through a process that both compels life and encourages attrition. Race becomes a determining factor in the state's attempt at "making" certain groups live while "letting" others die in the name of optimizing the population. From the vantage point of the state, Latinas/os compose a population subject to both maneuvers—a paradoxical position that reflects the utility and disposability of Latina/o bodies. Whereas Latina/o studies scholars have focused on how the logic of biopower is predicated on the *exclusion* of pathologized or threatening bodies through policies such as the forced sterilization of Latinas in the seventies, anti-immigrant ballot initiatives, mass deportations, and efforts to overturn the Fourteenth Amendment, I argue that military recruitment demonstrates an alternative logic of biopolitical *inclusion* that takes particular interest in Chicana/Latina biological and social reproductive capacities. I focus specifically on the maternal Chicana/Latina body and its role in fortifying neoliberal militarism's attempts to optimize and militarize Latina/o communities, a population that is often perceived as an internal threat to national security.

THE CHICANA SOLDIER AND THE ANTIWAR ACTIVIST: BODIES IN WAR AND BODIES IN PROTEST

Bodies at War focuses on two figures that receive little scholarly or public attention in discussions of war: the Chicana soldier and the antiwar activist. Yet, despite this neglect, Chicanas and Latinas are increasingly becoming the face of U.S. militarism and humanitarian interventionist propaganda. In January 2013, secretary of defense Leon Panetta announced the Defense Department's landmark decision to mandate that all military branches open combat roles to women by 2016 or provide evidence to justify the prevention of full gender integration. In anticipation of what will undoubtedly become a historic shift in military culture, each military branch has begun recalibrating its advertising strategies to make a broader appeal to potential female recruits. According to the most recent demographic study of the armed services, 15.5 percent of accessions and new enlistees were Hispanic, compared with 21.1 percent of the Hispanic civilian cohort in the age range of eighteen to twenty-four years.[85] The percentage of Latinas who serve in the military has always been smaller than their percentage of the civilian population; however, their enlistment numbers have been steadily increasing. In 1975, 6 percent of military servicewomen were Hispanic, whereas in 2002 that figure rose to 14 percent.[86] Although the number of Hispanic women serving in the military is relatively small, they make up a larger percentage of enlisted women than do Hispanic men within the cohort of enlisted men.[87]

The rise in Latina enlistment corresponds to an increase in images of the Latina soldier. In 2013, news of a leaked e-mail triggered a minor controversy among observers of the military. In a message to Colonel Christian Kubik, chief of public affairs for the army's Training and Doctrine Command, Colonel Lynette Arnhart critiqued the use of "attractive women" in the army's communications strategy. The article she was referring to appeared in the November 2013 issue of *Army* magazine and featured information about the army's "Soldier 2020," which is the army's study of how to integrate women into military occupational specialties that were previously off limits. As deputy director and senior military analyst at Fort Leavenworth, Kansas, Colonel Arnhart oversaw the study of institutional and cultural factors affecting gender integration.[88] In her e-mail, Arnhart encouraged military publicists to select photographs of more "average looking" women: "There is a general tendency to select nice looking women when we select a photo to go with an article. . . . It might behoove us to select more average looking women for our comms strategy. . . . For example, the attached article shows a pretty woman, wearing make-up while deployed on duty. . . . Such photos undermine the rest of the message (and may even make people ask if breaking a nail is considered a hazardous duty)."[89] Colonel Arnhart was widely criticized for her comments. Congresswoman Jackie Speier tweeted that the e-mail was "another example that @USArmy just doesn't get it as it debates if pretty girls should be used in pamphlets."[90] Yet, what Congresswoman Speier "doesn't get" is that the issue of militarized femininity has always been crucial to the military's investment in policing the intimate spaces of women's bodies. Colonel Arnhart's e-mail is only one more example of the kind of intense surveillance and disciplining that female bodies undergo in processes of militarization.

The "pretty woman" in the advertisement is Corporal Kristine Tejeda of the Third Advise and Assist Brigade, First Calvary Division, who, according to the caption, "provides security for a tour of the ancient city of Ur, Iraq" (figure 2).[91] Corporal Tejeda's image is superimposed on the front page of an article about the Soldier 2020 program.[92] To the right of her image is a description of the program's rationale, which is to open "previously closed positions and occupational specialties to women while maintaining our combat effectiveness."[93] The article reminds readers that women have served in the military for "generations," and that in the wars in Iraq and Afghanistan, 150 women were killed in action and 800 were wounded. Given the history of service, the casualty and injury rate, and the "few practical limits to the vital contributions women can make in our Army formations," the article asserts that there are no legitimate objections to implementing the Pentagon's policy. As the face of gender integration in the army, Corporal Tejeda's

FIGURE 2. Cpl. Kristine Tejeda, Headquarters Battery, Second Battalion, Eighty-Second Field Artillery Regiment, Third Advise and Assist Brigade, First Cavalry Division, Task Force Steel Dragon, providing security for a tour of the ancient city of Ur in Dhi Qar province, Iraq, September 24, 2013. Photo by U.S. Army/Pvt. Andrew C. Slovensky. From Gen. Robert W. Cone, "Soldier 2020," *Army*, November 2013, 29.

image plays a significant symbolic role. Like the Chicana soldier body discussed at the beginning of this chapter, the uniform (in this case, desert camouflage fatigues) represents an inclusive military vestment that marks the Latina body as a member of the national defense team and a citizen of the nation. Through her soldier body, Tejeda enables the army to promote itself as both racially and gender inclusive, and because the army welcomes the Pentagon's policy change, it can also appeal to liberal feminists who advocate for equality within the ranks.[94] Thus, the Latina soldier body allows the army to remake its public image as a progressive institution as it simultaneously competes with the other military branches for the most desirable youth demographic: the Latina/o population of service age.

From Colonel Arnhart's perspective, the black eyeliner and subtle shade of lip gloss undermines Tejeda's warrior pose. Tejeda's status as a "pretty woman" signals a larger discourse about how Latina embodiment has been historically associated with hypersexuality and reproductive threat. Through their depiction in mainstream media, Latinas "often perform a safe yet exotic sexualized femininity because of their racial and ethnic ambiguity."[95] However, the sexualized Latina bodies depicted in the media as "globally consumable docile bodies subject to the erotic and voracious gaze of the United States" introduce conceptual problems for traditional renderings of the U.S. soldier body.[96] Perpetually marked by an "exotic sexualized femininity," the Latina soldier icon embodies disjunctive discourses of race, gender, sexuality, and citizenship. Perhaps this is the real reason that Corporal Tejeda's image produces such a destabilizing effect in the Soldier 2020 ad. As a metonym of the state, the soldier body has been traditionally perceived through a white male iconography. By displacing this universalized somatic norm, the Latina soldier body disrupts stabilized discursive associations between white masculinity and the nation. The race and gender of the Latina soldier complicate the traditionally masculine and white iconography of the American soldier, thereby limiting the Latina's capacity to represent the nation, even when her body is vested in the symbolic power of the military uniform. Yet military advertisers, in their single-minded pursuit of new recruits, seemingly disregard the contradictions inherent in the Latina soldier body. Instead, military propagandists use the image of Latina soldiers to depict the military as a multiracial, feminist, and progressive armed force.

Tejeda's racial and ethnic identity was taken for granted in the debate over female beauty, suggesting that the image of a Latina in fatigues has become socially acceptable and unremarkable. But the process behind such normalizing gestures is fraught with tension and anxiety. I examine the labor that goes into naturalizing images of Latinas in uniform and the ideological role these images play in militarizing Latina/o communities. Military recruitment advertising is a science, after all, in which military advertisers rely on national surveys, commissioned demographic reports on the economic and social composition of Latina/o communities, and sophisticated instruments that measure service propensities, accessions, and attrition rates, among other metrics. As Colonel Arnhart's e-mail suggests, entire conversations and debates are taking place behind the production of military advertising. The focus groups, interviews, literature reviews, surveys, experiments, and other modes of data gathering and analysis reveal how military advertising relies on an extensive intellectual industry to collect, analyze, and disseminate information that could be used for recruitment. As Enloe warns, the intellectual labor that goes into recruitment advertising should prevent us from making the "lazy" assumption that "either tradition or culture was at work—*and* that neither tradition nor culture required explicit decisions for their maintenance." Rather, once we realize that the claims made in recruitment ads are "the result of memos, not tradition, it will be harder to treat the consequences as apolitical."[97]

Perhaps contrary to expectations, many military recruiters and advertisers are interested in the unlikely and usually ignored figure of the Latina mother. Inderpal Grewal's work shows how mothers in particular become critical to national security because of their role in raising citizens who may become soldiers and because they serve as "both the subject and agent of security through new surveillance technologies that emphasize the governmentality of security."[98] Given the mother's symbolic and functional role within the family, under neoliberalism she becomes "essential to the privatization of welfare and security."[99] I examine how Chicana/Latina mothers are conscripted into national defense through military recruitment advertising. In chapter 4, I explore the science of military recruitment to show how Chicana/Latina mothers' reproduction—both biological and social—is crucial to national security in the post-9/11 era. Through the symbolic function of her maternal body and her role in socializing her children for war, the militarized Chicana/Latina mother becomes an ally to the neoliberalized security state.

I want to return one more time to the image of Corporal Tejeda to highlight the implicit violence of the photo. The automatic weapon that Tejeda confidently holds in her hand is not an innocent prop and thus should dispel any essentialist notion of female nonaggression that we may have. In other words, Corporal Tejeda's image forces us to come to terms with the motives and consequences of Chicana/Latina violence. As bell hooks rightly points out, while "men continue to commit the majority of violent acts in war," the "sex role division of labor does not necessarily mean that women think differently than men about violence or would act significantly different if in power."[100] Because this is so, I do not presume that all women disfavor war, especially since women in the United States are raised within the same militarized culture as men. I make space for this position in chapter 2, because Elena Rodriguez's *Peacetime: Spirit of the Eagle* (1997) illustrates the ways in which many Chicanas identify with military culture even as they seek to challenge its misogynistic traditions. Because I take their views seriously, I am prevented from making sweeping generalizations or broad-based assumptions about Chicana opposition to war and militarism. Instead, I take the more productive route of studying how Chicanas are positioned and position themselves in multiple ways within systems of state power and in relation to state violence. As hooks reminds us, "In times of national crisis, women fight in combat globally and do not show any predisposition to be more nonviolent."[101] But the tension between antiwar, anti-imperialist feminists and feminist militarists exposes a vital conversation that we need to have as more women join state and subaltern militaries around the world. Although it is important to criticize state violence, we cannot lose sight of women's use of violence as a mode of self-defense, for achieving social justice, or for other reasons. As the proceeding chapters on Chicana soldiers and Zapatista women make clear, Chicana and Mexican women's engagement in militarism is sometimes a matter of survival. In such instances, a new set of questions arises: When is violence justified? How does it leave its mark on the Chicanas and Mexicanas who are no longer the recipients but the perpetrators of violence? What are the consequences?

In *Bodies at War*, I juxtapose the warring Chicana body, one trained in and committed to carrying out violence on behalf of the state, with the activist body, an equally important public figure that makes ethical and political demands in the service of peace. Like the Chicana soldier body, the Chicana antiwar activist body is equally troubling to normative gender roles. "The 'activist body' is not on the list of appropriate feminine traits," writes Sutton, because it challenges society's idealized notion of the "docile feminine body."[102] By occupying public space in sometimes unruly ways—that is, voicing forceful critiques of state policy in often loud, raucous public demonstrations—the Chicana antiwar activist transgresses cultural boundaries of propriety. But perhaps the activist's more disruptive quality lies in how she publicly announces her engagement in the process of subject and citizen formation. Sutton notes that "out-of-place bodies shape both the political landscape and the embodied consciousness of participants."[103] The Chicana antiwar activists and authors that I examine here reshape the political field by participating in the democratic practice of public contestation and open debate. While their political demands center on changing U.S. foreign policy and criticizing the predatory nature of military conscription and recruitment in their communities, they also make moral pronouncements against the military's indiscriminate use of violence. Thus, they make an ethical call for peace that transcends their national identities as citizen-subjects, an act that undermines wartime nationalism's insistence on symbolically compliant and vulnerable women who justify the violent protectionist actions of the national security state.

In Chicana poet Gina Valdés's poem about the U.S. war in Viet Nam "Hearts on Fire," she demonstrates how Chicana poets and activists tried to cultivate empathic connections by exploring the perceived affinities that connect the peoples of two nations at war. The poem begins with a direct address to a child named Nuoc, born in Saigon to a "Vietnamese dancer" and an "American soldier," and continues as the narrator recounts a series of events that occurred in 1968, the year of Nuoc's birth.[104] In describing the year's events, the narrator commemorates the repertoire of tactics that activist bodies draw on to protest violence. It was 1968 when

> some hearts broke
> into chants, others
> into flames.

Valdés's decision to use "hearts" as a synecdoche for the bodies of antiwar activists underscores the point that protest is not just political but emotional, or rather, that the distinction between the two is false to begin with. Her consequential enjambment emphasizes the play on words in which the phrase "hearts broke" doubles in meaning. In the move from the implied adjective (*broken* hearts) to verb ("some hearts *broke* into chants"), Valdés demonstrates how turning grief into action is not only possible, but also ethically imperative.

The poem continues with the narrator's recognition of Nuoc's birth: "I circled your birth / with thousands of students / chanting to Ho Chi Minh." Here, the "I" becomes part of a larger community, engaged in what some people no doubt considered treasonous speech. The narrator then moves on to describe the voices of revered Vietnamese Buddhist monk and peace activist Thich Nhat Hanh, Martin Luther King Jr., César Chávez, and Dolores Huerta, who all offer prayers for an end to war's violence. The poem's recurrent use of the fire motif—"flames," "exploded" prayers, and "ashes"—culminates in the last stanza with a reference to the most devastating examples of protest from the era: "Monks and nuns / opened their lotus hearts / and caught fire."[105] The reference is, of course, to the Buddhist monks and nuns who set their bodies on fire in protest to the war, leaving behind indelible images of the ultimate form of bodily protest.

But the year is also significant to the narrator for another reason. Simultaneous to personal protest is personal loss, as we learn in the sixth stanza that 1968 was also the year that

> Cousin Rudy's prayers exploded
> in a mine, next to a Vietnamese boy

whose father planted rice,
same as tío José[106]

While the last line of the stanza emphasizes sameness ("same as tío José"), an important first step in creating empathic connection, the poem moves beyond narcissistic recognition toward an attempt to reach a deeper understanding of Otherness and one's vulnerability to another's Otherness. In other words, Nuoc's birth and the various forms of protests engaged in around the world that year help frame the narrator's understanding of Cousin Rudy's death. Death equalizes Cousin Rudy and the nameless Vietnamese boy, while grief devastates the fathers of both young men. Cousin Rudy's death also presents the occasion for the narrator to join a broader community of loss, one that reaffirms shared vulnerabilities and compels a search for an end to violence. Butler reminds us that to "be injured means that one has the chance to reflect upon injury, to find out the mechanisms of its distribution, to find out who else suffers from permeable borders, unexpected violence, dispossession, and fear, and in what ways."[107] Valdés's narrator actively seeks to know how others grieve and uses injurability as a basis for solidarity rather than for retribution. And after understanding how injury is disproportionately distributed, the narrator joins others in protesting war. Injury becomes an opportunity to acknowledge vulnerability and enables the call for "global political community."[108] As the poem begins with a birth resulting from military occupation and ends with the deaths of self-immolating monks and nuns, we can trace the narrator's attempt to relate to others across the voluntary or involuntary destruction of bodies and across the cultural and national differences that impede solidarity. By traversing those borders, the poem resists the official enframement of the war.

Throughout *Bodies at War*, I show how in various ways Chicana war literature attempts to halt the narrative violence done to injurable bodies by "fram[ing] the frame," a narrative process by which Chicana authors question a dominating interpretive frame and "expos[e] the orchestrating designs of the authority who sought to control the frame."[109] Because of a war narrative's need for continuous reproduction, it contains the conditions of its own transformation and demise. Butler contends that reproducibility can generate risk just as it can promote war: "Frames are subject to an iterable structure—they can only circulate by virtue of their reproducibility, and that reproducibility introduces a structural risk for the identity of the frame itself. The frame breaks with itself to reproduce itself, and its reproduction becomes the site where a politically consequential break is possible."[110] Put differently, though states mount powerful and convincing versions of martial histories, they can never determine how those stories are perceived or recirculated. Even the most enduring frames must submit to the uncertainty of confronting sites where unauthorized reiterations or renegade interpretations are produced. Although states are ideologically invested in war narratives, individuals and communities are equally invested in war stories that differentially inform their understandings of cultural identity, collective memory, national belonging, and gender constructions. They tell different stories about war, often without regard for inconsistencies with official versions.

A compelling example of war narrative's mutability can be found in the material and literary iterations of the soldadera. Often described as camp followers or actual combatants, soldaderas were Mexican women who participated in the Mexican Revolution. While most soldaderas were treated as anonymous figures in the background of war, some became famous, including La Adelita, a woman from Durango, Mexico, who eventually inspired one of the most popular corridos of the revolution.[111] In Mexican and Chicana/o literature and art, the soldadera is both revered and romanticized. More recent attempts have been made to refer to Latina soldiers in the war on terror as descendants of the soldadera. Yet, the Mexican Revolution does not necessarily make a convincing or appropriate analogy for the Iraq War. Jorge Mariscal explains why: "U.S. invasion and occupation of Iraq bears little resemblance to the Mexican Revolution in which common people rose up to take back control from a corrupt government and foreign influence."[112] Mariscal's point in describing the incongruence between these two wars is to consider the representation of Melissa Valles and Ana Laura Esparza, a Chicana and a Mexicana "green card soldier," respectively, who were killed during the Iraq War in 2003. Were these women "Adelitas" simply because they took up arms in a military campaign? Or does the soldadera more accurately symbolize a subaltern position against government corruption and U.S. imperialism? "History alone will tell us," Mariscal writes, "if Valles and Esparza—these new 'Adelitas'—gave their lives in a righteous cause or in an unjust act of arrogance and political miscalculation."[113] The issue of whether Chicana soldiers represent the new soldaderas raises an even more important question about the political work of cultural symbols. How has the revolution come to provide the symbolic language used to imagine imperialist wars of expansion into foreign territory? What gender models does the revolution offer and how do they inform contemporary behaviors and practices? Much of the Chicana war literature examined in *Bodies at War* relies on the Mexican Revolution as a metanarrative—at times, an imperfect one—for interpreting later wars, militarisms, and militancies. In some ways, the Mexican Revolution's lack of similarity to the war on terror is not as pertinent as the symbolic value attributed to soldaderas. As Guisela Latorre points out, "Regardless of whether *soldaderas* were appropriate predecessors to Chicanas struggling for equality in the here and now, it is their *symbolic* potential and their malleable category as icons" that are important to how and why Chicana artists and activists use them.[114] Literary reclamations of the soldadera or La Adelita are examples of how past wars are reinterpreted for new wars as Chicana authors and activists produce new understandings of women's relationship to war. I show how Chicana war literature often uses the revolution as a lens to analyze class, race, gender, and sexuality in war narratives and to envision forms of agency and identity.

The soldadera is also the ideal vehicle for a study on Chicana and Mexicana embodiment because so many competing values coalesce in her image. She is a symbol of Mexican nationalism, a Chicana/o nationalist icon of antiwar activism, a feminist representation of political subjectivity, a role model for female soldiers, and a transnational figure for anti-neoliberal movements. The chapters in *Bodies at War* follow the soldadera's literary and cultural iterations over time, beginning with antiwar protest during the U.S. war in Viet Nam and ending with U.S. military advertisements of Chicanas and Latinas in the global war on terror. Yet, in all her cultural and national specificity, the soldadera helps us learn something about how militarism delimits access to political rights, shapes the meaning of citizenship, and transforms women's relationship to the state.

MAPPING GENEALOGIES

In chapter 1, I examine Chicana antiwar protest and fiction about the United States' war in Viet Nam. The chapter begins by looking at three examples of antiwar activism during the sixties and seventies to frame a discussion about militarism's circumscription of the public sphere. I focus on Delia Alvarez, Nina Genera, and Lea Ybarra—all Chicana activists who had brothers serving in the war. As the sister of the longest-held prisoner of war (POW), Alvarez negotiated official demands by the Richard Nixon administration that relied on framing POW families' grief in a way that would mitigate public opposition to the war. While Alvarez expressed her antiwar views in the national press and media, Genera and

Ybarra expressed their opposition to war by creating and distributing an antidraft pamphlet entitled *La batalla está aquí* (The battle is here) (1972), which included graphic pictures of Vietnamese war victims. I analyze how their pamphlet and Alvarez's public opposition, through speeches and interviews, attempted to reframe official discourse about the war. More importantly, I read this example of Chicana antidraft activism as a challenge to the neoliberal rationale for ending the draft. In other words, while neoliberals and Chicana activists both opposed the draft, Chicanas grounded their opposition in an ethical argument against imperial U.S. violence rather than one based on the principle of self-interested choice. I then examine the Chicana antiwar collective known as Las Adelitas de Aztlán and their public performance of mourning during the 1970 Chicano Moratorium in Los Angeles. I also look at more recent Chicana poetry and literature, including Stella Pope Duarte's *Let Their Spirits Dance* (2002), a novel about a Chicana mother's journey to the Vietnam Veterans Memorial Wall, to examine how the state's management of bereavement works as a form of political repression that Chicanas subvert by publicly expressing unauthorized displays of mourning. Through a reading of Chicana activism and literature, I examine the state's attempt to reproduce gendered citizenship through the regulation of grieving Chicana bodies. At the height of its war-making powers, the state attempted to determine who should grieve publicly, who could be grieved for, and where grieving should properly take place. I argue that Chicana activists and writers rejected the regulatory reach of the state and instead illustrated how sisters and mothers of soldiers made larger ethical claims about corporeal vulnerability that undermined the warring state's furious efforts to frame certain lives as beyond bereavement. As a result, they turned the intimacy of private grief into public claims of political grievance as their grief extended to the Vietnamese victims of U.S. military aggression—a process that reconfigures the nation-bound meaning of citizenship and restores the democratic practice of dissent.

As chapter 2 makes clear, structural and ideological changes that occurred at the end of the war in Viet Nam set the stage for significant changes in the U.S. military. As the war ended, so did conscription; in its place the military switched to an all-volunteer force. The AVF obligated military planners to satisfy personnel needs by focusing on the economic behavior of potential recruits to attract enough enlistees from the civilian workforce. In the nineties, the decline in the welfare state coincided with the rise of women's enlistment in the military. I draw on the work of feminist war scholars who demonstrate how the articulation of neoliberal policies pushed many women of color and the working class into the military, as was the case with the protagonist of Elena Rodriguez's autobiographically inspired novel *Peacetime*. In the novel, we read about Private Medrano's induction into army culture and the transformation of economically impoverished and racialized female enlistees, who develop a militarized feminist stance that emphasizes self-reliance and personal responsibility rather than questioning the social structures that limit their options. I also examine the more recent experiences of Mickiela Montoya, a young Chicana army veteran, whose time in basic training and in the Iraq War reveal the intense disciplining of female soldiers as they endure the army's culture of violence against women. Through these examples of Chicana soldiering, we can witness the corporeal and ontological transformation of Chicana bodies in the military, a transformation that I argue is indicative of a fundamental reconfiguration of citizenship currently at work within neoliberal militarism's regime.

Whereas Rodriguez's novel centers on the formation of the neoliberal citizen-soldier, Graciela Limón and Lorna Dee Cervantes attempt to resuscitate the political citizen-subject whose spheres of action include domestic and transnational politics. Chapter 3 focuses on how Limón's *Erased Faces* (2001) and Cervantes's "Coffee" (1998/2006) reconnect the self-managed neoliberal subject—a figure withdrawn from the realm of coalitional politics, unable or unwilling to forge alliances in the service of social justice—with transnational social movements. Limón and Cervantes expose the ravages of neoliberalism in the Americas by focusing on indigenous resistance to neoliberal reform, particularly through the Zapatistas. I briefly examine the Zapatistas' form of subaltern feminist militarism and how it inducts women into militarized violence. Limón's and Cervantes's texts enable an analysis of how women negotiate the transition from victim to aggressor and how such transformations illustrate the ethical limitations of resistant violence. Moreover, I show how their texts focus on Chicana and Mexican indigenous women whose bodies are marked by histories of colonialism and heteropatriarchy, legacies that manifest into what Walter Mignolo refers to as the "colonial wound," or the physical and/or psychological scars resulting from the lingering process of modernity and coloniality.[115] In short, my reading of both texts explores how women experience transgenerational violence and how they themselves wield violence for particular personal and political ends.

As the foregoing discussion on military recruitment advertising suggests, the body of the Chicana soldadera takes on new symbolic meaning as it becomes representative of imperial aggression in the global war on terror. Like the Chicana soldier body, the Chicana/Latina maternal body also serves the military and the nation, but in different ways. In chapter 4, I examine military recruitment campaigns to trace the influence of neoliberal militarism and its peculiar mix of neoliberal and neoconservative discourses best exemplified in ads that feature the militarized Chicana/Latina mother. The military's interest in fertility patterns and its market research on Latina/o parenting practices reveal its belief that to militarize (and recruit) Latina/o youth, one must first militarize the Latina mother. My focus on the Chicana/Latina maternal body enables a larger discussion on how home, homeland, and home front get reconfigured in a post-9/11 context, becoming critical concepts that undergird the spatiality of neoliberal militarism. Another way to put this is to say that neoliberal militarism has a multiscalar logic that begins with the smallest scale (the body) and moves to increasingly larger extrapolations (the nation). Focusing on the home and its variants as a space that is actively produced and productive enables my analysis of the sociospatial formation of militarized subjectivities. I use a cultural and literary archive to show how militarized Chicana/Latina motherhood gets performed in the space of the home, homeland, and home front, and how some of these texts challenge the stability and security connoted in the word *home*. While Graciela Tiscareño-Sato's bilingual children's book *Good Night Captain Mama/Buenas Noches Capitán Mamá* (2013) features a Chicana/Latina active-duty air force pilot who transforms the family home into a training camp for the next generation of citizen-soldiers, Virginia Grise's *blu* (2011) undermines the logic of home and defense by using a queer Chicana mother to question the notion of domestic security and by collocating the national homeland with Aztlán, the Aztec homeland that Chicana/o cultural nationalists revere as their territorial inheritance. Both homelands come under scrutiny as Grise uses pre-Cortesian myth to critique patriarchal violence and the militarization of space.

In the conclusion I examine Chicanas' evolving relationship to the state. As more women join the military, we must reckon with their willing participation in state violence now that militarized liberal feminism has facilitated their entry into previously banned combat positions. To counterbalance the bleak notion of an increasingly militarized future, I study the artwork of Favianna Rodriguez and Nao Bustamante, who recuperate the figure of the soldadera as part of a Chicana antiwar imaginary. I argue that through the soldadera, we can begin to imagine a peace-affirming future.

I turn first, in chapter 1, to Chicana authors and activists who attempted to shine light on the state's genocidal imperial practices during the U.S. war in Viet Nam by learning from the wounded bodies of conscripted Chicano soldiers and injured and mutilated Vietnamese children. These authors and activists' ethical call for relationality provides the first glimpse into a more hopeful antiwar future.

1

THE ETHICS OF CHICANA GRIEF AND GRIEVANCE

Activist and Literary Responses to the U.S. War in Viet Nam

Were each of us spontaneously and, as it were, inherently non-violent, there would exist neither ethics nor any prohibition against murder.

ROGER BURGGRAEVE, "VIOLENCE AND THE VULNERABLE FACE OF THE OTHER"

Revolutions and riots often begin with a funeral.

GAIL HOLST-WARHAFT, *THE CUE FOR PASSION*

You cry like our ancestors. . . . They cried with their souls, not their eyes. That is the way to mourn, to mourn with all your heart.

STELLA POPE DUARTE, *LET THEIR SPIRITS DANCE*

IN THE POEM "UNTITLED," María Herrera-Sobek opens with the somber image of deceased Chicano soldiers returning from Viet Nam: "We saw them coming / in funeral black bags / body bags they called them."[1] Given the high rate of Chicano and Latino casualties, the image became ubiquitous within countless Latina/o communities, as did the new vernacular of *body bags* that accompanied it. Unsurprisingly, many Chicanas/os began to question long-held community beliefs in the dignity of military service, the honor of dying for one's country, and the value of patriotism. Poems like Herrera-Sobek's "Untitled" refuse to compartmentalize violence by relegating it to the battlefield and instead expose the links between imperial and internecine violence that challenge the fiction of a cohesive, unified polity. For example, the narrator describes the way "USA guns / turned inward" targeting the Chicana/o youth who lay "Dead in the streets / Dead in the battlefields / Dead in the schools."[2]

In the face of economic disparities and political repression, the presumably female narrator describes the impulse to protest. Herrera-Sobek's "Untitled" is one of a series of poems on the U.S. war in Viet Nam that highlights the experiences of the Chicana/o antiwar activist. In her poem "Vietnam," Herrera-Sobek presents the antiwar activist as a foil to the U.S. soldier. While soldiers marched to the "rat-tat-tat / Of firing machine guns," activists "Marched to the tune / Of peace / In their sandaled feet."[3] In the poem, "Vietnam—A Four-Letter Word," Herrera-Sobek continues to focus on the protesting body and its function as a public political signpost to be read semiotically. While chanting "Hell no, we won't go," protesters not only reject the military uniform, but also profane the symbols of national unity, as they wear "peace / On their foreheads / Love on their sleeves / And American flags / On their behinds."[4] The protesting body thus plays a critical role in physically occupying public space to engage in collective acts of solidarity. I focus on the Chicana activist body and its various modes of protest to reveal how "political resistance involves, first and foremost, putting the material body in action to affect the course of society."[5] But, as Herrera-Sobek suggests in her poem "Chicana Vietnam Blues," public protest also requires the willingness to take bodily risks. The opening lines of that poem begin with a reference to the Kent State University shootings on May 4, 1970, in which members of the Ohio National Guard opened fire on student protesters, killing four and injuring ten others. Closer to home and only three months after Kent, antiwar activists experienced another act of state-sanctioned violence when, on August 29, 1970, the Los Angeles Police Department disrupted and attacked the Chicano Moratorium, killing three people, including Rubén Salazar, a well-regarded journalist for the *Los Angeles Times*.[6] Approximately thirty thousand protesters participated in the moratorium, making it the largest antiwar demonstration organized by a minority group. The protest revealed not only the Chicana/o community's mass rejection of U.S. policy, but also the willingness to physically proclaim that rejection and the risk protesters faced for doing so. With deadly police repression of the moratorium and with "the scream" of the Kent State shootings echoing in the background, Herrera-Sobek's Chicana antiwar narrator continues to dance and march, "drug dazed," as a public act of defiance, while making symbolic sacrificial offerings of her own blood "In competition / With the killing fields / Of Vietnam."[7]

Herrera-Sobek's antiwar poetry helps us understand how Chicana protesters challenged national patriotic affect and asserted their citizenship through public embodiment. We learn about the forms of literal and symbolic wounding that protesting bodies endured as they shaped and were shaped by political unrest at a time when the state's war-waging agenda depended on public unity. The fiction of public unity, as Iris Marion Young points out, is critical to war's success: "Under threat from outside, all of us, authorities and citizens, imagine ourselves a single body enclosed on and loving itself."[8] Social critique, under these conditions, not only undermines unity, but "worse yet, it is ungrateful." This chapter focuses on various examples of "ungrateful" Chicanas who protested the U.S. war in Viet Nam, and who did so by performing a kind of mourning that transformed grief into political grievance and activism. I use the descriptor of "ungrateful" to characterize these Chicana activists and writers because it captures the rejection and condemnation that many Chicanas, and others, faced for voicing their opposition to war. It also speaks to the courage they mustered to face such denunciation. As Butler reminds us, "Dissent is quelled, in part, through threatening the speaking subject with an uninhabitable identification. Because it would be heinous to identify as treasonous, as a collaborator, one fails to speak, or one speaks in throttled ways, in order to sidestep the terrorizing identification that threatens to take hold."[9] This theme of betrayal—to the nation and to the Chicano nation—runs throughout Chicana antiwar activism as Chicanas were seen as traitors for speaking out of turn against the war and against patriarchy.

Herrera-Sobek's poems introduce us to the image of Chicana antiwar protesters—a group that rarely receives popular or academic attention. Marginalized because of their gender and their exclusion from the draft, the Chicana antiwar protesters discussed throughout this chapter experienced warfare through indirect forms of personal, political, and social violence. Living in a wartime economy meant that funding for critical social services and infrastructure was redirected away from the working class and communities of color, who relied more heavily on state aid. Thus, the war indirectly impacted Chicanas by shifting economic burdens from the state to Chicana/o families and households. Like the women discussed in this chapter, many Chicanas also had sons, brothers, cousins, and other loved ones fighting in the war. For a variety of political and personal reasons, Chicanas became critical members of the larger Chicana/o antiwar movement and participated in massive demonstrations and antiwar protests. Chicanas wrote against the war in editorials, small publications, local newspapers, and in poetic and other literary forms. By forming and participating in protest communities, many Chicanas developed a political consciousness that helped them challenge the social, educational, and political inequalities that plagued their communities. What has been less understood in the research about Chicanas in the movement is how Chicana antiwar activists deliberately deployed their positions as sisters, wives, mothers, and cousins of servicemen to mount effective rhetorical and emotional campaigns against the U.S. war in Viet Nam. Their filial bonds to men who were caught up in the war machine raised the stakes of their activism as they fought to keep their loved ones off the battlefield and to reduce the staggering casualty rates that were devastating the larger Chicano familia. Chicanas' motives, political stances, and ethical views, as well as the cultural challenges they faced as women, are glossed over in most accounts that focus on the Chicano soldier or veteran perspective. This chapter refocuses attention on Chicana antiwar activism and literature to reframe Chicano movement narratives and, more significantly, examine how a generation of Chicana activists and authors leveled powerful political, cultural, and ethical critiques of warfare.

As these political and cultural workers struggled along with other protest communities to bring an end to an unpopular war, they emphasized the war's devastating effects on young Chicano men and Vietnamese victims of U.S. aggression. Through the performance of public mourning and other modes of protest, Chicana antiwar activists used political, cultural, and affective appeals to foment a change in the Chicano community's reverence for military service and "warrior patriotism." They used poetry, literature, antidraft activism, protests, and other expressive modes to perform a form of mourning that reimagined wartime notions of citizenship, gender, and imperialism. I argue that these displays of mourning and grief reveal a deeper understanding of human vulnerability and ultimately promote the kind of ethical awareness needed to make moral and political claims on the state. Grief became a defining component of what I describe as Chicanas' antiwar aesthetics, a practice that merged activism with different forms of artistic representation and performance to evoke ethical and political awareness within the Chicana/o community. Among the tactics used by Chicana antiwar activists were deployments of art to stir ethical responses to violence, uses of atrocity photography and visual framing to arouse sympathy and personal accountability, public performances of mourning, and writings of poetry and literature to lament loss and challenge state memorializations of Chicano casualties. Through this multifaceted and body-centric mode of protest, Chicana antiwar activists challenged neoliberal militarism's logic of war. The sixties and early seventies was a period of great social tumult for many people. As Herrera-Sobek's narrator in "Chicana Vietnam Blues" puts it, "no one left / The decade / Unscathed / Unscarred."[10] Her poem reminds us that war and protest were written on the Chicana antiwar activist's body in sometimes violent ways. The poem's title also suggests that Chicana protesters mourned the casualties and social turmoil wrought by U.S. warfare. In the following sections, I focus on the interventionary value of the Chicana activist body—often scathed and scarred and made vulnerable to state violence—and the public performances and literature that she produced. I show how such figures as Chicana activists were able to turn their "blues" into action, or transform their grief into political grievance, to impede the war's negative effects on the Chicana/o community and on the people of Southeast Asia.

NATIONAL AND NATIONALIST FAMILIES AND THE HOME FRONT OF WAR

While Herrera-Sobek's poem "Untitled" is about the war, it is also about the war's impact on the Chicana/o family. The poem's narrator laments that it was "our / brown men / shot / in a dishonest war" while the U.S. government posed as the antagonistic force that destroyed entire families: "For *they* had the guns / and the power / to send our boyfriends / fathers, brothers / off to war."[11] Through an emphasis on oppositional pronouns ("we," "our," and "they"), the poem expresses the agonistic stance that Chicana/o activists took against the state. Rather than offer praise for Chicano military service as previous generations had done, the narrator describes how the war broke up her family and others like hers as Chicanos were impressed into service. Representing a presumably female collective, the narrator emphasizes the romantic and kinship bonds that animate her activism by speaking as the lover to "boyfriends" and as the relative of "fathers" and "brothers." Yet, Chicana activists' relationship to the family has always been fraught with tension given how certain Chicano activists have wielded the concept to perpetuate male privilege. In *Next of Kin: The Family in Chicano/a Cultural Politics*, Richard T. Rodríguez provides the most detailed study of how Chicano nationalists imagined the Chicano people as "a 'nation' defined within the contours of domesticity," wherein the "archetypal Chicana would necessarily provide a feminine spirit of maternal consolation (in spite of her suffering) while ensuring the procreation, hence survival, of Chicano culture."[12] Rather than serve as an empowering model of collectivity and egalitarian relations, the Chicano nationalist family often attempted to manage women's sexuality by imposing cultural gender norms and dichotomies. For example, Chicana activists who rejected the idealized submissive and passive models of womanhood embodied in figures like La Virgen de Guadalupe were often charged with betraying the movement's goals, or as Lee Bebout puts it, "Nationalist discourse scripted Chicanas as always already potential Malinches."[13]

As scholars have argued, Chicanas have consistently struggled against the limits of Chicano nationalism's version of la familia, questioning its heteropatriarchal presumptions and its binary gender roles, which bound women to static notions of traditional female behavior. Yet, challenging nationalist conceptions of family did not entail or require abandoning the family altogether. Rather, as Benita Roth points out, "Chicana feminists also inverted ideas about what being part of a *traditional* Chicano (movement) family meant, arguing that the Chicano family was never the repository of machismo that anti-feminists made it out to be."[14] In *¡Chicana Power! Contested Histories of Feminism in the Chicano Movement*, Maylei Blackwell shows how Chicanas contested nationalist proscriptions of gender roles and their accompanying iconography, such as the "Revolutionary (m)Other"—a common image in anticolonial struggles depicting women's participation in revolution as being "defined by their role as reproducers of the nation"—by recovering and actively reinterpreting historical figures to open up new spaces for Chicana political agency.[15]

Just as Chicano nationalists envisioned the family to be critical to the formation of the Chicano nation, the family was also invoked in wartime narratives of national defense. Natasha Zaretsky argues that the family had always served as an important private realm of heteronormative militarized citizenship production: "It had to prepare children for the duties of liberal citizenship and democratic participation, it had to instill a healthy work ethic and a sense of military honor into boys, and it had to socialize girls for the demands that would one day be required of them as wives, mothers, and homemakers."[16] Protecting this sacred and foundational institution of national regeneration helped war makers justify their military pursuits abroad. In most wartime narratives, women are critical not only to maintaining the nuclear family unit, but also as symbols of vulnerability. They become part of an inextricable dyad that Enloe refers to as "womenandchildren," a phrase that captures the infantilizing tendency of war discourse to imagine women as "family members rather than independent actors, presumed to be almost childlike in their innocence about international *realpolitik*."[17] From a conservative patriarchal perspective, the family was in peril from foreign enemies and from domestic forces, including the feminist movement, the gay rights movement, and an interventionist welfare state—all of which threatened to displace the father as family patriarch and upend traditional gender roles. In this sense, Chicano nationalists and the purveyors of official and dominant wartime nationalism expressed a common concern over the dissolution of the heteropatriarchal family that undergirded their ideological claims to collective identity, national defense, and male privilege. This convergence of interests, Rodríguez reminds us, is not so surprising since subaltern nationalisms that "rail against the state" often "adhere to similar ideologies around gender and sexuality."[18]

Chicana/o antiwar activists also posed a threat to the nation-as-family as the state became increasingly preoccupied with quieting antiwar protesters. Jennifer Correa describes how the Brown Berets, along with other radical groups, including the Black Panthers and the American Indian Movement, were targets of FBI investigations and subjected to the state's arsenal of illegal and covert tactics of intimidation.[19] The state justified its probe into these groups by labeling them as subversive Communist organizations and therefore threats to national security. Even when it was proved that many of these groups had no Communist ties or that they were vulnerable to dissolution because of their own internal conflicts, they remained troublesome reminders of social unrest. In Correa's words, the state practiced a form of parens patriae to govern the Brown Berets, a group that "proved to be 'unruly'" because it challenged its "'father' figure—the state."[20] Thus, Chicana/o antiwar activists and the broader social protest movement posed a significant challenge to the state's fiction of a united public.

The Chicana antiwar activists, writers, and poets discussed in this chapter reveal the ways in which many Chicanas were empowered by their kinship ties and inspired to protest the war in Viet Nam. In addition to developing sophisticated understandings of U.S. foreign policy, kinship to Chicano soldiers or potential draftees was an important ground for their political subjectivity. Yet, Chicana antiwar activists often contested what Blackwell calls the "family melodrama of nationalism," even as they redeployed the symbolic meaning of the family to protest war and state violence.[21] Their specific attempts to keep individual Chicana/o families unified by opposing the draft, militarism, and "warrior patriotism," rather than willingly sacrifice Chicanos for the protection of the larger national family, put them in direct conflict with the needs of the state. Moreover, their public condemnation of U.S. war policy ran counter to the state's desire to marshal the representational power of compliant (and grateful) women in need of protection. To war planners, sisters and mothers of soldiers were particularly significant for their culturally symbolic function as grieving women who represented the sanctity of individual families and, by extension, the nation-as-family.

MOVING FROM GRIEF TO GRIEVANCE: THE GRIEVING CHICANA BODY IN PUBLIC SPACE

Grief is an emotion, and mourning, usually expressed in the form of rituals, is the performance and often the containment of grief.[22] As a performance, mourning allows for a public recognition of one's grief and loss. When imposed by official or social institutions—through memorials or parades, for instance—mourning also acts as a safety valve to help carefully manage grief's emotional volatility. From the perspective of the state, this management is critical because "if grief is artificially inflamed or prolonged, or if the expected conclusion is never satisfactorily achieved," it can move from causing chaos within the family or intimate social circle to causing instability within the larger society.[23] Throughout history, different states and powerful religious institutions have attempted to regulate grief by imposing or banning certain mourning rituals to avoid turmoil or to incite action.[24] Thus, mourning can be read as a form of politics that involves the manipulation of emotional loss for specific objectives. Moreover, women are central to this emotive politics because the "almost universal art of mourning is usually performed by women."[25] I draw on this history to understand the political import of Chicana bodies in mourning and how public performances and expressions of grief formed the foundation of their antiwar aesthetics. This history also helps us avoid thinking about grief in reductive terms or as a disempowering, immobilizing, or even pathological mental state. For Chicana antiwar activists and writers, mourning the loss of Chicano soldiers and the deaths of Vietnamese people enabled important forms of gendered political agency. This chapter shows how they used an antiwar aesthetics to transform grief into grievance.

My discussion of the transformation of grief into grievance is inspired by Anne Anlin Cheng's beautifully rendered *The Melancholy of Race*. She argues that seeking grievance for racism involves demanding public recognition for wrongs committed and "often takes the form of transforming the marginalized, racialized person from being an object bearing *grief* to being a subject speaking *grievance*."[26] Yet, for Cheng, subjecthood is never really achieved in this process:

> The promise of acquiring public recognition, while not without its potentials, cannot really grant subjecthood to the disenfranchised since, strictly speaking, to be "recognized" is still to occupy an object position. To be recognized means that there has to be a recognizing agent, authority and dominant culture. . . . Hence while grievance can be calculated and named, the underlying structure of differentiation continues to generate its history of abjection and coercions.[27]

She goes on to argue that grievance is a "double-edged solution," which promotes the view of aggrieved racialized persons as reveling in their own victimization. Consequently, "the gesture of granting agency through grievance confers agency on the one hand and rescinds it on the other."[28] While Cheng reveals the limits of grievance-based strategies, her analysis prompts questions of its own. Is public recognition always the goal of grievance, or is it just a means to an end, the end being social change (in this case, the end to racist draft boards and the end to an imperialist war)? Is social and political change possible without first seeking recognition? Although seeking recognition does leave one in an "object position" (indeed, can one ever truly escape that positionality?), it does not follow that one cannot also become a subject in the process. I raise these questions because the personal and political development that Chicana antiwar activists experienced seems too important to dismiss. We cannot disregard the organizing, consciousness raising, and intellectual and creative labor they performed as they challenged patriarchal, nationalist, and cultural nationalist attitudes and sought public recognition *and accountability* for the disproportionate deaths of Chicano soldiers. The state, as a "recognizing agent," may have retained its authority to grant recognition, but this did not necessarily negate the subjecthood and agency that Chicanas exercised as they petitioned the state for an end to the war.

Cheng's analysis of the psychoanalytic and political dimensions of grief and grievance is important because it problematizes any celebratory or simplistic notions of agency. Taking up a psychoanalytic view of mourning also reveals its political potential for social change. Here, my use of mourning draws not from Freud's initial definition of mourning—a "healthy" time-bound process of decathexis—but from his later views on mourning's complex entwinement with melancholia. In this revised interpretation, melancholia—the inability to move on from the lost object—is what constitutes the ego. As David Eng and David Kazanjian explain, because the "ego is composed of the residues of its accumulated losses," melancholia is "the precondition for both the ego and the work of mourning."[29] This notion of loss's lingering residues can be "productive rather than pathological."[30] Eng and Kazanjian further argue, "Avowals of and attachments to loss can produce a world of remains as a world of new representations and alternative meanings." If loss can enable "volatile potentiality and future militancies," then we can read Chicana antiwar mourning practices as a political and an ethical gesture toward an unknown future.[31] We can begin to see how Chicana activists' profound attachment to loss enables the imagination of a future without war, body bags, or body counts. I am thus proposing that we read the Chicana antiwar activist as a melancholic figure who apprehends multiple forms of loss and whose own grieving body gets inscribed with competing national and cultural nationalist claims as she questions the ethical consequences of state violence.

But public mourning is never a neutral practice. It is often perceived by some as an unwelcome display of emotion that can determine one's legitimate membership within the nation. I borrow here from José Muñoz's notion that affect is a largely unrecognized yet critical component of citizenship. He asserts the existence of a kind of "'official' national affect" premised on an unmarked white middle-class subjectivity that deems "ethnic affect as inappropriate."[32] In particular, Latina/o affect's impropriety stems from its description as being excessive relative to the normative affect of whiteness, which is staid and subdued. Rather than debate whether Latina/o affect is excessive or not, Muñoz's larger point is to show how affect is a way to perform, or "do," citizenship.[33] I demonstrate in this chapter how affect became a political resource that helped Chicana antiwar activists perform citizenship through their bodies. As they cleared a public space for the feeling brown body, they challenged the limitations of official national affective codes and reimagined the meaning of the nation and of citizenship. Furthermore, Chicana antiwar activists and writers added another dimension to the politics of mourning by interjecting ethics into the discussion of agency, grievance, and public recognition. Because their grief extended to so-called enemies of the state, their mourning became a mode of ethical awareness of human vulnerability, a counter to neoliberal militarism's biopolitics of body counts and general disregard for the value of human life. They rejected the us-versus-them rhetoric of wartime patriotism and instead urged their community to adopt a more stringent moral stance against violence. This capacity to use mourning to "do" citizenship, to envision more liberatory and just futures, and to arouse an ethical response to violence is what makes Latina/o affect both socially and politically consequential.

CHICANA ANTIDRAFT TACTICS AND ANTIWAR ETHICS

Chicana antiwar activists were pushing for change at a time when the military was holding significant internal debates around the issue of conscription. These debates coincided with and were a substantive part of the formation of the neoliberalization of the U.S. military.[34] This convergence should come as no surprise considering that Milton Friedman, one of the leading theorists and proponents of neoliberal economics, was a member of the President's Commission on an All-Volunteer Armed Force, formed by Richard Nixon in response to his campaign pledge to end the draft.[35] Referred to as the Gates Commission, after its chairman, former secretary of defense Thomas Gates Jr., the panel of military officials and academics convened throughout 1969 and early 1970 to examine ways to end conscription. The commission recommended the formation of an AVF that would attract enlistees by "making entry-level military compensation competitive with civilian wages," which would theoretically maintain the military's racial composition and high-caliber personnel.[36] Although commission members disagreed about the transition from conscription to volunteerism, they ultimately proposed measures to ensure the feasibility of an AVF.

The commission's report, presented to Nixon in 1970, reveals how neoliberal thinking eventually led to significant institutional change in the U.S. military. According to George Flynn, the report "reflected the ideas of Milton Friedman and Adam Smith. The preamble expressed the principles of classical liberalism and fears of government domination of individual freedom."[37] The commission's rationale rested on arguments about choice, tax burdens, and financial incentives that continue to inform current recruitment campaigns. The report rehearses many of Friedman's arguments in favor of the AVF—a topic that he had been writing about as early as 1962—with emphasis on two primary and related neoliberal concerns: economic freedom and individual freedom.[38] Because the report focuses on the need to protect the potential draftee's economic freedom, a cost-benefit analysis displaces any moral considerations about citizen obligation or war. Instead, the commission devotes an entire chapter to explaining the various hidden costs assumed by draftees under conscription and emphasizes the need to factor implicit costs into the actual budgetary expenditures of the draft program.[39] The commission argues in the report that draftees were being "taxed by conscription."[40] The conscription tax, a notion attributed to Friedman, describes how draftees were "coerced into serving at levels of compensation below what would be required to induce them to volunteer. They are, in short, underpaid. This underpayment is a form of taxation."[41] From the perspective in the report, the government was financially taking advantage of servicemen in the sense that servicemen were disproportionately paying for the war in lost income potential and were subsidizing the nonserving public for an estimated tax amount of $2 billion per year, or an average of $3,600 per draftee.[42] This notion of turning service into a tax is a hallmark of neoliberalism's tendency to regard all action in monetary terms. It also frames conscription as the ultimate form of governmental penalty and, for neoliberals, the most detestable kind: taxation. The AVF represented a feasible solution to the nation's military needs, but only if it made service financially worthwhile. Thus, the commission's primary recommendation to Nixon was to raise the salary for military personnel—a change, members argued, that should be instituted whether or not the AVF was adopted. With such a change, the "all-volunteer force will attract men . . . who will [volunteer] when military service imposes less of a financial penalty than it currently does."[43]

The report also maintains that conscription is a form of governmental coercion that minimizes free choice: "Compelling service through a draft undermines respect for the government by forcing an individual to serve when and in the manner the government decides, regardless of his own values and talents."[44] For Friedman and other neoliberals and libertarians, the draft represented the ultimate affront to individual liberty.[45] Because individual and economic freedom are so closely intertwined within neoliberal philosophy, the issue of limited individual choice is framed as a matter of hidden costs, which are attributable to the deferment system itself:

> Young men distort their career and personal plans to take advantage of opportunities to postpone or avoid being drafted. They enter college when they otherwise would not. They stay in school longer than they otherwise would. They accept employment in positions they otherwise would not take. They marry and have families before they otherwise would. There is no doubt that the costs of these distorted choices are real.[46]

Under the draft, young men who do not want to serve are forced to make "distorted" life choices that impinge on their true desires and goals and their freedom of self-determination. Coerced military service obviously interferes with a conscript's ability to self-engineer his future within a free market; instead, he becomes an unwilling participant in an uncompetitive, low-wage military labor market. And although the commission admits in the report that these costs are incalculable, it insists that they should nonetheless be considered when comparing the real costs of the draft and the AVF.

The Gates Commission report is most striking in how it depicts recruits as chiefly economic beings rather than patriots, and military service as primarily a job. The commission minimized the notion of national duty as it formulated the idea of a sustainable AVF based on incentivized service and economic self-interest. Many members of the military community did not welcome the move to an AVF in 1973 precisely because it emphasized labor-market rationality to the detriment of a civic obligation ethic. David Segal explains what civic republican militarists regarded as the stakes involved in relying on the self-interested enlistee:

> Instead of being motivated to serve his country and make the world a better place, he is concerned with pay, benefits, and the quality of working life. The nature of the individual's relationship to the organization is transformed, with the traditional implied contract of mutual obligations between the service person and the service being replaced by an explicit contract in which work and time are exchanged for economic remuneration. The military installation, base, or post is seen less as a community and more as a work place, in which the uniformed employee spends only his working hours.[47]

The discomfort that civic republican militarists felt over the AVF reflects how neoliberalism's emphasis on individualism challenges the meaning of citizenship.[48] The military's shift to "a labor-market model of military manpower and a human-relations orientation to management" required the adoption of civilian and industrial employment strategies, including a reconfiguration of military compensation, training, and other workers' benefits. No longer did the military primarily promote a traditional collectivist and patriotic ethos, which defined military service "as something other than a civilian job."[49] Instead the rationalized military came to reflect more general neoliberal trends and behaviors within civilian life that privileged individualism at the expense of traditional notions of national pride and civic obligation. Those who advocated a civic republican conception of the citizen-soldier ideal viewed the AVF as bankrupting the ethos of the military and of service. The civic republican tradition, according to R. Claire

Snyder, conceives of "military service and civic participation" as necessary components of citizenship.[50] The citizen-soldier, universalized as a white heterosexual male, is seen as the ideal embodiment of this preferred form of citizenship because his service lies in nonpecuniary commitments to the political community to which he belongs. His motives for service are based on deep-seated beliefs in "liberty, equality, camaraderie, the rule of law, the common good, civic virtue, and participatory citizenship."[51] Thus, the concept of an all-volunteer force, particularly one based on market rather than political principles, offends the civic republican tradition of civic obligation. From that perspective, service must be viewed not as an economic choice, but as an obligation to the polity.[52]

The draft complicated both the neoliberal and the civic republican philosophies in its selective coercion of military service. But for Chicana antidraft activists, both philosophies failed to address the economic and political realities that limited the choices draft-eligible Chicanos could make. In their view, the burden fell heavily and disproportionately on the Chicana/o community—a sentiment based on the perception of high casualty rates among Chicanos. The self-managed potential draftee that Friedman imagined is quite different from the Chicanos and other working-class men of color who found themselves facing conscription. Friedman's potential draftee is a man with options (he can simply *choose* to enter college or, if already enrolled, stay longer), who can easily maneuver within the free labor market. The high unemployment rate, underfunded public education system, housing segregation, political disenfranchisement, and racial discrimination also made the civic republican notion of participatory citizenship and civic obligation uncompelling to a newly politicized generation of Chicana/o youth, who began to question the values of earlier generations for whom military service epitomized citizenship and national belonging.[53] Although Chicana antidraft activists may have shared with neoliberals like Friedman a desire to end the draft, their motivations and their philosophical and political principles differed from neoliberal and civic republican rationales. For many activists, the draft represented a predatory system in which the predominantly white local draft boards were more likely to send working-class men of color to war than middle-class white men.[54] Therefore, early efforts to protest the high casualty rates of Chicanos in the war focused on reforming the draft boards. Critics began lobbying for more diverse racial and ethnic representation on the boards. Yet, even though greater diversity was gradually achieved, the Selective Service System still privileged middle-class and elite white men through a deferral system for full-time college students—a benefit that few Chicano students could take advantage of given the group's low rates of college attendance. Moreover, men who failed to pass the Armed Forces Qualification Test (AFQT) were also not exempt from service after 1966, when the military instituted Project 100,000, a program that lowered the minimum required scores on the AFQT.[55] Ironically, for these men with limited options, military service was regarded as a way to promote self-engineering and self-management. Men in the Project 100,000 program would learn skills that were "marketable in the civilian economy and pay well."[56] They could become "automotive mechanics, construction workers, telephone lineman, truck drivers, policemen, cooks, and skilled workers in many other civilian occupations."[57]

Spurred into antidraft activism by having brothers who served in Viet Nam, Lea Ybarra and Nina Genera founded Chicano Draft Help, "one of the [Chicano] movement's longest-running anti-draft efforts."[58] Ybarra had one brother and more than twelve cousins in the military, and Genera saw her younger brother denied a hardship deferment despite the draft board's knowledge of their mother's terminal illness.[59] Genera and Ybarra were further influenced as students at the University of California, Berkeley, where they were exposed to antiwar protests and Chicana/o student organizing through the student organization Movimiento Estudiantil Chicano de Aztlán (MEChA). After attending training to become draft counselors, Genera and Ybarra began their antidraft activism by meeting busloads of draftees arriving at the Oakland Army Induction Center. There, they faced the daunting task of trying to convince as many men as possible to consider applying for deferrals:

> Their main tactic was to "bombard" the men with visions of their own mortality in hopes that they would at least stop and examine their available options. "We would say, 'Do you want to die?'" Genera recalled, and mention evidence of disproportionate Chicano casualty rates. Although the vast majority of men completed the short walk from the buses to the induction center, some turned around. The women provided these men with basic information about possible deferments.[60]

Ybarra and Genera expanded their antidraft tactics by writing, printing, and distributing a bilingual pamphlet entitled *La batalla está aquí: Chicanos and the War* (1972). While its most extensive section focused on Selective Service classifications, deferments, and advice on how Chicanos could use them to postpone or avoid being drafted, the pamphlet also included images of Chicana/o antiwar protesters, corridos, drawings and paintings by Malaquías Montoya and other artists, and photographs of dead or injured Vietnamese children. Ybarra and Genera included critical commentary on how the war specifically and disproportionately harmed the Chicana/o community, and they offered strong critiques of Richard Nixon's military escalation and his mishandling of negotiations over the release of U.S. POWs. As a document that combines legal advice, visual arts, and political commentary, *La batalla está aquí* represents an important multilayered rhetorical artifact of Chicana antiwar activism. It signals the sophisticated political engagement of Chicanas who opposed the war on legal and moral grounds. It also exemplifies the ethical commitment to valuing all human life that many Chicana/o antiwar activists and artists held and promoted through their work.

Chicana antidraft activists, and the Chicana/o antiwar movement in general, also posed political and ethical challenges to the war. In Oropeza's extensive reading of Chicana/o print culture from the sixties and seventies, she identifies the major themes found in Chicana/o war writing, including a strong anticolonial critique of U.S. imperialism. Oropeza points out that many Chicana/o antiwar activists were inspired by the Vietnamese people's resistance to foreign invasion.[61] Chicanas/os' new sense of attachment to the land through the concept of Aztlán further strengthened their allegiance to the Vietnamese struggle for independence. Movement activists first learned of Aztlán at the Chicano Youth Liberation Conference held in Denver in 1969. Chicano poet Alurista first introduced Aztlán to attendees through his poem on the mythic homeland of the Aztecs, presumed to be located in the present-day U.S. Southwest. The concept enabled Chicanas/os to claim an indigenous connection to the land that transcended geopolitical borders and predated Spanish and U.S. conquest. The concept's liberatory potential was further cemented in El Plan Espiritual de Aztlán, the manifesto produced at the 1969 conference, which outlined Chicana/o demands for economic, political, and cultural autonomy. For some, Chicanas/os and the Vietnamese were engaged in parallel anticolonial struggles for autonomy from U.S. imperialism. This inspired many Chicana/o activists to identify the Vietnamese as "kindred spirits" in battle against U.S. imperialism rather than as enemies of the state.[62] Many Chicana/o antiwar activists also formulated ethical critiques of the government's execution of the war, expressing dismay at Vietnamese casualties and the destruction caused by U.S. weapons. The publication of graphic images of Vietnamese casualties—many of whom were children—in news outlets forced the public to confront the horrors of war.

As Chicana antiwar activists like Ybarra and Genera grappled with the human carnage resulting from their government's actions, they deployed an antiwar aesthetics to foreground an ethical appeal to the larger Chicana/o community to end the violence. On the dedication page of *La batalla*, Ybarra and Genera explain that the impetus behind their collaboration on the pamphlet was to help "a los de *Mi Raza* a hacer valer sus Derechos de Ciudadano, exigiendo la Igualdad y Fraternidad, en ésta Sociedad Opresiva que siempre nos ha considerado inferiores en un país que [era] hace tan sólo 125 años era" (the people of my race value their rights of citizenship, and demand equality and fraternity in this Oppressive Society that has always considered us to be inferior in a country that is only 125 years old).[63] For Ybarra and Genera, citizenship was expressed not through patriotic military service or civic obligation, but through knowledge of how to avoid conscription using legal deferments. The pamphlet also infuses the discussion of a rights-bearing citizen with an emphasis on informed criticism of U.S. imperialism and of the community's complicity in perpetuating blind patriotism. The pamphlet speaks simultaneously to multiple audiences, using graphic photos of war casualties to bolster political critique with an ethical address.

Because the pull of militarized masculinity was so strong, Ybarra and Genera relied on a combination of different rhetorical appeals to convince young Chicanos to consider deferment and to break the community's reverence for military service. For example, one tactic was to reaffirm yet redirect militarized masculinity by highlighting the need for defenders of the community. By naming their pamphlet *La batalla está aquí*, Ybarra and Genera borrowed the rhetoric of war and masculinist protectionism to frame deferment as an equally courageous option for young men rather than an act of cowardice.[64] They also used the neoliberal logic of cost-benefit analysis to present an economic rationale for their antidraft and antiwar position. For example, they briefly describe the financial cost of the war and the subsequent misallocation of money: "Nixon will spend seven billion dollars more on this war this year alone. . . . Every time we blow up a village in Vietnam we are spending enough money to build a new hospital or library here. . . . And war has brought inflation—you know how much more food costs now than five years ago."[65] Although this critique of the war's effects on government spending and personal finances resonates with the neoliberal principle of economic self-interest, Ybarra and Genera quickly move on to the more significant costs of the war. The "real cost," they argue, has been paid by the Vietnamese. Ybarra and Genera note that while the United States had lost fifty-five thousand men, the Vietnamese had "lost over a million persons, a third of them civilians."[66] The activists note that many survivors were being confined to refugee camps, and they describe how U.S. chemical weapons were destroying farmland and other resources. Although these "hidden" costs of the war were not factored in to Friedman's accounting of externalities, they contributed to Ybarra and Genera's ethical critique of the human toll of the war.

While the risk of injury or dying in battle that U.S. soldiers face is also strangely absent from Friedman's cost-benefit analysis, Ybarra and Genera emphasize what they argue is the disproportionately high Chicano casualty rate. Using Ralph Guzman's study *Mexican American Casualties in Vietnam*, Ybarra and Genera point out that "Chicanos have accounted for more than 20% of this country's casualties while they make up only 10% of this country's population."[67] The activists further highlight the Chicano casualty rate by including the lyrics to Daniel Valdez's "The Ballad of Richard Campos," a song that not only laments the death of a Chicano soldier, but also questions the social value of that loss. The corrido, or ballad, begins with the line "You are dead, Richard Campos, you are gone," and then proceeds to ask how the state would have treated Campos if he had lived: "Would they treat you the same? / Or send you on your way with a medal stuck in / your hand."[68] In the figure of Richard Campos, potential draftees are forced to confront their own mortality. The lyrics ask them to consider whether the trappings of military recognition ("a medal stuck in / your hand") adequately compensate for the risks of death and bodily injury they face. The last stanza then highlights the social injustice Chicanas/os face in the United States:

> Now should a man
> Should he have to kill
> In order to live
> Like a human being
> In this country?[69]

The corrido ends by suggesting that to live "like a human being / in this country," which is to say living a dignified life with access to the full benefits of citizenship, requires committing violence on behalf of the state. While service is described as a "debt" that must be paid to Uncle Sam, first-class citizenship is conditional for the Chicano soldier.

But the last stanza is about more than a matter of the Chicano soldier's social or citizenship status. It actually presents the potential draftee with a moral quandary. Whereas the song begins by lamenting the loss of Chicano life, it ends by describing the Chicano soldier's capacity and willingness to take life. Here, the Chicano soldier is not asked about killing for the lofty goal of defending the nation and its values. Rather, killing the Other is framed as a requisite for securing one's own living standards. That is, the stanza presents the soldier with an ethical encounter between the Other and the self, in which the Chicano soldier is confronted with the dilemma of either refraining from violence or pursuing his own self-interest. By inserting "The Ballad of Richard Campos," Ybarra and Genera move from the language of cost—both economic and personal—to an insistence on ethics.

This ethical address continues with a full-page reproduction of Rupert García's *¡Fuera de Indochina!* (1970). Located on the pamphlet's back cover, García's image of a presumably Asian face in pain immediately exposes the reader to the indescribable toll of human suffering caused by the U.S. war in Southeast Asia (figure 3). It is important to note that García was a Viet Nam War veteran "who served at a secret air base in Indochina from 1965–66."[70] In a later interview, García explains how he was inspired by the Chicano movement to "get involved with society and make images that were understandable by us the artists and also the folks in the neighborhood."[71] He thus translated his war experience into one of the most powerful yet simple images of the Chicano antiwar movement and sent copies of the poster to the organizers of the 1970 Chicano Moratorium in Los Angeles.[72] In *¡Fuera de Indochina!* the abstract outline of the face in two-toned color provides enough visual details to delineate eyebrows arched in pain or anger, eyes that look upward as if in supplication, and a gaping mouth shaped in the form of a loud lament or an angry shout. Other distinguishing features are deliberately omitted; we do not know the face's gender, for example. Instead, we are confronted with an enigmatic face, contorted in pain, that emerges from a black abyss. The silence of the image on the page is in an uncomfortable tension with the imagined sounds of pain, anger, and fear implied by the agape mouth. Although there is only one face, the figure's solitary cry represents the admonition of the people of Southeast Asia in their entirety as the mouth seemingly forms the words "¡Fuera de Indochina!" (Get out of Indochina!). Thus, in García's image we are given a clear political command to end foreign invasion and colonialism, as referenced by the explicit use of Indochina to refer to the region. The appeal is made in Spanish, suggesting that a Spanish-speaking Latina/o community is the intended audience, with the capacity and obligation to heed the command.

FIGURE 3. *¡Fuera de Indochina!*, screen print by Rupert García, 1970. Image courtesy of Fine Arts Museums of San Francisco; Rupert García; Rena Bransten Gallery, San Francisco; and Magnolia Editions, Oakland, California.

We are also ethically hailed by the face in pain. We can read García's image of an agonized countenance as an example of what philosopher Emmanuel Levinas called "the face of the Other."[73] For Levinas, the face is not visually reproducible; it is representationally evasive and cannot be captured by an image. Yet this figure that eludes our ability to visually discern it represents a "conversation" between the I and the Other, which forms the basis for an ethical encounter.[74] Our inability to visually identify the contours and features of the face of the Other disarms us from the power to define and categorize, a power that is often used to engender violence. Instead, we stand before the face without the security of being in control or having authority: "The expression the face introduces into the world does not defy the feebleness of my powers, but my ability for power. . . . [T]he face speaks to me and thereby invites me to a relation incommensurate with a power exercised, be it enjoyment or knowledge."[75] But the face is also vulnerable. Indeed, its utter vulnerability is what draws our attention and sets up the context for an ethical encounter: "The being that expresses itself imposes itself, but does so precisely by appealing to me with its destitution and nudity—its hunger—without my being able to be deaf to that appeal."[76] The "destitution and nudity" is critical to the ethical encounter. Because of it, we come to understand something about the vulnerability of the Other. We become, as Judith Butler puts it, "awake to what is precarious in another life or, rather, the precariousness of life itself."[77] In García's image of the agonized visage, we encounter the extreme vulnerability of the Other because the face is denuded of all markers of self-control and self-possession; instead, pain, the outward manifestation of vulnerability, is nakedly apparent to behold. And this state of abject defenselessness prevents us from "being able to be deaf to that appeal." As viewers, we are unable to turn away from the face's expression, and after recognizing its vulnerability, we feel obligated to learn more.

The Levinasian face also voices an important interdiction. With all its defenses laid bare, in its extreme openness, the face makes a "primordial expression" that commands: "You shall not commit murder."[78] Strangely, the command presumes the will or intention to commit violence on the part of the "I." The presumption—a response to a belief that our own self-preservation depends on harming the Other who may do us harm—suggests that peace requires an active suppression of our violent inclinations.[79] This suppression becomes the basis for ethics: the struggle between self-preservation and recognizing the vulnerability of the Other. Importantly, the face's ethical appeal to refrain from murder is only an appeal, with no physical or juridical power to enforce it. Roger Burggraeve explains, "The term 'appeal' expresses . . . a call to human freedom as good will—that is to say, as a will that can override its own self-interest and stand essentially open for the other than itself, but that can also, again as free will, cast this appeal to the wind."[80] In other words, we can act in our own self-interest by harming the Other, or we can subsume our self-interest by recognizing the vulnerability of the Other and refraining from violence. The Levinasian face presents us with an uncomfortable ethical choice. Much like Richard Campos, we are forced to weigh our own needs and actions against those of the Other.

The antiwar ethics that Ybarra and Genera employ in *La batalla* contrast sharply with the neoliberal ethics of self-care exemplified in Friedman's rationale for the AVF. Neoliberalism should not be regarded as nonethical, despite the violence it engenders; rather, it closely adheres to the Greco-Roman understanding in which "concern for the self and care of the self were required for right conduct and the proper practice of freedom," as Foucault explains. "In antiquity, ethics as the conscious practice of freedom has revolved around this fundamental imperative: 'Take care of yourself.'"[81] Neoliberalism is only an updated and extreme version of this form of ethics. With self-care as the basis for a neoliberal morality, radical individualism and economic self-interest become the ideal principles to guide personal conduct and decision making. Through ballads, art, and photography (discussed in the following section), Ybarra and Genera present an alternative ethical regime as the basis for their antidraft activism. Rather than privilege the ethic of self-care, their antiwar aesthetic prompts an encounter between the self and the Other and uses vulnerability and suffering as the basis for action and moral conduct. By emphasizing this encounter—through the Levinasian face and "The Ballad of Richard Campos," for example—*La batalla* calls for an end to violence through an appeal that one is free to deny but cannot easily ignore. The vulnerability of another's suffering guides choice making and does not rely on cost-benefit analyses. In other words, there is no economic logic to refraining from violence; rather, the face of suffering calls on different impulses for action. In this way, Ybarra and Genera replaced the neoliberal ethics of self-care with a humanist ethics of care for the Other. As I argue in the following section, Chicana antidraft and antiwar ethics would prove necessary in helping the Chicano community reject the dehumanizing and demoralizing practice of body counts.

COUNTING BODIES

"We have been charged with excessive quantification in respect to measurement of progress in Vietnam," said Robert McNamara, secretary of defense from 1961 to 1967.[82] But, he went on to aver, "I have no apologies whatsoever for attempting to measure progress." As a former Harvard Business School professor and president of Ford Motor Company, McNamara believed in the power of quantification and a rationalized approach to achieving President John F. Kennedy's and then President Lyndon B. Johnson's objective of victory over Communist encroachment in Viet Nam. McNamara had served in the Statistical Control Office (SCO) of the U.S. Army Air Corps during World War II, an experience that had perhaps convinced him of how mathematical models could rationalize the process of waging war. After the war, he recruited some of his SCO colleagues to work at Ford, where he "introduced various military techniques into business management."[83] The cross-fertilization between the corporate world and the military came full circle when President Kennedy tapped him to become defense secretary in 1961. According to Jonathan Neale, McNamara "ran the war like the Ford Motor Company. You had the capital, you had the hardware, and you had the men—they were just labor."[84] Once settled at the Pentagon, McNamara established the Office of Systems Analysis, where a group of civilian and military personnel were tasked with conducting cost-effective analyses on various military functions to provide "empirical data to support McNamara's assessment of the war's progress."[85]

McNamara's belief in statistical certitude complemented and contributed to the rise of the neoliberal military. Although the military had used data analysis before, McNamara's tenure as defense secretary ushered in a "technocratic, corporate rationalizing agenda to the Pentagon" that, one could argue, fetishized numerical rationality.[86] Statistics offered McNamara a comforting form of measuring progress and promoted the false belief that war could be as efficiently managed as the performance of workers on the shop floor. Applying a corporate mentality, including business management principles and industrial productivity techniques, to nonbusiness sectors (in this case, war) has since become a familiar neoliberal practice. At the time, however, running the war "like the Ford Motor Company" had devastating consequences, leading to strategic blunders and clouding an accurate assessment of the war's mission and conduct, all of which resulted in the loss of hundreds of thousands of lives. My specific focus here is on how this practice of compulsive quantification enabled the language of empirical data, epitomized by the phrase *body counts*, to obscure the human toll of the war. Although body counts had been used during the Korean War, and although McNamara's Pentagon collected and analyzed various data on numbers of bombs dropped, attacks on infiltration routes, and other indices, the dominant indicator of success in McNamara's war of attrition was the enemy body count.

McNamara later acknowledged his overreliance on body counts: "People have criticized me for stressing this very brutal concept of body count."[87] He went on to admit, "It was, in a sense, a terrible thing." But, as the defense secretary in charge of managing a war of attrition, "it is important to try to understand whether you are accomplishing the attrition or not."[88] Because the U.S. war in Viet Nam was considered to be an unconventional war fought against nationalist insurgents, the traditional ways of measuring victory in war (i.e., through territorial gain and advancement) were thought to be largely inapplicable in Viet Nam. Instead, military planners waged a war of attrition in which, Marilyn

Young explains, the "goal was to reach a 'crossover point' at which more enemy soldiers were being killed than could be replaced. Only body counts would indicate when that point had arrived."[89] The accuracy of body counts and kill ratios, however, were eventually called into question during the war, as it was revealed that soldiers and commanders were inflating the body counts to claim successful missions.[90] The obvious failure of this metric eventually prompted McNamara to doubt the data: "I didn't have any confidence in any of the figures, within considerable margins of error."[91]

For the purposes of this chapter, what interests me more is not the reliability or veracity of the data, but how the blunt yet veiled military speak used to quantify death became part of official and public vocabularies of war. According to Daniel Hallin, "Every Thursday the Public Affairs Office in Saigon released the weekly casualty figures, or 'body count.' And for years the networks put them up, every Thursday, usually next to little American, South Vietnamese, and NLF or North Vietnamese flags. In later years of the war, however, they began apologizing in various ways for the coldness of the numbers."[92] In this manner, the language of body counts—originally spoken among military planners and in the battlefield—"aspire[d] to the condition of the framing language" of war in public discourse.[93] As part of war's reductive idiom, body counts became part of the official and popular framing of war, which designated acceptable ways of speaking of and thinking about the wounded and the dead. The biopolitical language of *body counts* and *kill ratios* altered the language of war, creating a duplicitous vernacular that simultaneously obscured the dead (by replacing bodies with numbers) and highlighted precisely what was at stake in war: the accumulation of vulnerable and killable human bodies.[94]

The framing of enemy and civilian deaths as body counts undoubtedly legitimated McNamara's approach to the scientific management of the war. As August Carbonella puts it, body counts "were used to sell the war to an increasingly skeptical U.S. public on the nightly news, in much the same way as production reports are used to bolster corporate standings in the stock market."[95] Enemy bodies were easily used to substantiate victory because of how the wounded human body functions in times of war. Elaine Scarry argues that the wounded body stands as the ultimate instance of reality: "The visible and experienceable alteration of injury has a *compelling and vivid reality* because it resides in the human body, the original site of reality."[96] Yet, the wounded body evades linguistic expression; language becomes impotent in the face of corporeal pain. Because of injured bodies' capacity to evade linguistic containment, they are characterized by their nonreferentiality or referential instability—their ability to lend credence and fixity to different contexts and ideas, or what Scarry calls derealized, disembodied, and unanchored beliefs. Simply put, the "reality-conferring" function of wounded bodies legitimizes state narratives of war because "wounding is able to open up a source of reality that can give [an] issue force and holding power."[97] The rising toll of dead and wounded Vietnamese bodies reconfirmed McNamara's claims of progress in the war, claims that were further bolstered by the seemingly objective veneer of numerical data.

While the occulting power of war's language enables the double erasure of injured bodies, both physically and verbally, the photos of atrocity act as a counter that exposes death, injury, and vulnerability. During the war, body counts remained largely unimaginable until a series of war photographs helped enflesh the abstraction. Both the original and the reprinted versions of *La batalla* appeared at a time when the public was exposed to what would become the era's most iconic photographs: Eddie Adams's 1968 photo of the execution of a captured Vietcong prisoner; army photographer Sergeant Ron Haeberle's photos of the My Lai massacre published in the final months of 1969 in *Life* and *Time* magazines; and Associated Press photojournalist Nick Ut's 1972 photo of Vietnamese children fleeing an aerial napalm attack.[98] Chicanas/os, like all other Americans, were being exposed to war atrocities through the publication of these photos as well as through media coverage, which provided viewers with what Susan Sontag refers to as a kind of "tele-intimacy" not experienced in previous wars.[99] Ybarra and Genera intensified that sense of intimacy in *La batalla*.

In an interview with Oropeza, Ybarra explains that many Chicana/o antiwar activists "were feeling badly about the Vietnamese."[100] Ybarra and Genera expressed their horror over Vietnamese casualties by including photos of injured and murdered children in *La batalla*. "Through such graphic images," Oropeza writes, "the authors also hoped to erode the automatic respect with which many Mexican Americans had long regarded military service."[101] In addition to questioning the long-held tradition of military service within the community, the images also provide the most striking revelation of the extreme precariousness of the Other. The photos work differently from García's artistic rendering of the Levinasian face. Instead, we enter a more complex ethical terrain created by the content, medium, framing, and instrumentalization of the photos. Although bodies can be used to anchor notions of progress and to substantiate numerical victories in battle, in the pamphlet Ybarra and Genera attempt to reappropriate the use-value of wounded bodies by questioning whether children's deaths and mutilation are equivalent to progress, and whether a victory that relies on those injuries is justifiable. Through the selective and strategic use of atrocity photos,

Ybarra and Genera infuse ethics into the cold spreadsheets of McNamara's accumulated bodies.

The images that confront the reader on the first page of the pamphlet are three captioned photos cut and pasted into a collage that takes up most of the page (figure 4). Only one image features a surviving child, "Little Nguyen Hong Tam, 2, victim of U.S. incendiary bomb."[102] The toddler's face cries in agony as he clutches onto an arm that holds his naked, scarred body. In the other two photos, we see four lifeless children, their mutilated and bloody bodies frozen in death. While the captions provide names to identify and humanize each child, they also explicitly name the weapons that caused the carnage: "U.S. incendiary bomb," "U.S. steel-pellet bombs," and "U.S. bombs." Naming the weapons reminds readers of the sophistication and technological superiority of U.S. weaponry but disabuses us of the belief that such weapons are used discriminately and with precision.

Susan Sontag describes how photos can corroborate the truth or serve as verifiable proof of body counts and the like.[103] Whereas numbers can be manipulated or inflated, photos of the dead stand as irrefutable. Yet, photos do more than verify attrition. They can, if properly framed, disrupt the language of body counts by invoking ethical witnessing, which intervenes in the practice of tallying bodies. Yet, the ethical value of atrocity photos is far from self-evident or undisputed. For example, Sontag argues that photos have delimited "ethical content," that their "emotional charge" tends to wear off over time, transforming photos into works of art. Moreover, they cannot provoke as deep an understanding as narrative can: "Only that which narrates can make us understand. The limit of photographic knowledge of the world is that, while it can goad conscience, it can finally, never, be ethical or political knowledge."[104] In Sontag's estimation, photos do not present the full story behind the image and thus offer only partial knowledge when full knowledge is needed to make informed ethical judgments. Moreover, photos can raise serious concerns about racialized subjects being further dehumanized through the conventions of photography. For example, the images discussed above harbor a kind of invasive quality based on the camera lens's proximity to the bodies. There is something indecent and almost forensic about the way the camera zooms into the bodies, occluding all background and context. In these photos, the wounds are privileged over the humanity of the children. As Sontag points out, this level of scrutiny is usually reserved for the "exotic" and the black and brown bodies of Others: "With our dead, there has always been a powerful interdiction against showing the naked face. . . . The more remote or exotic the place, the more likely we are to have full frontal views of the dead and dying."[105] Such atrocity photos exhibit a level of exposure that is not afforded to white American bodies.

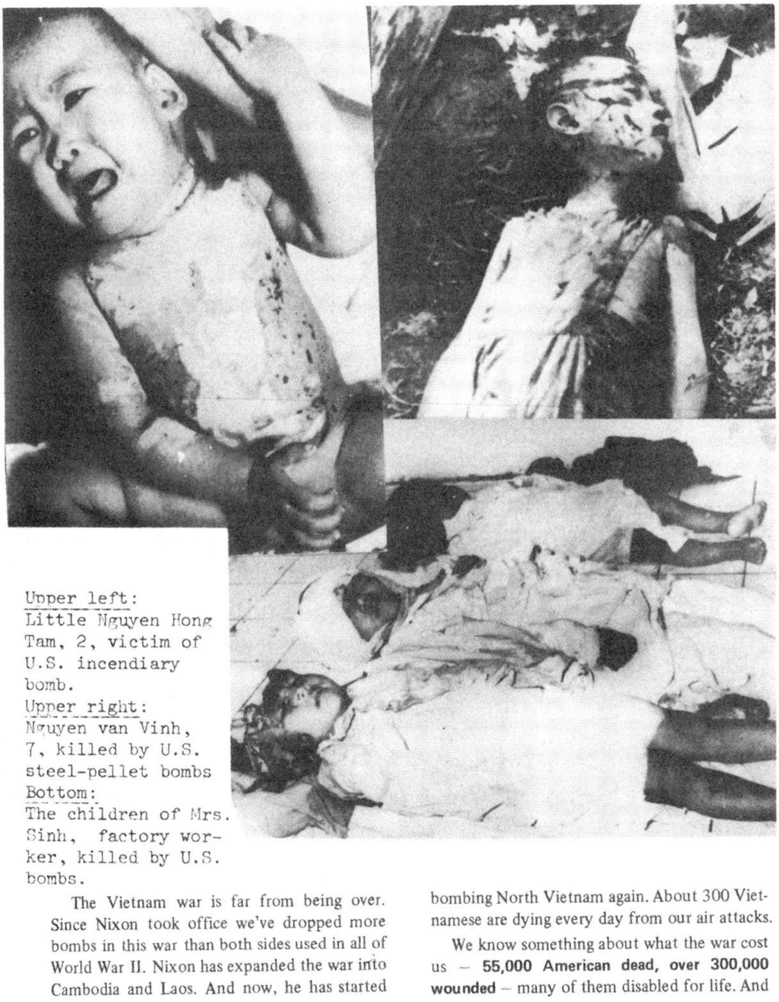

Upper left:
Little Nguyen Hong
Tam, 2, victim of
U.S. incendiary
bomb.
Upper right:
Nguyen van Vinh,
7, killed by U.S.
steel-pellet bombs
Bottom:
The children of Mrs.
Sinh, factory wor-
ker, killed by U.S.
bombs.

The Vietnam war is far from being over. Since Nixon took office we've dropped more bombs in this war than both sides used in all of World War II. Nixon has expanded the war into Cambodia and Laos. And now, he has started bombing North Vietnam again. About 300 Vietnamese are dying every day from our air attacks.

We know something about what the war cost us – **55,000 American dead, over 300,000 wounded** – many of them disabled for life. And

FIGURE 4. Page 1 of antiwar pamphlet, *La batalla está aquí: Chicanos and the War*, by Lea Ybarra and Nina Genera, 1972, featuring images of Vietnamese children injured or killed by U.S. bombs. Courtesy of Lea Ybarra.

Instead, the "exotic" Other, "even when not an enemy, is regarded only as someone to be seen, not someone (like us) who also sees."[106]

For Ybarra and Genera, the photos were meant to perform multiple tasks. On the one hand, they were selected to inspire sympathetic reactions among Chicano viewers. On the other hand, their function was to evoke responsibility for that suffering. Through a series of directives, Ybarra and Genera forced viewers to realize that they had the power to end the suffering through deliberate and conscious actions within their own community. The pamphlet itself offered the community ways of diminishing the misery of war either directly (by applying for deferrals from service) or indirectly (by discouraging young men from defining their masculinity through military service). Thus, every member of the community was implicated in contributing to a broader culture that enabled and condoned warfare. For this reason, Chicano community members were forced to bear the discomfort of looking at torment if they had any intention of alleviating it. Viewers became, in a sense, wounded by the images of suffering. Obviously, this wounding was drastically different by degree and kind from that of the bodies in the photos, but it was a kind of wounding nonetheless, an "assault on the sensibility of the viewer" that served the specific purpose of awakening moral culpability.[107]

Ybarra and Genera were careful to move their viewers beyond sympathy and into action. The close-up shots of most of the images give the impression of being near enough to touch the battered bodies of children, awakening an instinctual gesture and desire to console the injured through human touch. Yet, as Sontag reminds us, the desire for or illusion of sympathetic proximity to suffering also obscures the power relations established through the image:

> The imaginary proximity to the suffering inflicted on others that is granted by images suggests a link between the faraway sufferers—seen close-up on the television screen—and the privileged viewer that is simply untrue, that is yet one more mystification of our real relations to power. So far as we feel sympathy, we feel we are not accomplices to what caused the suffering. Our sympathy proclaims our innocence as well as our impotence. To that extent, it can be (for all our good intentions) an impertinent—if not an inappropriate—response.[108]

Sympathy can be just as dangerous as antipathy if it leads to complacency and impotence. Focusing on one's grief can devolve into a self-centered, solipsistic gesture that further decenters the victims of violence by privileging one's own emotions. Ybarra and Genera seemed aware of the risk of sympathetic inaction that *La batalla*'s photos might engender. To show how the Chicano community was implicated in the atrocities of war and therefore the suffering of Vietnamese victims, Ybarra and Genera provided specific steps to take to challenge the militarization of their community.[109] In this way, they ensured that viewers could use their sympathy in productive ways.

The framing of the atrocity photos in *La batalla* is critical to channeling viewer sympathy into action. Ybarra and Genera's inclusion of photos of children burned by U.S. chemical weapons exemplifies the role of framing in the pamphlet's antiwar aesthetic. For example, one pair of photos features nine-year-old Hoang thi The and thirteen-year-old Tran van Tang, wounded by U.S. phosphorous and napalm bombs, respectively (figure 5). Their wounded bodies are the focus of each photo. In one, we can see where napalm seared away the skin of Tran's outer right thigh, exposing damaged muscle and bone as his emaciated body lays on a bed, his facial expression betraying none of the physical anguish that presumably wracks his young body. While viewers are confronted with each child's gruesome injuries, their eyes are also directed above and to the left of the photos, where text in large, bold display type asks readers, "What Can You Do to keep chicanos [*sic*] from going to Viet Nam and killing or mutilating beautiful children."[110] The phrasing of this rhetorical question emphasizes Ybarra and Genera's insistence on personal responsibility. The question highlights Chicanos' role in committing violence against children like Hoang and Tran. It suggests that military service is not about honor and family tradition, but about transforming young men into agents of death—an unsettling reality for the families and loved ones of soldiers and potential draftees to contemplate. Here, Chicano soldiers are not absolved from the violence they commit against "beautiful children," a phrase that recognizes and humanizes the vulnerability of bodies marked as Other. In contrast to McNamara's tallying of anonymous quantifiable bodies, the photos in *La batalla* are of identifiable, individualized, and vulnerable bodies whose "beauty" lies in their shared humanity.

While the bold question indicts Chicano soldiers in the violence, it also implicates the Chicana/o community in the war. As a direct address made to the nonsoldier, the question urges readers to overcome any sense of impotence they may have as well as the false sympathetic proximity that atrocity photos inspire. In other words, the photos of dead and injured children ask readers to feel, while the large bold text asks readers to act. Ybarra and Genera, in answer to their own question, directly address specific segments of the community: parents, women, and employers. For example, the pamphlet advises fathers not to shame their sons into service with phrases like "'Que no eres hombre cobarde?' 'Aren't you a man, coward?'"[111] Meanwhile, mothers are asked not to view the military as a way to get their sons "off the streets." Parents, in general, are advised to resist the social pressures of a militarized society by putting their family above the needs of the state: "Parents must begin to place the love of their sons before their for the Chicano to obtain, in comparison to the Anglo, in the case of the Selective Service System, Chicanos have received deferments when they have obtained proper counseling as to their legal rights.

What Can You Do to keep chicanos from going to Viet Nam and killing or mutilating beautiful children

Upper right:
Little Hoang thi The, 9, Quang Van commune, wounded by U.S. phosphorous bombs.

Lower left:
Tran van Tang, 13, a school boy of Thuong Son hamlet, seriously burned all over his body by napalm bomb in a U.S. air raid.

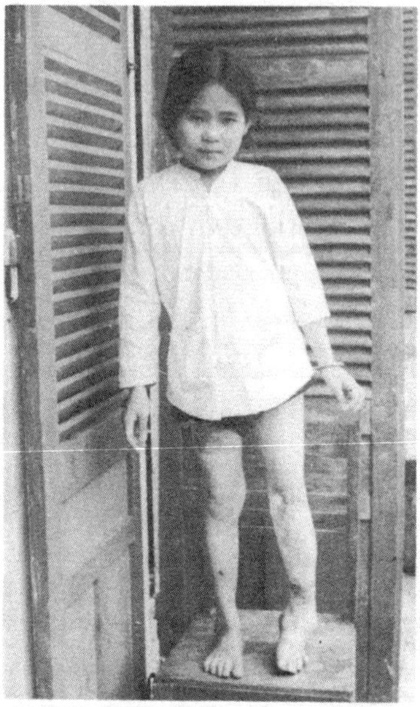

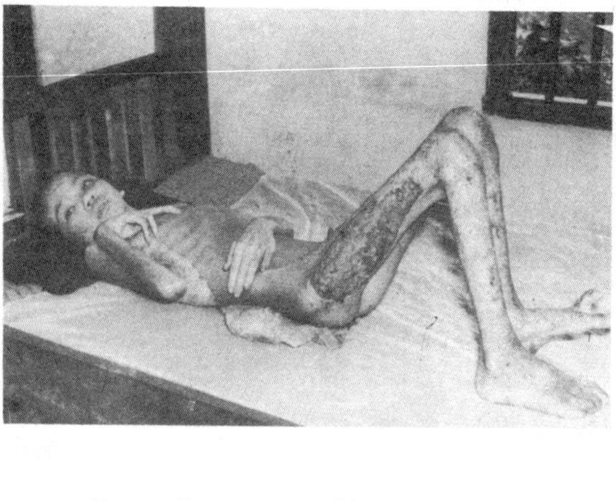

WE ONLY LOSE OUR MEN AND OUR HONOR AND PRIDE BY PARTICIPATING IN OR PROMOTING THE KILLING OF THOUSANDS OF MEN, WOMEN, AND CHILDREN.

5

FIGURE 5. Page 5 of antiwar pamphlet, *La batalla está aquí: Chicanos and the War*, by Lea Ybarra and Nina Genera, 1972, featuring a call to action juxtaposed with photographs of Vietnamese children severely injured by U.S. bombs. Courtesy of Lea Ybarra.

fear of the government." Women are also encouraged to use their relationships with draft-eligible men to discourage service: "Women, we can be very influential in convincing, encouraging, and supporting our husbands, brothers, boyfriends, cousins, nephews, in seeking legal alternatives to the draft."[112] Meanwhile, employers within the community are advised to hire any potential Chicano draftee because "a deferment and no job isn't going to feed him or his family or pay his bills."[113]

In addition to these specific suggestions, Ybarra and Genera include various photographs of Chicanas/os protesting the war. Directly opposite the images of Hoang and Tran is a photo of Chicanas/os marching and holding protest signs (figure 6). The protesters feature Chicanas/os of all ages, including a woman in the foreground (presumably a young mother) who looks down at a young girl and boy at her side—an indication to readers that antiwar marchers include entire families and are not some radical fringe element of the community. The young mother's sign, which reads "Viva la Revolucion," contrasts with a sign directly behind her, which reads "Raza Si, Guerra no." While the two signs seemingly hold opposing messages, their incongruity is easily explained by considering the Mexican Revolution's symbolic meaning. For Chicana/o protesters, the revolution represented an instance when the underclass and exploited peoples of Mexico rose up to overthrow a corrupt and oppressive state. It proved that by working as a collective, the Mexican people can effect change in favor of social justice. The "Viva la Revolucion" protest sign suggests that ending the U.S. war in Viet Nam will require similar collective effort.

Despite the inherent limits of the medium, Ybarra and Genera demonstrate how photographs of atrocity can be used to evoke ethical responses. Their deliberate framing of the photos is important to note because, as Sontag points out, photos in and of themselves do not help us understand. Rather, meaning is, in a sense, curated by the framer to achieve a particular interpretation and, ultimately, to elicit a particular response and action.[114] Yet, frames are vulnerable because they must be reproduced. Reproduction creates new contexts, which open up new meanings and affects. This is the hope of an antiwar aesthetic. The hope is to capture and reshape an image, even if only for a brief time, to engage in what Butler calls the "critical instrumentalization" of the image.[115] The difficult images that Ybarra and Genera include in *La batalla* are themselves reframed within a collage of Chicana antiwar commentary, photographs of Chicana/o community protesters, and images of Chicana/o protest art. The photos of Vietnamese suffering take on new meaning in their new home in *La batalla*, as they force viewers

to Vietnam, in proportion to the total population, then they send off their own white youth . . ." 10

Daniel Valdez in a song entitled *THE BALLAD OF RICHARD CAMPOS,* also expresses this same sentiment when he states,

You are dead, Richard Campos, you are gone
You are dead, and I bid you good-bye
But now that you're gone, there's a doubt in my mind
What would have happened if you never would have died?

Would they treat you the same?
Or send you on your way with a medal stuck in your hand
Saying "Thank you, boy, thank you very much,
You have paid your debt to Uncle Sam"?

Now should a man
Should he have to kill
In order to live
Like a human being
In this country?

One need only remember the Chicano moratorium throughout California and the Southwest and especially the Chicano Moratorium in Los Angeles in August of 1970, when thousands of Chicanos marched to protest the Vietnam war, to realize that there is a growing awareness among Chicanos concerning the war. Unfortunately, although this awareness is growing, it still involves relatively small numbers, and the majority of young Chicanos are still being drafted or are enlisting because they think that they will eventually get drafted anyway, and that there is nothing they can do about it. The point is, something **can** be done. The Chicano can use the Selective Service regulations to his own advantage by learning the legal procedures necessary to apply for and receive deferments. Realizing, of course, that any type of legal justice is always more difficult and sometimes impossible

4

FIGURE 6. Page 4 of antiwar pamphlet, *La batalla está aquí: Chicanos and the War,* by Lea Ybarra and Nina Genera, 1972, featuring an image of Chicanas/os, including families with children, protesting the Vietnam War. Courtesy of Lea Ybarra.

to consider cross-cultural awareness and, more critically, to acknowledge the Chicana/o community's complicity in state violence. Through careful selection, formatting, and organization, Ybarra and Genera curated the photos of wounded children to elicit moral outrage and personal accountability. Juxtaposing photos of wounded children and Chicana/o protesters helped to prompt both sympathy and action in their readers. Readers were given different models of action to take that ranged from drawing on private family relationships to making public pronouncements against the war. Moreover, Ybarra and Genera's use of atrocity photos challenges Sontag's assertion that photos can never provide "ethical knowledge." Ybarra and Genera show that by careful selection, captioning, collaging, and narrative framing, such photographs can elicit empathy, discomfort, and ultimately outrage within viewers—emotions that form the basis for ethical action.

Whereas Ybarra and Genera used various rhetorical and visual tactics in *La batalla* to galvanize antiwar sentiment within the community, Chicana antiwar activist Delia Alvarez found herself at the center of a movement to protest the Nixon administration's handling of POWs. I move now from a discussion of how Chicana activists used grief and sympathy to mobilize their community to an examination of how the state attempted to harness the symbolic power of grieving POW families to support its agenda. In the following section I focus on how Alvarez strategically reclaimed her grieving Chicana body in public interviews and protests to challenge the state's war policy.

PUBLIC MOURNING, FAMILY BETRAYAL: DELIA ALVAREZ AND POW ACTIVISM

On August 2, 1964, North Vietnamese forces allegedly torpedoed the USS *Maddox* in the Gulf of Tonkin. Three days later, twenty-six-year-old Mexican American navy pilot Everett Alvarez Jr., from Salinas, California, was shot down from the sky after dropping bombs on North Vietnamese targets in the Gulf of Tonkin. Alvarez was quickly captured by North Vietnamese forces and held captive for the next eight and a half years, making him the second-longest-held prisoner of war to be captured in North Viet Nam. As the war progressed, other U.S. POWs joined him at the North Vietnamese prison they would come to call the Hanoi Hilton. Although the Alvarez family soon learned that Everett had indeed survived, many other families continued to anxiously await news about their POW. Not knowing a loved one's fate and knowing that one's son, brother, or father was being held captive by enemy forces were two forms of emotional torment that many U.S. families experienced. While the state sympathized with the desperation and grief of POW families, it was initially wary about how the public display of grief might affect the war effort. The increasing number of U.S. POWs was a sensitive issue for the succession of administrations that would eventually oversee the war.

According to Natasha Zaretsky, Everett's capture, like that of subsequent POWs, did not receive much news coverage until 1966.[116] During that time, the Johnson administration advocated a policy of "quiet diplomacy," in which the families of POWs were encouraged to "stay out of the public eye, refrain from contacting the press," to avoid affecting negotiations with the North Vietnamese.[117] But Melvin Laird, upon replacing Robert McNamara as secretary of defense, convinced a newly elected Richard Nixon that the policy of "quiet diplomacy" had been a failure. In 1969, Laird launched the Go Public campaign, bringing attention to the plight of POWs by encouraging their families to publicly grieve the absence of their loved ones. The campaign's goal was "to highlight North Vietnam's intransigence and violations of the Geneva Conventions for refusing to provide information on American POWs and for barring impartial international inspections of prisoner-of-war camps."[118] The campaign emphasized not only how the North Vietnamese were violating international standards, but also that by doing so, they were devastating the innocent families of POWs by keeping fathers away from children, husbands away from wives, and sons away from parents. In Zaretsky's analysis of the Go Public campaign, she shows how the administration relied on the symbolic value of grieving families to reframe the debate about the war. By focusing on the emotional cost that POW families were paying for the captivity of U.S. servicemen, the "campaign vilified the North Vietnamese and portrayed America as victim rather than transgressor" and "constructed the private world of the family as a wounded and violable space of national injury, one under threat from a foreign adversary."[119] Moreover, Zaretsky argues that these grieving families provided sentimental cover for a series of U.S. atrocities (including the My Lai massacre) and violations.[120] By appropriating POW families' grief as its own, the state transformed itself into a nation-as-family, which necessitated and justified a continuation of the war while providing a moral claim to outrage against humanitarian abuses.

Women were central to maintaining this analogical fiction between family and nation because of their capacity to symbolically embody innocence and vulnerability. Women in mourning were figures whose private grief was meant to be read as an apolitical appeal for sympathy and support. The grieving mother and other female kin who supposedly act out of the purity of their love rather than out of rational or political motivation wielded the power of moral condemnation. Everett's mother, Soledad, and his older sister, Delia, along with other POWs' female family members, were expected to perform this emotional labor in public and on behalf of the state. In the early years of Everett's captivity, Delia's sisterly love for him defined her view toward the war: "I guess you could say I was apolitical then. I just thought about my brother, defending his country, and falling into the hands of the enemy."[121] Delia not only complied with the policy of "quiet diplomacy," she also believed in the state's rationale for the war: "I believed in the domino theory. To tell you the truth, I never questioned anything."[122] Her initial response as concerned sister and as unquestioning citizen suited the goals of the Go Public campaign. Eventually, however, family bonds compelled rather than quelled Delia and Soledad's demands for more information, not only about Everett's status, but also about the war itself.

For Soledad, her long-held interest in the California mission system helped her draw comparisons between the Spanish colonizers in Mexico and the succession of colonizers in Viet Nam, a history she learned only by reading everything she could find about Vietnam.[123] Through her own self-initiated and self-directed study of Vietnamese history, she was able to question U.S. war policy and even relate with the Vietnamese struggle. In Everett Alvarez's co-authored autobiography, *Chained Eagle: The Heroic Story of the First American Shot Down over North Vietnam*, he describes his mother's developing views on colonialism: "There was even something comparable in her mind between the poorly armed Mexicans who fought for their sovereignty against a much better equipped army, and the out-gunned Vietnamese who appeared night after night on her television screen."[124] Soledad's view of the war was not solely or simply shaped by her role as the mother of a POW; rather, her maternal love for her son became the impetus for her transformation into an inquiring and well-informed citizen capable of forming trenchant political analyses of her government's policies. In the early years of Everett's captivity, however, she and the rest of the Alvarez family never voiced their questions or criticisms outside their home. They were aware of their role as a POW family and the importance of maintaining the appearance of a family united in their faith in government and its policies: "Forever conscious of the boundaries between private license and public constraints," the Alvarezes "dared not expose the family free-for-alls to the watchful and critical eye of the public."[125] To fully engage in the democratic practice of public debate, however, the family would have to voice their objections in public. Delia's own political evolution and her role as the family's designated spokeswoman soon facilitated the family's break from the "public constraints" of a prowar culture.

Delia's transformation from an "apolitical" sister began when the United States escalated its bombing and troop deployment in North Viet Nam. At that point, she started questioning the sincerity of the government's efforts to free her brother.[126] Despite McNamara's numerical certainty in a high body count, the Alvarez family recognized that "the enemy showed no sign of giving up nor any readiness to negotiate."[127] In addition to doubting the strategy of attrition, Delia also grew frustrated with the lack of information about her brother. During Everett's eight and a half years of captivity, Delia's worldview was further shaped by her own experiences and community activism. After graduating from college, she worked at the Santa Clara Welfare Department, where she witnessed firsthand the lack of opportunities for her community, including for the young men who were being drafted because, unlike Everett, they did not attend college and thus could not benefit from student deferments.[128] In 1967, she left for a short European vacation, which turned into a twenty-month journey that exposed her to international criticism of the U.S. invasion of Viet Nam. This exposure to U.S. flag burning and anti-American sentiment further influenced her broader perspective on both the war and her country's judgments and motives. Upon her return to the United States in 1969, she helped organize a petition of more than seventy thousand signatures demanding that the United States take "more forceful, positive action" toward the release of Everett and the other POWs.[129] Delia also grew critical of the National League of Families of American Prisoners and Missing in Southeast Asia, an organization of POW families established in 1970, and opposed their tactics, which were based on the belief that "the best way to help their men [was] to try to make life better for them while they [were] captives."[130]

Delia's activism became increasingly public as she spoke at rallies in support of antiwar naval airmen and women and appeared with Jane Fonda and antiwar veteran John Kerry.[131] She also joined the Chicano movement which, as we have seen, had an active and committed antiwar component. Indeed, she attributed her activism and political critique to the movement: "My involvement with the Chicano movement has done more than anything to open my eyes to things as they really are."[132] Like Soledad, Delia began to identify similarities between the conditions of Chicanas/os and the Vietnamese: "The mentality that calls Vietnamese 'gooks' is the same mentality that calls brown people 'spics.' It's the same battle."[133] In her provocative public statement, she implied that because the Vietnamese and Chicanas/os are in the "same battle" against U.S. racism, they are allied against a common enemy. Linking domestic forms of discrimination to U.S. foreign policy clearly placed Delia's activism outside the views of most POW families. Delia and Soledad, as a result of these views and their calls for an end to the war, felt "alienated" from other POW and military families. Delia described being in a "rough position" as an antiwar activist and a sister of a POW: "If you spoke out against the war, people would think you were unpatriotic, or were being unfaithful to your brother."[134] Delia also believed that she had "drawn the ire of the families because of her activities with the Chicano movement."[135]

Her status as the sister of a POW afforded her the opportunity to occupy local and national stages of protest. She frequently appeared in local and national print and TV interviews. The public's interest in her views may have been initially based on her POW family status, but she undoubtedly also attracted attention for her ability to articulate an oppositional political critique of the administration and the war. She was granted a moral authority based on kinship, which she used to make political demands on the state rather than on its behalf. Because of her dissidence, however, she faced various threats. Zaretsky describes how "POW wives appeared at meetings where Alvarez was a featured speaker to publicly scorn and ridicule her. She received hate mail and anonymous phone calls accusing her of being a communist traitor."[136] Thus, her decision to enter the public sphere as an antiwar protester, to use her body to selectively perform affect, entailed the risk of emotional and physical harm.

Delia's critique of the war and the Nixon administration extended to the Go Public campaign. In one interview, she accused the administration of publicly releasing the names of POW families to use them "as a public tool to create emotionalism."[137] Thus, she recognized the state's attempt to manipulate her family's grief and refused to publicly perform the emotional labor that was expected of her as the sister of a POW. Delia's refusal to mourn appropriately over the captivity of her POW brother was a direct challenge to the state's directives as well as a rejection of performing the prescribed national affect. By national affect, I am referring to José Muñoz's notion of a national feeling associated with hegemonic white middle-class subjectivity that "positions itself as the law" and as the normative basis for citizenship.[138] Here, I read patriotism as the highest expression of state-sanctioned national affect. Being labeled "unpatriotic," as Delia and Soledad had been, demonstrates how they failed to perform the expected national affect appropriate for the female relatives of a captured solider. Delia does not let Everett's status as a soldier obscure the discrimination that Chicanas/os face in the "battle" against U.S. racism. She also does not let the national esteem for her lionized brother obscure the violence of his chosen occupation as a navy pilot. Rather than perform the grateful and patriotic sister or the grief-stricken sibling, in many of her print and TV interviews, she performs a kind of stoicism and skepticism that contrasts with the Go Public campaign's promotion of weeping and forlorn families.[139] Delia's stoicism or lack of affect served as a political rejection of Nixon's attempt to appropriate the emotions of POW families. If, as José Muñoz argues, "standard models of United States citizenship are based on national affect," Delia's stoicism and her unpatriotic behavior called her own citizenship into question.[140]

Ironically and dismissively, Everett attributed Delia's antiwar activism to her emotions. During his first press conference after his release, he was asked if there was any tension between him and Delia as a result of her activism. He responded, "I was glad to be home and she was glad to have me home, for sure. I'm convinced that to a large degree, her activities were based largely on emotion. We were there for a long time and she wanted us home. She wanted me home."[141] Despite Everett's conciliatory tone, his later memoirs show clearly that Delia's antiwar activism caused him great consternation. In his memoir *Code of Conduct*, he writes, "Dealing with my sister Delia's defection from the cause I'd nearly died for and suffered a long time for was more difficult" than dealing with news that his wife had left him for another man.[142] Everett's remarks at the press conference attempted to explain away Delia's political critiques of the war by relying on age-old gendered stereotypes of the irrational, emotional woman. Interpreting what he viewed as his wayward sister's misguided actions as based on her excessive love for him was a way to excuse and process the sense of betrayal he felt.

It is important to understand that Delia's refusal to mourn appropriately also had an ethical dimension. Though she would not grieve on the state's terms, she did grieve nonetheless for the Vietnamese victims of the war. When asked about her brother's release, she replied, "Everett will return when Vietnamese children will be able to look at the sky and clouds and not fear that a bomb will drop that will burn and tear their bodies. Everett will return because the Vietnamese will live! Because the Vietnamese will win!"[143] Like Ybarra and

Genera, who used photos of injured Vietnamese children to evoke moral outrage, Delia shows similar concern for the innocent victims of U.S. aggression. In graphic detail, she describes the burning and tearing of children's bodies as a rhetorical strategy to highlight the violence of the war. Interestingly, her reference to bombs falling from the sky is either an ironic statement or a veiled indictment (or both) of her brother's role as a navy pilot conducting his own bombing mission on North Vietnamese targets before he was shot down and captured. She also conditions Everett's return upon U.S. defeat, a defeat she jubilantly expresses as a Vietnamese victory: "the Vietnamese will win!" Delia's comments reflect a preoccupation with "enemy" lives that transcends her own national identification and family loyalties. She expresses an unauthorized concern for the wrong bodies, which places her at odds with the state.

The state was not alone in attempting to invoke and use the symbolic power of grieving Chicana bodies. In the next section, I examine how Chicanas also had to contend with the cultural nationalist demand for the Chicana-in-mourning. Chicana antiwar activists, however, also understood the symbolic, political, and cultural value of their embodied emotions and chose to perform them selectively to assert their citizenship and to arouse ethical awareness.

MOURNING CHICANO DEATH: LAS ADELITAS DE AZTLÁN

In Say Burgin's study of women in the antiwar movement, she argues that antiwar activism became a new terrain where "men and women participants re-worked social and political meanings of gender, as well as gender-based anxieties."[144] For many male antiwar protesters, such anxieties were the result of having their own masculinity called into question by war supporters for refusing to fight in the war. If war was regarded as a rite of passage for men, protesting war was viewed as a sign of emasculation and cowardice. Allaying anxieties over masculinity often resulted in compensatory forms of male domination within the antiwar movement. Because men—not women—were targets of the draft, many men were emboldened to assert themselves as the presumptive and logical leaders of the movement who could then determine strategy. Burgin shows how male members of the New Left, the Students for a Democratic Society, and other antiwar movements often "delegate[d] tasks and roles to women that were bereft of decision-making and characterized by underappreciated work, such as typing and preparing food."[145]

Elizabeth Armstrong and Vijay Prashad explain that in some antidraft groups, women's contributions were so devalued that women were banned from participating altogether.[146] To further shore up their embattled masculinities, many men resorted to or condoned the sexual exploitation of women. Treated as "secretarial and sex staffers," many women left to join other organizations or to form their own.[147]

Facing similar forms of male chauvinism, Chicana activist Gloria Arellanes and other Chicanas broke away from the East Los Angeles Brown Beret chapter to form Las Adelitas de Aztlán so they could practice their activism on their own terms.[148] Dionne Espinoza explains that before the Adelitas left the Berets, they had already served as "the administrative backbone of the National Chicano Moratorium Committee (NCMC)," helping to organize marches and protests against the war in Viet Nam.[149] As the newly formed Adelitas, Chicana activists continued their antiwar activism by redeploying the cultural role assigned to the Adelita. "As members of the NCMC," Las Adelitas de Aztlán

> prepared for the 28 February 1970 moratorium march by strategizing about how they could communicate the urgency of the struggle against the war in Vietnam. After a group brainstorming session, they chose to dress themselves as revolutionary women in mourning, wearing black, . . . and carrying crosses, which they made available to other march participants as well. The crosses bore the names of *carnales*—cousins, brothers, and friends (Chicana veterans were not discussed)—who had fallen in Vietnam. On that day, as they marched under the banner of Las Adelitas de Aztlán, they symbolically invited the community to mourn with them.[150]

Espinoza's description reveals how the Adelitas' embodied activism included not only the daily work of strategizing, planning, and organizing (underappreciated activities that require specific abilities, demands, and sacrifices of the body), but also their bodily presence in street protests. Pictures from the march show how the Adelitas performed history by wearing rebozos, the shawl typically worn by soldaderas, and carrying crosses as they walked in a mock funeral procession. Using costumes and props, the Adelitas enacted a kind of political theater for the community, performing an affect of grief that acknowledged the community's loss. Through this rescripting, the Chicana soldadera's body carried the weight of the community's sorrow for the thousands of young Chicanos who had been drafted or killed in the war. By wearing the named crosses of Chicanos killed in action, the women transformed the Adelita from a hypersexualized revolutionary sweetheart to a woman in mourning who embodies the implicit ethical condemnation that accompanies images of grieving women.[151] Through their political performance as bereaved women, Las Adelitas counted on the rhetorical force of female grief to "communicate the urgency of the struggle against the war in Vietnam."

Their acts of public mourning must also be read as a way of "doing" citizenship because, as Sutton explains, "activists' bodily performances, capabilities, and vulnerabilities during political protest produce social, cultural, and political effects."[152] The Adelitas used their bodies as "political 'arguments' or 'text,' as symbols that convey political meanings" to be read visually and viscerally by participants and observers.[153] The Chicana soldadera became a culturally specific marker of agony that reminded the community of how warfare has long shaped Mexican and Chicana/o identities. By occupying public space, they asserted a Chicana feminist presence that revised the historical personage of the soldadera while invoking the historical precedence of Mexican popular resistance to state power. They used this historical consciousness to call the community into action against the war. Rather than affirm the state's national motives for war, the Chicanas' grieving bodies promoted a cultural nationalist critique of U.S. military aggression. Thus, the grieving Chicana bodies of Las Adelitas de Aztlán and other Chicanas who mourned publicly and privately become important indexes of how communities experience communally shared pain and the ways in which many women challenged the state's management of bereavement.

The Adelitas' performance was part of a larger Chicano antiwar movement that focused on mourning. Grace Kyungwon Hong argues that this movement was specifically organized around protesting the high Chicano casualty rate in the war and the state's indifference to the value of those deaths. She shows how activists recognized the discrepancy between official efforts to revere war casualties and the marginalization that Chicano soldiers faced in life and death. Despite nationalism's reliance on concepts such as the Unknown Soldier—a figure that epitomizes obligation and sacrifice to the state and whose anonymity suggests the irrelevance of race, class, and ethnicity—Chicana/o activists recognized the "difference between the racialized specificity of the Chicano soldier and the supposedly universal soldier as the ultimate citizen of the U.S. nation-state."[154] In a sense, these activists wanted to de-universalize (or particularize) the Chicano soldier to prevent his symbolic containment in state narratives of honor and patriotism as well as to highlight the hypocrisy of national reverence for Chicanas/os who, in life, were treated as marginalized second-class citizens.

Mourning was obviously critical to the interpretive and symbolic struggle over the meaning of Chicano death. Hong goes on to trace the antiwar movement's nationalist impulse to use mourning to invoke and bind a Chicana/o collective identity. Indeed, she argues, the Chicano antiwar movement's form of cultural nationalism emulated the state's nationalism in that both relied on managing mourning to constitute a community "by providing one irrefutable meaning for, and one possible affect—earnestness, mournfulness, grief—toward, death."[155] But nationalism's—both state and subaltern—anxious attempt to control the meaning of death and the mourning practices of individuals inevitably leads to exclusionary and even oppressive practices. To prove this claim, Hong points to the first national Chicana conference held in Houston, Texas, in 1971, where more than six hundred Chicanas from across the nation gathered to discuss issues and to adopt resolutions that addressed their specific needs and demands.[156] Hong points to the debate between Chicanas who wanted to focus on the Chicano movement's broader goals rather than on gender-specific concerns that they deemed "trivial when compared to the plight of marchers on César Chávez's pilgrimage from Delano who were getting shot at and of Chicanos dying in the Vietnam War."[157] The debate between what Chicana historian Vicki Ruiz calls Chicana "loyalists" and "feminists" was a continuation of a conflict that had begun at the 1969 Denver youth conference, where a contingent of Chicanas declared, "It was the consensus of the group that the Chicana woman does not want to be liberated."[158] Chicana "loyalists" accused Chicana feminists of wanting to be liberated *from* the community rather than *within* it. Chicana feminists were also accused of lacking commitment to the community and even betraying its advancement. In Hong's view, the act of mourning Chicano death became one more litmus test that Chicana feminists faced to prove their loyalty to the movement: "The sanctity of Chicano death came to be the delimiting boundary for Chicano/a identity and community, which had to be defined in a singular way, brought together around shared mourning and grief around Chicano death. Chicana feminism's interrogation of community boundaries was then figured as a betrayal and as insufficiently respectful of Chicano death."[159] Hong argues that the movement's insistence on mourning led to disciplining the emotions and commitment of activists by ensuring that they demonstrated the proper cultural nationalist affect. The deaths of Chicano men were prioritized over the needs and concerns that Chicanas had and required activists' full attention and energies. In this view, Las Adelitas' public performance of mourning was both sufficiently respectful of Chicano death and compulsory.

Hong goes on to frame this compulsory mourning as a form of grievance in which the grieving Chicana/o subject, who is interpellated by state nationalism, "approach[es] the state to regain a power to which it presumes it is entitled but has lost."[160] This reading of Chicanas' public mourning practices relies on the notion of official recognition and compensation for loss. Moreover, the redress of loss requires the reappointment of patriarchal power. According to Hong, the compensation for Chicano death "comes with the reassertion of one's 'rightful' place as patriarch of a family, narrated as the regaining of 'traditional' culture."[161] In other words, through state recognition and redress of loss, the Chicana/o community can return once more to the sense of wholeness it experienced before encountering loss, a return to the normalcy of traditional male-dominated communal identity.

While Hong's analysis of Chicana/o mourning practices is persuasive, her analysis of grief has limitations that underestimate the power of women's performance of mourning and their motives. As I have shown, Chicana activists such as Lea Ybarra, Nina Genera, and Delia Alvarez had personal and political motives for publicizing their grief; their public expressions of mourning may have aligned neatly with Chicano nationalist demands, but they were not overdetermined by them. Rather than presume that Chicana activists acted out an imposed cultural nationalist affect, we could read the performance of groups like Las Adelitas de Aztlán as deliberate political staging of Chicana antiwar activism. Hong's analysis also presumes a one-dimensional interpretation of grief (grief as a demand for redress or compensation) that does not account for its ethical dimensions. Moreover, grief need not lead to the resurrection of patriarchy. Rather, mourning opens up new modes of Chicana political agency and ways of revising gender roles. Burgin explains how "gender becomes reconstituted as much *through* antiwar experiences as it acts as a predictor *for* those experiences."[162] While some may have assumed that women were naturally suited to mourn death, the reasons that compelled the Adelitas' actions and the meanings they ascribed to their performance tell us more about how they redefined gender roles through their activism in the movement.

This redefinition occurred through their symbolic and public recasting of the Adelita figure. Through art and in print culture, Chicana activists during the movement struggled to redefine the soldadera's legacy. The image of the soldadera, and more specifically the Adelita, was fraught with gendered associations that were often problematic for the Chicana activists who adopted and resignified these political icons. Maylei Blackwell describes how the soldadera "functioned as a conservative model of the role Chicanas were expected to play in the movement. . . . [L]a Soldadera was construed as a foot soldier in the movement who would follow the party line and carry out orders on the ground level."[163] The Adelita, on the other hand, represented "the revolutionary sweetheart whose role was to inspire and support her compañeros." Norma Cantú explains that these images of soldaderas as followers were false and largely propagated by literature and Mexican films. The disempowering perception, Cantú argues, became a "self-fulfilling prophecy . . . in the minds of contemporary Chicanos and Chicanas who feel that women must follow."[164] At the same time, the soldadera was an alluring and anomalous figure whose marginality resonated with many Chicana activists. Guisela Latorre argues that many Chicanas felt a special affinity for the soldadera, who was, after all, "a woman of color trying to survive in a hostile patriarchy," something that Chicanas were trying to do "within the Chicano Movement and the dominant U.S. mainstream."[165]

The soldadera therefore became an attractive transgressive figure for Chicanas "seeking a revised version of Mexican history that will better serve them in their contemporaneous struggles of the 1970s."[166] Part of this revision included reworking the Chicano nationalist family. Espinoza describes how Las Adelitas de Aztlán used flyers and banners to advertise the organization as a "familia de hermanas" (family of sisters).[167] Working within the movement's family rhetoric, the Adelitas showed how the familia could be redefined "as a term of political kinship that did not require male dominance or even male presence, but did require communitarian ethics."[168] Eschewing traditional notions of the family—and the gender hierarchy and division of labor it entailed—the Adelitas showed that, contrary to the claims of Chicana loyalists, it was possible to bridge Chicana feminism and community advancement. They showed how insisting on feminist demands and mourning for the community's losses were not antithetical activities, that mourning need not be used as a disciplinary tactic, but that it could instead open up space for Chicanas' creative and symbolic expressions of political dissent. While it may be easy to read the Adelitas' actions as conforming to Chicano nationalist demands (following the orders of male leadership as soldaderas were said to have done) or as performing the traditionally and presumably passive role of women in mourning, Sutton reminds us that to "understand whether women's embodied practices have a transgressive effect or not, it is important to examine the social context of activism."[169] The Adelitas' defection from the Brown Berets, their role in organizing the February 1970 moratorium march, and their strategic political decision to perform as a sisterhood of mourning soldaderas in public space all attest to how these Chicana activists vigorously reworked the meaning of both gender and mourning within the Chicano movement. Finally, their actions showed that grief did not necessarily lead to the reassertion of the patriarchal Chicano family, but that it was possible to "recast the concept of 'familia' in constitutively egalitarian and woman-identified terms."[170]

In the following section, I return us to the state's attempt to manage the mourning practices of its citizens as illuminated by contemporary Chicana fiction about the Chicano casualties of the U.S. war in Viet Nam. Stella Pope Duarte's *Let Their Spirits Dance* (2002) helps expand our understanding of how state memorialization of the Chicano soldier relies on the compliance of grieving mothers and sisters to justify and legitimate its war policies and legacies.[171] The novel reflects what this book's earlier sections on Chicana activism have shown: Chicanas ascribe different meanings and values to their mourning practices, which often pose a political and ethical critique of state wartime nationalism. In the process, they redefine and reassert an embodied citizenship and ultimately challenge the cost-benefit logic of neoliberal militarism. In other words, while Friedman and other neoliberals viewed the conscript's dilemma as an issue of future lost wages, Chicana activism and literature show how the true cost of war is the devaluation of life, and that this cost, which is poignantly illustrated through grieving Chicana bodies, is ultimately borne by all of us.

REPRODUCING CITIZENSHIP AND MONUMENTALIZING MOURNING AT THE VIETNAM MEMORIAL

On November 13, 1982, the deputy director of the Veterans Administration and former POW Everett Alvarez Jr. stood before a crowd of 150,000 people gathered for the official dedication of the Vietnam Veterans Memorial.[172] In his speech, he lamented the poor public reception of returning veterans. With the dedication of the memorial, however, he noted that more than ten years after the end of the war, "America is saying, 'Welcome home!'" For Alvarez, the occasion was particularly powerful. In his dedication, the memorial concretizes and venerates the deaths of fifty-eight thousand U.S. soldiers while also upholding the state as an object worthy of the deaths of its citizens. His sister Delia's challenge to Nixon's policy of public mourning reminds us that grief over the death or captivity of a loved one carries the potential to undermine state policies if that grief is not carefully circumscribed by official practices of bereavement. Such attempts to manage grief or, we might say, to militarize mourning occur at places like the Vietnam Memorial, a state-sanctioned site of mourning where the deaths of soldiers are embedded within the nation's history through monuments located at the National Mall.

Stella Pope Duarte's *Let Their Spirits Dance* is a grief narrative that focuses on the Vietnam Veterans Memorial as the site of mourning the death of a Chicano soldier. The novel centers on Jesse Ramirez, who dies in Viet Nam. Forty years later, his mother, Alicia, hears his voice and makes a *manda*, or promise, to God that she will travel to the Vietnam Memorial to touch her son's name before she dies. Her manda comes in response to a miraculous phone call from the government through which we learn that the Ramirez family is to receive a check for ninety-two thousand dollars as a result of an error that occurred decades ago. Not only did the government initially send Jesse's remains to the wrong address, but they had also sent half the required bereavement payment to the wrong family. After discovering the mistake all these years later, the government now owes the Ramirez family ninety-two thousand dollars in accrued interest. The family uses the money to pay for a week-long caravan from Phoenix, Arizona, to Washington, D.C. Memories of Jesse recur throughout the text as the narrator, Teresa Ramirez, spends decades coming to terms with her brother's death and its effect on the family.

The novel portrays what Lauren Berlant calls "pilgrimage-to-Washington" narratives, in which citizens journey to the nation's capital and learn the lessons of national history by gazing at monuments of past conflicts or historical figures. For Berlant, citizens are created "through technologies of national memory."[173] By viewing monuments and thereby learning the official narratives of the events and political figures they represent, cynical citizens are transformed into ideal citizens. The "pilgrimage to Washington is," Berlant writes, "already all about the activity of national pedagogy, the production of national culture, and the constitution of competent citizens."[174] The Vietnam Memorial exemplifies the pedagogic function of national monuments. Through monuments, the state attempts to impose meaning on the deaths of military personnel by interpreting them as examples of patriotism and national service, which citizens are encouraged to revere and emulate. This notion of creating citizens through national culture is played out in the novel as Teresa, a second-grade teacher, leads her class in a unit on Viet Nam. In addition to researching the country's history, the students also recreate the Vietnam Wall out of butcher paper and black crayons, etching in Jesse's name. Through this lesson, the schoolchildren are inducted into a citizenship that requires knowledge of national history and the proper behaviors and meanings associated with the nation's commemorative practices.

While the Vietnam Memorial is part of the national pedagogy, it is also a significant and emblematic site of the state's religion: nationalism. Benedict Anderson argues that like most religions that transform "fatality into continuity" by offering spiritual forms of immortality and regeneration, nationalism also seeks to legitimize itself by venerating its founders and notable citizens, endowing them with immortality through patriotic reiteration.[175] Through memorials to fallen soldiers, the state constructs secular yet highly reverential and consecrated sites that not only teach individuals how to be citizens, but also how to worship the state. Within nationalism, death can only be read as sacrifice, a meaning that imposes reverence for the deceased and for the object of sacrifice: the state. *Let Their Spirits Dance*, however, proposes Catholicism as a counter to this form of state religion. As I will show, Catholicism—with its attendant beliefs in suffering and sacrifice—challenges both the pedagogical function of the war memorial and the nationalist narratives of sacrifice that attempt to appropriate Jesse's death and turn his mother and sister into faithful citizens.

Aside from his given name of Jesus, Jesse is immediately identified as a Christ figure when Teresa associates his death with a passion flower that miraculously blooms out of season in the family's front yard. Then, in a parallel narrative, Duarte associates Jesse with the Aztec warriors who were sacrificed to the god of war Huitzilopochtli. In the novel, Don Florencío, a *tlachisqui*, or *curandero*, and "direct descendant of the Aztec people," envisions a "warrior with a plumed headdress" on the day of Jesse's birth.[176] It is through Don Florencío that Teresa learns about Aztlán and the long trek the Aztecs made to Tenochtitlan—a myth that she will repeatedly use to characterize the group's journey to the Wall. These dual narratives of sacrifice—of the Christian Christ and Aztec warrior—overshadow if not displace the national narrative of sacrifice that often accompanies pilgrimage-to-Washington narratives.

If Jesse's character represents Christ, Alicia becomes the *mater dolorosa*, the Mother of Sorrows, who is consigned to suffer interminably over her son's death. Through Alicia's religious devotion we learn about other Catholic female figures associated with suffering and pain. For example, images of Saint Rita with a thorn from Christ's crown stuck in her forehead and statues of Our Lady of Sorrows with a dagger piercing her heart decorate Alicia's home. Alicia also expresses her religious devotion through membership in the Guadalupanas, a sisterhood of penitent older women who venerate La Virgen de Guadalupe through prayer and ritual. Wearing gold medallions engraved with the image of La Virgen, Alicia and her *comadre*, a fellow Guadalupana, accompany the caravan to Washington and insist on stopping at sacred sites along the way. Alicia's membership in the Guadalupanas and constant references to Catholic narratives of female suffering reinscribe Alicia's own grieving maternal body as a site of religious devotion. And like Saint Rita, who asked to suffer as Christ had suffered, Alicia accepts, indeed welcomes, suffering as a fact of her life, but also as a form of proximity to God. Rather than fear suffering, Alicia's acceptance of pain is almost beatific and serves as a model for confronting pain and finding meaning in it. Teresa explains how the caravan travels with pain: "La manda, my mother's promise, is changing our landscapes forever. It's suffering in motion. . . . Suffering is our map, it's why we're on the road. Men and women in pain stand close to Christ, the man of sorrows. . . . We wouldn't be on the road if it weren't for war and suffering. We're part of some unearthly plan to balance the scales of suffering, to release a spring in our souls that will free us from the fear of suffering."[177] Teresa's description of "suffering in motion" complicates the traditional pilgrimage-to-Washington narrative by interjecting a narrative of religious suffering and penance.

In Katrina White's analysis of *Let Their Spirits Dance*, she describes the religious references as being "confusing" and "largely irrelevant to the true issues at hand in the novel."[178] While White views the female characters as disempowered women who "rely heavily on the saintly virgin's will and guidance rather than their own agency," I argue that the religious references actually form the basis for the novel's critique of state violence by dislodging the state religion of wartime nationalism with a Catholic tradition of sacrifice and suffering.[179] It is through La Virgen that Alicia asserts her agency as a Guadalupana who mourns the loss of her son to the state's imperialist violence. She views her suffering not as a voluntary sacrifice to the state but as a spiritual connection to God that leads ultimately to reunification with her son.

Duarte's choice to focus on Alicia's suffering is significant because maternal symbolism has often represented a threat to militarism's circumscription of public discourse. As Sara Ruddick points out, the mater dolorosa is a frequent icon in wartime discourse. She not only "mourns war's suffering, she also holds lives together despite pain, bitterness and deprivation."[180] The mater dolorosa epitomizes the loving yet helpless mother who is powerless to stop the violence that besets her family. The state has often tried to impose meaning on that suffering by labeling it as a sacrifice made in the interest of the nation. It is important to understand how mothers can be inducted into national belonging through grief if their mourning aligns with state objectives that perpetuate war or if they see their son's death as a sacrifice instead of as a murder or as a careless and costly abuse of state power. For example, it was at the end of the Civil War when Abraham Lincoln established the gold star mothers to elevate maternal suffering as a selfless act of national commitment.[181] Alicia is also cast in the role of mater dolorosa by the media, who follow the family's cross-country pilgrimage. Traveling while in poor health and thus risking her life, Alicia is praised for "answering her son's call to get to the Wall." As one character puts it, Alicia is "a symbol of all the other moms who lost their sons in Vietnam." The loss of her eldest son endows her with a kind of power that commands respect. Teresa even refers to her as a "Chicana Rosa Parks" as she gains enough strength to stare down a racist police officer who threatens to arrest her younger son: "This country already took one of my boys, Mr. Policeman. You can't have the other one."[182]

While Alicia is unwillingly and unwittingly transformed into a national heroine because of her maternal suffering, she simultaneously rejects the national narrative of heroism imposed on her son because of his service and death. She keeps Jesse's neglected service medals—Silver Star, Purple Heart, and Bronze Medal—in a dusty curio cabinet, and when Teresa asks to borrow them for show-and-tell, Alicia unleashes her bitterness: "I hate those medals! . . . They never brought him back! Those men, what did they know? Pendejos! [Idiots!] They said, here, take these medals in place of your son. What were they thinking? I never wanted the medals. I wanted my son!"[183] Throughout the novel, she rejects the state's multiple forms of military recognition. For example, when she is told that President Clinton wants to meet her and pay tribute to the Hispanic soldiers who served in Viet Nam at a special ceremony at the Wall, Alicia wryly replies, "Era hora" (It's about time). Teresa describes how the "money and the medals meant nothing to her."[184] Unlike the proper gold star mother, Alicia views the posthumously awarded medals and the belated ceremonies as hollow gestures of national inclusion. She refuses to venerate her son's death through state recognition and, in the process, rejects the interpretation of her grief as a willing sacrifice to the state or an expression of patriotism. Instead of upholding wartime nationalism's need for the sacrificial mother, the novel portrays Alicia's suffering as a sacred mission. When a reporter asks Alicia about the trip, she replies, "My mijo [*sic*], that's Jesse. He didn't call me here for nothing. . . . It's la manda, my promise that's making me strong. I made a promise to get there, and I'm going to keep it. God is leading the way, and La Virgen."[185] Military recognition does not motivate Alicia's journey to the Wall; rather, her trip is a spiritual quest to reunite with her son. And because she dies at the end of her journey, that reunion takes place in the afterlife.

Alicia's role as the grieving mother never conforms to official narratives of the war. Perhaps the strongest sign of Alicia's rejection of wartime nationalism is the fact that she never actually reaches the Wall. Instead, soon after arriving in D.C., she passes away. Before she dies, however, she learns that Jesse had married a Vietnamese woman and that they had had a son together. She meets Jesse's family in the hospital for the first and last time. As she holds her daughter-in-law's hand and learns about her son's final days in Viet Nam, we realize that she has completed her manda to touch her son's name. It is not the memorial that contains Jesse's memory, but the family that survives his death.

Jesse rejects wartime nationalism even more forcefully. Throughout the novel, we read the letters he wrote Teresa in 1968. In them, he describes the hardships of soldiering and his budding romance with Thom, the young Vietnamese woman he would eventually marry. In one letter, Jesse tells Teresa about his inability to shoot or hit the "enemy":

> I tell the guys shoot, cover yourselves, but it's hard when you look at the Vietnamese in the face. They're farm people, they look like a bunch of migrants bending over the rice paddies. They look so pathetic. Gabachos [white Americans] who have been here for a while say it's all a cover. They punch them around, beat them up, even the women. I can't, sis, it would be like hitting my nana or tata [grandmother or grandfather].[186]

In his final letter, he describes how he is often mistaken by the Vietnamese for being one of their own: "These people look at us los Chicanos like we're one of them. We look more Vietnamese than American, that's for sure."[187] Jesse's sense of affiliation to the Vietnamese, his ability to view them as potential family members rather than as the Other, interferes with his function as a soldier. This moment of recognition in which a Chicano GI highlights personal and historical points of identification with the Vietnamese is a defining feature of Chicana/o war literature, distinguishing it from the larger genre of American Viet Nam War literature. George Mariscal examines multiple instances of such moments of recognition in Chicano war writing. He argues that whether portrayed in simplistic or nuanced ways, these moments unveil the "intolerable contradictions" in narratives about the Chicano soldier's experience of war. Mariscal cautions against reading such moments as naïve instances of solidarity or as examples of the victimized veteran or the "good veteran," whose narrative can whitewash the atrocities committed during the war. Rather, Mariscal argues that acts of recognition, such as those found in Jesse's letters, produce new knowledge and transcend nationalism, thereby creating ideological ruptures within dominant wartime nationalisms: "The capacity for recognizing in the enemy specific 'shared' racial and class affiliations—e.g., farm worker/peasant, racialized minority/racialized foreigner—takes place during episodes in which characters (and through the process of analogous configuration, readers) find themselves in situations where inherited ideological structures break down."[188] These are the moments when characters reject the ethnocentric, white supremacist, and imperialist discourses that characterize much of this genre. I would add that the process of breaking down received ideologies is when these acts of recognition open up spaces for ethical engagement. Jesse has difficulty "look[ing] the Vietnamese in the face" because he recognizes the humanity and vulnerability of his supposed enemies—an ethical awareness that interferes with the military objective to kill.

His act of recognition culminates in his marriage to Thom. The creation of their biracial and binational family attests to Jesse's recognition of Vietnamese humanity and his rejection of wartime ideologies of violence and domination. It is important to note that Jesse's act of recognition is made through the body of a Vietnamese woman. Kalí Tal argues that in most novels about the Viet Nam War written by veterans, the Vietnamese woman is a silent one-dimensional character subject to violence, rape, and torture. In some novels, she is "developed in order to demonstrate that the soldier/killer is still worthy of love and capable of loving."[189] Even when she plays the more benign love interest, she has "no real life before she meets her soldier and none that is pursued after."[190] We meet Thom only at the end of the novel, when she says a few words to comfort Alicia, so we could read Thom's character as a mere prop demonstrating Jesse's capacity for ethical awareness. Yet, the novel also attempts to follow in the tradition of Chicana antiwar activists by traversing the national borders meant to impede such acts of recognition. The birth of Thom and Jesse's son signifies, in some sense, the Chicana/o's place within a larger global family that transcends the more insular and exclusionary national family on which wartime nationalism depends.

White argues that the novel provides a "conformist" and "apolitical" narrative of multicultural incorporation and national belonging. For her, the caravan of multiethnic characters embarks on a "patriotic pilgrimage that reaffirms the travelers' sense of national belonging as well as their U.S. citizenship."[191] Not only is the specificity of the Chicana/o experience of war lost, White argues, but the novel also fails to "achieve a truly critical Chican@ consciousness due to its emphasis on the war memorial." Yet, I argue that as a pilgrimage-to-Washington narrative, the novel surprisingly ends on a note of failed citizenship. That is, the novel ends with Teresa's description of the memorial and the hidden narrative of racist recruitment and drafting practices made manifest by the Latino names inscribed in the Wall: "As I walk by I see more and more men with Spanish last names. 'Oh, my Christ . . . look at all the Spanish names! They cleaned out the barrios for this war!'"[192] The litany of Spanish surnames continues until Teresa eventually finds Jesse's name. Charles Griswold and Stephen Griswold remind us that the Latin root for monument, *monere*, not only means "to remind," but also "to instruct."[193] In the scene described above, the lesson that Teresa learns at the Wall is not about patriotic commitment. Rather, Teresa realizes that the war waged in Viet Nam was dependent on the internal war against Latino communities, that the state "cleaned out the barrios for this war." For Teresa, grief turns into shock and horror as the Wall comes to represent a devastating abuse of state power rather than the revered monument meant to contain her brother's memory. After viewing the Wall, Teresa is not inducted into a national culture through the proper veneration of soldier death. If, as Barbara Correll argues, the "monument is constructed like—or is read as—a language," the Vietnam Memorial is "failed speech."[194] Through the litany of names, the Wall fails to speak in the voice of national unity. For Teresa, Jesse's name is one of many who did not sacrifice for the state but who was sacrificed by the state. It is also important to remember that Jesse's dead body underwrites the trip to the memorial. Were it not for the ninety-two thousand dollars from the state, the caravan would not have been possible. But like the service medals that Alicia refuses to honor, the check is part of the inappropriate logic of compensation reminiscent of Milton Friedman's cost-benefit analysis of the draft. While Friedman urged the state to account for the hidden costs accrued by draftees who lost possible future earnings in the civilian labor market, the hidden and incalculable cost of potential death was left out of the equation. If the state cannot approximate the value of life through monetary compensation, it can, at least, endow death with symbolic value through monumentalization, a process in which "bodies are symbolically exchanged for the abstract knowledge of the monument."[195] Though the novel emphasizes the Wall as the narrative's destination, Alicia's failure to arrive suggests rejection of the memorial's citizen-making function. Alicia refuses to embrace the state's appropriation of her mourning when she rejects Jesse's status as a bemedaled war hero. By refusing to perform the role of the grateful yet grief-stricken gold star mother, she further calls her own citizenship into question. Thus, if the novel's intent is to celebrate national belonging, then it fails to fully reproduce characters who are properly reverential citizens.[196]

The significant structural and ideological changes that occurred during the end of the war in Viet Nam—including debates over the draft and the military's transition to an all-volunteer force—set the stage for the ascent of neoliberal militarism. While Chicana antidraft activists found themselves in strange company, with Milton Friedman, in their opposition to the draft, they opposed the neoliberal ethic of self-care at the base of Friedman's push for an AVF and instead promoted an ethic of relationality, recognition, and vulnerability. Because their grief extended to the Vietnamese victims of the U.S. military, their public outcries proved inconvenient for official narratives. The Chicana antiwar activists featured in Herrera-Sobek's poetry show how Chicanas deployed grief as a humanitarian tool for social justice by lamenting the pain of others—an ethical move that places human suffering above national identity. The grieving mother and sister in Duarte's novel further demonstrate how the state perceived female family members to be a critical site of military planning and wartime citizenship production, as well as how Chicanas have actively contested that role. As neoliberalism came to replace Keynesian economic philosophy and became further entrenched as a political ideology in the decades following the war, a new generation of Chicanas found themselves entangled with the neoliberal military in the nineties, when the decline in the welfare state coincided with the rise of women's enlistment in the military. I turn now from the state's attempt to form citizens through the manipulation of grieving Chicana bodies to an alternative site of citizenship production—the army boot camp—where the process of military induction in the AVF produces Chicana soldiers who internalize a neoliberal ethics of self-help and self-management.

2

"YOUR SAFETY NET IS YOURSELF"

Neoliberal Militarism in Elena Rodriguez's *Peacetime*

PERHAPS THE ONLY WORK of literature that focuses on a U.S. Latina soldier, Elena Rodriguez's *Peacetime: Spirit of the Eagle* (1997) reconfigures the militarized space of an army boot camp to assert Chicana cultural identity and female empowerment within a patriarchal institution predicated on racial, class, and gender hierarchies. At one point in this autobiographically inspired novel, two Chicana enlistees invoke the history of Mexican soldaderas as cultural references to understand their own role as U.S. Army soldiers. When the protagonist Eliza Medrano asks her friend, the aptly named Adela Canela, if she is ever scared, Adela replies, "Dealing with fear is part of life. I'm sure that even the soldaderas were scared."[1] She explains to Medrano that soldaderas were women who "fought during the revolution in Mexico" and who are part of a Chicana/o military legacy: "You know, Eliza, we come from a long history of bravery. Our men have received more Medals of Honor than any other group." The characters Adela Canela and Eliza Medrano find solace in these examples of Mexican and Chicano bravery as the two women struggle to endure the army's sexist and patriarchal structure. For these Chicana soldiers, the stoic soldaderas represent female empowerment and cultural pride, which enables Canela and Medrano to accept their own place in the U.S. military.

Elena Rodriguez's *Peacetime* appeared in print near the end of a significant decade for female soldiering and was published the same year *G.I. Jane* appeared in movie theaters. For the Chicana characters in *Peacetime*, the soldadera was a more culturally familiar model of Mexicana militarism than the character of Lieutenant Jordan O'Neil, played by Demi Moore, an antifeminist female candidate undergoing Navy SEAL training. Yet, both the novel and film reflected the public's interest in the increasing enlistment of women in the military. Rodriguez was one of many women who enlisted and filled the state's peacetime military personnel. The increased participation of servicewomen like Rodriguez as well as dual-career military couples during the 1992 Persian Gulf War was in part the result of recruitment strategies during the eighties, which targeted women "to compensate for the decline in the pool of eligible young men" who were "high school graduates, drug-free, [and] non felons."[2] But the increased attention on female soldiers was also the result of milestones and scandals that had exposed the military's deep-rooted masculinist and misogynistic culture. In August 1991, Congress passed legislation that ended "the formal ban on women flying combat airplanes."[3] One month later, elite navy carrier pilots, known as *tailhookers*, held what would become a notorious convention at a Las Vegas hotel, where female naval personnel and female civilians were sexually assaulted and harassed as they were "forced to run the tailhookers' frightening and humiliating hotel corridor gauntlet."[4] In 1996, a legal challenge forced the Citadel, an all-male public military college in South Carolina, to admit Shannon Faulkner as its first female student.[5] The decade also saw the perennial debates between social conservatives and military feminists and their sympathizers over the issue of women in combat—a debate dramatized in *G.I. Jane*. Rodriguez's *Peacetime* provided a much-needed reflection on Chicanas' experiences that seemed to go unnoticed in public conversations on women in the military.

Rodriguez's *Peacetime* follows Private Eliza Medrano's induction into army culture and her transformation from an economically vulnerable Chicana to a self-reliant citizen-soldier. This chapter also moves forward in time to the Iraq War to examine the experiences of Mickiela Montoya, a young Chicana army veteran, whose experiences at basic training and in Iraq reveal the intense disciplining of female soldiers as they endure the army's culture of violence. My reading of *Peacetime* and of Montoya's experience focuses on the military's claim of producing self-sufficient leaders, a claim that I challenge by problematizing the notion of self-reliance and linking it to the larger ethos of neoliberal militarism. Both the novel and Montoya's published interviews demonstrate how, within the province of the military boot camp, neoliberal militarism provokes intense corporeal and ontological disciplining. This disciplining produces subjects who are trained to become inured to committing and receiving violence, trapped in the economic margins of society, compelled to practice traditional gender norms, and encouraged to adopt conservative forms of feminism that maintain patriarchal institutions while emphasizing liberal notions of individualism, leading them to view the military as a progressive institution rather than the purveyor of violence that it really is. Through examples of Chicana soldiering, we can glean the corporeal and ontological transformation of Chicana bodies in the military and how neoliberal militarism attempts to use this as a model for the transformation of society as a whole.

FEMALE ENLISTMENT AND THE ILLUSION OF CHOICE

If the AVF supposedly offered choice to individuals, that choice became increasingly circumscribed by the eighties and nineties, as neoliberalism—along with the state's divestment in social welfare programs—limited employment options and economic support systems for poor and working-class communities. For many, the notion of choosing between military service and civilian employment was a false choice to begin with. As Zillah Eisenstein puts it, women's enlistment signals the constriction of democracy "if democracy means choice and opportunity."[6] Eisenstein explains how high unemployment and limited options for social mobility and advancement curtail women's choices and make the military appear to be a viable solution to economic stratification: "The military—given this militarist stage of global capital—is a main arena where working- and middle-class women can find paid work. These women are looking for ways to get medical and housing benefits, educational resources, career training." Ilene Rose Feinman further argues that women turn to enlistment to offset the "loss of unionized industrial-sector employment to overseas manufacturing's highly exploitative labor practices, and the proliferation of part-time service-sector jobs," which leave "little in the way of quality occupation and prospects for women's work."[7]

Neoliberal entitlement reform further delimited the options women had to support themselves and their families. For example, with the passage of the Personal Responsibility and Work Opportunity Reconciliation Act of 1996, the Bill Clinton administration ushered in the concept of *workfare*, which Julie MacLeavy and Columba Peoples describe as a "more castigatory policy mechanism that emphasizes self-sufficiency and individual requirements to work."[8] The concept of workfare is one of the markers of the state's widespread adoption of neoliberal principles when it comes to providing for the economically precarious. MacLeavy and Peoples describe how workfare has "not only made employment the primary means of response to social and economic inequality, but stipulated it as an individual responsibility."[9] The stricter regulations embedded in neoliberal welfare reform indicate not only a streamlined government role in social provision, but also the state's "responsibilization of its citizen subjects"—a process of neoliberal governmentality that shifts the social and economic burdens produced by neoliberal policies onto marginalized communities (particularly women and children), who have little choice but to shoulder the weight.[10]

Military enlistment becomes, for many, a way to gain access to state-funded support and to do so without incurring the social stigma attached to nonmilitary welfare.[11] Part of that stigma comes from the notion that social welfare weakens the concept of citizenship. David Segal argues that in the sixties, the term *benefits* was legally replaced with *entitlements*, in a move that emphasized the idea of citizenship rights over obligations: "The rationalization of citizenship rights in the welfare state virtually stripped the conception of citizenship of any notion of obligations that accompanied the rights."[12] If soldiers and veterans received welfare, that welfare was construed as benefits in return for service rendered, through either conscription or civic obligation. Thus, society and the government did not denigrate soldiers by attaching to them the stigma that accompanies nonmilitary welfare:

> Whereas the clients of other welfare institutions were regarded as less than full citizens, military personnel were regarded as good citizens. Clients of other institutions who were taken care of because they were outside the productive economy were looked down upon, whereas military personnel were cloaked in the social honor that derived from their association with the military institution and the myths that legitimized it. Because benefits that were received—whether housing, medical care, education, or disability insurance—were regarded as earned entitlements in exchange for the fulfillment of a citizenship obligation, the solider was not looked down upon for accepting them.[13]

Segal's characterization of nonmilitary clients of social welfare existing "outside the productive economy," however, downplays the ways in which racialized and patriarchal capitalism has actively pushed white women and people of color outside the "productive economy." Furthermore, Segal's description leaves out the possibility that military personnel who receive welfare are not stigmatized because they are predominantly white men. As M. Jacqui Alexander reminds us, "Race, class, and gender have historically operated as powerful markers to distinguish between the undeserving poor" and other groups who receive entitlements, such as the "deserving elderly."[14] In this case, the deserving male soldier enjoys full citizenship and state support without the stigma of being associated with the "undeserving poor."[15]

With the rise of female soldiering, many women are also becoming "good citizens" and are gaining access to state benefits as they, too, become "cloaked in the social honor" once reserved exclusively for men. Embodying a combination of civic republican and neoliberal principles, the soldier is the neoliberal standard bearer of choice, self-reliance, and service to the state. "Paradoxically," as Deborah Cowen and Amy Siciliano note, "the soldier offers a model of entitlement, but one that is organized through responsibility and contribution."[16] Although Cowen and Siciliano refer to a Canadian context, their observations appropriately describe U.S. militarization, where "rebuilding the military is part of a broader recasting of entitlement in citizenship."[17] Or, as M. Jacqui Alexander puts it, the "military has been positioned as the new citizenship school for women and men removed from public assistance."[18] Under neoliberal militarism's regime, the soldier epitomizes the free individual who voluntarily chooses service and whose choice demonstrates a capacity for self-management and self-reliance—two qualities that make it possible for the neoliberal state to withdraw its support from the social reproduction and welfare of its citizens. Elena Rodriguez's *Peacetime* helps illuminate the physical and ontological processes that go into forming these neoliberal citizen-soldiers through military service. In the novel, we see how Chicana and other female soldiers learn that to be good citizens, they must volunteer to fight and die on the state's behalf yet refrain from questioning how the state perpetuates social structures that limit their economic choices.

DISCIPLINING THE CHICANA SOLDIER: ELENA RODRIGUEZ'S *PEACETIME*

In Rodriguez's *Peacetime*, enlisting in the army is an option of last resort for most of the female characters. For the Native American soldier, Morningstar, the army was the most viable option on the reservation for earning desperately needed income. She tells Medrano that she enlisted to help support her sister's children after her sister's husband abandoned the family. Medrano joined the army to earn money for college and to help provide for her family. That she does not have any children of her own to support astonishes the army recruiter who initially inducts her:

> "No kids at all?" His eyes showed surprise. "No. Is the Army only taking people with kids these days?" "No," he said laughing, "Of course not. I was just surprised that a Mexican American female like yourself doesn't . . ." "Not all of us have ten kids, you know," Medrano said with her voice dripping resentment.[19]

Medrano's exchange with the incredulous recruiter emphasizes the common stereotypes about fertile Chicanas that circulate within society. More importantly, it highlights the issue of child support, which compels many women to seek income and benefits by enlisting in the military. As more and more women seek ways of providing for their families in the face of limited alternatives, the military finds a steady and inexhaustible pool of potential enlistees who join the military because, as Morningstar puts it, "poverty is not fun."[20]

By limiting the time and setting of the novel to Medrano's seven-week stay at boot camp, Rodriguez focuses on the process of military induction, through uniforms, training, and regulations that standardize the enlistees' physical appearances. According to Carol Burke, the boot camp's function is to sever the recruits' ties to civilian life and to eradicate their individuality as they are subsumed into the military's corporate identity: "Boot camp transforms recruits from jocks and nerds, boys from the 'hood and women from the suburbs, into knockoffs of model soldiers by stripping them of their clothes, shaving off their hair, forbidding them their accustomed freedoms, and instilling military discipline in them as second nature."[21] If the military boot camp is a site of fundamental transformation, where the civilian becomes a soldier, Rodriguez's novel demonstrates how that transformation is fraught with difficulties for Chicanas and other female enlistees.

In the early pages of the novel, Rodriguez alludes to the visual and ideological value of sartorial uniformity and reiterates what Melani McAlister calls "military multiculturalism," in which the military presents itself as an example of one of America's progressive race-blind institutions. After looking around at her peers, Medrano comments on the equalizing effect of the army uniform among the racially diverse platoon of women: "She walked into the barracks, and the variety of races hit her. She was still in awe of the different races represented in the Army. Sergeant Acosta had told her something that struck Medrano in a special way. He said there was only one color in the Army and that was green. Differences among the races were not as pronounced as soon as soldiers put on their uniforms, since all dressed the same. They were going through the same experience. So at that time, they seemed more alike than different."[22] The scene evokes the crucial function of military multiculturalism, which is to simultaneously recognize and sublimate racial difference. That is, racial difference is not completely obscured but strategically celebrated. The army heralds ethnic identity to reinscribe its value, to transform the racialized and gendered soldier into a defender of the nation. The army's "variety of races" signals the plurality of American society, whose racial tensions and economic disparities are subsumed by service to the state. The military thus becomes a model of egalitarianism for a society still divided along racial lines. The passage suggests that as part of the multiracial platoon, Medrano will ostensibly transcend her racial identity by donning the army green.

But the novel calls into question the notion of military multiculturalism by taking on a military feminist perspective that articulates race, class, and gender. Burke reminds us that the process of transformation that boot camp instates also relies on culturally familiar gender codes. She describes how drill instructors denigrate recruits by "infantilizing" them and, "if the recruits are male, feminiz[ing] them through the kind of humiliation designed to impress on them that to be degraded is to be female ('Come on, ladies')."[23] Throughout the novel, Rodriguez puts pressure on the military's limited embrace of gender difference and its misogynistic practices. She depicts the Fort Jackson base in South Carolina as the site for Medrano's bildungsroman, the place where the protagonist learns to test her physical fortitude and build emotional strength. Medrano struggles to endure seven weeks of intensive training with her platoon members, which include Anglo, Latina, African American, and Native American women from working-class communities, who enlisted to avoid a jail sentence, support children, or, in Medrano's case, travel the world and earn enough money to pay for college. For Medrano, attending college and enlisting in the army represent female independence from the family. The military is the ideal site for her personal empowerment, where she can earn an education and learn skills that will enable her future economic success and independence from men.

Medrano begins her limited feminist reconfiguration of the predominantly white male institution by casting it as a space to develop and assert a strong sense of her Chicana identity. This transformation is facilitated by the introduction of

Adela Canela, the novel's moral center and source of cultural knowledge. Adela, described as a "petite" Chicana whose "confidence made her look taller" and whose "eyes were introspective as if preoccupied with a million deep thoughts," joins Medrano's platoon in week three. She tells Medrano that Sergeant Grimes had transferred her from his platoon for insubordination: "We didn't get along. Grimes hated me, and I hated his racist, SEX-ist guts!"[24] Eventually we learn that Adela, originally from El Paso, had spent time in Medrano's hometown of Sunland Park, New Mexico, and that both women actually knew each other's families through church. Adela immediately lets Medrano know that she is not the typical El Pasoan who looks down on Sunland Park's economically impoverished community: "Don't you ever feel[,] Eliza, that you need to justify living in Sunland Park. There are jerks out there who think being poor monetarily means being poor in spirit. They are the same idiots who think money buys you class. That it buys you soul—as if it's a sin not to have a bunch of money. As if money makes you a better person. What a bunch of crock!"[25] With this statement, Adela aligns herself with the class politics that befit her namesake. As the designated soldadera—in both name and spirit—Adela becomes the instructor in Medrano's education in economic justice. Yet, unlike the soldaderas who fought against elite exploitation of Mexico's poor and working classes during the Mexican Revolution, Adela limits her criticism to crass materialism. She rejects the notion that money determines a person's worth, but her outrage stops short of a real critique on the structures of impoverishment.

Adela's function is to insert a strong dose of female empowerment into the novel. Through Adela, Rodriguez attempts to expand the symbolic reach of the soldadera. Here, the soldadera becomes more than a figure preoccupied with class warfare. Rather than serve as an object of romantic fetish, she actively challenges the military's sexual harassment of women. Through various conversations and encounters in the novel, Adela engages in a war against female oppression. Her primary nemesis is Sergeant Grimes, a character who vocalizes and enacts the institution's degradation of women in its ranks. In one scene, Sergeant Grimes publicly berates a woman for being discharged during the fourth week of training, assuming that she is quitting because she is mentally weak. Adela risks being reprimanded for speaking out of turn and, more importantly, speaking back to a drill sergeant by telling him, "I just hope you never have a child with cancer and have to be discharged from the service to take care of her, Sergeant Grimes." Adela's remark catches him off guard, turning his face "beet red" as "dozens of disgusted eyes bored into him." The moment becomes a significant, if fleeting, reversal of power, as Grimes experiences the shame of being a spectacle, similar to how he turned women into spectacles by the way "his eyes paw[ed] the females" in his platoon.[26] In the face of the institution's tacit acceptance of female degradation, such victories take the place of real punishment for harassment.

In another scene, Adela again confronts Sergeant Grimes when he vows to personally discipline a woman who forgets to snap her helmet strap:

> "I'll fucking have to cram some brains into you myself! Be in my tent after chow tonight, and we'll see if I don't smoke your sorry ass until you lose your stupidity!"
>
> "Why does she have to go to your tent, Sergeant Grimes?" asked Canela angrily.
>
> "Who the hell gave you permission to fucking speak, Canela? You are even stupider than this one!"[27]

Adela's confrontation once again exposes Sergeant Grimes's abuse of authority and his constant use of sexual harassment and intimidation. Adela is familiar with Grimes's history of sexual assault having come from his platoon originally. She tells Medrano that Grimes "knows better than to try anything with me," yet she remains concerned for the women who stayed in his platoon: "I don't have proof—the others don't say anything about it—but I'm pretty sure it's happening. I think they are scared."[28] Through a permissive institutional culture of violence, the women are disciplined into silence, as the menacing presence of Sergeant Grimes throughout the novel underscores the condoned forms of violence and harassment that female soldiers endure. Adela's repeated public humiliation of Grimes speaks to her courage in facing down the novel's most incorrigible drill sergeant. It also illustrates her defiance of authority—a trait that the military has no tolerance for and instead tries to eradicate through a relentless regime of emotional, psychological, and physical training. Through the undisciplined soldadera, Rodriguez critiques the misogyny inherent in the army boot camp.

In addition to Adela's courageous confrontations with Sergeant Grimes, Medrano herself frequently subverts military culture and protocol, even as she learns to follow its rules and conventions. Medrano's repeated challenges to masculinist practices emphasize the incongruous fit of female soldiers and military culture, as well as how women's bodies become disruptive to the military's protocol. Medrano explicitly describes female bodily functions and how women adjust to procedures not intended to accommodate them. In the opening pages of the text, we read about Medrano's straining and perspiring body as she struggles to do male push-ups during army PT, or physical training: "She detested male pushups. They were not the female kind where the knees were bent. These were the macho kind where the weight of the body was placed on the shoulders."[29] The scene foretells the various physical exertions Medrano will endure over seven weeks of PT as she emphasizes female physical difference in a male-dominated institution. For example, she expresses her gratitude that her period did not occur during a training session, because "having to change pads during bivouac would've been a nightmare," although the "many pockets in her uniform had made it easy to store pads."[30] In similar passages throughout the text, Medrano highlights her female body's limitations and functions, underscoring her perseverance and adaptive skills.[31] Her constant references to her body also highlight how, as Heather Höpfl puts it, the "military organization is not, it seems, a place for women with physical bodies which produce menstrual blood, breast milk, maternal smells." Instead, women must suppress and quietly manage the "disruptive power of the female body" to minimize the disequilibrium that their presence creates in the masculine world of boot camp.[32]

Medrano's female perspective on military maneuvers extends to weapons training, where her struggle to master her M16 weapon represents a complex symbolic negotiation with violence and female sexuality. For example, she undoes the traditional association between gun and phallus in her description of her rifle. Rather than mimic the common military refrain, "this is my weapon, here is my gun; one is for fighting, the other's for fun," Medrano asks her M16 for help after she continuously fails to shoot the required number of targets to pass the weapons test: "'We have not been the greatest friends, but we can change that. I need you to pull through for me, so I can qualify and get out of basic. From this day on, I'm baptizing you Midnight—dark, mysterious, and beautiful.'"[33] Medrano's baptism of her M16 not only renames but regenders the literal and metaphorical phallic weapon, altering its association with male virility and sexual dominance over women. Instead, Medrano's M16 becomes an extension of her own body and an equally suggestive symbol of female sexuality that is "dark, mysterious, and beautiful."

Although Medrano's resignification of the phallic weapon reads as a feminist reversal of power, it calls to mind what Kelly Oliver describes as culturally entrenched associations between women's bodies, sex, and death. She notes that the link between women and weaponry draws on "age-old fears of women and the fantasy of female sexuality as a threatening weapon."[34] Such fantasies help explain the proliferation of military aircraft nose art and the designation of popular Hollywood actresses as "bombshells" during World War II. In a more recent and disturbing example, the military has used women's sexuality as part of its interrogation repertoire against detainees at the U.S. prison in Guantanamo Bay, where female interrogators reportedly used "'sexual touching,' 'provocative clothing' (including miniskirts, bras, and thong underwear), and 'fake menstrual blood' to 'break' Muslim prisoners by making them unclean and therefore 'unworthy to pray.'"[35] Medrano's renaming of her M16 merely reaffirms the association between female sexuality/female bodies and violence. Once again, what feels like a feminist reinscription of power falls short of meaningful critique. Instead, we are left to marvel at militarism's adaptive capacity to appropriate a feminist challenge to normative male power and state violence. Furthermore, her bond with her M16 makes it that much easier for her to carry out the state's violence. Midnight may help Medrano pass her weapons test, but she will be shooting at targets with no thought as to what those targets represent.

Perhaps the most revelatory instance of female disciplining in the novel is the makeup lesson that comes in week three of basic training. In this scene, Medrano is taken to "a lecture room full of females from all the platoons," where she is instructed on standard military cosmetic procedures: "A mirror and make-up tray sat in front of each female. They were being taught how to apply make-up by a beauty consultant. . . . Medrano started applying blush the way the beauty consultant instructed. Next came eye shadow. She chose a shade of brown for her lids. With a disposable mascara wand, she applied black mascara to her eyelashes." Immediately after the cosmetics session, soldiers are told to return to their barracks to wash off the makeup and report immediately for weapons training, where they are to learn "how to adjust the sights on their M-16s."[36] Rodriguez reveals the extent of the military's concern with normative signs of femininity as it incorporates and thus oddly equates makeup lessons with weapons training. That the army would find it imperative to teach women how to apply mascara suggests the value military officials place on women's bodies and appearances. Medrano and the other women are puzzled by the need for such a lesson but go along without asking questions or realizing how the military's investment in maintaining proper gender norms is necessary to upholding militarism itself.

The army's control over its soldiers' physical appearance requires extensive regulation of every aspect of the soldier body. A glance at the U.S. Army's most recent manual on uniforms and insignia reveals the level of detail involved in monitoring the presentation of male and female personnel. In it, we learn about what the army considers to be appropriate displays of gendered identities and the limits of self-expression necessary to maintaining uniformity. For example, the following guidelines detail the acceptable uses of cosmetics for women:

> As with hairstyles, the requirement for standards regarding cosmetics is necessary to maintain uniformity and to avoid an extreme or unmilitary appearance. Males are prohibited from wearing cosmetics, to include nail polish. . . . Females may wear cosmetics if they are conservative and complement the uniform and their complexion. . . . Females will not wear shades of lipstick and nail polish that distinctly contrast with their complexion, that detract from the uniform, or that are extreme. Some examples of extreme colors include, but are not limited to, purple, gold, blue, black, white, bright (fire-engine) red, khaki, camouflage colors, and fluorescent colors. Soldiers will not apply designs to nails or apply two-tone or multi-tone colors to nails.[37]

The army's manual on appearance uncovers fissures in the maintenance of gender difference. That a statement on the prohibition of cosmetics and nail polish for men is even necessary suggests that some men have attempted to or might contemplate breaking the militarized norms of masculine appearance. Meanwhile, the restriction on "extreme colors" of makeup and multihued nail polish for women also reveals the army's moral judgment on how "conservative"-looking women should present themselves. "Bright (fire-engine) red" lipstick apparently crosses the line of acceptable military cosmetics, perhaps because it connotes a sexually active (read: sexually loose) woman intent on seduction.

Cynthia Enloe argues that militarized cosmetic application is not anomalous but is part of a "bureaucratic campaign" in which military officials write memos and have meetings about the serious business of eye shadow and blush. Special committees are tasked with creating the standards for properly feminized soldiers. While the Marines require women "to tweeze their eyebrows in a regulation arch," other service branches stipulate the appropriate length and style of hair.[38] In addition to regulating outward appearances, the navy, in a memo Enloe describes, recommends standardizing women's undergarments to prevent female soldiers from wearing "fancy panties and half-bras."[39] Hillman adds that in 1975, the Air Force Academy made the disastrous attempt to "find a single-size bra that it could issue to all enlisting women." It also mandated that women wear pumps or high heels on certain occasions to retain female cadets' "'feminine' appearance," even if this meant placing "femininity over function."[40] These attempts at designing uniforms for servicewomen and advising them to wear what the Naval Academy calls "conservative cosmetics" reveal the "difficult process of trying to reconcile a normative ideology that vilifies 'feminine' characteristics with the reality of female bodies."[41] The military's adoption of civilian cultural beauty standards reifies those standards within the military; more importantly, the fact that entire committees are devoted to such concerns suggests an intense level of regulation and control over female bodies.

Medrano seemingly disregards the makeup lesson without fully contemplating how militarism relies on normative notions of gender. The careful lessons on eye-shadow application provide clear examples of how "regulatory norms materialize 'sex' and achieve this materialization through a forcible reiteration of those norms."[42] In an institution overly reliant on aggressive hypermasculinity and intent on producing male soldiers who embody those traits, the presence of properly feminized women is critical. It matters to military officials that women look recognizably feminine so that they are not confused with men. More importantly, feminized female soldiers project the military's image as an institution that protects dominant gender codes: "To be 'mannish' is to be a freak, a defiler of femininity, an offender of both respectable women's and respectable men's sensibilities. In short, a mannish woman is a threat to the proper order of things."[43] Culturally legible femininity protects the military's gender and sexual hierarchy and what Butler calls "the consolidation of the heterosexual imperative" that sustains the military.[44] Feminized female soldiers give the appearance of a heterosexual female soldiery, and since gender constructs are relational, the feminized female soldier protects rather than undermines the necessary construction of masculinized men.

Yet, the military's attempt to regulate the most intimate spaces of the female body and the minutest details of its display exposes an unstated institutional anxiety over the fragile nature of militarized genders. The necessity of reiterating norms, Butler argues, is itself a "sign that materialization is never quite complete, that bodies never quite comply with the norms by which their materialization is impelled."[45] Thus, the cosmetics scene in *Peacetime* reflects the hyperregulation of the female body and the vulnerability, and therefore potential overturning, of militarized gender norms. As I discuss later, however, some women attempt to defeminize their body's appearance as a matter of emotional and physical protection from the onslaught of sexual harassment on base, rather than to rebel against the imposition of traditional norms of femininity.

Medrano's descriptions of restrictions on and violence against women's bodies belies feminist egalitarian militarists' claim that women's presence can democratize the military. Yet, democratizing the patriarchal structure of the military is not Medrano's actual goal. Rather, she views the army as a way of achieving social mobility through education benefits and a steady income. Thus, the novel focuses on her adaptive abilities, her perseverance, and the survival skills she learns—skills that will help her survive not in a combat zone, but in the patriarchal civilian culture to which she will eventually return. Despite the multiple threats of sexual violence, boot camp is ironically depicted as a relatively safe space compared to civilian life because of the female camaraderie that develops within the platoon. We see this particularly at the end of the novel, after Medrano's multiracial platoon completes basic training. As the women discuss their future assignments, Adela questions the importance of their singular accomplishments in the context of insurmountable social disparities: "The world is all screwed up with wars, racism, sexism, diseases, rapes, mutilations, child abuse, wife beating, sexual harassment, and so on! What's the use? What's the purpose?"[46] Adela's list of concerns moves from large-scale conflict to intimate forms of violence, linking war with specific forms of race- and gender-based oppression. Ironically, Adela does not acknowledge how the military is implicated in the violence that she decries. Instead, the passage curiously distances the military from social disorder while presenting the military as the solution.

Medrano dispels Adela's negativity by reaffirming the army's meritocratic ethos of self-empowerment and responsibility, as she tells Adela that "your safety net is yourself."[47] With this statement, Medrano implies that the purpose of boot camp is to instill self-reliance rather than to question the larger systems of power in place. By focusing on the individual, the novel deflects attention away from institutional accountability—a move that preserves the military's image as a progressive social institution while suggesting that aggrieved communities should "be their own safety net." Judging from Medrano's response, we can read her embrace of the military's "bootstrap" mentality as a reflection of her induction into what Wendy Brown calls neoliberal citizenship. Brown describes how neoliberalism's economic rationality is not confined to economics but permeates all spheres of social life as it interpellates citizen-subjects, and in this case, the citizen-soldier, into neoliberal citizens. By this process, she writes, neoliberalism "figures individuals as rational, calculating creatures whose moral autonomy is measured by their capacity for 'self-care'—the ability to provide for their own needs and service their own ambitions."[48] As we have seen in the previous chapter's discussion of neoliberal ethics, this ethic of "self-care" acts as a cover for neoliberalism's insistence on privatization, which enables the state's abdication of responsibility for ensuring that everyone has access to basic resources.

Earlier in the novel, the roles between Adela and Medrano were reversed, when Medrano explained why she joined the army: "In high school I always felt I had to get top grades, so I could get into college. My parents couldn't help me with homework. They don't have much education, and they couldn't afford to help me financially for college. I never had a safety net."[49] In response to Medrano's assessment of her predicament, Adela says, "your safety net is yourself, Eliza." The conversation takes place at the beginning of week four, or the midpoint of basic training. By the end of week seven, we see that Medrano has adopted Adela's motto to the point where she can now repeat it to Adela herself. What Brown shows us is that the military's ethic of self-reliance correlates with neoliberal citizenship, as Medrano learns to assume all responsibility for her life choices: "The rationally calculating individual bears full responsibility for the consequences of his or her action no matter how severe the constraints on this action, e.g., lack of skills, education, and childcare in a period of high unemployment and limited welfare benefits."[50] Medrano's response best exemplifies Brown's assertion that neoliberalism's moralizing rhetoric of responsibility lays the weight of full accountability onto individuals, thus "depoliticizing social and economic powers and at the same time reduc[ing] political citizenship to an unprecedented degree of passivity and political complacency."[51] In this light, Medrano's depolitical response to Adela's catalog of social disparities suggests an inward turn to individual initiative rather than an outward critique of institutional accountability, which eventually limits the possibility for coalitional activism and social justice.

In Ben Olguín's analysis of *Peacetime*, he reads the female unity that culminates in the novel's ending as the formation of a "female GI body" organized in resistance to "the pornographic gaze and attendant sexual violence mapped onto their bodies by their fellow heterosexual male GIs." Despite the potentially empowering notion of a "collective body of soldaderas" working in unison, Olguín argues that the "women in *Peacetime* ironically may be facilitating their own containment within the U.S. Army, since the convergence of their individual identities into one body—the GI unit—is the very objective of boot camp."[52] My reading of the novel's female collectivity, while different from Olguín's, reaches similar conclusions. As I have argued, neoliberal militarism accommodates the contradictory pairing of liberal individualism and the military's esprit de corps.

As long as the corporate GI body—and the discipline required to achieve it—is wielded in the service of protecting profit, individual freedom, and the illusion of choice, the ideological contradictions between neoliberalism and militarism are manageable. The women in the novel have been inducted into the military corps, into one body trained to carry out the state's violence. They have achieved the collectivity that the army desired, even if that collectivity is critical of the institution's misogynistic practices. But they have also acted as the kind of individuals that neoliberal militarism requires. In the era of the AVF, almost every woman made the individual "choice" to enlist—a choice circumscribed by state divestment in social services and the structural impoverishment of women and children. Each woman is individually trained in committing violence (and in becoming the target of violence) without considering how their participation in that violence maintains oppressive power structures. In the end, both Medrano and Adela practice a disempowered, depoliticized militarized feminism that must be satisfied with the illusion of progress as it chips away at a patriarchal institution without ever reaching its core. Finally, both Chicana soldiers have internalized neoliberal militarism's ethos of self-sufficiency and self-care—the hallmarks of a neoliberal citizenship that allows the state to transfer its moral, social, and economic responsibilities to individuals.

Although Rodriguez's characters are trapped within what Olguín describes as an "unresolved tension between containment and resistance," the undisciplined Chicana soldadera has the most potential to seriously disrupt neoliberal militarism's hegemony.[53] Adela's historical knowledge about women's agency, her cultural pride, her class consciousness, and her defiant challenge to the pervasive culture of sexual harassment signals to readers the kind of feminist politics that the soldadera represents for Rodriguez. Through Adela, Rodriguez presents the most forceful, yet limited, critique of neoliberal militarism. In an argument with another woman, Adela retorts, "Hell, I'm not here by choice. That's for sure. . . . I don't think any so-called 'minority' or women should join until the system works better for us."[54] Adela boldly describes her enlistment as being antichoice, thereby highlighting the façade of voluntarism that undergirds neoliberal military recruitment practices. More intriguingly, she denounces enlistment for women and people of color—two groups most commonly targeted by neoliberal policies. Her recognition of a failed system suggests a political awareness of structural racism, sexism, and class exploitation. Unfortunately, Adela's radical social critique is underdeveloped in the rest of the novel. Instead, she becomes neoliberalized as Medrano convinces her to be her own safety net. Ultimately, her broad structural critique is narrowed to the confines of the boot camp, where she engages not in a revolution against the state, as did her soldadera antecedents, but in a battle against sexual harassment and violence in the military—a battle she is condemned to always lose.

"I'M A SOLDIER, NOT A GENDER": THE STORY OF MICKIELA MONTOYA

Although Rodriguez's novel is a fictionalized rendering based on the author's personal experience of boot camp, it nevertheless provides a glimpse into military induction for the uninitiated. Sadly, Rodriguez's novel resonates with the horrific conditions that many servicewomen currently face in today's military. One such woman, Mickiela Montoya, is a young Chicana veteran of the Iraq War who, in a series of interviews with Helen Benedict and others, describes her experiences inside U.S. Army basic training at Fort Leonard Wood, Missouri.[55] Through Montoya's experience, we see how the military disciplines the female soldier body through a pervasive misogynistic culture of sexual violence. Her story helps emphasize the point that neoliberal militarism is not gender neutral. While the economic component of neoliberal militarism engenders a self-supporting individual who can be his or her own safety net, the neoliberal militarist project continues to rely on deeply ingrained violent codes and practices of female oppression.

Montoya, a Mexican American woman from East Los Angeles, was only seventeen years old when she forged her mother's signature to enlist in the California National Guard in September 2002. Coming from a troubled family life marked by an absent father, drug-addicted and neglectful mother, and constant shuttling from relative to relative, Montoya unsurprisingly gravitated to an institution that promised stability, guidance, and income. After her grandmother's death and a bout with self-destructive and rebellious behavior, she turned to one of the ubiquitous military recruiters operating at her high school. Montoya describes enlisting under the assumption that she would be committed to the guard for six years and would be "fighting forest fires, helping with floods, and protecting her country from terrorist attacks, all at home in California."[56] Instead, she was committed for the standard eight years of service and was soon sent to Iraq.

Montoya describes how the nine-week period of army basic training was divided into three phases called Red, White, and Blue.[57] The first day of the Red Phase (weeks one and two) begins for sleep-deprived recruits with shouting drill instructors giving contradictory commands to pack and unpack lockers and personal belongings, clean and reclean floors and barracks, and incessant yelling and insults about personal appearances.[58] Recruits acclimate wearily to days that typically last sixteen hours and are characterized by constant physical exercise, which is used as both training and punishment for failing to execute sometimes-impossible orders. During this first phase, recruits memorize the seven "army values" and the "warrior ethos," and repeat D&C, or drill and ceremony practice, which requires recruits to "stand, march, and reflexively obey orders, and is derived from the age-old practice of training soldiers to load and fire weapons in precise coordination." Benedict notes that while some criticize D&C for being obsolete, "most commanders defend it, saying it prevents military units from degenerating into murderous mobs."[59]

In the second phase of boot camp, known as the White Phase (weeks three through five), recruits are exposed to CS gas and train in combat maneuvers and weapons. For Montoya, the experience of shooting her M16 rifle was empowering: "The first time I shot my weapon, I felt powerful. It changed me forever."[60] Through weapons training and bayonet fighting, she was gradually inducted into the role of killer. To help desensitize her to this new role, Montoya learned marching chants that helped transform her actions into an automatic response without ethical deliberation:

> What makes the green grass grow?
> Blood, blood, bright red blood
> What makes the pretty flowers bloom?
> Guts, guts, gritty grimy guts[61]

The chants, or military cadences, Montoya learned are often referred to as "Jody calls." They have different themes and serve multiple purposes. While the rhyme scheme and rhythm help marching recruits walk in unison, the contents speak to the intense desensitization to violence that individuals endure to prepare to kill other human beings. The chant makes no logical sense, but its gruesomeness and repetition achieves its ultimate purpose. As Montoya notes, "You say these words so much they lose their meaning. It felt unnatural at first, but you do it so much you don't even think what the word *kill* means after a while."[62] By emptying out the words' content, Montoya and others learn to psychologically distance themselves from the violence they will commit. They learn to eschew civilian standards of decency in favor of a militarized vernacular of butchery and carnage.

This militarized vernacular of violence also includes misogynistic language, which, Benedict argues, "is so deeply engrained in military culture as to be reflexive."[63] For example, it is used to refer to the garrison cap worn by women (the "cunt cap") and is perhaps most prevalent in cadences and Jody calls, such as the infamous "Candy Man":

> Who can take a chainsaw
> Cut the bitch in two
> Fuck the bottom half
> And give the upper half to you?[64]

The lyrics are sung to the tune of the popular song "The Candy Man," featured in the 1971 film *Willy Wonka and the Chocolate Factory*, in a perverse attempt to banalize the dehumanization of women. The military song epitomizes the heightened levels of aggression, violence, and women hating required to produce killer men. Sex and death become synonymous. In the song, men share a disarticulated female corpse, emphasizing that male bonding, in this context, necessitates not only the absence of women, but the sexual violation and destruction of women. For some, the song may be a harmless, albeit tasteless, set of lyrics, but as Henri Myrttinen reminds us, "Violent masculinities are actively constructed, with the aid of words and weapons, through social and cultural institutions."[65]

It is important to examine the disciplining function of violent rhetorics for their role in culturally producing and conditioning female bodies to become vulnerable to violence. For example, Montoya shares her exposure to her male counterparts' taxonomy of women: "There are only three things the guys let you be if you're a girl in the military—a bitch, a ho, or a dyke."[66] Women are categorized based on their perceived or actual sexual availability to men. Each category is denigrated, leaving no desirable option for women to choose. The categories are socially enforced through male gossip in such a way that even if a woman tries to ignore the misogynistic taxonomy, she cannot. Her refusal to define herself in sexual terms earns her the label of "bitch" or "dyke." Montoya learned this lesson firsthand: "In the beginning, I was considered a ho because I was nice, and then later on because I realized what they were saying about me, I became a bitch because I was not mean, but I didn't go along with what they were saying."[67] Her niceties were misconstrued by her male friends, who "took it the wrong way." Eventually, she learned that these supposed friends were saying that she was a "stripper" and a "hooker." These misogynistic utterances are so overwhelming that they often put women at risk of internalizing the labels. For example, Kayla Williams's memoir *Love My Rifle More than You: Young and Female in the U.S. Army* (2005) opens with the psychological struggle of negotiating labels: "Sometimes, even now, I wake up before dawn and forget I am not a slut. The air is not quite dark, not quite light, and I lie absolutely still, trying to will myself to remember that that is *not* what I am. Sometimes, on better mornings, it comes to me right away. And then there are all those other times. Slut."[68] The pervasive atmosphere of female degradation transforms women's self-perceptions to the point where women like Williams will themselves to avoid identifying with misogynistic descriptors, as they cope with the psychological damage that comes from the constant devaluation of their identity and human dignity.

For the men who use these words to sufficiently degrade others, the next logical step is to act on their verbal targets. Benedict explains that amid strenuous training and indoctrination, women and men who are "labeled gay or emotionally weak" are subjected to constant sexual harassment: "When they run obstacle courses, men line up to ogle their bodies. When they walk into the food hall, hundreds of eyes undress them. When they reach or bend to pick up something, men whistle, groan, and stare."[69] Williams also describes the experience of having "their eyes on you all the time, your breasts, your ass—like there is nothing else to watch, no sun, no river, no desert, no mortars at night."[70] For Montoya, the discomfort was long lasting: "When I would go to the lunch hall, and that's where a lot of times because you would be walking and then it just felt like you were like on stage or something. It made me uncomfortable when I got back into the United States."[71] In response to being scrutinized, Montoya altered her own bodily comportment, hoping to deflect unwanted sexual humiliation: "There's so many guys watching you walk, so I had to learn to do it with no girlyness at all."[72] In this striking admission, we see how female bodies (and feminized male bodies) become targets of sexual intimidation and violence within an overall environment that is inhospitable to women.

Montoya's comment also points toward the active processes of defeminization and masculinization that many women voluntarily undergo in the military. Of course, many women are attracted to the military's promise of gender neutrality. After years of enduring gender-based discrimination, their desire for fair treatment makes perfect sense. Montoya's desire to be "a soldier, not a gender" is an explicit call for equity and respect. Unfortunately, she asks the military to behave in a way that is fundamentally antithetical to its history, structure, and ethos. As previously discussed, the military relies on clearly defined genders, on carefully crafted masculinities and femininities that maintain patriarchal order. The strict maintenance of militarized genders leaves female soldiers in the untenable position of performing culturally accepted femininities that open them up to the violence of sexual harassment. The alternative is to undergo defeminization, to deliberately fail to practice the physical expressions, mannerisms, and multiple modes of performing dominant femininities. For Montoya, walking in a non-"girly" way helped her maintain a sense of protection through invisibility.

In Heather Höpfl's analysis of the 1997 film *G.I. Jane*, she describes how defeminization is portrayed as feminist success. In the film, the female Navy-SEAL-in-training, Jordan O'Neil, achieves androgyny and becomes an "ungendered" body through grueling physical training, cursing and swearing with high proficiency, shaving her head, and denouncing feminism itself. Indeed, she becomes what Höpfl calls a "phallic feminist" as a result of her relentless pursuit of phallic power.[73] Because Jordan's desire is to obtain access to the privilege and power of male superiority rather than challenge the patriarchal system itself, her masculinized body is both anomalous and disempowered. Although Jordan defies the military's strict maintenance of gender norms for women—a move that signals gender's inherent vulnerabilities—the "triumph" of her masculinized body only further bolsters the patriarchal domination and denigration of the feminine. Rather than undergo a productive crisis, patriarchal militarism remains intact and reveals its capacity to accommodate isolated cases of gender transgression without jeopardizing its norms, value systems, or power.

Nonetheless, Jordan's "homomorphic" transformation comes at a high cost. As Höpfl explains, "The phallic feminists have little appreciation of the extent to which they are incorporated into the mechanisms which maintain male culture by their faith in androgyny and, worse, lose any valuation of what is lost of the feminine by this ready capitulation to male order."[74] This aspiration for androgyny resonates with Montoya's desire to be "a soldier, not a gender." If soldiering has always been culturally defined as synonymous with male combatants, then it is implicitly gendered to begin with. Yet, Montoya's statement portrays the soldier as nongendered, while the term *gender* stands in for woman—a subject position that she willingly casts off. We find the same sentiment expressed in

Jennifer Silva's interviews with female ROTC cadets, as one respondent stated, "When I am in the uniform I want to feel like *an officer*, I don't want to feel like, oh *she's* an officer. But outside it I want to feel more feminine, but when it comes to my job I don't want to be feminine."[75] Taken together, these statements suggest that soldiers and officers are antithetical to women and the feminine. *Soldiering* and *women* become antonyms, and as Silva points out, "for women, being a 'gender-neutral' soldier requires constant awareness of oneself as *either* a person or a woman."[76] By participating in this mode of self-denigration, these women accept the false claim of gender neutrality and internalize the military's antifeminine position to the detriment of their own subjectivities. Ultimately, this devaluation of the feminine is hard to put into words. Though men can be emasculated, as Höpfl astutely reminds us, "there is no term which describes the taking away of women's power."[77]

Gender neutrality, as difficult to achieve as it may be, does not guarantee protection within the military's culture of male impunity. As Montoya's near-encounter at an Iraq base reveals, the possibility for sexual assault is constant. While walking to her trailer along with her "battle buddy," a buddy system intended to help female soldiers protect themselves from attack *by fellow soldiers while on base*, her male "buddy" told her, "You know, if I was to rape you right now, nobody could hear you scream. Nobody would see you. What would you do?"[78] Montoya intimated that she had a knife (which she did not) and that she would stab her would-be assailant. When asked in a later interview if she carried a knife from that point forward to protect herself from Iraqis, Montoya responded, "I never intended on using the knife for an Iraqi. I had my M-16 for that. But my knife, I always just kept it for another soldier, because any time I would have any type of strong sexual harassment words spoken, I just mainly felt a little bit more secure, and it was visible, too, to the other soldiers."[79] Montoya's experience gives us a glimpse of the kind of psychological terror many servicewomen endure daily as they operate with a heightened sense of vigilance, both on and off base.

Obviously, not all service members are violent misogynists or condone violence against women through passive behaviors. Nevertheless, my focus here has been on the documented cases of sexual assault, rape, and intimidation that permeate all branches of the U.S. military and that serve as examples of how women's bodies are inscribed by an institutional culture of sexualized violence. The level of violence meted out against servicewomen is horrifying. For example, in July 2005, the bruised, raped, and partially burned body of nineteen-year-old

LaVena Johnson was found in a storage tent on a U.S. military base in Balad, Iraq. She had been shot through the mouth with an M16. Although the army declared her death a suicide, Johnson's parents, who petitioned for autopsy and crime scene photos, argued that the photos reveal bloody boot prints, defensive wounds and scratches on her arms, a badly beaten face, and a "caustic substance appears to have been poured on her vagina . . . to eliminate signs of rape."[80] For the Johnsons, the army's own forensic evidence contradicted its official findings. In 2007 the burned corpses of Marine corporal Maria Lauterbach and her unborn fetus were found in the backyard of Cpl. Cesar Armando Laurean, the man she had reported for raping her. It is suspected that Lauterbach's pregnancy resulted from the rape.[81] These grisly examples of rape and violent retribution against rape victims only scratch the surface of a larger systemic practice of condoning, if not enabling, rape through the military's lax, insensitive, and ineffective policies.

Montoya's transformation from a neglected, rebellious Chicana teenager to a specialist in the Army National Guard is an important story to tell about the disciplining of the militarized Chicana body. By the time Montoya completed the Blue Phase (weeks six through nine) of basic training, she had undergone institutional indoctrination, psychological conditioning to violence, and physical alteration of her body and movement. Benedict provides a thorough explanation of what Montoya, and others like her, endured, and it is worth quoting at length:

> She was deprived of sleep to make her susceptible to suggestion and keep her too exhausted to rebel. She was screamed at by her superiors and made to shout, "Yes, sir!" in reply to humble her and accustom her to functioning in an atmosphere of constant aggression. She was humiliated, made to obey capricious commands, and to endure arbitrary punishments to stoke her anger while prohibiting her from venting it, thus building up aggression. She was treated like a child to give the drill sergeant the authority of a parent. She was kept from the news to keep her ignorant and malleable. Her uniform, rules about hair, and the fact that she was no longer called by name but only by rank, "recruit," or the last four digits of her social security number, were all designed to erase her civilian identity. She was made to sing bloodthirsty songs and chants to inure her to killing. She was kept in constant physical pain to break down her will and accustom her to the harsh conditions of war. And while she was punished for independent thinking, such as

> asking questions, she was rewarded for complying with group behavior or sacrificing herself for others.[82]

Benedict lays out for us the complex relationships between physical, emotional, and psychological modification that goes into militarizing a body in basic training. Each minute task and every verbal command collectively compose an overall hostile and hierarchal environment theoretically meant to prepare recruits for the extreme conditions of warfare. There is a breaking down of the body, its previous identity, physical limits, comfort zones, and individuality, in favor of cultivating a human body that responds to and emits aggression, unquestioningly obeys orders, and privileges the group over individual needs or desires.

Through *Peacetime* and Montoya's descriptions of basic training, we see how military power explores the Chicana soldier body, manipulating and transforming it into a serviceable body for the state. Benedict's description of military training describes the tactics used to fulfill what Foucault calls a "military dream of society," in which individuals become the "meticulously subordinated cogs of a machine" managed by "permanent coercions" and "indefinitely progressive forms of training" that result in "automatic docility."[83] Through training, the body develops new capacities and aptitudes, as well as a newly developed power that must be tempered by disciplinary control into a condition of "docility-utility."[84] The multiple forms of coercion and minute control that Chicanas experience are meant to foster the "military dream" of utility and obedience. As we have seen with the undisciplined Adelita who confronts predatory drill instructors and Montoya's defensive maneuvers against sexual harassment and her attempt to conceal her "girly" gait, isolated moments of disobedience are not only possible, but occasionally tolerated. They are also, however, quickly subsumed. While Foucault's analysis of the docile soldier body is useful, it presumes a white male body rather than account for the disciplinary tactics applied to Chicana and female soldiers in general. It does not account for how disciplinary power maintains gender differentiation and gender subordination or how female docility is presupposed before boot camp and then compounded in basic training. The experiences recounted in *Peacetime* and in Montoya's interviews demonstrate how intimidation, violence, misogynistic language, military cosmetics instruction, and the regulation of women's appearance and movement discipline Chicana soldier bodies into compliance with military standards and heteronormativity, which help maintain the viability of the military. Without women's subordination—achieved through various methods, of which sexual harassment is but one—the neoliberal military becomes dysfunctional.

If a neoliberal "dream society" were to exist, it would require disciplinary methods to produce obedient yet responsible subjects. Neoliberals, Lisa Duggan argues, place a high value on personal responsibility. They view "'private' *competition*, *self-esteem*, and *independence* as the roots of *personal responsibility*, and excoriat[e] 'public' *entitlement*, *dependency*, and *irresponsibility* as the sources of social ills."[85] After enduring seven weeks of boot camp, Medrano and Adela achieve the neoliberal dream of personal responsibility and self-sufficiency. Rather than rely on state support or question its policies or its perpetration of military violence, the Chicana soldiers in *Peacetime* become their own safety net.[86]

Military training is also responsible for Montoya's transformation from a troubled Chicana teenager to a self-managed soldier-citizen. Like the Chicana characters in *Peacetime*, Montoya also learns to become her own safety net, but only after being denied support services upon her exit from the military. After serving in the army for seven years, Montoya became a twenty-four-year-old single mother and homeless veteran. Her military career ended when she decided to leave because she could not secure childcare for her two-year-old daughter: "I went to the VA [Veterans Administration] to ask if they had any type of daycare help or resources and they said no, she's not a veteran, we have help for veterans."[87] Not being able to find a job that would cover her living expenses and childcare costs, Montoya became one of an estimated 6,500 homeless female veterans. According to Lisa Fletcher and Felicia Biberica, the fact that one in three servicewomen "report they were raped or sexually assaulted while serving" partly accounts for female veterans being "four times more likely than their male counterparts to wind up homeless."[88] These statistics represent the tragic reality that military women are often disciplined to endure the psychological and physical traumas of sexual violence and to suffer the consequences with little if any support. In addition to this harsh lesson, Montoya and others learn that, despite being a "good citizen"—as defined by voluntary military service—neoliberal policies have eviscerated the concepts of entitlement and earned benefits: "My friends went to college and now they have careers. . . . I dedicated seven years of my life to the military and it's as if it were for nothing."[89] What Montoya has sadly learned is that under neoliberal militarism, the state is not interested in carrying out its ethical, social, and economic obligations. Instead, individuals like Montoya must acquire the skills necessary for self-sufficiency and self-management—corollaries to the principle of free choice.

Taken together, *Peacetime* and Mickiela Montoya's experiences demonstrate how neoliberal militarism is predicated on the debasement of women. Both accounts describe a pervasive misogyny overlapping the process of military indoctrination, with women's bodies treated as threats and as objects used for male sexual release. Neoliberal militarism also thrives off the economic oppression of female civilians, servicewomen, and veterans. Although the ideological architects of the all-volunteer force envisioned enlistment as an individual's choice among other options, the reality of harsh neoliberal policies delimited the options available to poor and working-class women and people of color. The constriction of choice worked to the AVF's advantage, as women increasingly joined the military to gain access to state services and income. But, as Montoya's homelessness illustrates, continued access to that support is hard to maintain. Ultimately, we learn from both *Peacetime* and the experience of contemporary Chicana servicewomen like Montoya that neoliberal militarism requires and aspires to reproduce economically vulnerable yet self-reliant subjects who refrain from making political demands on the state.

In the next chapter, I turn to Chicana transfronterista literature to examine how women challenge neoliberal militarism by forming cross-border solidarities. While U.S. militarism fosters misogyny, women in other countries have tried to disarticulate patriarchy from militarism. Although Mexicana insurgents undergo a process of weapons training and physical transformation similar to that of their Chicana enlistee counterparts, the insurgents identify neoliberalism as a source of oppression and actively challenge state policies. Through a study of comparative militarisms, we can see how women are differently implicated in systems of power and how they are remade through violence.

3

WAR, TIME, WOUND

Anti-Neoliberal Militarism in the Work of Graciela Limón and Lorna Dee Cervantes

I'm five hundred and two years old, cabrón!
CAPTAIN IRMA FROM GRACIELA LIMÓN'S *ERASED FACES*

Adelita es la mujer to destroy los capitalistas.
EL VEZ AND THE MEMPHIS MARIACHIS, "MISERY TREN"

IN 1994, THE ZAPATISTA ARMY of National Liberation (Ejército Zapatista de Liberación Nacional, or EZLN) waged what they described as the "Fourth World War" against neoliberalism. By launching their assault on military posts in several towns in the southern Mexican state of Chiapas, on January 1, 1994, the day Mexico was to begin implementing neoliberal reform through NAFTA, this group of indigenous insurgents turned the world's attention to the political, economic, and ethnic crisis in the region. Drawing on Mexican and Mayan worldviews and histories, the Zapatistas' emergence left many of its earliest critics skeptical.[1] The notion of an astute and organized Indian-led army proved to be a conceptual challenge for dubious officials and intellectuals and led to what José Rabasa calls the "impossibility" of the Zapatistas' radical emergence. Rabasa discusses press coverage during the early days of the rebellion, in which some critics believed the Zapatistas were being led by non-Indian agitators: "How could Indians understand NAFTA without foreign advisors?"[2] The Zapatistas' impossibility is also based on their demands for a radical reorientation of Mexican culture and politics, one that calls for justice and democracy. Their "call for justice is in the realm of the incalculable," as Rabasa puts it. "What could make amends for the oppression of indigenous peoples over the past five hundred years?"[3] By proposing "the impossible as a utopian horizon of alternative rationalities to those dominant in the West," the Zapatistas are out of sync with the nation in their timing and in their political demands.[4] Given the Zapatistas' expansive historical coordinates of resistance, temporality is a significant part of their liberatory project.

The Zapatistas have had a significant impact on Chicana/o political activism and expressive culture, inaugurating what could be called the genre of Chicana/o Zapatista fiction.[5] Works such as Graciela Limón's *Erased Faces* (2001) and Lorna Dee Cervantes's "Coffee" (1998/2006) focus on the struggles and persecution of Zapatista communities.[6] Events in *Erased Faces* are set in the years leading up to the Zapatista attack on San Cristóbal in 1994; however, the novel emphasizes the historical context of indigenous resistance to the multiple forms of colonial and imperial wars throughout Mexico's history. Focused on Afro-Chicana photographer Adriana Mora and Zapatista leader Juana Galván, a Tzeltal woman who encourages Adriana to use her camera to document the Zapatista insurgency, Limón's novel underscores the importance of history and memory to current narratives of transnational resistance and, importantly, places women's lives at the center of the war story. In Lorna Dee Cervantes's six-part poem "Coffee," the Chicana and Chumash feminist poet focuses on the 1997 state-sponsored massacre of forty-five Tzotzil Indian men, women, and children in Acteal, Chiapas, who were suspected of being Zapatista supporters. The Acteal massacre was one of the government's most brutal assaults since the 1994 uprising.

My analysis of *Erased Faces* proceeds in two phases. In the first section, I focus on the novel's depiction of Zapatista feminism and its ethical limitations. I use accounts of the founding of the EZLN and of its female leadership to show how Zapatista militarism promises ontological transformation to its female insurgents similar to the promise U.S. neoliberal militarism holds out to Chicana soldiers. While the Zapatistas' early attempt to imagine and practice a militarism divorced from misogyny and patriarchy seemed to offer women a true form of power and agency, these efforts were undermined by the Zapatistas' use of violence, a tactic that they later abandoned and replaced with nonviolent forms of action. This history is critical for understanding Limón's meticulously researched novel about Zapatista women. It provides the background for examining Juana's personal transformation and her induction into violence. I argue that while the novel positively depicts Juana's use of force, its ending undermines a fully celebratory or romanticized reading of resistant violence. Rather, the narrative forces us to contend with the ethics of women's violence and reveals militarism's capacity to appropriate the feminist goals of female empowerment and equality. In the second part, I focus on how the novel depicts violence as transferable over generations, as Juana and Adriana inherit the scars and memories of persecution from colonized indigenous women who lived in previous centuries. I argue that Limón uses these moments of repetition as more than a structuring trope. Rather, through the novel's focus on an embodied form of transhistorical violence, *Erased Faces* portrays alternatives to the linear progress narrative of the modern/colonial nation and the straight time of heteronormativity.

Cervantes's "Coffee" is also concerned with reimagining how time works, by layering disparate histories into a poetic narrative of contemporaneity. The poem ultimately fosters the development of a historical consciousness that promotes a capacious, asynchronous view of time—one that uses historical memory as recourse to neoliberalism's disregard for the past. Both works are equally preoccupied with rejecting Western conceptions of linear time in favor of alternative and indigenous understandings of cyclical time and allochronic events. By challenging modernity's periodization, both texts signal the existence of alternative value systems and thus of alternative visions for the future that include life beyond neoliberal militarism.

Existing scholarship on *Erased Faces* focuses predominantly on the novel's transnationalist and postnationalist perspective. For example, Elizabeth Cummins Muñoz and Ignacio López-Calvo draw on U.S. Third World feminism to analyze the novel's use of gender and sexuality in deconstructing the nation. Through the characters' active struggle against racist, sexist oppression, Cummins Muñoz argues, Adriana and Juana, along with the other Zapatistas, form a "collective that comes to replace the traditional role of national affiliation."[7] As exemplars of Chicana Zapatista fiction and poetry, *Erased Faces* and "Coffee" are rooted in a vibrant literary tradition of transfronterista, or cross-border feminist fiction and poetry inspired by U.S. Third World feminism. Developed alongside of and in response to the mainstream women's movement of the sixties and seventies, U.S. Third World feminism countered the movement's nation-centered and Eurocentric tendencies. Chela Sandoval explains how U.S. feminists of color juxtaposed two seemingly antithetical regions—the United States and the Third World—to foster "a geopolitical upheaval of the nation-state and its social imaginaries, and an innovative pulling together again of what [they] hoped could be a trans-national, -gendered, -sexed, -cultural, -racial, and coalitional political site."[8] This paradigm shift in methodology, praxis, and focus enabled a Chicana feminist political vision that transcended borders—a vision that inspired Chicana and Latina transfronterista literature, poetry, and film in the closing decades of the twentieth century.

Although Limón's and Cervantes's Chicana/o Zapatista literature is thematically concerned with transnational coalition building, I examine the relationship between bodies and time as Limón and Cervantes reveal how alternative temporalities are played out on the wounded bodies of women and girls. In their texts, the wounding of female bodies is a point of identification that enables and compels cross-border solidarities between Chicanas and Mexican indigenous women. Through a focus on wounded bodies and multiple temporalities, Limón and Cervantes challenge the Mexican state's narrative control of the revolution's legacy and reclaim the figure of the soldadera for an anti-neoliberal agenda.

"AN ARMED WOMAN COMMANDS THEM": THE ZAPATISTA WAR ON NEOLIBERALISM

While Zapatistas are perhaps most recognized for their iconic ski masks, they are also notable for their ability to crystallize complex economic analyses into succinct, often colorful, yet rhetorically sophisticated descriptions of neoliberalism's violence. In broad, Manichean rhetoric, their spokesperson Subcomandante Marcos describes an all-encompassing struggle that marks an impending phase of destruction for humankind: "Today, we suffer a new world war, a war against all peoples, against humanity, against culture, against history. It is an international war, of Money versus Humanity, carried out by a handful of financial centers, without homeland and without shame. Now, this international terror is called neoliberalism—an international economic order that has already caused more death and destruction than the great world wars."[9] The Zapatistas have recognized the destructive potential of NAFTA since its inception. Yet, as Courtney Jung explains, the neoliberal turn in the Mexican economy began before the implementation of NAFTA and can be traced at least to the wake of the 1982 debt crisis.[10] Under the onslaught of neoliberal policies, the living standards among the Mayan communities in Chiapas began to deteriorate precipitously.[11] Through the privatization of land ownership, the Zapatistas, like Emiliano Zapata, their namesake and hero from the Mexican Revolution, faced the loss of their land holdings and cultural traditions based on communal ownership. Hence, Zapata becomes a particularly apt symbol for the Indian communities who faced then president Carlos Salinas's (1988–94) neoliberal reforms to land tenure. In 1992, Salinas eliminated one of the most significant accomplishments of the revolution when he oversaw the repeal of Article 27 of the 1917 Constitution, which had redistributed land collectively to peasants in a form of land tenure known as ejidos.[12] Salinas's neoliberal reform prevented collective petitioning for land and enabled individuals to sell their parcel of land. The repeal of Article 27 was particularly devastating to Indians in Chiapas because one-third of the state's population lived on ejidos, most of which were located in the Lacandón region. Salinas's embrace of neoliberalism in the form of NAFTA further decimated the chances for improving the lives and livelihoods of Indian communities. Although geographically removed from the centers of power, the Zapatista communities in the Lacandón recognized the regression in their standard of living by observing that the "Mexican countryside is worse than ever and the campesinos more screwed than under Porfirio Díaz. . . . Instead of improving," they noted, "the social rights which were won in the revolution of 1910 now make one sad . . . and courageous."[13] Their critique of the state should also be read as a critique of its modern progress narratives, since conditions for Native peoples in the Lacandón have not just stagnated but regressed, a critique underlying Marcos's rhetorical phrasing: "Are not the indigenous demands a worrisome stain on history, dimming the splendor of globalization?"[14]

By attacking six towns in Chiapas on January 1, 1994, the Zapatistas recognized that their initial acts of violence would catch the attention of a previously disinterested Mexican government. In a communiqué dated January 20, 1994, Marcos writes,

> Our form of armed struggle is just and true. If we had not raised our rifles the government would never have preoccupied itself with the Indigenous people in our lands, and we would have continued on in poverty, forgotten. Now the government is very preoccupied with the problems of Indigenous people and campesinos, and that is good. But it was necessary for the Zapatista rifle to speak so that Mexico could hear the voice of the poor Chiapanecos.[15]

With carefully executed attacks on the state capital, the Zapatistas entered national memory as historical agents, subject to the scrutinizing gaze of the state.[16]

Legibility and the subjectivity it enables are particularly important for the indigenous women in the EZLN. For the Zapatistas, it is significant that the commander who led the takeover of San Cristóbal de las Casas was Comandante Ramona, a Tzotzil woman and member of the Clandestine Indigenous

Revolutionary Committee of the General Command (CCRI-CG) of the Zapatistas. The notion that an armed indigenous woman led the assault on the state capital forced the state to recognize the presence, indeed the power, of indigenous women. Through violence and militarism, indigenous women become decipherable to the state. Importantly, the forms of violence that indigenous women often endure also become legible once women take up arms. For example, in Marcos's account of the women's role in the attack on San Cristóbal, he describes how Capitán Insurgente Laura, a Tzotzil woman and captain of an all-male unit, "carries in her hands a carbine that she has taken from a policeman, he who only saw someone to humiliate or rape as he gazed upon her, an indigenous woman. After surrendering, the policeman ran away in his shorts, the same one who until that day believed that women were only useful when pregnant or in the kitchen."[17] The policeman's "gaze" upon the indigenous female body changes when Capitán Insurgente Laura's body becomes a weaponized and threatening body. She has disrupted the calculus of power by taking up arms and challenging the state's monopoly on legitimized violence.

In the face of military violence, women in the Zapatistas have taken up arms to protect themselves and their communities against the state's economic onslaught and the military's saturation of the region. Published interviews with Zapatista women reveal the extent of military training that all Zapatistas receive. For example, Infantry Major Ana María, who became a Zapatista at the age of twelve or thirteen, describes the education she received in weapons and politics: "They taught us to walk in the mountain, to load a weapon, to hunt. They taught us military combat exercises, and when we had learned that, they taught us politics. Then we went to the communities to speak with our people."[18] Márgara Millán Moncayo's study of indigenous women in the EZLN shows that the majority of Zapatista women, like Infantry Major Ana María, join when they are young girls. For many, the decision to take up arms with the Zapatistas is based on the potential opportunity to redress the conditions of abject poverty that devastate their lives, as is the case with Laura, a captain of Zapatista troops: "I was very young when I heard about the EZLN. I was working the land with other women who got together to grow some food. That's where we started talking and began to understand why we live in poverty and cannot find a better way of living. . . . I joined out of conscience, to fight for the poor; it is not right that children go on dying."[19]

Like the Chicana soldiers in boot camp discussed in the previous chapter, Zapatista women undergo exhausting physical transformation as their militarized bodies gain proficiency in warfare. The descriptions of Zapatista training show clearly that Zapatista militarism also induces an internal transformation, one that ontologically alters individuals. For example, in Marcos's tribute to some of the key women leaders in the EZLN, he describes Comandante Ramona's transmogrification into a Zapatista:

> In December 1984, not yet twenty years old, she arrives in the mountains of the Lacandon Jungle, carrying the marks of the whole history of indigenous humiliation on her body. In December 1984 this brown woman says, "Enough is enough!" so softly that only she hears herself. In January 1994 this woman and several thousand indigenous people do not just say, but yell, "Enough is enough!" so loudly that all the world hears them.[20]

In this description, Ramona is depicted as a young, soft-spoken "brown woman," whose marked body represents the collective experience of indigenous women's suffering. During her time in the mountains of the Lacandón, she matures into a Zapatista leader, skilled in weapons, combat training, and military maneuvers. Although we are not given specific details about her life before she joined the Zapatistas, we presume that she endured a history of gender- and race-based violence, one that is not only individually felt, but also representative of a larger collective experience. Before her military training, she could only whisper her defiance in a muted, isolated voice. But afterward, she develops a voice that shouts in unison with an equally adamant collective voice to condemn a history of indigenous repression and exploitation. Thus, Zapatista militarism is characterized as a physically and ontologically empowering process of self-actualization, particularly for the indigenous women who join the EZLN.

The Zapatistas' insistence on women's personal self-transformation marks the form of militarism they deploy as radically new. Zapatista women feel empowered to question all areas of life in which they experience gender-based oppression and abuse. This includes upending cultural traditions and family practices that perpetuate patriarchal power. While most militarisms are predicated on violence against women and the feminine, the Zapatistas are attempting to disarticulate armed defense from patriarchy and misogyny. Zapatista women initiated this process in 1993 by drawing up a list of women's rights and demanding that it be included as integral to the Zapatista platform. Indeed, the year before the Zapatistas made their debut on the world stage, a revolution had already taken place within their ranks, as women rebels mandated the disarticulation of militarism and masculinity through a ten-point list of demands called La Ley Revolucionaria de las Mujeres (LRM), or the Women's Revolutionary Law.[21] The LRM's significance lies in its assertion of women's rights within the EZLN, the various indigenous communities, and the individual families to which Zapatista women belong. The LRM and the Zapatista men and women who abide by it debilitate patriarchal militarism by acknowledging women's "specific situation of discrimination" and by placing "the corresponding responsibility for gender subordination" onto men.[22] The inclusion of women's rights—for all women, not only Zapatista women—as part of Zapatismo is a significant break from the kind of militancy practiced during the Mexican Revolution. Whereas the original soldaderas' contributions, needs, and political demands were marginalized during and after the revolution, the Zapatista women have an active and coequal role in shaping the political objectives of the group. "Compared to other revolutionary struggles," Mariana Mora argues, "the EZLN is not telling women to wait until the revolution triumphs to become a priority, but rather includes women's rights as a central part of their objectives—the reconstruction and redefinition of power in order to include the excluded."[23]

The Zapatista women's efforts at gender integration raise important questions about the nature of militarism. Namely, can antistatist militarism exist without patriarchy? In contradistinction to the U.S. military's form of neoliberal militarism discussed in the preceding chapter, the Zapatistas propose a different model of militarism that eschews organizational structures based on patriarchal orders, misogynistic practices, or masculine privilege.[24] Both *Peacetime* and *Erased Faces* depict liberal feminist claims of gender integration and equality; however, only Zapatista militarism is organized around the ideology and practice of dismantling political, social, and familial forms of patriarchy. Thus, while Adela in *Peacetime* attempts to reshape U.S. militarism into an antimisogynistic practice of state power, the Zapatista women—who are also part of a soldadera genealogy—attempt to forge an antipatriarchal, anticolonial, and antiracist form of militarism. Moreover, the Zapatistas' intersectional critique of neoliberalism promotes a collective vision of justice, one forged through communitarian struggle, while neoliberal militarism fosters an individualist ethos of self-management and personal responsibility. Yet, just like U.S. military induction, Zapatistas undergo weapons and combat training as they learn the art of warfare.

While Zapatista feminism provides a strong critique of neoliberalism and the various forms of oppression that women experience, I argue that its goals remain unachievable whenever it resorts to resistant violence. I begin by analyzing what

Srila Roy calls the "gendered logic of resistance," and how Zapatismo relies on disempowering notions of gender even as it attempts to overturn them.[25] Marcos's descriptions of Capitán Insurgente Laura and Comandante Ramona illustrate how the gender presumptions of power undergird Zapatista militarism. While ostensibly positive, his characterization of both women actually relies on familiar discourses of women's victimhood. Marcos describes Capitán Insurgente Laura primarily as an indigenous woman whom the policeman sees only as "someone to humiliate or rape." His description of Comandante Ramona also focuses on how she "carr[ies] the marks of the whole history of indigenous humiliation on her body." In both cases, the women are initially reduced to victimhood defined by sexual vulnerability. Both are characterized by a kind of abject passivity—indeed, the premilitarized Ramona is rendered virtually mute, as she speaks "so softly that only she hears herself"—that erases any sense of autonomy and multidimensional identity they may have had. For most Western readers, Marcos's description merely reaffirms stereotypes of the voiceless and oppressed Third World woman. Such stereotypes often animate paternalistic forms of charity and support that further affirm positions of power and privilege. Thus, Marcos's rhetoric unwittingly perpetuates disempowering discourses of gender and race while describing the very women he seeks to praise.

While meant to serve as images of liberation, his depictions of their resort to armed insurgency do little to challenge existing gender norms. In his account, their empowerment is primarily based on the weapon they carry and the potential for violence it enables. Yet, armed insurgency—like all militarisms—relies on the presumption that combat and soldiering are synonymous with masculinity. Kimberly Hutchings explains that discipline, rationality, aggression, and self-sacrifice are qualities associated with militarism, and that these are "instilled through their identification with idealized forms of masculinity in contrast to a denigrated feminine other."[26] Moreover, militarisms gain legitimacy by claiming to protect a defenseless civilian population that is often associated with women. While Marcos's descriptions of Laura and Ramona ostensibly challenge these gender roles, the depictions show only how women are successful at adopting forms of violence associated with militarized masculinity, thereby leaving in place larger notions of gender dis/empowerment. In Marcos's account, we get the impression that Laura and Ramona are anomalous examples of armed militants, while male soldiering is taken for granted. As anomalies, their roles in Zapatista leadership do not fully represent women's empowerment because, as Hutchings argues, the roles of soldier and civilian are stabilized by long-standing gender norms. Marcos's narrative of female empowerment portrays Zapatista militarism as being progressive and inclusive; however, it also shows how even anti-neoliberal militarism seeks to appropriate feminist goals by speaking in the language of women's agency.

In addition to reconfirming gender norms, the Zapatistas' use of violence had the opposite and unintended effect of spreading more violence in the communities they wanted to protect. In the days following the January 1, 1994, attacks, the Mexican military retaliated against indigenous communities in the region whether they had ties to the EZLN or not. In addition to waging a low-intensity counterinsurgency war against the Zapatistas and civil society in Chiapas, the military deployed sixty thousand troops, who were stationed among the three hundred camps and thirty military bases installed throughout the state. The state also enlisted the help of nine paramilitary groups "trained by the army and police and recruited by the cattlemen and their allies among the loyal 'good' indigenous in the PRI-controlled peasant organizations."[27] Marcos describes how, as a result of intense militarization of the region and violent confrontations, "the people from the cities went out into the streets and began shouting for an end to the war." The Zapatistas listened to their supporters and allies, "who were telling us to try to reach an arrangement or an accord with the bad governments, so that the problem could be resolved without a massacre. . . . And so we set aside the fire and took up the word."[28] To demonstrate their respect for their supporters' "demand [for] demilitarization and justice instead of bullets and soldiers," the Zapatistas began "endorsing the bullfighter's vocation, . . . making passes with our capes at assault helicopters, bombers, tanks, and tracking dogs."[29] In their Sixth Declaration of the Selva Lacandona, the Zapatistas reaffirm their "commitment to an offensive ceasefire" and vow that they will "not make any attack against government forces or any offensive military movements." Thus, the Zapatistas practice what can only be called a paradoxical and peculiar form of militarism. It is a militarism that is "against militarism" and is practiced by an army composed of insurgents who are "soldiers so that one day soldiers would not be needed."[30]

Thus, the Zapatistas recognize that violence is not the only path toward subject formation. To illustrate the multiple forms that resistance can take, Marcos includes the anonymous figure of "She" in his tribute to Zapatista women leaders. "She" has "no military rank, no uniform, no weapon." Rather, "She" is part of "that amorphous yet solid part of society that says, day after day, 'Enough is enough!'"[31] Like the Zapatista women who have chosen to take up arms, "She" is weary of political oppression and economic exploitation. But "She" also seeks an end to male domination, for "She has already fought against everyone—against her husband, her lover, her boyfriend, her children, her friend, her brother, her father, her grandfather." In Zapatismo, "She" sees a feminist solution to patriarchal control and the possibility of realizing a truly liberatory society: "She discovers that she is born on January 1, 1994. From then on she feels that her life—and what was always said to be a dream and a utopia—might actually be a truth."[32] Like Comandante Ramona, "She" experiences a rebirth, but unlike her fellow Zapatista, her transformation does not rely on militarized violence to achieve its power.

MILITARIZED ZAPATISTA FEMINISM IN *ERASED FACES*

Chicana author and activist Graciela Limón, known for her carefully wrought historical novels, is the first Chicana/o novelist to make the Zapatista rebellion the central focus of a novel.[33] *Erased Faces* follows the lives of three characters—Adriana Mora, Juana Galván, and Orlando Flores—and their eventual involvement with the Zapatistas. The novel is organized around flashbacks that fill in the personal histories of each protagonist, such as Orlando, who spent his childhood working as a servant and later as a *boyero* (mahogany logger). After decapitating his sadistic overseer, Orlando lives life as a fugitive, working as an itinerant laborer in villages throughout the Lacandón until he eventually joins the group that would become the Zapatistas. The emphasis on these characters' childhoods and years of struggle is a deliberate attempt to privilege the motivations for armed militancy rather than romanticize revolution. Scenes of conflict with cruel overseers or violent husbands demonstrate the interconnections between individual struggle and collective struggle. Although the novel avoids discussions of economic doctrine, globalization, and political philosophies, neoliberalism is its silent subtext and context.[34] Instead, Limón depicts the intimate consequences of economic inequities and power imbalances. The wars being waged in *Erased Faces* are explicitly against women's oppression, indigenous exploitation, and the lingering presence of modernity/coloniality. The novel shows us how one form of domination rests on others, and how, by winning singular battles over enslavement or personal choice (e.g., choosing who, when, and if to marry), individuals move one step closer to dismantling larger systems of oppression. By focusing on Juana's struggle to overcome patriarchal traditions and domestic abuse, Limón's novel highlights the redefinition of militarism that the Zapatistas employ.

The novel tracks the transformation of characters and the evolution of their radical consciousness. In light of their individual struggles, the characters ultimately conclude that war is the only solution. When the bishop holds a rally to try to quell the rising unrest that he sensed among his indigenous congregation, Juana silently questions his plea for pacifism: "*Is he not recognizing the enormity of grief suffered by our people for so many centuries? Is he not acknowledging that we are the ones to ultimately take control of our own lives? Why can he not admit that war is the only way to solve the grievous problems afflicting our people? War is the only way that will lead to defining our own history.*"[35] For Juana, the unbearable conditions of depravity that the elite inflict on her people call for extreme action. The outrage that she, Orlando, and others experience, known as "*kap jol*, the anger of the people," permeates indigenous communities and eventually leads to "*tzak' bail*, the armed movement against *los patrones*."[36] Importantly, Juana also connects the present injustices with the centuries of exploitation resulting from modernity/coloniality. The fact that time is stagnant during the continual persecution of indigenous communities is the novel's overall critique of the Mexican state's failed progress narrative.

Lest it be misunderstood that Zapatista men (or indigenous men, in general) easily and wholeheartedly accepted gender integration and women's equal rights in society, Limón depicts the initial turmoil that women's inclusion creates within the community. After Orlando explains to a group of potential recruits that fighting the patrones will require "men and women willing to fight a war, and even to die," someone yells out: "Women? That's crazy! ¡Estás loco! Women are useless in war! In fact, why are women here? War is not for women! This is none of their business!" The women at the meeting respond in outrage: "We have endured not only the fist of *el patrón* but that of our fathers, our brothers, our husbands. We have earned the right to be in the war!"[37] As Juana silently listens to the exchange, she grows increasingly attracted to the clandestine movement that values her rights and encourages her independence. When Orlando initially meets Juana, he frames Zapatismo as a movement to end exploitation and oppression, including the forms that affect women. His recruitment pitch consists of a series of questions that are no less revolutionary despite their simplicity: "Are you not tired of being told whom to marry and when to do it? Would you not want to choose your own partner? Would you not want to say when you are to have children, and how many?" Juana realizes that her own struggle against an arranged marriage and an abusive husband has prepared her to face the larger struggle for social justice. After all, "She had already fought a war when she defied her husband" by escaping from a violent forced marriage.[38]

Upon joining the Zapatistas, Juana undergoes a kind of boot camp training that prepares her for combat against the Mexican military. The training requires gender and cultural transformations necessary to make combatants more effective. Like the female soldiers in *Peacetime*, Juana learns to adapt her female body to wearing combat fatigues. "Wearing pants and a man's shirt posed a difficult obstacle for her"; however "she soon realized that dressing like a man also gave her more mobility and protection than did her long dress." Juana learns that soldiering requires new modes of mobility that only men's pants can facilitate, such as "slither[ing] on her belly, almost silently, and crawl[ing] on her hands and knees as she approached mock targets, or enemies." The shift to men's clothing is a challenge not only to gender norms, but also to her traditional form of dress: Tzeltal woolen skirts, huipils (embroidered cotton blouses), and huaraches (sandals). While the new uniform has the effect of defeminizing her and other Zapatista women, the purpose seems to be for combat effectiveness rather than privileging male dominance by erasing women's presence or their bodies. For example, wearing combat boots initially blisters her feet, but eventually Juana "enjoyed being able to step on sharp or prickly rocks and plants without worrying about her soles or ankles."[39]

Through this process of induction, we see how militarism gradually transforms Juana's body in physical and psychological ways as she learns to become an agent of violence. This transformation is most evident when she first learns how to carry and use a rifle. The foreignness of handling this kind of weapon is highlighted by her body's physical reaction to it: "Her elbows bled, and her hands and arms ached from the pressure of carrying the unaccustomed weapon until her skin became coarse, scabbing over with new bleedings on top of those wounds."[40] Unlike Eliza Medrano of *Peacetime*, Juana does not develop a special bond with her weapon, but she does endeavor to master it by "shooting long hours, beyond what was expected, until she was able to place the bullet on the exact mark on the designated tree or branch." Through her perseverance, Juana eventually excels at combat training, so that "it could not be denied that no one could match Juana's accuracy and speed during maneuvers."[41] Yet, the training Juana undergoes requires the same form of abstraction that state militaries promote when training soldiers to kill. Although there are no denigrating marching chants or pervasive sexual harassment at the Zapatista training camp, Juana is trained to view the violence that she is learning to inflict as an abstraction, as something she does to "mock targets" on tree branches. Learning to distance one's self from the violence done to another's body is part of all militarisms—state or subaltern—and becomes the inevitable source of ethical conflict.

Limón depicts Juana's military training as an important physical and emotional period of growth. She is "transformed from the girl who had sustained the blows of a morose husband into a woman now trained as a guerrilla." Juana gains a sense of personal independence through physical training and the literacy and Spanish-speaking skills she learns at the camp. Her transformation also comes with a nom de guerre, Teniente Insurgente Isabel, and a position within the Zapatista leadership. The transformation from a girl-wife to a guerrilla leader prompts Juana to reconsider her former life as a marginalized woman and to confront the source of her former oppression: patriarchal traditions. On one of her many missions to transport matériel to base camp, she decides to finally confront her father over his decision to sell her into marriage when she was fourteen. Although she had spent years "obsessed by the memory of her father bartering her," only after Juana's transformation into a new soldadera is she capable of confronting him and the oppressive traditions he once practiced.[42] After years of not seeing her father, Juana's interaction with him is terse and strained:

> "A daughter should not question her father."
> "*Tata*, why did you sell me?"
> "I did not sell you! It was an exchange!"
> "Were you exchanged for the price of a mule by your father?"
> "I'm not a woman!"[43]

By questioning her father's choice, Juana is also questioning the larger community's practices, because arranged marriages happened "to her mother, to her sisters, to all the women she knew."[44] Juana's confrontation with her intractable father exposes the forms of male privilege that operate within families and communities. Marginalized because of their gender, women become objects to barter in exchange for mules and other farm animals in a system that protects male dominance and control. Asking her father why he sold her into marriage is a significant act for Juana because it enables her to voice her rejection of patriarchal traditions. Focusing on such patriarchal practices thus becomes central to the

Zapatistas' project of liberation. Even though she knows her father will never change his views, the confrontation frees Juana from an overwhelming sense of rejection, "liberating her to follow the path of insurgency."[45]

Juana's internal transformation is representative of most of the women who join the Zapatistas. While spending time with the EZLN as their designated photographer, Adriana notices the changes that the women go through as they become committed members of the movement:

> She admired their confidence in what they did, whether it was practice shooting or exchanging ideas. She frequently thought of the many village women she had met during the past months, of their reticence and passivity, and she wondered how it was that the women of the force had transformed themselves, how they had built the bridge necessary to cross such a huge separation. It seemed to Adriana that she was seeing two species of women, each one from a different people, from a different land, from a different time.[46]

The contrast between Adriana's previous encounter with what she viewed as timid village women resigned to their own oppression and the spirited Zapatista women she now observes suggests that the EZLN promises the potential for radical ontological transformation. Although concerned with the existential threat that neoliberal militarism poses to their communities, the Zapatistas focus on arming women and others with the knowledge of how to name and confront their specific oppressions. The novel also challenges the perception of indigenous women as reticent and passive by emphasizing a genealogy of women agitators and leaders who, through the centuries, have confronted Spanish colonialism and the whip of the *patrón*.

Ironically, Juana's newfound sense of empowerment also enables the state's appropriative attempt to insert her into its national narrative. Limón incorporates the Zapatistas' attacks on January 1, 1994, into the novel by focusing on Juana, who is assigned to the rebel column in charge of attacking the town of Ocosingo. "With an M-1 carbine held in the assault position," Juana and her squad take over the town radio station and its garrison of federal troops. After only minutes, the insurgents collect the surrendered weapons of the federal troops and corral them into a central patio, as Insurgent Captain Irma yells out to the garrison commander, "*¡Feliz Año Nuevo, cabrón!* [Happy New Year, asshole!]." Juana observes the commander's shock at the early morning surprise attack, particularly the people who executed it: "How would he explain that it had been a woman who had disarmed him, reviling him, calling him a son of a bitch? Even more humiliating, how would he admit that she was an indigenous woman?"[47] The coordinated attack forced the government to reconsider its underestimation of indigenous men and women. Captain Irma's disarming of the garrison commander is also symbolic of the kind of *kap jol* (anger) that indigenous women harbor from centuries of oppression. Only by taking arms themselves do these women feel they can collectively challenge the state's monopoly on violence. The triumphal description of Captain Irma's role reversal compels us to approve of Juana's participation in the armed takeover of Ocosingo—an act that we might regard as a "good" use of antioppressive violence. Yet, even while Juana's participation partially challenges the image of the masculine protector, it does not undo the association between militarism and masculinity. Rather, it facilitates militarism's ability to selectively incorporate women into violence while perpetuating gender hierarchies.

While we might be inclined to regard the Zapatistas' resistant violence as legitimate and justified, I argue that the novel actually demonstrates the limitations of ethical violence. Hutchings describes how this form of violence presumes a subject who can not only identify particular ends as ethical, but also can "control the means she is using (violence) in the service of those ends only, and keep herself and her ends uncontaminated by the means of violence."[48] On the latter point, I argue that Juana has already compromised an important human disposition toward life. Through her weapons training, she learned to treat violence as an abstraction and thus became "contaminated" by the means of violence that were also supposed to lead to her empowerment. The most striking example of Juana's transformation is when she confronts her estranged husband, Cruz Ochoa. After years of tracking her down, Cruz finds Juana bathing in a river. Yet, before he can reach her, Juana senses his presence and reaches for her concealed gun: "As Cruz lifted his arm in hostility, Juana drew the weapon with both hands and pointed it at his face. The sight of the gun unnerved him as if he had been struck by an invisible fist." Juana then tells him, "Turn around, Cruz Ochoa, head for your village and never return. If you do, I'll kill you. *Te lo prometo* [I promise you]." Cruz recognized that Juana "had changed" as her "words cut into his brain, convincing him of her determination and ability to kill him."[49] Yet, we should also read her newly developed "determination and ability to kill" as a significant development in her ontological formation. The training she has received enabled a certain ethical distancing from life that is ultimately corruptive. Through violence, she has gained power. Yet power is not inherently good. She has subscribed to the notion that violence is the most effective way to resolve conflict, a view that forecloses other options she might have had to seek security and justice.

"WE REPEAT OURSELVES": THE TWO WRISTWATCHES OF SUBCOMANDANTE MARCOS AND THE COLONIAL WOUND

Benedict Anderson most famously proposed the relationship between the nation and time or, more specifically, simultaneity. As one of the preconditions for the rise of nationalism, the notion of *temporal coincidence* enables the modern conception of the nation as "a solid community moving steadily down (or up) history."[50] Yet, the idea of simultaneity that Anderson describes too easily dismisses the internal tensions over conflicting histories, memories, and practices that require a reconceptualization of how people occupy the time of the nation. The claim of synchrony is particularly inadequate for characterizing the multiple views of time in Indian Mexico. For example, in a 2006 interview with Carlos Loret de Mola, Marcos explained why he wears two wristwatches at once: "This is the watch that marks your time and this is the one that marks our time. This is a symbol that the movement will end when the two watches correspond, when society recognizes our place as Indian peoples. We are moving forward and you have to catch up to us. When we reach the same destination, then there will be only one time."[51] In referencing the difference in inhabited times, Marcos reveals what Homi Bhabha calls the "disjunctive temporality of the nation."[52] Rather than depict a synchrony of plurals moving together in the same calendrical and clock time of the nation, Marcos emphasizes the heterogeneous voice of the Indian communities that operates in a different temporality from that of the neoliberal state.

The symbolism of Marcos's two wristwatches opens a space for questioning the presumed mono-temporality of the state. Rather than define the Zapatistas as postmodern—a label that is popular with many scholars and academics—José Rabasa encourages us to think of the movement in terms of nonmodern (rather than *post-*, *pre-* or *anti-*modern). For Rabasa, the "contemporaneity of the modern and nonmodern enables us to conceive of modernity (that is, capital, the state, history) as just one temporality, even when it aspires to absorb all life."[53] The idea that capitalism, the state, and history do not include all temporalities, particularly the kind of temporality experienced by the Zapatistas' "indigenous communalism," leaves open the possibility that there are modes of thinking about and living in time that are outside modern progress narratives. Rather than a deficit, Rabasa argues, being a people "without" history can instead be viewed as a "productive exteriority," a position that places one outside the teleologies of "histories of salvation, civilizing missions, national formations, development, and market economy."[54]

But even if the Zapatistas operate outside modern time, they are still subjected to its violence as the state struggles to impose modernity onto the bodies of marginalized groups. The body becomes a site of regulation as the state imposes normative conceptions of time through what Elizabeth Freeman calls "large-scale periodizing mechanisms" that define acceptably managed lives. Freeman further describes how the "colonial state intervened early into temporality, inscribing itself into and as the bodies of 'the people' directly via the calendar, skewing indigenous rhythms of sacred and profane and representing these rhythms as backward and superstitious."[55] Those colonized bodies that accommodate the regulations of foreign institutions and practices of managing time endure a kind of physical and epistemic violence as "institutionally and culturally enforced rhythms, or timings, shape flesh into legible, acceptable embodiment."[56] Female bodies in *Erased Faces* resist the state's temporal conditioning by reliving colonial encounters in dreams and in the flesh. For example, the history of sixteenth-century Spanish colonialism is relived as late-twentieth-century Mexican neoliberal militarism.

Erased Faces is a novel that formally resists the propulsion forward in time. It is a novel of flashbacks, dreams, and the unconscious memories that constantly interrupt plot and, by implication, the time of the novel. This constant looking backward is also accompanied by the repetition of wounded bodies and forbidden desires compelling us to consider how the "body's microtemporalities," according to Freeman, "let in histories of pleasure as well as pain."[57] The repetition of scarred bodies, of women lashed at the stake, explicitly evince the generational physical wounds of colonial oppression as the characters reoccupy bodies throughout epochs. We see this in Adriana's recurring nightmare, as she imagines running through a forest with indigenous men and women in an effort to escape some unknown force. Despite the nearly paralyzing fear of being captured, she stops to search for something she lost: "It had been she who had lost something precious, something loved and so riveted onto her heart that reliving the dream made her feel pain beneath the nipple of her left breast."[58]

Before coming to Chiapas, Adriana's life was defined by this gnawing sense of loss—the object of which remains unknown until the end of the novel—and by this undecipherable nightmare. On hearing her dream, Chan K'in, the Lacandón elder, tells her the story about an unnamed indigenous woman who lived during the time of the Spanish invasion. This woman, a Chiapaneca who had been captured and displaced by colonizers, witnessed the hanging of Lord Cuauhtémoc, the last Aztec emperor, and the aftermath of the fall of the Aztecs. Eventually she returns to Chiapas, where she joins her people in a war against the Spanish. With arrows and rocks, the Chiapanecas are unable to hold off against Spanish cannons and canines. Rather than surrender, they commit mass suicide by jumping into ravines.[59] Yet, before everyone can make it, the Spanish and their dogs chase down the remaining survivors—including the unnamed woman—and condemn them to a life of slavery. A burn scar on the left arm distinguishes the unknown woman, a scar similar to the one Adriana has as the result of her abusive foster mother pouring boiling water on her when she was eight years old. Limón provides her understanding of the Lacandón philosophy of repetition through Chan K'in: "The people of this forest know that each one of us has lived not only once, but in other times. What is happening to us now is a repetition of what happened to us then. We also know that in each life we might have a different face or name, be a child or very old, or even be a man this time, and a woman the next. We repeat ourselves. You also have a repeated life."[60] For Adriana, living a "repeated life" connects her to the past—a significant grounding for a young woman who has been an orphan since the age of four. Living a "repeated life" is also a paradigmatic shift in conceptualizing time, one that demonstrates an alternative conception of how time functions.[61] It also undermines the national and postcolonial narratives of progress that make no room for repetition in their sequential ordering of events.

Like Adriana, Juana bears scars that link her to earlier generations of women. Years before the scar above her left eyebrow develops—the result of a vicious blow from her abusive husband—Juana recalls hearing stories about a similarly scarred woman living in colonial times. As a young girl, Juana heard stories from her mother about "a special woman, singled out by her resistance to the bosses, as well as by the scar that marred the skin above her left eyebrow." The story recounts the woman's daily labor of carrying stone-filled baskets from a rock quarry for the construction of the church in Ciudad Real. After long hours of hauling stone from sun up to sun down, the woman followed the others from her shift to evening mass at the Church of Santo Domingo, where "she joined the women and men of her tribe, squatting on the stone floor, backs bent, eyes drooping under the weight of fatigue."[62]

In a later scene, Juana asks Orlando Flores, the man who recruited her to join the Zapatistas, how women can overcome the power of the patrones. He answers her with a story about a Tzeltal woman who was brutally whipped because "she had received and told of visions of freedom for [her] people." As she "endur[ed] the searing pain of the whip, her forehead pressed against the pillory in such a way that the scar over her left eyebrow began to ache almost as much as the lashings." Orlando describes how the people came from surrounding villages to witness, with indignation, the violent whipping. Their indignation turned to revolt as they attacked the soldier and the priest who had ordered the whipping. The assault eventually became known as the 1712 rebellion of Cancuc, Chiapas, when surrounding villages united to temporarily overthrow the Spanish colonizers. Eventually, the Spanish and mestizos regained control. The story ends with the scarred woman fleeing the Spanish and their dogs.[63]

Adriana's and Juana's "repeated lives" are of women who witness and endure the violence of Spanish colonialism. The stories of these women reveal the cruel conditions of slavery, forced labor, and conversion. Yet they are also stories of resistance, with women playing prominent roles in the history of indigenous rebellion. The scarred bodies can more aptly be described as bearing what Mignolo calls "colonial wounds," which result from the violent encounter with European invaders, an encounter better known among Quechua and Aymara speakers as Pachakuti. For indigenous peoples of the Americas, Pachakuti defines the "violent destruction, relentless invasion, and disregard for their way of life—a convulsion of all levels of existence and the moment of *the founding colonial wound of the modern/colonial world*."[64] In line with what Franz Fanon calls the "wretched of the earth," Mignolo describes how the "wretched are defined by the *colonial wound*, and the colonial wound, physical and/or psychological, is a consequence of *racism*, the hegemonic discourse that questions the humanity of all those who do not belong to the locus of enunciation."[65] Moreover, the colonial wound transforms the body into a living document, on which pain is made to speak for itself. If the indigenous communities of Chiapas are presumed to be a "people without a history" because they lack a legitimized written historical record, then the body itself is the scroll on which historical memory is written. The wounds inscribe the history of colonial oppression and simultaneously the pain of that violent system. In *Erased Faces*, the characters inherit the bodies of women marked by colonial violence. By embodying this inheritance, Adriana and Juana bridge the past and the present with their flesh. The repetition of these wounds is important because, as Mignolo asserts, "Indigenous peoples in the Americas have not stopped struggling with that initial wound and are making their presence felt today."[66]

Yet, while inheriting the historical suffering of others, Adriana and Juana's wounds tell their own significant stories of present-day violence, racism, and oppression. Adriana's burn scars were inflicted by a foster mother who constantly degraded her: "*¿Qué vamos a hacer con esta niña? Es hija de negro, y su madre fue asesina* [What are we going to do with this girl? She is the daughter of a black man and her mother was a murderer]."[67] The foster mother's efforts to shame Adriana for her Afro-Chicana biracial identity and for her mother's actions culminate in a malicious act of abuse. Adriana's physical scars are accompanied by other manifestations of the psychological turmoil she experienced at the age of four when her biological mother shot and killed her father and then killed herself. Unable to unlock the door, Adriana remained trapped in the apartment with the decomposing corpses of her parents until neighbors eventually found her. As a result of her ordeal, she stopped speaking for years and developed asthma. Adriana's corporeal responses to the traumas she suffers continue into her adulthood and are reanimated as she once again encounters death, loss, and abandonment, this time in the mountains of Chiapas.

For Juana, the scar above her eye is a constant reminder of her forced marriage to an abusive man, Cruz Ochoa. In an early scene, we witness how days after having her third miscarriage, Juana is attacked by Cruz as she washes clothes at the river: "The force of the blow knocked her unconscious. She did not feel the pain of her face scraping against a rough surface, nor was she aware that Cruz had leaped into the current, grabbed her by the neck, and dragged her limp body from the river. Had she not been unconscious, Juana would have resisted him, hoping that her wish to be erased might have come true by drowning."[68] Juana's marriage to Cruz is defined by rape and torture, making death a desired reprieve from daily violence. Adriana's and Juana's wounds—both physical and psychological—are as critical as the colonial wounds they inherit. Their contemporary wounding bespeaks the pain and violence that occur within families and homes, the kind of pain that makes women seek alternatives to oppression, abandonment, and fear. It is the kind of pain that fuels revolutions.

Throughout the novel, Adriana and Juana draw meaning from their wounds. Frequently touching their scars, they recall the scars' origins, reminders of the oppression they suffered and hope to overturn. Each woman's constant reminder of violence produces the kind of "radical subjectivity" that Guidotti-Hernández describes. Drawing on the work of Elaine Scarry, Guidotti-Hernández argues that "radical self-awareness is produced through having pain inflicted upon the body from an outside source."[69] The wounds that Adriana and Juana carry are critical to their subject formation and their political commitments. Indeed, the novel refuses to emphasize healing as the primary goal, suggesting that the nature of colonial wounding requires living with the memory of pain. On the other hand, these characters are not trapped within dysfunctional, damaged bodies that consign them to lives of debilitation and disempowerment. Rather, the "pain, humiliation, and anger of the continuous reproduction of the colonial wound generate radical political projects, new types of knowledge, and social movements."[70]

DISRUPTING HETERONORMATIVE TIME

As the novel moves to the years following the 1994 uprising, Juana and Adriana are disheartened to see oppressive conditions remain in Chiapas. As witnesses to the profound dislocation of refugees within the Zapatista region, uprooted by the state's counterinsurgency campaign, Juana and Adriana commit themselves to providing humanitarian aid to the isolated mountain communities in Chenalhó and Acteal. The latter would eventually become the site of a state-sponsored massacre, on December 22, 1997, when paramilitary groups sponsored by the Mexican government would attack the town, killing forty-five Tzotzil Indian men, women, and children. The victims, most of whom belonged to a Catholic pacifist organization called Las Abejas (The Bees), were falsely suspected of being Zapatista affiliates. The fact that Limón dedicates her novel to the memory of those massacred at Acteal and makes the scene of violence the novel's climax suggests her desire to simultaneously memorialize the victims and expose state murder. In the novel, Juana and Adriana stand as horror-stricken witnesses to the massacre before one of the killers turns his weapon on Juana.

While the massacre is traditionally viewed as an example of the state's terror against the Zapatistas' call for political and economic justice, Limón interjects an additional rationale for the violence in the novel.[71] Palomón Cisneros, the military officer who assassinates Juana, hates her not only for being a Zapatista, but also for being a lesbian. By this point in the novel, Juana and Adriana have realized and established their love for each other. Before the massacre, Juana receives a warning that "enemies" outside the community have been talking about Juana and Adriana's relationship. This explains why Cisneros targets Juana and shouts, "*¡Manflora! ¡Come mierda!* [Eat shit!]."[72] The derogatory term *manflora* is one of the last words Juana hears before she dies, but it is not the first time she encounters it. Earlier in the novel, Orlando tells Juana a story about how his master, Don Absolón Mayorga, had his own sister stripped naked, whipped in front of the servants, and then cast into the jungle for being a lesbian. By recounting this story of lesbian persecution, Orlando introduces Juana to the word that violently marks her sexuality: "She was a *manflora*, a woman who loved one of her own kind. I remember that he shouted for everyone to hear that what she did, what she was, and what she called love was a sin, that it was repugnant, that she was an animal with no reason to live."[73] The reduction of the lesbian body to animality in this scene prefigures the vicious satisfaction that Cisneros feels when he shoots Juana. The presumed animality of colonized bodies and the insistence on colonial heterosexuality enable and justify obscene acts of violence, like the one M. Jacqui Alexander provides in her description of Spanish conquistador Vasco Núñez de Balboa's arrival in the Panamanian village of Quarequa in 1513. After his army had successfully killed the village's force of six hundred warriors and their leader, "Balboa killed and then fed to his dogs forty more Indians, whom he found dressed in 'women's apparel.'" The indescribable carnage leads Alexander to state that "militarism requires such staunch adherence to heterosexual masculinity that it resorts to violence in excess even of its own norms of killing." The suspicion of sodomy, its status as a sexually aberrant act, and "the threat of contamination" it posed to this newly founded colonial outpost required a swift and violent response. As Alexander explains, protecting and propagating heterosexuality becomes the unstated objective as the "incipient colonial state . . . sought to anchor heterosexual sexuality as the official sexual story, while turning homosexuality into violent spectacle."[74]

The excessive vitriol Palomón Cisneros emits when he murders Juana is an updated example of how "heterosexuality animates militarism."[75] Limón reimagines the massacre at Acteal, like the carnage wrought by Balboa at Quarequa, as a violent colonial attempt to maintain gender and heterosexual hierarchies. Adriana, writing in her journal days after the massacre, interprets the events at Acteal as state revenge for indigenous women's power: "*The massacre at Acteal was about hatred for women, for* mujeres indias *who had proven themselves as leaders, activists and movers of their people. . . . Juana's murder was caused by hatred, but it was even more than loathing because dangling from it, like poisonous snakes, was the repugnance and disgust for women like us. . . . She was erased because she had been strong, because she had been a leader, because she was* una india, *but most of all because she had committed the forbidden act: She had been in love with another woman.*"[76] For Adriana, Acteal was the state's rebuke against feminist agency and same-sex desire—both of which require violent acts of repression if state militarism and heterosexual masculinity are to maintain their power. Female militancy and lesbian desire undermine the patriarchal and heterosexual hierarchies that constitute state authority. To neutralize the threat that Zapatista feminism poses to the social order—and that same-sex desire poses to heterosexual masculinity—the Mexican state reenacts the violence of Spanish colonial rule: "*They unleashed their rabid dogs, the paramilitaries, to prowl the land, looting, raping, and burning* palapas. . . . *And their special targets were mujeres, because they were the ones who recognized those dogs even after they disguised themselves like laborers, like* campesinos."[77]

I read Limón's depiction of the Acteal massacre also as the novel's internal critique of Juana's induction into resistant violence. We have already seen how gender norms and discourses shape our ethical valuation of "good" and "bad" violence, and that even "good" violence merely reinforces a gender order predicated on women's subordination. Ethical violence is also hard to justify given that violence begets violence. In the context of the novel, Zapatista militarism leads to increased state militarism and the massacre of a pacifist community, including children. The instrumental use of resistant violence also presumes a kind of foresight and control that simply do not exist. Hutchings explains how ethical violence assumes that the agent is detached from her environment and can predict the outcome of her actions. Yet, "we do not know the future, our information is always partial and imperfect, and our control of events is limited."[78] These realities are perhaps the most convincing reasons for seeking alternatives to antioppressive violence. The novel's culmination in a spiral of violence suggests that Acteal is the tragic unintended consequence of Zapatista militarism. Ultimately, Juana's own participation in violence fails to ensure her own personal security or her political objectives. Read through a Chicana antiwar feminist lens, the novel illustrates our urgent need to disarticulate both violence from the search for justice and agency from violence.

Violence forecloses Juana's and Adriana's ability to live full lives committed to the Zapatista cause and to each other. Importantly, the violent repression of lesbian love further marks how time is embodied, for, as José Esteban Muñoz argues, the present "is impoverished and toxic for queers and other people who do not feel the privilege of majoritarian belonging, normative tastes, and 'rational' expectations."[79] Faced with multiple forms of homophobic violence, like the kind that Juana experiences, queers are also subjected to the reproductive imperative of straight time.[80] Though the present is "toxic" for queers, the past is equally inhospitable. But if pain can mark the body's relation to time, so can pleasure. In other words, just as Juana's and Adriana's wounded bodies connect them to the colonial past, so can their queer desire link them to a queer futurity free of the violence of heterosexual neoliberal militarism. Because Juana and Adriana lead "repeated lives," a kind of futurity is already guaranteed; they will encounter each other anew in different bodies. For Muñoz, queer utopianism can be glimpsed by identifying "a certain surplus" in a work of art "that promises a futurity, something that is not quite here."[81] Through the temporality of repetition, Limón's novel depicts the kind of queer desire that simultaneously exceeds the present and is forward dawning. Emma Pérez argues, however, that the "repetition of struggles, of oppression, seems endless, as if never to gain movement forward into another future, one where change would be hopeful or better. Perhaps all one can really hope for is survival."[82] Given the centuries-long struggles against colonial, patriarchal, racial, class, and sexual oppression, Adriana and Juana's relationship seems doomed from the moment it begins to flourish. But Muñoz's notion of queer futurity tempers the pessimism of Pérez's statement and helps to remind us that Adriana and Juana's shared histories and the intimate pleasures that proved to be in excess of the heteronormative present ultimately mark their path to a queer future of hope and desire.

"ESTÁS SON MIS ARMAS": LORNA DEE CERVANTES'S POETICS OF FEMINIST SOLIDARITIES IN THE ERA OF NEOLIBERAL MILITARISM

Eliza Rodríguez y Gibson describes Lorna Dee Cervantes's poetry as grounded in a "global Chicana feminism," one that "includes a concern for entire communities, including children, and articulates forms of solidarity with men, which characterizes both Chicana and Third World feminisms."[83] In "Coffee," Cervantes provides the transfronterista perspective needed to understand the destructive effects of global capital and to locate a politics of solidarity. The poem uses multiple stories of genocide to map the trajectories of neoliberal militarism in the Americas. Whereas section 1 describes the coffee crop's evisceration of Mayan lands in Guatemala, sections 2, 3, and 5 focus on the 1997 massacre in Acteal. Section 4 centers on the experience of a Jewish German refugee in unoccupied France, and the final section focuses on a young Latina activist in the United States who protests against neoliberal militarism. Thus, the poem asserts connections between seemingly disparate historical events and periods to present the long view of genocide and resistance. Each section is further linked either obliquely or directly to the act of producing, consuming, or boycotting coffee—a commodity that represents the privileged consumer tastes of North Americans and the cash crops that have decimated the ecologies and economies of various Latin American countries.

Cervantes insists on tying consumerism to the violent processes of production in order to unite the severed ties between our daily consumptions, political privileges, and the atrocities committed in the distant and more recent past. To do this, she employs a poetics of witness that links rather than isolates the histories of state violence against hunted and exploited peoples to situate distinct massacres in a global asynchronous temporal frame. So, the pairing of a 1997 massacre in the highlands of southern Mexico with the impending Nazi invasion of France in 1940 makes sense within a broader frame of violence and human memory.

The opening section narrates the violent transformation of Guatemala's "medicinal land into coffee" and the "deforested plantations" that puncture the countryside.[84] The stanza emphasizes the ecological and cultural devastation that goes into producing cash-crop export economies. In this opening stanza, Cervantes establishes seeing and being seen as dominant tropes that will contribute to her poetics of witness throughout the poem. In one scene, a victim is shown in the cross hairs of a gun:

> Golden epaulets glint
> in the fluorescent offices, crystal
> skulls shine in the eyes of the man
> with the machete, within the site
> of an AK-47.[85]

While the scene depicts the victim's vulnerability (here, the machete is more of a marker of labor than a weapon), it also aligns us unwillingly with the position of the shooter, by forcing us to imagine the *machetero* through the sights of an AK-47. Cervantes's use of synecdoche further heightens the sense of violence that campesinos endure. That is, "Golden epaulets" stand in for state militarism while, elsewhere in the poem, "Forty five [*sic*] pair of shoes" grimly represent the victims. The selective use of synecdoche shows the inhuman nature of the violence (by replacing people with things), but it also literalizes that violence. In other words, Cervantes's descriptions of "Matted hair cling[ing] / to the coffee plants," the popping of "melon heads," and an eye "dislodged from its skull" are necessary because they expose how the military really does mutilate bodies, how soldiers physically dismember human beings in a grotesque display of bloodlust.[86]

Beginning in Guatemala and ending on Wall Street, the opening stanza's cartography expands across national borders to collapse the distance between consumers and producers. As if dispelling the celebratory embrace of globalization, Cervantes ends the stanza by showing how what really connects us is the violence of neoliberal consumption: "While on Wall Street, / the black sludge of a people trickles through / cappuccino machines like hissing snakes."[87] Cervantes's reference to Wall Street recalls the role of U.S. capital in Mexican politics as seemingly regional, local issues within Mexico catch the attention of investors thousands of miles away. Here, I refer to Riordan Roett's 1995 Manhattan Chase Bank memorandum, in which the academic consultant outlines the Zapatista threat to the corporate investment climate in Mexico: "While Chiapas, in our opinion, does not pose a fundamental threat to Mexican political stability, it is perceived to be so by many in the investment community. The government will need to eliminate the Zapatistas to demonstrate their effective control of the national territory and of security policy."[88] In this sense, the Zapatistas' use of violence makes them legible not only to the state, but also to capital. The Chase memo exposes the level of financial, corporate, and government collusion involved in repressing labor and social justice movements. Two years after the Chase memo, President Ernesto Zedillo ordered the massacre at Acteal.

With section 2, Cervantes begins her poetic interpretation of the Acteal massacre. The stanza is set in the aftermath of the bloodshed. The remnants of violence are described using the imagery of children: the "plastic sandals of a child" stuck in mud and the bullet holes "the size of a baby's tender fists" do the labor of describing an incomprehensible brutality—a juxtaposition of innocence and death that denaturalizes military violence. Because justice must begin by naming the culprits, Cervantes inserts the names of state officials and generals responsible for carrying out the orders and for the cover-up. She names Homero Tovilla Cristiani, who was secretary of the interior for the state of Chiapas, and General Jorge Gamboa Solis. The former helps cover up events by telling concerned inquirers, "There is no massacre in Acteal."[89] The statement of official denial, delivered with such certitude, adds a layer of violence to the massacre that animates Cervantes's poetics of witness. Importantly, the poetic persona first appears in response to official denial: "I hear / nothing happened in Acteal. / And if it did / no one knows who they were."[90] The lyric subject's appearance at this point in the poem emphasizes the poet's role in exposing state deception. The enjambed line ending with "I hear" becomes a statement of solidarity with those victims whose voices are delegitimized as the government "lie[s] to the cameras." Yet, the poetic "I" is not the only voice privileged in the poem and capable of describing the abuse of power, for while the stanza is about death, it is also about surviving. Merely "Twenty yards / away" from the lying government press machine, "the survivors are speaking / the names of the men paid 600 dollars" to commit the slaughter against this indigenous community. Giving testimony to incriminate the guilty becomes an empowering act of survival. The lyric "I" does not appropriate or supersede the survivors' testimony; rather, the poet's job is to "hear" it and to enable us to "hear" it, too.

As with the first stanza, the stanza that follows also includes a standoff between victim and shooter. In this instance, a woman and an infant stand in the path of a killer's bullet:

> The first woman in line gazes into the coked-up eyes
> of her assassin projecting his automatic weapon
> into the ear of the whimpering baby at her breast.
> 500 years of history gets written in her eyes, as a Tzotzil
> mother wedges her sleeping newborn into the hole.[91]

Cervantes's repeated imagery of mother and child, a Pietà of sorts, disrupts neoliberal militarism's antiseptic effacement of women's and children's bodies. As the mother defiantly gazes back at her assassin, the recurring imagery of eyes and vision serve as critical tropes of witness. Because the woman in this scene is the active subject (she is the one who gazes), we are narratively aligned with her focal point of view. In this way, Cervantes ensures that we become implicated through a poetics of witness that positions us as silent observers to the execution of women and infants.

While the press silences incidents of state-sponsored criminality, Cervantes's poem insists that the poet's mandate is to recoup the events of December 1997 from official denials and historical oblivion. But exposing genocide is perhaps easier than compelling others to care about it. As the lyric "I" explains, if a massacre did take place, "no one knows who they were."[92] While Cervantes attempts to help us know the victims through tropes of seeing, she also employs the act of naming in order to transcend the imposed anonymity of the dead. Section 3 presents the complete list of names of the nine men, twenty-one women, and fifteen children who were brutally shot, stabbed, impaled, and hacked to death with machetes by Mexican-sponsored paramilitaries. Through official denial, we see the management of grievability, for without the recognition of death, we cannot grieve those whose lives were lost. The state's refusal to acknowledge the forty-five indigenous men, women, and children illustrates what Judith Butler says in a different context: "There is less a dehumanizing discourse at work here than a refusal of discourse that produces dehumanization as a result." If silence dehumanizes the deceased, it is not accidental; rather, the "differential allocation of grief serves the derealizing aims of military violence."[93] The poem's list is not quite an obituary; it does not have the accompanying details of life experiences nor does it provide us with access to the personalities attached to those names. But the act of naming is important. The names force the reader to recognize and thus humanize the victims of state violence. They force readers to repeat the mesmerizing multisyllabic Spanish and indigenous sounds, to notice the repetition of surnames, and to imagine the decimation of entire families:

> Rosa Vázquez Luna
> Verónica Vázquez Luna
> Mícaela Vázquez Luna
> Juana Vázquez Luna[94]

According to Edith Vásquez, the act of naming is also an exhumation that enables "a process of mourning, traditional rites, and proper burial."[95] Rodríguez y Gibson further describes how we are invited and indeed compelled to mourn along with the survivors as "Cervantes articulates solidarity grounded in poetic empathy" through a solemn enumeration of the slain.[96]

Section 4 disrupts the narrative trajectory of the Acteal massacre by turning our attention to the account of a Jewish man in France, saved at the last minute from Nazi capture by Varian Fry, a U.S. citizen often referred to as the "American Schindler." The section describes Hans Sahl, a German Jewish poet sitting at a café in Marseille, spending the day writing poems on "coffee splotched napkins" before he receives word that Varian Fry has arranged for his escape from France.[97] Following on the list of those massacred at Acteal in 1997, this section on 1940 unoccupied France seems out of place. The obvious connection is that both events reference acts of genocide. Although one instance is better known than the other (no national monuments or museums commemorate the genocide of indigenous peoples in the Americas), Cervantes is not interested in making facile comparisons. Her intent is to honor survival and remembrance. Furthermore, like the rest of "Coffee," this section reveres transnational solidarities practiced in the name of human rights. Indeed, we are told that the rescued Hans Sahl, who sits in a Greenwich Village café by the end of the section, "vows to spend the rest / of his days praising the man who defied the orders / of nations, Nazis, industry, collaborators, / gendarmes, and the United States Consulate."[98] The death of the man who helped Sahl escape by forging his exit visa compels the grateful poet to spend the rest of his life reflecting on the magnanimity of such selfless sacrifice.

Cervantes incorporates one of Sahl's poems, entitled "Sprich" ("Speak"), into the section, a poem that, according to a footnote, Cervantes "copied from a napkin on display in the Varian Fry exhibit at the National Holocaust Museum." The poem within a poem constitutes an important expressive response to violence and reminds us of Theodor Adorno's oft-misinterpreted statement that poetry is impossible after Auschwitz. If, as Adorno understood, indescribable violence cannot be represented in poetry or other forms of art, he also insisted that we have the responsibility to make the attempt. Therefore, Cervantes's inclusion of a poem within her own poem suggests poetry's always-flawed-yet-compulsive attempt to depict the face of evil. Sahl's "Sprich" captures the paradox of living in the moment of genocide. On the one hand, the poem encourages a self-defensive posture against those who seek one's destruction: "Not to lost causes present your heart. / Guard yourself until your hour's here."[99] On the other hand, the poem's title, "Sprich," functions as a declarative statement: in the midst of facing one's annihilation, one must speak. Cervantes, through her multilayered poetics of witness, suggests that poetry must be made to speak for human suffering, because words are all we have. Despite their seeming ephemerality (poems written on napkins), Cervantes suggests that poetry can speak across borders and temporalities.

The section on Hans Sahl's story—a disruption in the narrative of the Acteal massacre—signals Cervantes's theoretical and poetic intervention into the framing of time and history. The story of Jewish genocide breaks up the present tense of the poem. With its inclusion, the poem enfolds previous temporalities, reproducing what M. Jacqui Alexander calls the palimpsestic nature of time: "The idea of the 'new' structured through the 'old' scrambled, palimpsestic character of time, both jettisons the truncated distance of linear time and dislodges the impulse for incommensurability, which the ideology of distance creates. It thus rescrambles the 'here and now' and the 'then and there' to a 'here and there' and a 'then and now.'"[100] Alexander's theorization of time brings multiple temporalities into contact, offering up the possibilities that emerge from a hybrid sense of time and place. If the "impulse for incommensurability" helps sustain power through an "ideology of distance" and difference, then through commensurability comes the potential for solidarity, coalition building, and ethical witness. "Coffee" positions the "here and there" (Guatemala, Acteal, Marseille, New York) and the "then and now" (1940 and 1997) to upend the forward-looking trajectory of global linear progress narratives. Moreover, the insertion of Sahl's story also functions as a layering of temporalities that disrupts neoliberalism's disregard for historical memory—a point that I will explore momentarily.

With section 5, Cervantes returns to the work of mourning in Acteal. Like the section featuring Hans Sahl, this section focuses on the survivors of genocide. Written in mostly complete sentences, and with little of the imaginative word play Cervantes is known for, the documentary quality of the section 5 stanza stands out. Cervantes's reliance on direct syntax, diction, and grammar is partly explained by her reliance on testimony from Acteal survivors collected in Rosalva Aída Hernández Castillo's *The Other Word: Women and Violence in Chiapas Before and After Acteal* (2001). Hernández Castillo translates and weaves the testimonies of women who survived the massacre into a literary narrative of vignettes that recount the horror the community experienced.[101] One of the accounts includes the experience of an eleven-year-old girl who is given the alias of Mícaela to protect her identity. Cervantes uses this resource as the basis for the second half of the stanza, which is narrated from the perspective of Mícaela, who survived the shooting and whose role now is "to be the mouth / of a people."[102] We learn that Mícaela had been praying in the chapel with her family when the gunfire started. Fleeing with her mother and younger siblings,

Mícaela witnesses their deaths and pretends to also be dead as she lies "under her mother's cooling huipil." Cervantes then allows Mícaela to speak in her own words as she accuses the men who assassinated the members of her community:

> "Diego,
> Antonio y Pedro. More than fifty from Los Chorros,
> Pechiquíl, La Esperanza, Acteal. They were dressed
> in black. The ones in charge had military uniforms."
> She testifies to the National Human Rights Commission.
> She testifies to anyone who works to listen. How they
> stripped the dead women and sliced their breasts,
> forced sticks between their legs, opened the wombs,
> passing the fetuses from machete to machete. . . .[103]

Because so much of Cervantes's poetic oeuvre centers on poetry as a form of witness, it is perhaps not surprising that she turns the eyewitness testimony of a young girl into poetry. Cervantes details Mícaela's harrowing loss during the massacre so that we can bear witness to her trauma. There is also an important evidentiary function at work here. That is, given the state's denial of involvement and the press's complicity in that denial, Mícaela's experience and testimony are accusatory and become evidence that would condemn the guilty if a trial were ever to take place. Mícaela boldly and clearly names the assassins, their communities of origin, and the state's indisputable role in the killing ("The ones in charge had military uniforms").

Although not enclosed in direct quotations, the lines about the paramilitary's desecration of women's bodies are also based on Mícaela's memory. The essay from which Cervantes draws tells us what happened after Mícaela's family was murdered. After the men left, she hid near an embankment, before they returned with machetes in hand: "They were whooping and laughing and talking among themselves, 'we have to get rid of the seed,' they were saying. They stripped the dead women and cut off their breasts. They put a stick between the legs of one woman and opened the bellies of the pregnant women and took out their babies and played ball with them tossing them from machete to machete. After that they left."[104] Cervantes inserts the descriptions of desecration they perform, nearly verbatim, and uses Mícaela's memory to impart the incomprehensibility of postmortem mutilation. Through Mícaela's memory we hear the cynical words of one of the defilers describing the need to "finish off the seed," to destroy the already lifeless bodies in order to cancel out the humanity and dignity of these indigenous women and the fetuses they carried. Through Cervantes's poem, Mícaela compels us to hear what happened in Acteal: "She testifies to anyone who works to listen." Cervantes's poetics of witness ensures that we, as readers, do the "work" of listening. As Ana Patricia Rodríguez points out, "The subject in pain must be allowed to tell her or his story and to exercise her or his agency, and we must be prepared to allow the narrative of trauma to reveal itself. The act of solidarity begins in letting others produce their own narratives out of their particular pain, injury, and situations."[105] Cervantes's incorporation of Mícaela's testimony honors this young girl's courage to relive and recount these tragic events. In doing so, Cervantes also avoids subsuming Mícaela's voice so that the grieving subject can speak on her own behalf.

It is no accident that neoliberal militarism, which targets women's bodies and is indeed founded on violence against women, is itself challenged by women. In the poem's final section, we hear another female voice protesting against neoliberal militarism, as "A young girl in trenzas [braids] sings outside / The Mexican Consulate in Denver."[106] Rather than distance herself from atrocities committed in other countries, the young woman draws connections between her tax dollars and covert U.S. military support, between U.S. corporations and unfair trade agreements:

> No more
> of my tax dollars that buys the man who drives
> the Humvee that transports the soldier who shoots
> the weapon that blinds the toddler, that enters the heart
> of Guadalupe López Méndez who dies in Ocosingo
> asserting her civil rights. No more Genocide
> in my name.[107]

The passage neatly describes the chain of occurrences and the network of people that link the violations of human rights abroad to the tax-paying citizen in the United States. The young Latina protests not only the Mexican government, but also the U.S. government's role in funding, arming, and training the militaries that commit genocide. Yet, Cervantes is careful to avoid privileging the educated, modern, and progressive U.S. Latina against the figure of the "third world woman," who, Chandra Mohanty argues, is often described in Western feminist scholarship as being a woman who "leads an essentially truncated life based on her feminine gender (read: sexually constrained) and being 'third world' (read: ignorant, poor, uneducated, tradition-bound, religious, domesticated, family-oriented, victimized, etc.)."[108] Cervantes's naming of Guadalupe López Méndez is also a deliberate gesture to emphasize that even the act of public protestation is a marker of privilege, as certain activist bodies are more susceptible to violence than others. López Méndez, a Tzeltal Indian, was one of the Indian marchers in the town of Ocosingo who protested the massacre in Acteal.[109] When police began firing into the crowd of marchers, López Méndez was fatally struck in the stomach while her two-year-old daughter was wounded. Here, Cervantes highlights the political, economic, and national distinctions between the Latina-in-trenzas and the indigenous Mexican women subject to violence in order to emphasize that feminist solidarity begins with recognizing one's own privilege and power. Although the Latina's membership in the nation is questioned (a passing car full of "gringos" shouts, "Go back to where you came from!"), she recognizes her membership among the "First World faces" in the picket line and the power that U.S. citizenship confers. For the Latina activist, the best way to form alliances is to use her privilege to advocate for an end to the violence of neoliberal militarism. Recognizing the multiple forms of power at her disposal, she foregrounds her membership in the polity to demand that the state uphold its obligations to its citizenry. The threat of withholding her tax dollars or at least questioning what they are used for is further bolstered by her status as a voting citizen.[110] Since she cannot be taxed without representation, her representation by elected officials at the local, state, and federal levels makes her political demands potent. Despite neoliberalism's attempt to liquidate national sovereignty and to dilute the meaning of citizenship, the Latina refuses to give up on the value of a civil and political rights discourse and the state's capacity (and obligation) to defend those rights.

At the same time the narrator has a "First World face," we can also properly call her a U.S. Third World feminist, whose political and ethical commitments to Guadalupe López Méndez and Mexican communities affected by neoliberal militarism exemplifies the kind of extranational solidarity that defines U.S. Third World feminism. Indeed, her form of feminism requires an expansive knowledge of geopolitics because, as the narrator points out, "the only end to bullets for profit is knowledge— / knowledge that will not appear wedged between / commercials for Taster's Choice."[111] Moreover, understanding the state (both the United States and Mexico) and corporate role in perpetuating genocide becomes critical to challenging neoliberal militarism, which, Enloe argues, relies on "women located in different social, economic, ideological, and cultural locations remaining uninformed about, unconnected to, or even hostile to one another."[112] Isolation ensures women's role in maintaining the social hierarchies of class, race, and nationality that help neoliberal militarism target and exploit marginalized communities of labor. But neoliberal militarism loses ground when a Latina citizen casts her lot with indigenous women in Mexico and seeks to build political networks of solidarity to end women's oppression beyond her nation's borders.

The Latina activist uses not only her tax dollars but also her consumer dollars to make political demands. She uses her limited monetary wealth to critique the neoliberal mandate for consumption and, in the process, expands her arsenal of political activist weapons to challenge the very system that incriminates her as an accomplice to genocide. Cervantes does this by defamiliarizing the familiar and ubiquitous consumer products that the poem's readers undoubtedly recognize and perhaps consume. For example, she repeats the line "Néstles makes the very best . . . MUR . . . DER!"[113] She also implicates the Sara Lee brand in the massacre of Indian communities: "Nobody Doesn't Like Sara Lee like the living body of / an indigenous child found two days after massacre / in a bullet-ridden cave."[114] Cervantes insists on tying consumerism to the violent processes of production and the control of labor and resources necessary for increasing profit margins. Subcomandante Marcos underscores this point when he states that Chiapas "bleeds coffee."[115] In the Sixth Declaration of the Selva Lacandona, the Zapatistas call for precisely the kind of exposure that Cervantes provides in her poem: "In the market, for example, *we see* coffee in its little package or its pretty little jar, but *we do not see* the campesino who suffered in order to harvest the coffee, and *we do not see* the coyote who paid him so cheaply for his work, and *we do not see* the workers in the large company working their hearts out to package the coffee."[116] Recognizing that what "we see" and "do not see" enables consumer privilege and capitalist exploitation, Cervantes insists on the importance of a poetics of witness throughout her poem. Like the Zapatistas, Cervantes demands the protection of human rights by challenging the occult powers of neoliberalism.

Cervantes's turn to consumer purchasing power in the last stanza of the poem is an important shift because, as Mohanty argues, "everyday feminist, antiracist, anticapitalist practices are as important as larger, organized political movements."[117] Cervantes reappropriates the image of the neoliberal consumer, a figure largely emptied of social conscience and civic responsibility, to emphasize the quotidian activities that enable gross injustices in the name of globalization.[118] Cervantes offers us a way to challenge the imposed role of what Arlene Dávila characterizes as "docile" Latina/o consumers by advocating for what we might call a politically informed consumerism, which makes demands by wielding purchasing power in favor of a social justice agenda. If choice facilitates consumer purchasing power, then the narrator in "Coffee" suggests a way to turn the neoliberal principle of choice against itself when she proclaims, "I will grind Zapatista coffee," and vows to boycott corporate brands that perpetuate violence:

> I will not bank
> with assassins. I will buy crafts, not Kraft,
> Néstles, Proctor & Gamble, McDonald's, Sara Lee . . .
> I will fight this way forever.[119]

Writing in the spirit of a long Chicana/o tradition of using boycotts to challenge corporate greed and labor exploitation, Cervantes compels her readers to become informed consumers and to acknowledge the consequences of personal choice.[120] For Cervantes, consumer choice becomes its own poetic statement, most notably in her one-word poem "On Why I Boycotted Cinco de Mayo": "Coors."[121]

Cervantes's "Coffee" is a counter to the privatizing, self-interested nonethical rhetoric of neoliberal militarism. The poem challenges its consumerist, presentist language. By *presentist*, I am referring to consumerism's emphasis on the here and now, on impulse purchases and credit cards, on immediate gratification and deferred payment. Fredric Jameson describes this form of presentism as the "end of temporality" brought about by late capitalist globalization and reflected in postmodern cultures.[122] He focuses on finance capital to exemplify the fixation on presentism, one that produces an inability to contemplate the future, or at least to care much about it. In their obsession with the stock market, the postmodern subjects that Jameson imagines are governed by "the anxious daily consultation of the listings, deliberations with or without your broker, selling off" and other "rhythms of quarterly 'profit taking.'" These compulsions—a result of finance capital's growing dominance under late capitalist globalization—produce the "narrowing and the urgency of the time frame," where maximizing profit in the present is all that matters. Finance capital and other processes of capitalist globalization produce "new rhythms [that] are transmitted to cultural production in the form of the narratives we consume and the stories we tell ourselves."[123]

Such an obsession with the present clearly clouds a vision of both the future and the past. We could also argue that part of late capitalism's—and, I would add, neoliberal militarism's—fixation with the immediate present is its injunction to forget, its belief that historical memory becomes superfluous to the commodity-obsessed individual. With Marcos's typical penchant for metaphor, he describes the conflict between neoliberalism and the past as two pugilists squaring off in a boxing ring. In one corner of the ring is the "Market" with "its conception of time denying both yesterday and tomorrow." In the other corner is "History." He describes how the Market, ruled by technocrats and "professional amnesiacs," privileges the present, ignores the past, and treats the future as an extension of the present: "In order to defeat history, the past is denied a horizon that goes beyond the neoliberal 'here and now.' There is no 'before' or 'after' today. The search for eternity is finally satisfied: the world of money is not only the best of all possible worlds, it is the only one necessary. For the 'neo-politicians' the only acceptable attitude toward history is a mixture of nausea and regret. The past should be devalued, ignored, eliminated."[124] While the present provides favorable conditions for the world of money, the past leads to regret, shame, and nausea. This is because confronting history entails the moral, legal, and political recognition of past injustices, of genocides committed in the name of the state and the market, and of the violence required to sustain modernity/coloniality. Knowledge of the past, if fostered and perpetuated generationally, has the potential to enrage and mobilize the masses, who must remain content with their role as docile consumers mired in the present. Neoliberal militarism uses force to help ensure the continued suppression of historical consciousness and the fragile reign of the neoliberal "here and now."

Cervantes's poem rejects the hegemony of the present and the wholesale abandonment of history it demands. Rather, "Coffee" insists on tying consumerism to the violent processes of production and the control of labor and resources necessary for increasing profit margins. But it also insists on historical memory as a critical intervention into the genocidal violence authorized by global capital and enforced by neoliberal militarism. Rather than capitulate to a postmodern condition stuck in the present, Cervantes presents an alternative understanding of how time works, a conception that recognizes how "various technologies of timekeeping and various narrations of time can exist within the same temporality, thereby provoking important disturbances to the hegemonic financial market time of modernity, for instance, whose passage is contemporaneously marked by militarized war time."[125] This understanding makes historical memory not only relevant, but also vital to re/constituting transnational affinities and enabling acts of ethical witnessing.

At the poem's end, the narrator appropriates the language of warfare to describe her modes of dissent: "Estas son mis armas: / la computadora, el video, la pluma" (These are my weapons: / the computer, the video, the pen).[126] While the martial rhetoric implies violence, the Zapatistas encourage and practice nonviolent acts of solidarity. Like "She," the Zapatista ally who has "no military rank, no uniform, no weapon," Cervantes's activist-in-trenzas uses the computer, the video, and the pen as instruments for disseminating knowledge, exposing atrocity, humanizing the massacred, and "writ[ing] the dark into dawn."[127] "Coffee" provides clues on how to construct lasting solidarities, beginning with recognizing one's own privileged location and how it can be used in the service of a social justice agenda. Such recognition and self-reflection begins with bearing witness to atrocities committed in the name of national and consumer privilege. It involves letting those who suffer speak their own trauma to avoid reinscribing the feminist "rescue narrative of privileged U.S. feminists."[128] It also entails developing a historical consciousness of global interconnections.

As a rebel group committed to nonviolence, the Zapatistas practice the gradual yet powerful dismantling of patriarchal privilege and raise new questions about women's relationship to militarism. And yet, despite their turn toward nonviolent mobilization and activism, Rabasa argues, "The power of their violence resides in the new world they call forth—a sense of justice, democracy, and liberty that the government *cannot* understand because it calls for its demise."[129] Thus, the Zapatistas' obsession with history is perhaps its greatest weapon. Their respect for history is also embodied. Cervantes's description of how "500 years of history gets written" in the eyes of a Tzotzil mother in the moments before her assassination is a striking poetic rendering of Capitán Insurgente Maribel's response to a Mexican official in the days after the Zapatista takeover of San Cristóbal: "Extending his hand to her, Commissioner Manuel Camacho Solís asks her age, 'Five hundred and two,' replies Maribel, who is as old as the rebellion."[130] For indigenous women in particular, history is inscribed in their bodies through in/visible wounds. "Political violence is a mode of transcription," Allen Feldman argues. "It circulates codes from one prescribed historiographic surface or agent to another." He goes on to describe how the body, "altered by violence, . . . reenacts political discourse and even the movement of history itself."[131]

Limón and Cervantes focus on how indigenous women carry political transcriptions on their bodies—manifested in colonial wounding—and how their embodiment of history often results in the state's violent repression. Operating in an interstitial space between an ethical embrace of the past and a hopeful utopian vision of the future, the decolonial neo-soldadera figures of the EZLN and those depicted in Limón's and Cervantes's work challenge neoliberal militarism in the present. While time is critical to neoliberal militarism, so is space. I turn now from an examination of the temporal to the spatial dimension of neoliberal militarism to show how Chicana and Latina subjects in the United States are corporeally incorporated into post-9/11 discourses of national security.

4

HOME/LAND INSECURITIES

Chicana/Latina Mothers and the Reproduction of National Security

everywhere you fuckin turn in the barrio—recruitment office. diversions game room—recruitment office right next door. south park mall—recruitment office right inside. the movies—recruitment office, same shopping center.

HAILSTORM FROM VIRGINIA GRISE'S *BLU*

Militarizing motherhood often starts with conceptualizing the womb as a recruiting station.

CYNTHIA ENLOE, *MANEUVERS*

AN ADVERTISEMENT IN *HISPANIC* MAGAZINE (June/July 2008) by Todaysmilitary.com features a one-by-two-inch black-and-white photo of a Latina mother and her young daughters as they stand in a kitchen preparing a meal. With slightly upraised eyebrows, the mother turns to her oldest daughter, who awaits her mother's response. In the center of the page, the ad copy contextualizes the photo: "Your daughter wants to enlist in the Military. You want her to go to college. Is this the end of the conversation? Or the beginning?" At the bottom righthand corner, the omniscient voice of the military offers counsel to a perplexed mother: "Make it a two-way conversation. Learn more at todaysmilitary.com." Perhaps more surprising than the fact that the military feels qualified to give parenting advice is that the advice is addressed to a Latina mother. The issue of enlistment is staged as a dialogue between mother and daughter; the father (presuming there is one) is absent from the discussion. Underlying the ad's appeal to progressive Latina mothers is a feminist subtext that highlights female agency. Although the women in the ad are confined to the kitchen and engaged in traditional female domestic labor, the topic of their discussion is socially transgressive.

The caption informs us that the daughter has just asserted her desire to enlist while the mother insists that she attend college. Both options require a level of female independence from the family and the home and therefore challenge traditional gender roles. By convincing the mother that both military service and education can be achieved simultaneously, the military positions itself as the ideal site for female empowerment.[1]

The subdued graphics in the "Your daughter" ad might make it a weak recruitment device that would fail to persuade most mothers. Yet, the ad's effectiveness is not necessarily in its design layout but in the war culture in which it circulates. Even if a mother remains unconvinced that the military is a viable option for her daughter, the pressure to consider it may be overwhelming: "If just government officials alone articulated these militarized maternalist expectations, a mother may not find it all that hard to resist them. It is the confluence of militarized family dynamics, a militarized popular culture, and a militarized state that makes the myths of militarized motherhood so potent."[2] Militarism encourages mothers to view their parenthood as a reflection of their own citizenship. The question remains whether the Latina mothers who see the "Your daughter" advertisement will be convinced that their motherhood is tied to the state's needs. To the extent that the Latina mother does not ask about the violence her daughter would participate in (and be subjected to), the mother will likely model the military's preferred behavior toward war.

The "Your daughter" advertisement takes place in the feminized domestic space of the family kitchen because home and family are two fundamental concepts that underwrite the logic of war. In this chapter, I consider how neoliberal militarism relies on the interanimating concepts of home and homeland to stabilize patriarchal norms and systems of power. These gendered and differentiated spaces enable the spatial logic of national security. They also empower the sociospatial formation of subjectivities, such as the Latina mother in the ad who must decide if military enlistment is advisable for her daughter and if it validates her own civic identity. Through an eclectic archive of military recruitment advertisements, a children's book, and a play, I examine how Latina mothers are militarized through neoliberal militarism's spatial practices of scaling.[3] Throughout the chapter I show how neoliberal militarism moves from the smallest scale (the body) to the largest scale (the nation) and how this process produces profound forms of insecurity for Latina/o communities.

I focus on Latina mothers to demonstrate how Latina fertility is transformed from biological threat to national resource, and how Latina reproduction and mothering practices sustain the future of military recruitment and personnel needs. Military market research reveals how the biopolitics of recruitment requires the study and surveillance of Latina mothers' fertility rates, education levels, social networks, and views on military service. These data then shape recruitment ads that specifically target Latina mothers. By analyzing various ads, I propose that the future of national security rests, in many ways, on militarizing a traditionally vilified and maligned subject: the Latina mother. I then turn to the phenomenon of the Latina soldier-mother: a mother who not only encourages her child to enlist in the service, but also enlists herself. Graciela Tiscareño-Sato portrays this figure in her bilingual children's book *Good Night Captain Mama/Buenas Noches Capitán Mamá* (2013), the first in a bilingual aviation adventure series. *Captain Mama* provides a compelling example of how the Chicana soldier-mother embodies maternal protectionist discourses while transforming the family home into a space of military indoctrination. As with the military recruitment ads I examine, *Captain Mama* reveals how neoliberal militarism distorts the ostensibly inviolable public/private binary that undergirds the concept of home, even as it relies on the gendering of domestic spaces.

I turn finally to Virginia Grise's award-winning play *blu* (2011), which addresses the concepts of home and homeland while challenging the supposed stability and security connoted in each term. Set in an unnamed barrio and taking place in the post-9/11 era, the play uses pre-Cortesian myth to describe the contemporary realities of disorder and violence within the Chicana/o community. The play reveals neoliberal militarism's spatial practices of scaling by brilliantly depicting the interconnectedness of seemingly distinct spheres—home and homeland, home front and battlefront—that overlap, like concentric circles, to reveal patriarchy, militarism, and nationalism as their nexus. If the word *home* in homeland is meant to represent refuge, then *blu* exposes the daily intimate and institutional forms of violence that undermine the meaning of home. This, in turn, undermines the logic of national security and the forms of patriarchy implied in discourses of defense. The play also challenges the meaning of homeland by juxtaposing Aztlán, the mythic Aztec homeland, with the intensely militarized space of the nation guarded under the aegis of Homeland Security. I argue that because the play critiques militarized notions of homeland, it also critiques both wartime nationalism and Chicano cultural nationalism by drawing parallels between violent patriarchal war cultures and institutions: the Aztecs, gangs, the military, and U.S. imperialism. While *blu* depicts a queer Chicana mother under duress amid the violence and chaos wrought by neoliberal militarism, it also rewrites myth to critique war and militarization and to point toward more emancipatory notions of homeland belonging.

HOME/LAND INSECURITIES

Only eleven days after the terrorist attacks on September 11, 2001, the term *homeland* entered official state discourse, as Pennsylvania governor Tom Ridge became the first director of the Office of Homeland Security. Because *homeland* is linked to mythical origins, it invokes an autochthonous sense of national belonging that raises the issue of defense to the level of existential threat. The state's choice to use *homeland* as a departmental moniker suggests how the discourses of national defense rely on figurative language, prompting us to consider the relationship between metaphor and material space. Metaphors function by suggesting a similarity between something that is known and something that is unknown. In spatial metaphors, space is often represented as a fixed and self-evident location that grounds the unknown association.[4] In this way, spatial metaphors tend to flatten and naturalize space rather than acknowledge its dynamic and socially constructed quality. The *homeland* in Homeland Security operates in a similar way. By comparing the nation to a home, *homeland* evokes familial ties and mythic connections to a domestic space, but as a spatial metaphor, it dissembles the gendering and racializing processes that go into the social construction of the home. In the United Stsates, the home has been symbolically linked to women, specifically mothers, since the founding of the nation. Notions such as republican motherhood and the culture of domesticity helped mark the home as women's domain, a space where mothers could exercise the power of maternal influence as they governed over children and households.[5] Designating home as the site of women's power helped naturalize women's exclusion from other public spheres of influence and reconfirmed men's ostensible control of public life. The idealized home—depicted in popular domestic novels of the nineteenth century, for example—was a Christian household headed by a morally upright white middle-class woman. The homeland trope gains its rhetorical and ideological force by retaining this unstated reference to the white home and the white woman inside that home.

I focus on the homeland metaphor to understand the relationship between space and metaphor and to make the shaping powers of space more visible. In particular, I argue that neoliberal militarism relies on the concepts of home and homeland to stabilize patriarchal norms and systems of power. The home is a gendered and seemingly transparent space of social reproduction, and the *homeland* depends on the ideological production of home and the subjectivities that form and are formed by that space. Challenging the transparency of the home is particularly important to understanding how the militarized maternal Latina body and the militarized home are both rendered as "naturally natural."[6] Wartime nationalism deliberately cultivates a notion of home as a female space worthy of defense and sacrifice to facilitate militarism and imperial foreign policies. Moreover, the home is supposed to be a safe space removed from the battlefield, which is in turn a public space of danger and violence. The promulgation of distinctive gendered spheres has secured patriarchal claims to power and is central to war waging because war relies on a discourse of oppositions: public/private, men/women, domestic/foreign, and us/them.

Neoliberal militarism requires spatial differentiation and scaling to organize social, economic, and political relationships and to induce the formation of militarized subjectivities. Spaces are not only striated by gender, but also delineated by size and shape to produce specific effects. Mary Pat Brady explains, "By demarcating spaces, by establishing limits and thus contents, and by fixing spaces within a framework of spatial relations, . . . scale narrates and thereby helps to organize and produce space."[7] The smallest scale I examine is the Latina maternal body because, as Neil Smith explains, the site of the body is where identities are formed, and the scale of the body is where control is exercised by the self and others.[8] For example, I show how the state expects Latina maternal bodies to internalize attitudes of defenselessness and vulnerability in order to perform militarized mothering practices. Through the reproductive efforts of her body—both biological and social—she is expected to impress militarized values and ideologies on her children. While this process is often subtle, it is not incontestable, for "scales ranging from the body to the neighborhood to the nation can thus become the center of struggle."[9] The home is often the most intimate and immediate scale where embodied identity formation takes place. For women, scales can be constrictive of both physical and social mobility. I examine the dialectical relationship between scales because, as Laura Pulido explains, "Places are produced by other places," and an analysis of larger systems of oppression, such as racism, requires a simultaneous multiscalar analysis that attends to the relationships between spaces.[10] My analysis of neoliberal militarism's spatial logic focuses on the relationship between the body and the home as well as both sites' relationships to the larger scale of the barrio and the homeland.

Iris Marion Young has argued that the national security state operates under a gendered logic of masculinist protection. This form of protection originates in the patriarchal household, in which men paradigmatically occupy the role of protector, while women and children occupy the position of protected subjects. "In return for male protection," Young argues, "the woman concedes critical distance from decision-making autonomy."[11] Masculinist protection often masks hierarchal relations of domination as it mobilizes fear to ensure the compliance of the protected. In Young's view, society emulates the subordinate status of women: "This stronger U.S. security state offers a bargain to its citizens: obey our commands and support our security actions, and we will ensure your protection."[12] The state then takes whatever measures it deems necessary, including the abrogation of rights, to fulfill its bargain. In addition to protecting its citizens from foreign danger, the security state protects them from domestic threats—internal saboteurs, conspirators, and dissenters who seek to wreak havoc in the homeland.[13] This practice of defending against external and internal dangers facilitates the militarization of the barrio and its subsequent transformation into an internal battleground. I extend Young's analysis to argue that masculinist protection is critical to neoliberal militarism's spatial logic, which is founded on the spatial and thus social subordination and confinement of women to the home.

In many ways, the military provides a model for how to understand what a multiscalar exploration of space looks like. In recent years, most of the military branches have switched to using the term *battlespace* rather than *battlefield* in their doctrinal literature. While *battlefield* suggests a more static notion of the theater of war, *battlespace* acknowledges the shifting character of a given location and how multiple variables influence its function and meaning. Stephen Graham describes how battlespace includes everything "from the molecular scales of genetic engineering and nanotechnology through the everyday sites, spaces and experiences of city life, to the planetary spheres of space and the Internet's globe-straddling cyberspace."[14] The all-encompassing conception of space, in which "nothing lies outside battlespace, temporally or geographically," suggests the military's understanding of how different scales are interconnected and reliant. It also exemplifies a more invasive and pervasive quest to dominate bodies, geographies, and stratospheres through military technologies of control, intervention, and surveillance. Although this breakthrough in spatial knowledge will presumably be used for legitimate defensive purposes, it should conjure a deep anxiety in those of us who question the ultimate purposes this new orientation will serve. But if we take our cue from the military, we can learn how it plans to conceive of and dominate multiple spatial scales so that we can then imagine alternatives and counter-geographies.

MARTIAL DEMOGRAPHICS: MILITARIZING LATINA FERTILITY

During the 2004 presidential campaign season, both Democratic and Republican candidates vied for the votes of a newly imagined construct: the security mom. Conservative syndicated columnist Michelle Malkin helped enflesh this political fiction by claiming to embody its very qualities: "I am what this year's election pollsters call a 'security mom.' I'm married with two young children. I own a gun. And I vote."[15] In her diatribe against weak and politically correct politicians, Malkin questioned whether presidential candidates "understand our demands for a president who will ensure that Islamic terrorists are kept out of our country and that criminal illegal aliens are kicked out for good." Conflating these two popular boogeymen of the post-9/11 era, Malkin's position, which Michele Rodino identifies as that of the *mater bellicosa*, helps delineate the security mom's multiple spheres of interest: her family, her home, and her country.[16] In contrast to Malkin's maternalist and xenophobic nationalism are the "peace moms," best represented by activist Cindy Sheehan. Upon the death of her son Casey Sheehan in 2004, she became active in the antiwar movement and founded Gold Star Families for Peace in 2005. Speaking as the rhetorically powerful figure of the mater dolorosa, which Sara Ruddick explains is an effective maternal symbol that antiwar groups often use to oppose war, Sheehan refused to accept the official framing of her son's death as patriotic sacrifice and instead made maternal dissent the basis for her own citizenship.[17]

Latina mothering, I argue, is often differently implicated in national security because of the cultural and political stigmatization of Latina reproduction. Latina fertility in particular is usually portrayed in popular discourse and treated in public policy as a biological and cultural threat to the nation. Latina mothers are often criminalized for their reproductive capacities in addition to their race, gender, class, and citizenship status. Leo Chavez describes how Latina reproduction is transformed into a discourse that "produces a limited range of meanings, often focusing on [Latinas'] supposedly excessive reproduction, seemingly abundant or limitless fertility, and hypersexuality, all of which are seen as 'out of control' in relation to the supposed social norm" represented by white, "modern" women.[18] The threatening nature of Latinas' "dangerous curves," as Isabel Molina-Guzmán calls them, is their hypersexuality. Chavez describes how this hypersexuality "supposedly combines with pronatalist cultural and religious values (that are static and immutable because of their lack of social integration, assimilation, and acculturation) to produce high fertility rates."[19] He points out that immigrant women's fertility has been a national concern for much of U.S. history, but in the past forty years, Latina fertility has been the target of certain environmentalists and the birthright movement, who view it as a menace to national interests.

These groups have attempted to convince the wider public that Latina reproduction merits extreme measures of social control. Their efforts amount to the securitization of Latina reproduction, or the framing of Latina fertility as a purported threat to national security that justifies extreme or extralegal measures. The birthright movement's attempt to revise the U.S. Constitution's Fourteenth Amendment to withhold citizenship from children born in the United States to undocumented immigrants epitomizes how public discourse and public policy securitize Latina fertility and reproduction. Latina fertility is also securitized in popular culture. The anonymously produced and posted video game called Border Patrol provides a horrifying depiction of the criminalization and dehumanization of reproductive Latina bodies (figure 7). It features a pregnant, presumably Mexican woman crossing the U.S.-Mexico border with two young children in hand. While she is running for her life, she is also running in the direction of the welfare office, where she'll take advantage of social services to provide for her growing brood of children and "anchor babies." Players of the game score points for accurately aiming their weapon's cross hairs at the maternal body and shooting the target. Successful shots are rewarded with points and with images of blood splattering from the bodies of the mother and her children. The game provides a racist and misogynistic illustration of how the Latina mother is regarded as an invading threat to the homeland because of her reproductive capacity.[20] Unlike Border Patrol, however, military recruitment advertising presents a challenge to securitizing efforts to control Latina reproduction. As I show in the following section, ads that feature Latina mothers are free of alarmist and xenophobic rhetoric. Instead the image most often projected is of a loving, responsible mother who cares about the personal growth and economic future of her children and who plays a vital role in raising upstanding citizen-soldiers.

In some sense, the military's focus on motherhood is not surprising. Jennifer Terry points out that the "concepts of the nation as mother to be guarded and

FIGURE 7. Screenshot of the online flash game Border Patrol, http://www.flashrolls.com/shooting-games/Border-Patrol-Flash-Game.htm.

protected and the mother, in turn, as the figure for nurturing and reproducing the nation have a long history in Western political thought."[21] Thus, military appeals to mothers are quite common. Enloe shows that the militarization of motherhood has always been a crucial component of recruitment strategies: "Insofar as women are presumed to be the chief caretakers of sons and insofar as political leaders wanting to raise armies need to persuade mothers to offer up their sons to military service, women will be encouraged to see their maternal duty as a public duty and to release their sons (and sometimes daughters) for some higher good."[22] Lorraine Bayard de Volo argues that militaries often employ maternal symbolism and direct appeals to mothers to mitigate "potential maternal opposition" to war. By creating constructs such as the "good mother," military planners attempt to "draft" mothers into supporting the war effort just as the military asks them to give up their sons and daughters to war making. Mothers who resist militarized motherhood are labeled "unpatriotic mothers." Their failure to condone warfare through the willing sacrifice of their child's life is deemed as a "selfish" expression that indicates an "excessive attachment to their sons [and daughters]."[23]

The science of military recruitment illuminates the motivation for focusing on mothers and the level of invasive inquiry required to appeal to them. As the 2003 report by the Committee on the Youth Population and Military Recruitment makes clear, "accurately ascertaining [mothers'] ideological stance together with fashioning recruitment messages that appeal to rather than counter their traditional attitudes may hold promise for more effective recruiting."[24] Military advertising, and the science behind it, provides striking examples of governmentality's reliance on representation and intervention.[25] That is, governmentality functions through the proliferation of knowledges, expertise, and data not only to quantify a domain of interest, but to actually will it into existence for the purpose of subjecting it to deliberation, regulation, and ultimately intervention. The military's interest in studying Latina/o communities is to understand the characteristics, habits, beliefs, and interests of the largest youth demographic in the country. To do so, the military amasses data and produces knowledge about Latinas/os to construct the ideal representations of Latina/o soldiers that it seeks to recruit. The production of knowledge and actionable information lead to target marketing and market penetration, methods that can only be described as aggressive recruitment practices. Here, I focus on how the amassment of data helps the military scale down to the site of the Latina maternal body. This process helps the military discern the Latina mother's intimate reproductive capacities, her emotional attachments and triggers, her social needs, and her personal and familial aspirations. Then, through inscriptive processes, which include surveying, tabulating, and other quantifying procedures, military marketers categorize and taxonomize Latina mothers' behaviors and beliefs, making the maternal body the most intimate site of knowledge procurement and production, transforming it into a domain of interest and an object in need of intervention. Thus, military recruitment involves an invasive spatial practice that begins at the scale of the body and moves to increasingly larger social groupings.

Hispanic recruitment analyses invariably begin with a discussion of Latina/o demographics and their potential impact on military recruitment and readiness. Citing what is by now the familiar population projections from the Census Bureau, military analysts describe how Hispanics are becoming the largest minority group in the country. Early reports present this fact in relation to decreases in other groups. For example, Lloyd J. Matthews remarks on the "eye-popping projection that Americans of European background, now comprising about 72 percent of the U.S. population, will diminish to about 53 percent by the year 2050, meaning that so-called 'white Anglo-Saxons' are headed for minority status."[26] While Matthews candidly expresses his surprise (or anxiety) over the impending "eye-popping" racial trends, he represents the interest that many military analysts have in the growth of the Latina/o population. Given the trends in youth population growth, Matthews proposes that "some units in the Army might eventually experience Hispanic representation on the order of 20 to 40 percent, the largest share of which could be of Mexican derivation."[27] More recent analyses continue to cite the demographic shifts and do so while emphasizing the potential for positive dividends in the future. In "Recruiting Hispanics: The Marine Corps Experience," Anita Hattiangadi, Gary Lee, and Aline Quester describe how the Hispanic population has grown "from 5 percent of the population in 1975 to over 12 percent in 2003."[28] Given the group's propensity to serve and their strong enlistment behavior (defined as high completion rates of boot camp and first term of service), Hattiangadi and colleagues assert that "expected increases in the Hispanic youth population should be good news for all the Services." Indeed, the Latino youth population is of particular interest to military planners because of its projected increase of more than 9 million by 2025. This projection "means that the future target population for military recruiting and advertising will be more diverse and more Hispanic than the population as a whole."[29]

As to the causes behind the growth, Joseph C. Jones notes that "immigration and fertility rates are indeed changing America's complexion, and such change will inevitably affect ethnic representation in the Army."[30] Paul Sackett and Anne Mavor report that in the next two decades, Latinas/os will significantly change the "ethnic composition of the youth population": "Based on recent fertility patterns, the percentage of young adults who are Hispanic, of whom the largest subgroup is of Mexican origin, will increase substantially."[31] Instead of causing consternation for military planners, these sources of population growth actually alleviate concerns over imminent demographic problems. Writing in *Parameters*, a journal published by the U.S. Army War College, George Quester writes that the most significant demographic factors facing the armed forces "will be the 'graying' of the population, . . . as lower birthrates and longer lifespans project that a larger proportion of the total population will be above what was viewed, until recently, as the normal age for retirement."[32]

Ascertaining the interests, motivations, and desires of the Latina/o youth cohort requires researchers and marketers to conduct or utilize nationwide surveys that target the entire youth population. From 1975 to 1999, the Department of Defense (DoD) administered the Youth Attitude Tracking Survey (YATS), an annual telephone survey of approximately ten thousand youth between the ages of sixteen and twenty-four.[33] In 2001, the Joint Advertising, Market Research and Studies (JAMRS) Youth Polls replaced the YATS for measuring youth propensity.[34] JAMRS also began surveying adult *influencers*, defined as adults between the ages of twenty-two and eighty-five who had regular interaction with youth and the capacity to influence their choices.[35] For researchers at JAMRS, parents were the most important influencers because of their impact on "attitude and social norm formation," and because they often "serve as a major environmental constraint/roadblock between youth who are interested in joining the military."[36] Of greatest interest to military planners and advertisers are mothers, because of their "greater reluctance to recommend military service."[37] For example, the 2003 Influencer Poll showed that 44 percent of fathers and 55 percent of mothers were less likely to recommend military service than other career options.[38] According to Sackett and Mavor, mothers are also the primary influencers on youth career choices. Using a variety of youth surveys, they note that both male and female civilian youth respondents "talked to their mothers most seriously about the occupation they wanted to enter and about the training or education required to enter the selected occupation."[39] Sackett and Mavor also cite surveys of army and air force enlistees in which both groups stated that their mothers, more so than their fathers, were the most supportive and significant influencers in their lives. The researchers conclude that mothers generally support youth career decisions, "but they are likely to do so only if their sons and daughters['] career decisions square with their own beliefs and values."[40] They argue that women are traditionally more pacifist than men and "may have less knowledge of military life and careers on which to advise their sons and daughters *responsibly*."[41] It will therefore presumably be the task of military advertisers to instruct mothers on military life so that they can "responsibly" parent their child.

These results prompted researchers to study mothers' subjective norms—that is, the level of support that they would receive from family and friends for recommending military service to their son or daughter. According to the data, mothers seemed to care about what others thought, which led the authors of the 2003 Influencer Poll to recommend that "efforts to increase their perceived level of social support will be beneficial" to overall recruitment efforts.[42] A subsequent poll found that mothers, more so than fathers, must be "convinced that their children have what it takes to be successful in the military."[43] In addition to gauging mothers' views on military service, researchers are also interested in their personal characteristics, including educational attainment. The increase in women's education levels is significant because, as Sackett and Mavor note, there is a positive correlation between maternal education and youth educational goals.[44] A 2009 report on recruiting in the AVF noted that "since 1980, college attendance rates of mothers have greatly increased"—a distressing trend for recruiters given that "youth with more educated parents are more likely to pursue post-secondary education, and are therefore less interested in military service."[45] While most of the findings are provided as aggregated data that rarely specify Latina mothers' responses, military planners have made clear their interest in targeting specific groups. In a 2009 annual diversity report, the Marine Corps Recruiting Command stated its concerted effort to "further understand the role of African-American and Hispanic influencers, especially the role of parents in prospects' decision-making and how their perspectives on the military, enlistment, and related issues affect decisions to join our Corps."[46] Hattiangadi and colleagues also cite a study of recruiters that found "Hispanic parents are more involved than non-Hispanic parents in their children's recruiting decisions."[47]

The focus on Latina fertility, educational attainment, social networking, and other data points help transform the Latina body as a critical scale open to invasive state inquiry. The Latina mother's positive effect on expanding the recruitable youth cohort enables the military to jump scales from the individual reproductive body to the population. I argue that the military's interest in Latina/o demographics is a form of governmentality that requires what Foucault calls "apparatuses of security."[48] He argues that the modern state's focus on the population required attendant technologies of power, or apparatuses of security, whose purpose was to evaluate and manage probabilities and cost effectiveness, and to achieve acceptable outcomes at the level of the population. This reorientation shifted the state's relationship to events. Whether the event is a plague or a decline in grain production, the state's responsibility is to manage rather than prevent events, with the goal of achieving the optimal outcome for the population.

While the logic of biopower requires that the state ensure the maintenance of the population—its health, longevity, and overall well-being—that maintenance is predicated on the exclusion of harmful or threatening bodies. Managing populations requires twinned yet contradictory processes whereby the state exercises power by affirming life and permitting death. Those bodies that have been pathologized through race, gender, sexuality, class, or citizenship status are subject to multiple mechanisms of social excision. For example, the involuntary sterilization of Latinas as a means of limiting the growth of the Latino population demonstrates how biopower works through exclusion. In hospitals like the Los Angeles County–USC Medical Center, Mexican-origin women were forcibly sterilized between 1968 and 1974.[49] Renee Tajima-Peña argues that for Latina/o families, delivery rooms functioned like "border checkpoint[s] for unborn babies."[50] The logic of biopolitical exclusion was redeployed in 1994, when Governor Pete Wilson of California proposed the end of prenatal health care for undocumented women as a budget saving measure. The governor's proposal would have resulted in a greater number of low-weight babies, premature deliveries, and abnormalities, as well as an increased infant mortality rate.[51] The proposal was in addition to Proposition 187, a ballot initiative referred to as the Save Our State initiative, which passed in the same year and barred undocumented immigrants from accessing nonemergency medical services and public education. Federal courts eventually blocked both proposals, but they remain significant reminders of how "saving our state" from unwanted and foreign bodies requires policies that expose certain lives to risk, exclusion, and death. Jonathan Xavier Inda reminds us that the "fight against the enemy takes place on the terrain of the immigrant woman's body, the aim being to eliminate the enemy through controlling its capacity to reproduce."[52]

While forced sterilization and the denial of prenatal care are stark examples of a biopolitics of exclusion, military recruitment provides an alternative form of biopolitical *inclusion* that takes particular interest in Latina biological and social reproductive capacities. It is important to note that what distinguishes an apparatus of security from strictly disciplinary modes of power is its permissiveness. Unlike juridical and disciplinary regimes of power that function through regulation, prescription, and prohibition, apparatuses of security require "not interfering, allowing free movement, letting things follow their course; *laissez faire*."[53] Foucault goes on to explain that the condition of freedom, "the possibility of movement, change of place, and processes of circulation of both people and things" are critical to the deployment of security.[54] Moreover, apparatuses of security accept existing conditions as value-neutral realities and "rely on details that are not valued as good or evil in themselves, that are taken to be necessary, inevitable processes, as natural processes in the broad sense . . . in order to obtain something that is considered to be pertinent in itself because situated at the level of the population."[55] In this light, we can see how the military's support for pro-immigrant measures that expedite naturalization is born out of its concern for maintaining military readiness. In direct contrast to California's punitive and xenophobic Save Our State initiative, the military's pro-immigrant stance exemplifies a biopolitical rationality that focuses on managing the circulation of people and attendant shifts in demography, rather than attempting to prohibit or deter the direction of change underway. Because its ultimate mission is national defense of the population, the military has developed a different relationship to un/documented immigrants and, I argue, to Latina fertility and mothering practices. Its approach to the Latina/o community is to accept what it portrays as the inevitability of a growing demographic. Rather than treat this fact with trepidation or alarm, military marketing discourse and research present the data either in judgment-free terms or in a manner that celebrates Latina/o culture. Thus, military recruitment and marketing provide a new context in which to understand how Latina reproduction has been militarized and how Latina fertility and motherhood are being redeployed to serve national interests.

The Latina body's transformation from biological, ecological, and reproductive threat to national resource can be found in the images that grace recruitment brochures, posters, and online advertising. While these images of Latina/o subjects are often fabricated approximations of reality, they also function as militarizing discourses that affect Latina/o communities. Not only do they promote military values and practices, but they also seek to visually contain the public anxiety over a growing Latina/o population that is often perceived as an internal threat to national security. In contrast to the vilified pregnant Latina in the Border Patrol game, military advertising depicts the Latina mother as a potential ally in the recruitment of future generations.

For example, the Marine ad in the September 2007 issue of *Hispanic* magazine illustrates the role that family and home are expected to play in the militarization of Latina/o youth. The ad features a traditional nuclear family tableau, with a son in uniform surrounded by smiling parents on either side (figure 8). In the background is the façade of a middle-class home, the front porch supported by Greek columns and surrounded by a manicured yard. In bold uppercase letters, a caption reads: "Su entrenamiento empezó en casa" (His training began at home).[56] A short paragraph, also written in Spanish, describes the kind of training the young Marine received prior to enlistment. In the ad, positive values are associated with Latina/o families: being well mannered and courteous, having respect for elders, doing good, and having a strong work ethic. Written in second-person point of view, the ad text praises good parenting but suggests that the son's growth is incomplete. In the Marines, he can gain self-discipline and leadership skills to complete the citizen training he received at home. George Lipsitz asserts that the state "borrows legitimacy and commands obligation by insinuating itself into family and gender roles."[57] By claiming to value and teach the same qualities, the Marines become an extension of the Latino family, a partner in the rearing of Latina/o youth. Yet, the ad recognizes the ultimate power of influence that Latina/o parents have over their child and thus implores the

FIGURE 8. "Su entrenamiento empezó en casa" (His training began at home), U.S. Marines advertisement, *Hispanic*, September 2007. The eagle, globe, and anchor emblem; term *Marines*; and slogan "The Few. The Proud" are trademarks of the U.S. Marine Corps.

parents to relinquish the child to the nation: "Denle la oportunidad de servir a su país" (Give him the opportunity to serve his country). While the ad focuses on the son's maturation into a citizen-solder, the parents' citizenship is also at stake. The Latino parents are thus performing their civic duty by forfeiting a son, an act that demonstrates not only good parenting, but also good citizenship.

The state affirmation of good Latina/o parenting is an important gesture of national inclusion. The ad's address being in Spanish displays the military's concerted efforts to appeal to a linguistically marginalized community to meet military recruitment needs. Latina/o parenting is praised as a national asset. Arlene Dávila has shown how these powerful and pervasive images of national belonging are critical to Latinas/os, "whose attainment of representation is essential to contemporary politics."[58] She argues that advertisements are "complex texts that, as stereotypical or outlandish as they may be, are always entangled with the interests, desires, or imaginations of those whom they seek to entice as consumers."[59] Military advertisements circulate within and draw from preexisting representations of Latinidad and participate in the discursive construction of Latina/o cultural identities, which are constantly re/negotiated in the social process of national belonging and in the political process of claiming citizenship, rights, and representation. The ad discussed here exemplifies what Dávila calls the "'coming-of-age' discourses" of thoroughly assimilated and upwardly mobile consumer citizens.[60] Military ads contribute to the circulation of images in which Latinas/os represent a class of uber Americans who continue to practice and believe in the purported American values of "family, democracy, upward mobility, and workmanship" that non-Latina/o Americans have themselves supposedly lost.[61] Through figures like the militarized Latina mother, Americans are further reeducated in the lost art of personal sacrifice, gratefulness, and promilitary commitment. The Latina military mother joins her counterparts in political campaign ads and detergent commercials to make up "a preponderance of tamer and more publicly palatable appeals and representations of Latinos that are less threatening to an imagined 'mainstream.'"[62] The tameness of the Latina military mother's depiction is significant because it juxtaposes media depictions of the threatening brown reproductive body with a patriotic maternal citizen. While the ads mostly depict comforting images of Latina/o families on the cusp of "coming of age" through a son's or daughter's potential enlistment, they also conceal the realities of economic inequalities and political marginalization that continue to plague Latina/o communities—conditions that, in fact, make vulnerable Latina/o families desirable recruiting targets. As Dávila points out, sanitized images of Latinidad are predicated on Latinas/os being "disciplin[ed] into the 'right' way of being an 'ethnic.'"[63] This disciplining often attempts to produce docile Latina/o consumers, distracted into political inactivity by the glitter of new TVs and shiny cars. But disciplining in military advertising also entails transforming Latina/o subjects into promilitary patriots who see militarization as not only natural, but also desirable.

I return to the image of the mother because she is the visual and moral center of the ad. We are drawn to her by her salmon-colored blouse, which contrasts with the stark black color of her son's crisp Marine uniform. Her warm maternal smile is inviting. Her significance to the ad's marketing appeal is highlighted by her son's white-gloved hand resting respectfully yet lovingly on her shoulder. Framed by the white Greek columns in the background, we see a family, but more specifically a mother, who is safely ensconced within her son's embrace and the family home. The visual message is that both home and mother need to be protected—a responsibility that the Latino son dutifully fulfills. The mother's warm smile and modest pose further illustrate what Jean Bethke Elshtain calls the Beautiful Soul. Borrowing from Hegel's formulation, Elshtain defines the Beautiful Soul as a figure who embodies purity and an innocence or naïveté about historical and world affairs. Elshtain argues that in Western culture, women have collectively served as Beautiful Souls, a socially fabricated identity that enables the discourse of war: "Pictured as frugal, self-sacrificing, at times delicate, the female Beautiful Soul in time of war has been positioned as a mourner, an occasion for war, and a keeper of the flame of nonwarlike values—and has thus been set up as a being, and a whole way of life, men both cherish and seek to flee, both need and despise."[64] The Beautiful Soul's innocence is partly attributed to her confinement in the family home, where she fosters "nonwarlike values," in this case, respect, courtesy, and good manners. From the military's perspective, the Latino son embodies these values; however, he must also learn the warlike values taught by the military and practiced in the public, male world of warfare. This points to an unspoken tension between the military and the mother because, despite her innocence, the Beautiful Soul poses a danger to patriarchal militarism. The military must negotiate with the Latina mother who, as the primary influencer, wields tremendous power over her son's actions and decisions. The mother's "nonwarlike values" are worthy of defending but must not dominate the social order or interfere with the national security state's objectives. Therefore, enlistment becomes critical to the son's citizenship and normative gender formation as it helps to determine whether he becomes a protective son or a "mama's boy."

The mother's own citizenship is bound up in her son's enlistment in various ways. Supporting and encouraging a son's enlistment directly assists the state in meeting its recruitment goals. Through this act, the mother is told that she is contributing to the nation's security and imperial mission. She becomes a "civic being; she is needed by others." This is what makes the ad so alluring. Its effusive praise and hagiographic depiction of Latina/o parenting offers the mother a positive civic identity and a state-sanctioned role in national defense. Elshtain explains how the mother "is told, without her unselfish devotion to country and family each would be lost." Elshtain further argues, "Many women yearn for public identities as civic beings serving ends that take them beyond the borders of private lives."[65] Given the fact that child rearing in the home often goes unappreciated, and that Latina reproduction and mothering are socially devalued, or worse, criminalized, the positive public and official recognition of her efforts is extremely seductive. She also performs her civic duty by willingly embodying the Beautiful Soul values of the innocent mother in need of male protection and by maintaining the idealized notion of the family home. As the Beautiful Soul, sequestered in the domestic space, the Latina mother in the ad becomes a powerful justification for homeland defense. But just as neoliberal militarism requires the distinction of public and private spaces, this ad undermines spatial dichotomies by asserting that the son's military training began *in* the home and that by encouraging a son's enlistment, "él completará lo que ustedes empezaron en casa" (he will complete what you began at home). Because the home is regarded as the mother's domain of influence, the ad implies that the mother is primarily responsible for inculcating the specific qualities that the Marines value. In this sense, not only is the home transformed into a boot camp, but the mother takes on the role of drill instructor.

Through advertising and various marketing efforts, the military has targeted the Latina mother as the primary hindrance to and ally in neoliberal militarism. The power of influence she wields over her child's identity formation and decisions makes her a critical component to military recruitment and thus to the nation's military dominance. For this reason, military advertising reveres her social and biological reproductive capacities as national assets. In this marketing realm, the Latina mother's child-rearing body is no longer a biopolitical security threat, but an important resource for sustaining military readiness and imperial projects.

MATERNALIZING MILITARISM: *CAPTAIN MAMA* AND THE RISE OF THE SOLDIER-MOTHER

In the post-9/11 context, security moms are women who self-identify as mothers explicitly concerned with national defense, domestic terrorism, and immigration control. In Michelle Malkin's view, the attacks on September 11 signaled a new era of threat that provided mothers with the mandate to protect both home and nation through maternal hypervigilance and surveillance. "Nothing matters more to me right now," Malkin writes, "than the safety of my home and the survival of my homeland."[66] Within Malkin's histrionics, we get an image of a security mom who is anxious yet pragmatic, protective yet angry, bellicose and patriotic. Importantly, Malkin's security mom also operates within a larger context in which the lines between private and public are further eroded. Amy Kaplan argues that homeland security provokes a nervous frenzy of national defense that produces "radical insecurity," in which "the home itself serves as the battleground": "Every facet of domestic life—in the double sense of the word as private and national—must be both protected and mobilized against these threats. Homeland security calls for vast new intrusions of government, military, and intelligence forces, not just to secure the homeland from external threats, but to become an integral part of the workings of home, a home in a continual state of emergency."[67] As a mother who "lives defensively" and who voluntarily surveils her own family and community, the security mom becomes the ideal agent for the neoliberal security state. Inderpal Grewal has shown how the neoliberal state cannot or chooses not to provide protection for its citizens, and thus it outsources the job of security to mothers. In this sense, governmentality is enacted through the figure of the security mom. Not only does she become the desirable self-managed neoliberal subject, but when protecting her home as part of the national security effort, she becomes a national and imperial subject.[68]

The rise of the Latina soldier-mother expands our notion of the security mom figure and the ways in which Latinas participate in neoliberal militarism. While the actual numbers of Latina soldier-mothers are hard to come by, we can get a sense of this cohort through scattered news accounts and interviews. For example, in an interview with the National Hispanic Veterans Advocacy Network, Marilyn Gonzalez Colon, a Puerto Rican woman from New York, describes how she always wanted to join the military, but "I thought I couldn't do it because of my kids."[69] After consulting with her family, she eventually enlisted, passed all the physical tests, and became a member of the Army National Guard at the age of thirty-five. Though she entered the military to fulfill her lifelong dream, doing so also helped militarize her family—four of her five children have also enlisted in the military. Private Carmen Egipciaco, age forty, from Kissimmee, Florida, also joined the Army National Guard as a mother.[70] Egipciaco actually completed basic combat training with her seventeen-year-old son. These examples of Latina servicewomen point to what is perhaps a growing phenomenon.[71] As part of the national security state, both Colon and Egipciaco illustrate the transformation of the Latina mother from an object needing protection to a subject providing protection. *Good Night Captain Mama/ Buenas Noches Capitán Mamá* (2013), a bilingual children's book written by Mexican American air force veteran Graciela Tiscareño-Sato, also helps us examine the phenomenon of the Latina soldier-mother and how the gendering of protection discourses supports notions of home and homeland security.[72]

Tiscareño-Sato's *Captain Mama* tells the story of a Latina officer and aircraft navigator who must put her young son, Marco, to bed before she leaves to conduct a nighttime flying mission. Marco asks a series of questions about her green flight suit, a conversation that leads to a detailed explanation of her duties as a captain within the Air Mobility Command, her travel to different bases around the world, and the meaning of the command patches on her uniform.[73] *Captain Mama* illustrates the conflicting yet conjoined discourses that produce the figure of the Chicana soldier-mother and, I argue, provides an important example of the militarization of Chicana mothering. The anomalous Chicana soldier-mother, depicted here as Captain Mama, is a cross between the civic republican mother and the security mom. She actively participates in the project of national security; her military service forms the basis of her civic identity and further demonstrates her patriotic commitment to the nation. But unlike the civic republican mother, her participation is not confined to the private space of the home; rather, her service is publicly displayed and recognized through her military uniform. Like the security mom, she is concerned with keeping both home and homeland safe. While explaining to Marco the meaning of the U.S. flag, she states, "I serve in our military to protect our country and to keep you safe." Unlike Malkin's xenophobic and fascist form of mothering, however, *Captain Mama* promotes a lukewarm, tempered nationalism that is appropriate for young readers.

Captain Mama also complicates the idealized figure of the Beautiful Soul. The green flight suit prevents us from associating her body with maternal innocence. Yet her characterization of her duties in the air force belies the violence of military power that she participates in and thus endows her with a kind of innocence associated with the Beautiful Soul. For example, she explains to Marco that she is "part of a big team all over the world." She moves people and supplies like food and fuel, and thus, she portrays military defense as "things [that] are needed to keep the people of America and America's friends safe." Her participation in the military is seemingly innocuous; although her function as a captain in the Air Mobility Command enables military violence, her characterization distances her from the scene of battle and from the death and destruction that war entails. In this sense, she can retain some of the purity and ingenuousness of the Latina Beautiful Soul. Indeed, this is largely possible because of the way her actions are framed as maternal protectionism rather than what Young calls masculinist protectionism. In *Captain Mama*, maternal protectionism is portrayed as a traditional feature of mothering. Yet maternal protection accrues different meanings and self-perceptions that align with normative gender behaviors and roles. For example, Elshtain explains how "men see edifying tales of courage, duty, honor, glory as they engage in acts of protection and defense." In contrast to male "heroic deed doing," women "see edifying stories of nobility, sacrifice, duty, quiet immortality as they engage in defensive acts of protection, the nonheroics of taking care of."[74] The unstated danger that Captain Mama faces as part of her military occupation (for example, she tells Marco, "We connect our airplane to another military airplane in the air and give it the gas it needs to get to where it's going"), and the violence made possible by her actions, are devoid of awe-inspiring or even pretentious heroics. Glory and courage are absent from Captain Mama's narrative of maternal defense. It is also important to note that her maternalist protection does not completely displace the traditional role of the father. Before she puts him to bed, Captain Mama tells Marco, "Papa is here overnight to keep you all safe. I'll be here in the morning when you wake up." Despite her high rank as captain, she shares the duty of protector with her husband. And although the father's protection is devirilized, it helps stabilize the normative gender roles that are thrown into disequilibrium by the soldier-mother figure. Thus, militarized maternal protectionism combines conservative, normative, and feminist discourses as the soldier-mother operates in both the domestic space of the home and the national space of the homeland.

The illustrations show us the interplay between scales—that is, between the uniformed maternal body and the domestic space (figure 9). We see how the domestic setting neutralizes the jarring figure of the soldier-mother as militarism insinuates itself into the space of the family home and the intimacy of bedtime rituals. Dressed in her flight suit, Captain Mama continues to perform the activities of a parent—tucking a child into bed, singing a lullaby, and reassuring the child's sense of security and stability. These functions become militarized through the ensuing discussion of her green flight suit. She allows Marco to wear her newest patch, which recognizes her squadron's participation in Operation

FIGURE 9. Illustrated page from bilingual children's book *Good Night Captain Mama*, showing Captain Mama in her flight suit, looking down at her son in her bedroom; the first sentence on the page is "What are you wearing, Mama?" Illustration by Linda Lens, from four-time award-winning *Good Night Captain Mama/Buenas Noches Capitán Mamá*, written by air force veteran Graciela Tiscareño-Sato (Hayward, Calif.: Gracefully Global Group, 2013), 4. Used with permission.

Restore Hope, conducted on the Souda Bay Naval Base on the Greek island of Crete—a gesture that transforms his pajamas into a uniform. Before he goes to bed, Marco salutes his mother and says, "Good Night Captain Mama." Once again, the family home functions as a boot camp, where a mother participates in the militarization of her child.[75] Unlike the denigrated reproductive brown body of the undocumented migrant woman, Captain Mama's mothering is socially valued. Her body does not illegally transgress national boundaries; it defends them. While her mothering affirms the national security state, however, she is equally susceptible to violence. Thus, the larger point here is that while the soldier-mother and the undocumented maternal border crosser are on opposite sides of the security state apparatus, both remain in the cross hairs of neoliberal militarism's violence.

HOME/LAND INSECURITY: VIRGINIA GRISE'S *BLU* (2011)

I turn now to Virginia Grise's *blu* (2011), which affords a critical reading of martial geographies and the interrelation of distinct, but not isolated, spatial scales that distend across the body, home, barrio, homeland, and nation. More particularly, *blu* exposes how these spaces work together to form a violent and militarized home/land that produces profound forms of insecurity for Chicana/o communities. The play focuses on a queer Chicana family coping with the loss of its oldest son, Blu, who dies in the Iraq War. The mother, Soledad, is the emotional center as she attempts to reconstitute her family after leaving an abusive and dysfunctional relationship with Eme, a former gang member now imprisoned. Soledad's new family includes Hailstorm, a two-spirited indigenous woman who helps raise Soledad's two sons, Blu and Lunatico, and daughter, Gemini.

I read *blu*'s dystopic post-9/11 barrio landscape as a critique of the Aztec homeland of Aztlán and the national homeland of the United States, both territories used to cultivate distinct forms of nationalism that are grounded in virulent militarisms. I examine the discourse of Chicano cultural nationalists during the Chicano movement of the sixties and seventies to show how Aztlán was often depicted as an embattled landscape under colonial occupation that necessitated masculinist defense. As we have seen in chapter 1, the Viet Nam War draft, economic marginalization, and underfunded social services, as well as racism and social pressures to assimilate to white America all contributed to a social malaise best characterized as *un desmadre*, a colloquial Chicano street term that literally means "an un-mothering" and signifies chaos, discord, and destruction. This history forms the setting in *blu*, where characters not only contend with the spatial legacies of Aztlán, but also negotiate the multiple and connected institutional forces that perpetuate their spatial marginalization—structural inequalities, militarized schools and policing, and ubiquitous recruitment centers. Local gangs further adopt state practices of territorial acquisition and control, adding to the spatial insecurity of barrio inhabitants. While the breakdown of society under neoliberal militarism—that is, the desmadre experienced by poor and working-class communities of color in a post-9/11 context—make mothering nearly impossible, *blu* insists that motherwork and the family are still necessary and critical to cultural survival and demilitarization.

Grise's turn to Aztlán contributes to a larger Chicana/o theater history, which includes playwrights Luis Valdez and Cherríe Moraga, who explored Chicana/o indigeneity through pre-Cortesian myth. Thus, Chicana/o playwrights have a history of exhibiting what Raúl Villa calls a "nationalist place-consciousness," in which Chicana/o authors interrogate the territorial boundaries of the nation-state while proposing a mythic and material reterritorialization of colonized space. I also read Grise's *blu* as an important addition to Chicana/o urban literature, a subgenre of Chicana/o literature that critiques urban development's social and spatial displacement of Chicanas/os and that exposes the "dialectical production of barrio social space."[76] Mary Pat Brady argues that Chicanas "write with a sense of urgency about the power of space, about its (in)clement capacity to direct and contort opportunities, hopes, lives."[77] I draw on both Villa's and Brady's theoretics of urban space to demonstrate how neoliberal militarism reproduces a geography of spatial injustice and immobility within the Chicano barrio, and how Chicana literature can help us imagine the demilitarization of spaces and subjectivities.

MARTIAL GEOGRAPHIES: MILITARIZING THE BARRIO

Examining the relationships between spatial scales helps us identify the heterogeneity embedded in homogeneous terms like *homeland*. While *homeland* suggests collective belonging and cohesion, it also controverts the marginalization of internal zones and the people who inhabit them. As Kaplan reminds us, homeland's "folksy rural quality" has "a decidedly antiurban and anticosmopolitan ring to it."[78] The implied opposition between the urban and rural (and suburban) demonstrates how landscapes are racialized by a series of local ordinances and state and federal policies that promote de/industrialization, segregation, housing discrimination, and white flight, resulting in the long-term development of racially segregated communities like the Latino barrio and the white suburb. The larger point here is that only certain spaces are included in the national imagined geography of the homeland. While white suburbia represents the idealized neighborhood that must be defended from foreign threats and domestic racialized enemies, the city becomes, in Stephen Graham's words, an "urban Hobbesian 'state of nature'" that requires militarized policing and other violent tactics of state control.[79]

In the nineties, military strategists began to focus intensely on cities as "a unique battlespace that provides both attacker and defender with numerous and varied avenues of approach and fields of fire."[80] Mike Davis explains that the attack on elite Army Rangers by "slum militias" in Mogadishu in 1993 forced the military to reassess its urban combat preparedness training, referred to as military operations on urbanized terrain (MOUT).[81] While strategists focused on cities like Beirut, Karachi, Kabul, and Lagos, they also targeted certain U.S. cities as sites of potential threat. Major Ralph Peters, in his article for *Parameters*, a publication of the Army War College, argues that the "future of warfare" lies in the "broken cities of the world," and then he proceeds to list "Tuzla, Mogadishu, Los Angeles, Beirut, Panama City, Hue, Saigon, Santo Domingo" as instructive examples of past urban conflicts.[82] The conspicuous inclusion of Los Angeles in the list of potential foreign hotspots alludes to the city's history of protest. This history, along with the city's subterranean infrastructure, presumably justified the military's decision to conduct MOUT training exercises in Los Angeles.[83] Yet the city's history of protest—which includes the Zoot Suit Riots of 1943, the Watts Riots of 1965, and the 1992 L.A. riots—is a direct response to how Los Angeles residents are racialized by a series of local ordinances and state and federal policies that promote de/industrialization, housing discrimination, white flight, and segregation policies that determine the racial character and economic opportunities within the city.[84] For MOUT strategists, the economic and social marginalization of racialized urban communities provides the ideal training conditions. For example, air force captain Troy Thomas recommends MOUT training in "our own blighted cities" where "massive housing projects have become uninhabitable and industrial plants unusable. Yet they would be nearly ideal for combat-in-cities training."[85] Thus, the city is not only racialized but also militarized, or perhaps more accurately, because the city is racialized, it is more intensely militarized. MOUT transforms the domestic city into an intranational military zone, where personnel are trained to combat foreign fighters by practicing on racialized and economically marginalized U.S. communities. The racial targeting of "enemy" domestic populations suggests that the metaphor of *homeland* is one that "valorizes a privileged national population of exurbanites and suburbanites, separated from racialized Others in both U.S. cities and colonial frontiers."[86]

The militarized barrio in *blu* reflects the historical process of urban re/structuring and attendant spatial processes of gender and racial formation. Given the play's possible setting in either Los Angeles or San Antonio, I focus here on the processes of militarization that are specific to Los Angeles but evident in other barrios across the country.[87] *Blu* reminds us that the violence and disorder of the barrio are not endemic to Chicana/o culture; rather, they are the result of deliberate planning and willful neglect, and, as I argue here, they are critical to neoliberal militarism's spatial practices.

Grise's portrayal of the barrio as a zone of chaos and violence implicates its unstated opposite—white suburbia—as a space of peace and order. Although white suburbanization is never referenced in the play, the barrio as a racialized space of violence cannot exist without it. Both urban and rural spaces were concomitantly formed from as early as the mid-nineteenth century, when residential mobility was partially determined by individual preference to live next to certain groups (and not others) and was facilitated by local policy, industrialists' interests, and federal programming. While racially restrictive covenants, redlining practices, and discriminatory federal mortgage-lending practices helped shape racial housing segregation, other policies, such as zoning laws, that concentrated industrialization in nonwhite areas—and in the case of Los Angeles, pushed Mexican American communities and industry to East L.A., transforming the barrio into an industrial district—determined the racial character and economic opportunities within city and suburban spaces.[88]

Larger economic ideologies and policies at the state and national level further shaped the formation of city and suburb. Defense spending during World War II produced enormous wealth, which enabled the government to pay for social welfare programs.[89] This economic philosophy, known as military Keynesianism, expanded and supported (albeit in uneven and iniquitous ways) the safety net for millions of people. Increased levels of military spending, sometimes financed through deficits, helped mitigate the threat of economic recessions until the seventies, when a series of national and international events produced rampant inflation, a rising unemployment rate, and a general economic slowdown.[90] Neoliberal policy makers and political elites attributed the economic crisis to government interference through practices such as social welfare spending and market regulations. The solution to righting the economy, they argued, was to adopt neoliberal policies.[91] The Right's critique of antipoverty programs was also spatialized, as it asserted a link between welfare programs, urban unrest, and the breakdown of the family.[92] Urban blight and rundown housing in ethnic neighborhoods as well as an individual's use of social welfare became a sign of cultural pathology and dependency that stood in contrast to the individual initiative, independence, and work ethic found in the inhabitants of white suburbia.[93] Ruth Wilson Gilmore argues that the Right interpreted urban protests, such as the 1965 Watts Riots in Los Angeles, as a national crime problem that necessitated the logic and tactics of national defense: "The Right had to interpret the turmoil as something it could contain, if elected, using already existing, unexceptionable capacities: the power to defend the nation against enemies foreign and domestic."[94] Moreover, the putative crime wave had "urban and racial qualities," as the racialized inner city and its inhabitants became the target of militarized policing and the prison-industrial complex.

The characters in *blu* are entrapped by the spatial legacies of criminalization, racism, and militarism as they negotiate what Gilmore calls "domestic militarization," or the state's overly aggressive repression of mostly poor people of color and its reliance on prisons as the foundation for this regime of violence.[95] While prison expansion is the state's geographic solution to resolving socioeconomic crises and containing surplus populations, it also contributes to the martial geography of the barrio.[96] The play dramatizes the confrontation with the carceral state when Lunatico, Soledad's thirteen-year-old son, tells Blu about how a police officer at his school arrested him for tagging in the school restroom. The cop arrests Lunatico after finding a blue marker in his pocket. While Blu criticizes the school's lack of funding for replacing broken windows and buying textbooks, Lunatico replies, "but we got enuf money to pay some punk ass cop to worry about me and my gotdamn [*sic*] blue marker?"[97] The brothers' conversation highlights the securitization of public schools and the school-to-prison pipeline, in which the school campus is transformed from a place of learning to one of surveillance and intimidation (the cop "carries a gun. Hits the lockers with the night stick").[98] The scene is also powerful for how it captures the psychological violence of criminalization as Lunatico recounts how the cop and vice principal arrest him in front of his class. The scene is written so that Eme, Lunatico's imprisoned father, co-narrates the moment of detention as he tells Soledad of his own arrest years before. Through an evocative deployment of ensemble narration used to emphasize the shared experience of various characters, Grise depicts repeating cycles of trauma as the family is disrupted by generations of incarceration.[99]

The emphasis on imprisonment also suggests the play's critique of homeland security discourses and exposes the interconnection between discrete spatial scales that makes neoliberal militarism possible. U.S. domestic prisons are often regarded as institutions critical to a liberal democratic society that values law and order.[100] They legitimize the state's use of force while "naturaliz[ing] punishment and death within the 'domestic' domains of the homeland security statecraft."[101] Yet, as Dylan Rodríguez argues, the prison is not and has never been isolated from the global. The prison and the military are not only domestic institutions, but they are also globally mobile modalities of power and violence. The infamous military prisons of the war on terror (the Abu Ghraib prison in Iraq and the Guantanamo Bay detention camp in Cuba) are the unstated analogs to the domestic U.S. prison, illustrating the portability of U.S. incarceration practices. They are also spatially complected. While the media converts the torture of detainees in Abu Ghraib into violent spectacle, the violence within domestic prisons is naturalized through discourses of public safety.[102] In this sense, the domestic prison "provides the discursive exterior space into which the Abu Ghraib tortures are situated." I argue that the prison in *blu* is meant to function as a signifier of the state's regime of power, which relies on the local and global incarceration of threatening brown bodies. Eme's incarceration and Lunatico's imminent detention illustrate how urban penality tracks the Chicano characters in the barrio, circumscribing their mobility and limiting their economic options as they traverse proliferating spaces of detention. Furthermore, the confinement of racialized citizens like Eme is a manifestation of a masculinist protectionist logic, which seeks to defend the sanctified notion of the white home, even as it destroys the homes and families of incarcerated brown and black folk.

Grise uses helicopters to depict the most dramatic forms of barrio militarization. All the barrio's residents are subject to militarized policing, as the repressive sound of a helicopter precedes most scenes in the play.[103] The helicopter functions as a tool of the state's masculinist protection efforts, facilitating state surveillance of internal threats. As "the premier symbol of Los Angeles's capitalized, militarized police force," the helicopter also becomes the omnipresent symbol of militarized urban space.[104] The *Military Operations* manual notes that while the basic combat principles of urban warfare have not changed in the past century, "the introduction of helicopters, fixed-wing aircraft, armor, and precision-guided munitions (PGMs) has altered some of the techniques associated with urban combat."[105] Thus, the helicopter operates within the foreign battlespace and domestic city as a signifier of state power. The helicopter also symbolically collapses the spatial distance between the barrio and the battlefield as we learn that Blu dies when the military helicopter he is riding in is shot down in Iraq. In *blu*, different manifestations of neoliberal militarism's spatial domination appear—in the school, in the prison, in the barrio, and on the battlefield—as a besieged Chicana family is connected through surveillance and death via the ubiquitous helicopter.

AZTLÁN AND THE SEDUCTION OF THE AZTEC WARRIOR MYTH

In Kaplan's examination of the mysticism surrounding the homeland metaphor, she notes that for deracinated individuals, one desires a return not only to the physical land of origin, but also to the mythic origin of one's collective identity.[106] This description of a geo-mythical connection to land perfectly illustrates the Chicano movement's ideological, cultural, and psychic investments in Aztlán. Living in what is now the U.S. Southwest, Aztec ancestors answered the prophetic mandate of the god of war, Huitzilopochtli, to travel to the new homeland of Tenochtitlan, located in modern-day Mexico City. The term began circulating among activists at the 1969 Chicano Youth Liberation Conference in Denver, after the authors of El Plan Espiritual de Aztlán, a political and cultural manifesto of Chicano autonomy, introduced Aztlán as the spiritual homeland of all Chicanas/os. For Chicano nationalists, Aztlán substantiated Chicano historical and material claims to the U.S. Southwest, allowing Chicanos to challenge nativist and xenophobic aspersions against their community and to articulate a connection to the land that superseded the state's practice of tying citizenship to territory. It also helped nationalists forge a collective cultural identity based on a presumed shared indigenous heritage.

The return, in both the physical and the mythical sense, is complicated by the uncanniness of the homeland, the notion that the homeland is haunted by past and future invasions.[107] In Anzaldúa's essay "The Homeland, Aztlán/*El Otro México*," she describes how after three hundred years of Spanish colonialism and a brief period of Mexican self-rule, the former territory of Aztlán encountered another imperial usurper. Beginning with Anglo encroachment into Texas in the 1800s and culminating with the U.S.-Mexico War of 1848, Anzaldúa shows how the ideology of Manifest Destiny led to the legal dispossession of property as well as the extralegal forms of "Anglo terrorism" that included the lynching of Mexicans.[108] This colonial cartography spurred a Chicano nationalist rhetoric of reterritorialization as the concept of Aztlán helped Chicanas/os to "denaturaliz[e] the U.S.-Mexico border, which had been naturalized through the continually vibrant ideology of Manifest Destiny."[109] Yet, the process of denaturalizing the land entailed a militarist response that often repeated the prophetic language of white Manifest Destiny. El Plan's preamble describes the Chicano resistance to the "brutal 'gringo' invasion of our territories" and the need for Chicano "civilizers of the northern land of Aztlán from whence came our forefathers" to reclaim the Southwest.[110] In the authors' description of how "Chicano defense units" will secure reclaimed territory, they employ a militaristic rhetoric of masculinist defense: "The front line defense will come from the barrios, the campos, the pueblos, and the ranchitos. Their involvement as protectors of their people will be given respect and dignity. They in turn offer their responsibility and their lives for their people. Those who place themselves in the front ranks for their people do so out of love and carnalismo."[111] As an urban and rural call to arms, El Plan militarizes the barrio by conceiving it as a "front line" in an intranational battleground.

By emphasizing Aztlán as a material geographic space, some Chicano nationalists adopted gendered notions of property, ownership, and defense that ultimately limited the radical potential of Aztlán as a sign of what Mary Pat Brady calls the movement's "anti-imperial geographic imaginary."[112] In other words, the tropes of invasion and defense often incited a set of practices associated with gendered forms of power and control. While protection can be performed by a man or woman, the implied Chicano "protector" who serves out of a sense of "carnalismo" is presumed to be male. As Young points out, there is a gendered logic behind the practice of protection that originates in the patriarchal household and masks hierarchal relations of inequity and domination.[113] In the passage from El Plan cited earlier, the authors venerate the warrior role by describing how all "protectors" will be respected for their physical sacrifice in service of the community. This selfless behavior must also be considered as a form of pastoral power in which, according to Young, the "gallantly masculine man is loving and self-sacrificing, especially in relation to women" and "readily risks himself in the face of threats from the outside in order to protect the subordinate members of his household."[114] But the protector-protected relationship requires an implicit bargain in which the protected willingly suspend individual liberties, judgment, and, as I argue below, physical mobility in exchange for protection.[115] Thus, in calling forth the ancestral homeland of Aztlán, Chicano nationalists not only called for a symbolic return to mythic origins, but also promoted a vision of modern-day Aztlán as an embattled geography that necessitated the gendered logic of masculinist protection.

Chicanas have long been skeptical of what Young calls the "benign masculinity of protection."[116] Anzaldúa provides a feminist alternative to the Chicano nationalist historiography by arguing that the journey from Aztlán inaugurated the eventual subordination of women. She describes how early Aztec society was, in fact, matrilineal and valued the "balanced duality" of male and female. The move from Aztlán constituted a shift toward patriarchal militarism in the guise of masculinist protectionism. Operating according to the dictates of Huitzilopochtli, the Aztecs "were to guarantee the harmonious preservation of the human race by unifying all the people on earth into one social, religious, and administrative organ. The Aztec people considered themselves in charge of regulating all earthly matters. Their instrument: controlled or regulated war to gain and exercise power."[117] The Aztec's militaristic society was predicated on military power and gratuitous death; it justified its desire for territorial domination by claiming to protect humankind from extinction through the constant sacrifice of human souls. This bloody mandate included the subjugation of both the feminine and women.

Grise skillfully alludes to historical layers of nation building and imperial hubris, showing the different forms that patriarchal violence takes in the quest for territorial expansion. The Aztec history of imperial land grabs is emulated in *blu* at a local level through gang warfare, which also involves territorial acquisition on a smaller scale. For Eme, Blu, and Lunatico, life is circumscribed by the need to defend 204th Street. Gang membership is treated like a male rite of passage, as each character receives his tattoo and experiences or prepares for ritualized initiation into the gang. Eme reminds Soledad that the gang life is indelibly inscribed in their children's lives: "there some things you can't erase. i'm their father, soledad. it's tattooed in skin. . . . family. brotherhood. the streets. those streets are home. they a part of who we is. they run in the veins of my children. their stories are written on the sidewalk."[118] In Eme's view, the gang is an alternative homosocial family whose identity is defined by its relationship to territory. Yet, Soledad refuses to buy into the male fantasy of domination and the gang's appropriation and perversion of kinship bonds maintained by violence. In a later scene, she exposes the gang's façade of ownership when she explains to Lunatico that family and street are not coterminous: "there some people never leave this neighborhood. . . . they start to act like they own it. claiming streets. claiming neighborhoods. like it mean something to our family. to our people. those streets aren't ours. we don't own them. ain't no one come from the streets."[119] Soledad recognizes that for gangs, violence compensates for dispossession, and thus she insists that Lunatico decouple territory from identity.

Rosa Linda Fregoso writes that as a "semiotic terrain, the street is often riddled with contradictions" for Chicanas. It can be a space "that engenders new subjectivities for women," such as *pachucas*, or female gangsters, whose mobility on public streets flaunted the notion that a young woman's proper place was in the home.[120] *Blu* reveals how the barrio streets could be an inhospitable place for women not because the play affirms the home as a safe haven, but because it attempts to critique the violence endemic to patriarchal territorialism. In *blu* the street becomes a male domain of power, patrolled by young men engaged in constant tests of manhood and loyalty, which involve hailing potential rivals with "wutcha claimin? wutcha down for?"[121] The set of questions, often a prelude to conflict, reflect the logic of street politics, which is based on one's ability to possess and protect gang turf. Gemini recounts to Blu her experience of being interrogated on the street by a "group of boys" who asked her, "what's your name? where you from? where you goin? wutcha lookin at? where you live?"[122] The desire to claim streets and to protect them from invading gangs reenacts official state surveillance, as gangs control and dominate inhabitants, particularly women's bodies. Gemini provides a horrific example of this when, in a fragmented prose that reenacts the trauma of violation, she describes being raped on the street:

> GEMINI: closed my eyes. sky black. my body outside this body circling. watched them. a group of homies. move closer. arms reach round me. push me up against the fence. broken pieces of styrofoam. caught. chain linked fence. an old pair of tennis shoes left hanging. throw me to the floor. hard. lie me down. kicked and screamed. they pushed up against my insides.[123]

The street becomes a space of terror as Gemini, who was a girl at the time of the incident, is encircled by a group of "homies" who strengthen their own camaraderie by participating in a collective act of violence. Gemini's body becomes part of the landscape, equated with the trash that litters the sidewalk. Unlike for her brothers and father, the street is not home. Yet, as a casualty of gang war culture, her tragic story is "written on the sidewalk."[124] Implicitly, Gemini's assault is a warning against female mobility in public spaces. Fregoso argues that Chicana domestic confinement, like Western women's immobility in general, is a feature of capitalism's structural segmentation of gendered labor into public and private spheres, where women have been traditionally consigned to perform the private, nonwage labor of child rearing.[125] Chicana territoriality is also rooted in Spanish colonization. Citing the work of Jean Franco, Fregoso explains how the Catholic Church and the Spanish Crown influenced notions of domesticity by promoting the home as a space where Spanish women could be protected from the threat of sexual taint posed by the Moors. Thus, the fear of miscegenation forms the historical basis for later understandings of home and practices of women's confinement. "Masked as a concern for their safety," Fregoso argues, "the confinement of Chicana young women to the home is first and foremost about protecting sexual property and policing sexuality."[126]

The scene of Gemini's assault further challenges the romanticized image of Chicano gang culture propagated in art and film. Within discourses of Chicano nationalism, pachucos, the forebears of the Chicano gangster, "have been celebrated as Chicano heroes, equals in the struggle against domination and conquest to the likes of Aztec warriors and Mexican revolutionaries."[127] The deployment of the Aztec warrior myth often ennobles the pachuco/gangster by changing the discourse from criminality to protectionism and defense.[128] But the Aztec warrior myth can also be read as a cultural narrative that compensates for a history of colonial sexual domination that, as Elizabeth Martínez reminds us, began with a hemispheric rape. For Martínez, this rape shapes a Chicano "colonized mentality" and informs notions of masculine power and politics: "We carry in us, consciously or not, the idea that to be conquered is to be *chingado* (screwed); that to become unconquered requires dominating—even screwing—others."[129] The subtext of this sexual metaphor is that domination is equated with castration. The scene of Gemini's violation underscores how patriarchal institutions (invading armies, gangs, etc.) use violence to control and dominate women's bodies, rendering the homeland a site of trauma.

Importantly, the U.S. military has also recognized the power of the Aztec warrior myth and has studied ways of manipulating Chicano claims to Aztec heritage to militarize disenfranchised youth. In Javier Hernandez's 2003 thesis for the Naval Postgraduate School, "An Exploratory Study of Hispanic Officer Recruiting in the Mexican-American Community of South-Central Los Angeles: Implications for the Officer Corps of the Future," he suggests how the navy can capitalize on the Chicano fascination with Aztec culture. He explains that during the sixties and seventies, "suddenly, Mexican-Americans were proud to associate with the warring Aztecs and deny their Spanish lines."[130] Hernandez then describes how the Aztec "warrior ethos" is currently manifested:

> There are no direct data to support a link between a cultural warrior ethos, inherited from the Spanish Conquistadores or Aztec warriors, yet something may

> exist. Belonging to a warrior group and establishing a solid identity may be some of the attraction that draws many Hispanic youths into gangs. . . . The military offers honor, respect, and a group identity, which are also elements that attract many Hispanic youths into gangs.[131]

Hernandez suggests that Chicanos' "descent from military empires" may explain why "Hispanic high school students have a relatively favorable opinion of the armed forces."[132] This genealogy can then be used to increase and diversify the ranks of the naval officer corps: "For Mexican-American youth, learning about their Spanish and Meso-American warrior ethos may be a source of pride. The Marine Corps has been very successful in appealing to young audiences with imagery of knights fighting dragons. A similar approach using Aztec warriors might also work to specifically attract the attention of Hispanics of Mexican descent."[133] Hernandez identifies these historical antecedents to explain Chicano youth propensities and how these cultural values can be used to support the state's imperialist projects. The fact that the military can appropriate Aztec warrior iconography to appeal to a certain formation of masculinity suggests how patriarchal collectivities, both small and large, operate through similar logics. Even though Hernandez shows how both gangs and the military are in competition for the same pool of recruits, he leaves the premise of violent territoriality unquestioned. Yet his comparative analysis illustrates the portability of masculinist protectionist discourse—that is, its ability to transcend different kinds of collectivities and nationalisms. Through the glorification of a male warrior ethos, the subaltern and antistatist Chicano nationalism—exemplified through Aztec warriors defending Aztlán—is not so different from the military's entreatment on behalf of the state. Thus, masculinist protectionism may serve opposing ends, but it can unify men through appeals to a violent masculinity that presumes the immobility and spatial confinement of women to the home/land.

Hernandez's work marks an important example of the spatial dimensions of military recruitment that targets the desirable demographic of marginalized Latina/o youth. Target marketing, as Caren Kaplan explains, is a spatial practice partially derived from military weapons technology, involving a "geographically based form of classifying neighborhoods through subsets of demographic information."[134] This helps explain why, according to Jorge Mariscal, the U.S. Army Recruiting Command aggressively targets Latinas/os "at about twice their rate in the general population," and why it is no accident that Los Angeles and San Antonio are the army's "top two recruiting battalion areas."[135] Grise portrays the spatial dimensions of military recruitment by depicting the barrio as a critical part of the state's "military labor geography," where spatially marginalized youth, such as Blu, are criminalized and then militarized through predatory recruitment practices.[136] In her attempt to dissuade Blu from enlisting, Hailstorm critiques the ubiquity of recruitment offices in the barrio: "everywhere you fuckin turn in the barrio—recruitment office. diversions game room—recruitment office right next door. south park mall—recruitment office right inside. the movies—recruitment office, same shopping center. not enuf money for books at cha school but there they be. posted outside the cafeteria. recruitment officers. they sellin it, homie. just didn't think you'd be buyin it."[137]

Grise stages a recruitment scene to examine the equivalencies between gangs and the military and to undermine the warrior tradition within the militarized barrio. In the scene, a recruitment officer attempts to tap into Blu's own sense of futility and desire to escape the barrio. He offers Blu the chance to "be a part of something." Blu responds by affirming that he is part of something and that his identity is secured by the gang turf he claims and defends:

> BLU: I'm from here. my homies they from here too. not from over there but from right here.
>
> RECRUITMENT OFFICER: don't you ever dream of leavin? city streets. concrete. bangin. all of it. stop fightin. stop frontin. just be.
>
> BLU: sometimes.[138]

The officer encourages Blu to exchange his street identity for a national identity by participating in a larger national effort that transcends neighborhood turf battles. Through military enlistment, he offers Blu social acceptance, national belonging, and relief from the fatigue of having to constantly perform a violent gang masculinity. He also gives the false promise of escaping violence, for in reality, Blu merely exchanges the insecurity of the barrio streets for that of the battlefield in Iraq. Blu is attracted to the idea of leaving the confining space of the barrio but questions the war itself. He tries to rationalize his decision by providing a list of reasons to Hailstorm: "healthcare. education. benefits. they don't sell that shit at the corner store you know." He finally provides what is perhaps the real reason for his decision: "don't wanna wind up dead or in jail. you know. not goin down. not goin down like that." For Blu, the barrio offers limited options for criminalized Chicano youth. Ultimately, Blu expresses what it is like to live in a constant state of insecurity: "been at war my whole life: i fight it here or i fight there. all the same."[139]

Hailstorm, however, recognizes the gravity of Blu's decision and tries to convince him to change his mind. When Blu defends his choice by describing the military as a "brotherhood," Hailstorm responds by pointing out that Blu is merely exchanging one gang identity for another:

> BLU: the military is like a brotherhood. forever. always faithful.
>
> HAILSTORM: is a gang. shave your head cholo bald. turn in your colors for a uniform. get a new tat. it's not like you doin different. is still a gang blu. and 'sides we at war.[140]

For Hailstorm, gangs and the military are both institutions that practice similar rituals of induction. The major difference is the military's capacity for killing and the state sanctioning of its violence. Hailstorm also attempts to expose the false conception of family that patriarchal collectivities reproduce. She insists that Blu has a family who loves him. But Blu (and Lunatico) refuses to accept the new queer family that Soledad and Hailstorm have created. Both boys constantly reject Hailstorm, ridiculing her for trying to be a "man" or for trying to replace their father. Blu prefers the promised "brotherhood" of the military and tells Hailstorm, "this ain't my house. not here wich you."[141] In the end, Blu and Lunatico reject the queer family because, in their view, it lacks a patriarch; instead, they search for the restoration of male power in gangs and the military.

UN DESMADRE EN AZTLÁN: SPATIALIZING VIOLENCE ON THE BODY AND IN THE HOME

In his description of Aztlán, Luis Leal explains how it represented a "paradisiacal region where injustice, evil, sickness, old age, poverty, and misery do not exist."[142] Yet, for many Chicano nationalists living in the U.S. Southwest during the sixties and seventies, the lost paradise of Aztlán was more like a dystopic wasteland. Rodolfo "Corky" Gonzales, in his popular movement poem "I am Joaquín: an Epic Poem, 1967," memorably describes how Joaquín, the emblematic Chicano, is "Lost in a world of confusion, / Caught up in a whirl of a / gringo society" and struggles to maintain his cultural identity in the face of "American social neurosis, / sterilization of the soul."[143] His poem catalogs the Chicanos' fall from glory, as the once proud descendants of Aztec kings now "lengthen / the line at the welfare door / and fill the jails with crime."[144] Rudolfo Anaya's retrospective analysis of the movement confirms the social malaise that Gonzales decries: "It was a time when we saw our community assaulted by poverty and oppression; the denigrating effects of racism ate away at our pride and stamina. Assimilation, on the other hand, only raised false hopes for our people, so it was a time of crisis."[145] In increasingly alarmist terms, Anaya goes on to explain how Chicano nationalists felt that "unless we re-established the covenants of our ancestors our culture was threatened with extinction."[146] The discourses of real and perceived existential crisis and extinction projected an overwhelming sense of fear that animated the call for masculinist protectionism. Concomitantly, the rhetoric of crisis and fear elevated the family home to a sacred place of refuge and rejuvenation. The Chicano family home became a haven within the occupied homeland, and in this nested sanctuary reigned the Chicana mother, who not only embodied cherished cultural values, but also inculcated them in her children. For example, in "I am Joaquín," Gonzales introduces us to a nameless maternal figure, the emotional center of the home, whose eyes become "a mirror of all the warmth / and all the love for me."[147] This maternal fountain of warmth and love is critical to Chicano nationalist discourses of defense because it is her presence in the home that makes it worth defending.

I characterize the deteriorating social conditions as *un desmadre*, a colloquialism that, in a Chicano context, describes a violent, chaotic world that disorients and enervates individuals. Alvin Korte describes how the term is a shorthand for the phrase "Te voy a partir de tu madre (I will tear you from your mother)."[148] He goes on to explain its psychological significance: "To threaten a child or another person with *Te voy a partir la [de tu] madre* is ominous because it represents being deprived of one's mother, her love, nurturance, and, worse, life itself. . . . In this sense, *desmadre* becomes the horrific representative of a threat, a deep, menacing, gnawing fear of being swallowed up by unknown dangers."[149] The term's etymology is a telling indicator of how the culture venerates the mother's role in maintaining the social and psychological well-being of the individual. This veneration produces a one-dimensional and semisacred figure whose self-abnegation is a voluntary and natural quality necessary to maintaining the spiritual and emotive needs of the family.

I propose that we regard *desmadre* as a spatial term that helps us understand the relationship between gender and space, and that further draws the parallels between state and Chicano nationalist discourses of defense. In other words, the mother's spatial confinement to the home provides the emotional and psychological comfort that justifies and fortifies masculinist defense. For the authors of El Plan, protecting the family home was so important that it became one of the organizational goals of the movement: "Our cultural values of life, family, and home will serve as a powerful *weapon* to defeat the gringo dollar value system and encourage the process of love and brotherhood."[150] The weaponization of the family home is premised on the mother's ability to provide emotional comfort ("warmth and love") and cultural rejuvenation in the face of "gringo" capitalism and assimilative pressures. The emotional labor she performs endows the home space with meaning. Alternatively, her absence, or the un-mothering of the home, portends cultural abandonment and social disequilibrium.

In *blu*, Grise subjects the Chicano family home to external and internal forms of violence as the characters navigate a dystopic setting that threatens to overwhelm them. Soledad's desire and inability to protect her children is a recurring theme in the play. Violence in the form of gang drive-by shootings permeates the walls of her house and destabilizes the notion of home as refuge. As bullets "ricochet off walls," Eme advises that they put the children's mattresses on the floor. Soledad tells Eme: "not gonna teach my children to be scared in they own house." While Soledad wants Eme to leave the gang life, his illicit gang activities provide the family with meager support yet exposes them to the daily terror of random bullets and street warfare. Every night while at work in a factory, Soledad prays to "diosito santo" to protect her children and rushes home after work to check their beds.[151] Powerless in the face of gang violence and poverty, Soledad relies on prayer and luck to secure her home and family. By prioritizing gang warfare in this scene, Grise suggests that the desmadre in Aztlán is partly self-inflicted. Chicano gangs cannibalize a community already besieged by militarized policing. The pervious walls of the family home further blur the presumed spatial distinction between public and private as gang violence moves from the larger scale of the barrio to the smaller scale of the home.

Soledad's and Eme's powerlessness is an additional critique of masculinist protectionism. If Eme's role is to protect the family from the threats lurking outside, then he fails miserably. Not only does he fail to protect, but he actually becomes an aggressor who puts Soledad's own safety at risk inside the home. At one point, in a bout of drunken hysteria over the ever-present helicopters in the barrio, Eme hits Soledad. Years later, Soledad tells Hailstorm about the incident and tries to rationalize Eme's abuse: "there's that split second. you know. that split second before someone, someone hits you. . . . their body. whole body tenses up. hold it tightly. all the years of anger and rage. disappointment. being looked down on. thought less of. every time they got beat up. beat down. the broken dreams." Soledad recognizes how the daily indignities of economically and politically marginalized communities exacerbate violence in the home. Moreover, she recognizes the cyclical nature of domestic violence when she describes her own father's abuse of her mother: "he'd bite down on his lip. open his hand. And pas. coffee table thrown. TV broken. on the floor. silently. eyes closed fist clenched. pas. pas. pas." However, she vows to stop the cycle when her daughter Gemini is born: "wasn't gonna let her grow up like that. so when he [Eme] got arrested. that was it. that was it. no more. i wuz done."[152] The play's exposure of domestic violence challenges the notion of home security and calls into question women's mobility practices in private and public spaces. Brady explains how "women develop individual mental maps, charting their routes" through "a series of risk-assessment scales" that help them determine that "they are safest at home and most at risk in public." Soledad's experiences demonstrate how these maps "chart the geography of crime incorrectly."[153] In *blu* the home is rendered as a site of overwhelming violence, where women are vulnerable to internal and external forms of danger, thereby making traditional practices of mothering in safety impossible.

The play further undermines idealized notions of home and family on which cultural nationalist and nationalist projects depend. In Fregoso's deconstruction of what she terms the "Chicano familia romance," she explains how early movement activists imagined the Chicano familia as "an indispensable support system capable not only of meeting the needs of its members but also of sheltering them from the violence, exploitation, racism, and abuse perpetrated in the external, public sphere of the Anglo capitalist world."[154] But such idealizations presumed that the home was a safe space for the mother, and that only the "Anglo capitalist world" committed violence—a view that absolved violence within the family. If a mother's presence forestalls disorder and destruction and instead provides love and security, then Soledad represents the impossibility of sustaining such fictions, because she reveals how mothers cannot provide security if they are themselves the target of violence. In this way, *blu* refuses to romanticize the Chicano home and homeland (i.e., Aztlán). Rather, the home becomes a site where disintegrative forces merge to fracture the family.

The play's depiction of *un desmadre en Aztlán* also makes the larger point that neoliberal militarism impedes successful mothering. Soledad's inability to perform the emotional labor of maternal solace for her children endangers not only the Chicano nationalist need for domestic refuge and psychic comfort, but also that of the national security state. Cowen and Gilbert argue that, in the wake of 9/11, public discourse and policy making have increasingly looked toward the family to serve as a "response to and means for managing the anxieties and insecurities generated in and through the War on Terror."[155] Under neoliberal militarism, every family becomes responsible for the economic and emotional welfare of its members. Women in particular perform the emotional labor of providing comfort, sustenance, and moral direction. These acts, performed in the private space of the home, are critical to the social reproduction of self-reliant, economically self-sufficient, and emotionally stable citizens. Soledad's inability to emotionally and physically secure her children undermines the security state's attempts to privatize domestic security and to govern citizens who can properly manage the social anxieties that neoliberal militarism and perpetual warfare generate. In this case, neoliberal militarism fails to achieve the privatization of security because of its own role in fomenting social disorder. The institutions that support neoliberal militarism (the prison-industrial complex, militarized schools, and the U.S. military itself) make the idealized notion of home/land security unattainable. The persistence of Chicano-on-Chicano violence and abusive heteropatriarchal families also contribute to the overall desmadre that ravages the barrio.

In refusing to invisibilize the daily violence women face in the private sphere, *blu* undermines the national fantasy of home as refuge. For the national security state to justify war, it must convince its citizens of the existence of a foreign danger that threatens the security of the national and domestic home. But for the logic of masculinist protectionism to function, the daily occurrences of violence within the home must be elided. In other words, neoliberal militarism requires the *mismapping* of private and public space as sites of violence.[156] In this sense, Grewal argues, the state's war-waging project enables the perpetuation of domestic violence by "suggesting not that home is a site of patriarchal violence but that the home must be protected against it." The exaggeration of a foreign threat enables the state to "externalize danger" by "displac[ing] the violence of the family" onto the racialized Other.[157] *Blu* challenges both the elision of violence and its displacement. Exposing women's daily insecurities deprives the security state of its justification for war. In other words, war is not necessary to protect the home/land from terror if the family home is already a space of terror.

REWRITING MYTH, REWRITING FAMILIA: IN SEARCH OF A CHICANA FEMINIST HOMELAND

Challenging the Aztec warrior myth requires the larger deconstruction of Aztec mythology, particularly the origin stories of war and death that explain the rise of one of the most powerful indigenous empires in the Americas. The founding of the bellicose Aztec society is based on what Jane Caputi calls "Goddess murder," or the killing of the moon goddess Coyolxauhqui (Painted Bells).[158] *Blu* rewrites the myth of Coyolxauhqui's sacrifice—a myth based on attempted matricide, fratricide, female dismemberment, and female betrayal—to challenge the power of patriarchal discourses and the role they play in perpetuating violence. Rewriting myth entails rewriting familia because, as the myth of Coyolxauhqui demonstrates, the origin of war and warrior culture is a broken family.

The details of the Coyolxauhqui myth come to us through the *teocuicatl* (divine song), which was recorded shortly after the Spanish conquest and which narrates the birth of the god of war, Huitzilopochtli. The song describes how the mother goddess, Coatlicue (Serpent Skirt), was sweeping the temple at Coatepec when a ball of feathers fell on her. She placed the ball in her bosom, and after completing her chore, discovered that the ball had disappeared. Unbeknownst to Coatlicue, the ball, which "symbolized divine semen," resulted in an immaculate conception.[159] Upon hearing of their mother's mysterious pregnancy at the temple, Coatlicue's children became upset. Her daughter, Coyolxauhqui, was particularly enraged by her mother's action and incited her four hundred brothers to punish their mother for bringing shame to the family: "My brothers, she has dishonored us, / we must kill our mother, / the wicked woman who is now with child. / Who gave her what she carries in her womb?" Hearing of her children's plot to murder her, Coatlicue becomes "frightened" and "sad."[160] Miraculously, her unborn son, Huitzilopochtli (Southern Hummingbird), also hears of the plot and reassures his mother that he knows what to do. When Coyolxauhqui and her four hundred brothers arrive at the top of Coatepec, Coatlicue gives birth to a fully grown Huitzilopochtli, who is dressed in battle gear. He kills or chases down his brothers and decapitates Coyolxauhqui, throwing her dismembered body down the hill. In their commemoration of this myth, the Aztecs constructed the Templo Mayor, a pyramidal temple dedicated to Huitzilopochtli and Tlaloc, the rain god, in which a large stone disc featuring a carving of Coyolxauhqui's dismembered body lies at the base. In the Aztecs' periodic blood sacrifices of enemy combatants, they would ritually enact the killing of Coyolxauhqui by ripping out the hearts of their captives and then throwing their bodies down the pyramid to land on the Coyolxauhqui Stone.[161] Thus, Coatlicue's pregnancy and Coyolxauhqui's death are at the heart of Aztec discursive and ritualistic practices, demonstrating how the control of and violence against the female body are critical to discourses of war and patriarchy.

Grise weaves mythology into her characters' lives and uses it to structure the plot. In *blu*, there are two Coyolxauhqui figures: Lunatico and Gemini. Lunatico, whose name means both "crazy" and "moon," is more closely aligned with the original mythic portrayal of Coyolxauhqui. Just as Coyolxauhqui disavowed Coatlicue for disturbing the normative structure of the patriarchal family, Lunatico rejects Soledad's attempt to create a new queer family with Hailstorm. Gemini is more overtly identified with Coyolxauhqui. Not only does she dream she is the lunar goddess, but she actively rewrites the myth of Coyolxauhqui. Throughout the play, Gemini sits atop the roof, where she listens to the omnipresent helicopters and imagines a world beyond the barrio. But the roof also doubles as Coatepec, the sacred mountain from which Coyolxauhqui's dismembered body is thrown. Grise dramatizes the moment of Coyolxauhqui's descent by having Gemini dream that she is Coyolxauhqui. With "arms extended in flight," Gemini dives off the roof: "Lights out before she hits concrete."[162] The reenactment of mythic sacrifice is then performed in the violent urban reality of the barrio, when Gemini is raped by a group of homies: "stopped saying no. tears turn to stone. i prayed. lying down on concrete. hard. please lord diosito santo."[163] Like the Coyolxauhqui Stone, which memorializes the goddess's brutal dismemberment, Gemini's violated body is inscribed onto the cold, hard sidewalk. While Blu was not present during the rape, he contributes to Gemini's trauma because he is the only person she tells about it afterward. Rather than offer consolation or even street justice, he stands speechless and refuses to look her in the face ever again. Thus, Blu, a representation of Huitzilopochtli, is implicated in Gemini's spiritual dismemberment. The rape scene underscores how women's bodies have always been vulnerable to violence in warrior cultures.

Gemini refuses to be a victim, however, and thus actively rewrites the Coyolxauhqui myth to imagine a more empowering future for herself, her family, and her barrio. She rejects Chicano cultural nationalism's tendency to sexualize women's roles in Aztec mythology when she tells Hailstorm, "i don't wanna be no aztec princess."[164] Instead, she embraces the identity of Coyolxauhqui and authors a new reading of female sacrifice, becoming what Laura Pérez calls a Chicana *tlamatini*, the Nahuatl term used to describe the scribes who recorded and deciphered the glyphs and codices of the Nahua ancestors.[165] She tells Lunatico, "i'm rewriting the myth. clipped his wings. because this time i do not die. this time he was the ultimate sacrifice. i cut out and eat his heart. even if more a moment, the war will end. the moon will swim. i've been dead too long. we've been dead too long, luna. i'm gonna resurrect. gonna resurrect me. not gonna die.

not this time, not gonna go down like that."[166] In Gemini's revision, Coyolxauhqui kills Huitzilopochtli and becomes the victor in the mythological sibling rivalry. But Coyolxauhqui's victory is not a triumphant reversal of power for selfish gain or a celebration of violence. Rather, she implies that it is necessary to kill Huitzilopochtli to end war and upend patriarchal violence. In other words, killing the war god ensures peace. In a poignant reversal of power, Grise equates Blu with the victims of war. Blu's name refers to Huitzilopochtli's battle color as well as to the blue paint victims were covered in before having their hearts ripped out and bodies cast down the temple.[167] Thus, Blu's death also signifies the tragic consequences of imperial hubris; his death represents the thousands of Latina/o soldiers sacrificed to U.S. imperial war. David Carrasco writes that the Aztecs honored warrior death as a way to justify their power: "Death on the battlefield was called *xochimiquiztli* (flowery death), reminiscent of the modern claim that it is 'good and noble to die for one's country.'"[168] Yet, Grise is careful to portray Blu's death not as patriotic sacrifice but as a critique of patriarchal militarism.

As Gemini authors her own future, she also rejects a culture that values death for one that privileges life and rebirth, for the mythic battle between Huitzilopochtli and Coyolxauhqui is also an astral war that pits the sun god against the lunar goddess.[169] In Gemini's account, the moon is associated with the ocean, both of which symbolize rebirth and healing powers. By privileging the triumph of the moon over the bloodthirsty sun, Gemini replaces the ritual of death with one of hope and regeneration. Gemini's rewriting of myth transforms the sky from a space that harbors a constellation of warring factions into a space of possibility; the sun, moon, and stars are no longer guerrilleras locked in ritual combat but vehicles that enable dreaming, self-transformation, and healing. Gemini's sanguine retelling of goddess rebirth (in contrast to "Goddess murder") marks her as a true Chicana tlamatini, for, as Moraga explains, "the scribe's task is to interpret the signs of the time, read the writing on the barrio walls, decode the hieroglyphs of street violence, unravel the skewed message of brown-on-brown crime and sister-rape."[170]

Gemini's resurrection denies a violent mythology predicated on dismemberment of its required female victim. Her spiritual death cannot be used in service of imperial power and patriarchal militarism. Instead, she exhibits an oppositional subjectivity that pushes back against prevailing expectations when she defiantly declares that she is "not gonna go down like that." I want to further insist that we read Gemini's revisionist mythmaking as a spatial practice, one that welds material and discursive spaces together. As Linda Flores explains, Chicana feminists have a history of revising and creating new narratives to construct a discursive space and home. If marginalized communities are beset by a public discourse that denigrates them, then "repudiating mainstream discourse and espousing self- and group-created discourse" becomes a way to recoup and revalue one's cultural and gendered identity. This act of discursive creation helps sustain and validate Chicanas' bruised and violated psyches. Flores contends, "When Chicana feminists refuse to accept mainstream definitions of themselves and insist that they establish and affirm their own identity, they build a space through discourse."[171] Moreover, once they establish this space, "they begin to turn it into a home where connections to those within their families are made strong." I read Gemini's (and ultimately Grise's) rewriting of the Coyolxauhqui myth as a repudiation of misogynistic discourse propagated not by the mainstream, but by Chicanos themselves, that opens up a discursive space for Chicanas to exercise the affirmatory power of self-authorship. Sitting on her rooftop perch, Gemini practices a form of revisionist mythmaking that reorients the meaning of the material and the metaphorical landscapes of Aztlán. That is, by rejecting the brutality of "Goddess murder" and the violent patriarchal territorialism that it instates, Gemini imagines a demilitarized Aztlán, one that is absent of imperial mastery and petty turf wars, of female confinement and immobility. Rather than abandon the idea of home and the comfort it connotes, she reimagines it as a liberatory and welcoming space. Unlike the Chicano nationalist ideal of home, this Chicana feminist home does not require maternal confinement, does not necessitate masculinist protectionism, does not condone domestic violence, and, finally, allows for the redefinition of families. Thus, rewriting myth entails the simultaneous rewriting of space and family. What Grise offers us through the mythical vision of a teenage Chicana from the barrio is nothing short of a "Chicana feminist homeland."[172]

Virginia Grise's *blu* exposes the constructedness of home and homeland to expose neoliberal militarism's dissimulative practice of producing spaces and subjectivities in often unacknowledged ways. In its depiction of a post-9/11 Chicano barrio under siege, *blu* attributes the immobility and control of characters to state practices of spatial injustice and to patriarchal policing of women's bodies. Ultimately, the play allows us to see how militarization and patriarchal territorialism—whether propagated by the state or by cultural nationalists—relies on and requires women's spatial subordination. Thus, perhaps it is fitting that Gemini develops a critical spatial awareness while being untethered from the ground, for when she sits atop her family home, she envisions new forms of attachment to land and space in contradistinction to both neoliberal militarism's spatial logic and the Chicano nationalist reterritorialization of a mythic homeland. Rather than embrace an uncritical celebration of a warrior culture that affirms male power and violence, Gemini provides a proleptical glimpse into the demilitarization of Aztlán.

In this chapter I have identified neoliberal militarism's spatial logic and how Latina mothers are militarized through the spatial practices of scaling. In other words, neoliberal militarism not only militarizes space, but also functions by connecting different spaces together in ways that promote the sociospatial formation of militarized subjectivities. I have focused on the body, the home, and the homeland as three interlocking sites of subject formation that undergird the logic of national security. We have seen, for instance, how Latina fertility changes status as it moves from biological threat to national resource. While neoliberal militarism relies on the separation of distinctly gendered spaces, it also embraces contradictions to expand and strengthen its ideological reach. Thus, the family home—revered as the mother's pacific domain and sequestered from the male world of warfare—is simultaneously a site of military induction, where mothers inculcate militarized values to future generations. The state's reliance on mothers reveals how it privatizes and outsources militarism to mothers like Malkin's security mom, a woman who vigilantly prepares her children for imminent danger: "We have educated our 4-year-old daughter about Osama bin Laden and Saddam Hussein. She knows that there are bad men in the world trying to kill Americans everywhere."[173] But Patricia Hill Collins would have us remember that motherhood is "both dynamic and dialectical."[174] While the state desires the kind of militarized mothering that supports its objectives, women can and often do practice a demilitarized form of motherhood. The methods of this practice differ, but they can include denunciating the seductive embrace of militarized citizenship. It can include a rejection of the state's obtrusive gaze and of patriarchy's immobilizing practices. It can entail critiquing the homeland and the role of masculinist protectionism in women's spatial subordination. Finally, it must involve reclaiming the home as a safe space where women can mother in personal security (not on behalf of national security), and where they can socialize children to value an ethics of nonviolence.

CONCLUSION

Oneiric Futures

Until we are all represented, respected, and protected by society and the laws that govern it, the status of the Chicana will be that of a countryless woman.

ANA CASTILLO, *MASSACRE OF THE DREAMERS*

Men think women have no love of country, that the desire for nation is a male prerogative.

CHERRÍE MORAGA, *THE HUNGRY WOMAN*

Although most feminists are highly critical of political violence, few are committed to absolute pacifism.

KIMBERLY HUTCHINGS, "SIMONE DE BEAUVOIR AND THE AMBIGUOUS ETHICS OF POLITICAL VIOLENCE"

IN ANA CASTILLO'S COLLECTION of essays *Massacre of the Dreamers: Essays on Xicanisma* (1995), she muses on the figure of the "countryless" Chicana. For Castillo, a Chicana's allegiance to a country is conditioned on her access to the full protections enjoyed by all rights-bearing citizens. Regardless of a Chicana's desire for national belonging, the state's disenfranchisement and disavowal of the Chicana renders her citizenship negligible. But the Chicana's status as a "countryless woman" does not mean that she does not harbor attachments to the land. Castillo notes that if she were literally exiled, "the core of my being would long for a return to the lands of my ancestors." Her "ethereal spirit" and "collective memory" would "yearn to *claim* these territories as homeland."[1] Castillo's countryless Chicana suggests the close relationship between the body and the nation, for it is in and through the body that desires, longings, and yearnings for national and cultural national belonging are (re)produced and manifested.

Interestingly, Castillo's reflection on the countryless Chicana is sparked by U.S. poet Adrienne Rich's reference to British modernist Virginia Woolf. Castillo begins her essay with an epigraph from Rich's "Notes toward a Politics of Location," which cites Woolf's polemic *Three Guineas* (1938). In that book, Woolf mounts a feminist critique of women's social, political, and economic marginalization. *Three Guineas* is also a pacifist critique of war, written using an epistolary conceit. Woolf responds to a male interlocutor who asks Woolf for her thoughts on how to prevent war and solicits her donation to the society for which he is treasurer.[2] For Woolf, the marginalization of women (their inability to obtain education and their economic dependence on men) generates women's different views on nationalism and patriotism and thus distinguishes their perspective from men on the value of warfare. Given the society's gender division, she suggests establishing a society for the daughters of educated men called the "Outsider's Society."[3] This society would promote an end to war using its members' limited modes of power, including indifference to patriotic appeals, which, she argues, have no purchase on women who are barred from the full privileges of citizenship. If the outsider were ever to be told by a man, "I am fighting to protect our country," Woolf imagines the outsider's response would be to ask, "What does 'our country' mean to me an outsider?" Indeed, the outsider's sense of alienation is so great that it would prompt her to declare, "As a woman, I have no country. As a woman, I want no country. As a woman, my country is the whole world."[4]

Castillo's adaptation of Woolf asks us to consider what "our country" means to Chicanas, who are often outsiders because of their racial, ethnic, gender, sexual, and class identities. The answer to the question is central to understanding Chicanas' views on war and militarism, because the willingness to serve in the military often presumes a feeling of obligation to one's country and usually a desire for national belonging and acceptance. While Woolf's outsider "want[s] no country," the same cannot be said for many Chicanas and Latinas. Gina Pérez, in her ethnographic study of Latina/o youth in Lorain, Ohio, introduces us to several Latina teens who are enrolled in their high school's Junior Reserve Officer Training Corps (JROTC) program and who negotiate the daily cultural experiences and national definitions of citizenship. Pérez's important work lays out the multiple and competing notions of service and citizenship that inform Latinas' views on national belonging and identity. She explains that young Latinas are motivated to enlist for many reasons, including economic mobility, college tuition assistance, travel, and a respect for family military legacies. Pérez's respondents also describe their desire to challenge the stigmatization of criminalized Latina/o youth by seeking affirmative public recognition through JROTC participation. Clearly, the desire for autonomy, self-mastery, and a basic sense of dignity often compels young Latinas to consider military service. Pérez's work is a critical reminder that Latina youth exercise their agency in different ways, as "they strategize, aspire, and organize their social worlds with the limited resources available to them." For many of them, military service is a primary way to "create meaningful and economically secure lives for themselves, their families, and their communities."[5]

Bodies at War reflects Chicanas' complex and heterogeneous views on war and militarism while also showing that nationalism engenders violence and that women are particularly vulnerable to violence committed by and in the name of the state. This book reconfirms and illustrates Chandra Mohanty's incisive description of how "nation-states invent and solidify practices of racialization and sexualization of their peoples, disciplining and mobilizing the bodies of women, especially poor and third world women, as a way of consolidating patriarchal and colonizing processes."[6] Advanced capitalist states, like the United States, monopolize and deploy violence in the name of national security.[7] Given the state's historical and continued use of violence against its own citizens as well as against peoples abroad, *Bodies at War* implores us to examine Chicana desires for national belonging through military service within the broader context of state-sanctioned violence and to grapple with the material, political, and ethical consequences of women's participation in war.

Women are not only subject to violence, but also subjects of violence—a fact that is often hard to accept. For example, in Woolf's defense of women's pacifism, she argues, "Scarcely a human being in the course of history has fallen to a woman's rifle."[8] Woolf explains to her male interlocutor that fighting has always been men's habit, not women's, and that this gender-based difference makes it impossible for women to understand the motivations for war: "Obviously there is for you some glory, some necessity, some satisfaction in fighting which we have never felt or enjoyed. Complete understanding could only be achieved by blood transfusion or memory transfusion."[9] Viewed from our current moment, Woolf's statements seem like naïve descriptions of a more simplified gender order. They seemingly question women's capacity for committing violence and thus provide women with a false sense of moral distance from the destructive effects of warfare. If it were ever true that no one had died from a "woman's rifle," that claim is impossible to make now. In response to Woolf's contention and to the U.S. use of torture on detainees in the war on terror, Cuban American performance artist and scholar Coco Fusco examines women's relationship to violence in *A Field Guide for Female Interrogators* (2008). Fusco asserts that there are "more American women waging war these days than there are those who try to prevent it."[10] Fusco's direct address to Woolf focuses on the military's deployment of female interrogators and how the tactics they use specifically rely on their female bodies and sexuality. Fusco begins by framing her inquiry with a discussion about the leaked photographs from the U.S. military prison in Abu Ghraib, Iraq, in which U.S. servicemen and women were seen posing with the tortured, sexually humiliated, or dead bodies of Iraqi detainees. She focuses on the image of servicewomen as co-perpetrators of torture, who were sometimes referred to as either "young, naïve white women" or "torture chicks" in the media. Their presence in the photos led Fusco to explore how the state actively compels female intelligence officers "to deploy sexuality as a weapon."[11] She describes how women are expected to use their bodies in various tactical ways to elicit information from Muslim detainees. These tactics include a variety of positions and proximities that deploy female sexual exhibitionism and aggression to help the officer establish dominance and control.[12] Fusco shows how these tactics are "aimed at 'breaking' detainees by means of an open attack on their masculinity."[13] Her account demonstrates that the military has figured out a way to use the female body for more than its symbolic power in popular discourse. It now weaponizes women's bodies and uses them as a tactical form of physical and psychological torture. Fusco attempts to understand how our culture's emphasis on seeing women only as victims combined with the feminist movement's insistence on women's freedom to express their sexuality and desires have contributed to the public's lack of outrage over women's participation in sexual torture. Fusco attributes this lack of outrage to our failure to imagine violent uses of female sexuality: "We don't really have a language for comprehending female sexual aggression as rape, which diminishes our ability to perceive it as such."[14]

Women's participation in state violence is easy to overlook given the way a militarized liberal feminism attempts to frame the issue of women in the military. The past six years have seen a paradigm shift in how the state and dominant society view women's capacity to soldier. In 2010, Congress voted to end the military's policy of "Don't ask, don't tell," which prohibited gay, lesbian, and bisexual service members from openly declaring their sexual orientation. As Elizabeth Hillman notes, this punitive policy was particularly detrimental to women, whose mere "appearance in uniform and career choice [could] trigger charges of lesbianism" and subsequent discharge from the military. Hillman explains that "lesbian-baiting" was then "used to silence, control, and intimidate women who report sexual assault and harassment or otherwise challenge male behavior within the military."[15] In 2013, Defense Secretary Leon Panetta announced lifting the combat exclusion policy. The repealed ban opened up new military occupations and career opportunities for servicewomen, along with access to the full benefits and honors that come with them. In 2016, the new defense secretary Ashton Carter announced that transgender service members would now be able to serve openly and that the military would pay for their gender transition–related health care. The next major military milestone will be requiring women to register for Selective Service. In 2016, the U.S. Senate passed a bill mandating that women turning eighteen years old on or after January 1, 2018, register for potential military service. The bill currently awaits a vote in the House of Representatives, where it is expected to pass after vigorous debate.

For militarized liberal feminists, these incremental shifts in military policy are victories in the struggle to achieve gender parity and equal access. For example, Terry O'Neill, president of the National Organization for Women (NOW), was an early advocate for repealing the combat exclusion policy: "Women in the military are exposed to the same kind of dangers that combat service exposes a soldier to, but the difference is that the women are not getting combat pay, and they're not getting combat-related opportunities for promotion." O'Neill goes on to argue that "it's only fair to recognize that women belong, as much as men do, in combat units."[16] The American Civil Liberties Union (ACLU), another champion of women's rights, has also supported women's access to all combat specialties. It has filed several lawsuits over the years on behalf of servicewomen who claimed that the prohibition against women serving aboard ships or in ground combat units is a violation of their constitutional rights. In testimony before Congress, ACLU representatives have stated, "Men do not have a monopoly on patriotism, physical ability, desire for adventure, or willingness to risk their lives. Until both the responsibilities and the rights are shared on a gender-neutral basis, women will continue to be considered less than full-fledged citizens."[17]

Taken together, these statements from NOW and the ACLU represent a militarized version of liberal feminism that views combat as a means of career advancement rather than state-sanctioned violence. From this perspective, the debate over women's service is primarily about equal access and fair compensation. It is also about removing barriers to personal choice and self-determination.

Thus, this brand of liberal feminism aligns neatly with neoliberal militarism, as both ideologies emphasize the freedom to choose and place a premium on individual merit and personal responsibility. Importantly, both are intensely concerned with the measuring, disciplining, and physical capacities of women's bodies. For example, the argument for women's inclusion in combat rested on three points: first, that women could meet comparable physical standards required of men; second, that servicewomen were already being exposed to injury and death in the field of battle, and therefore it was only fair that they receive equal compensation and employment opportunity for that risk; and third, that women could and did display a "willingness to risk their lives" for their country.[18] Unlike Woolf's disaffected outsider, liberal feminists argued that "men do not have a monopoly on patriotism" and that servicewomen had voluntarily proved, and continued to prove, their national loyalty through bodily sacrifice.

Bodies at War has shown that liberal feminism's embrace of militarism avoids the more urgent ethical implications of gender equality in the military. While I have examined texts like *Peacetime* and *Captain Mama*, which view women's inclusion as a way to obtain self-empowerment and first-class citizenship, I have also insisted that we not lose sight of war's multiple casualties. We can agree that a series of complex factors often motivates women to enlist, but we must also acknowledge that as the state's most expansive and destructive arm of power, the military is not a neutral institution for self-improvement and gender equality. Even while military service has enabled marginalized groups to achieve significant social advances, those advances come with a cost—occupation, displacement, oppression, and death for someone else, somewhere else.

In some ways, the militarized liberal feminist focus on the fitness, endurance, and strength of women's bodies deflects attention away from the purpose of such physical training. Moreover, perhaps without fully appreciating it, militarized liberal feminists have helped open up women's lives to more opportunities to experience and engage in violence and even death through their advocacy for women's participation in combat. When Congress requires women to register for Selective Service—which many military observers believe is an eventuality—women in the coming generations will no longer have the choice to serve in times of national crisis. They will be compelled to register under the threat of economic sanctions, heavy fines, and criminal prosecution.[19] More importantly, they will experience what Kathleen Barry calls an expendable life.[20] For Barry, mandated Selective Service registration is a state-sanctioned depreciation of men's lives, which requires them to accept the possibility of injury, death, or taking life on the state's behalf. It is an involuntary form of self-sacrifice tied to an aggressive notion of masculinity that requires men to suppress their own valuation and their internal prohibitions against harming others. Barry pointedly asserts that the experience of expendability potentially alters men's moral and ethical compass, as the socially accepted "devaluation of their lives and their own fear make disconnection safer than compassion, violence more realistic than connection."[21] Expendability has also become normalized as a "natural" transition from innocence to obligation, as young men are socialized to view registration as a requirement of manhood. My main point here is to consider how future generations of women will experience the social and ethical implications of expendability. How will the potential for compulsory service redefine notions of femininity? How will women reorient themselves to state violence? How will this reorientation manifest itself in our personal and interpersonal relationships and alter our ethical values? We have seen how Chicana antidraft activists have been at the forefront of challenging the state's practice of military induction on ethical grounds. Their use of affective and embodied modes of protest should serve as emulative examples as we confront the military's expanding definition of potentially draft-eligible individuals.

Sadly, many Latinas have already experienced the violence of military expendability. In journalist Lizette Alvarez's report about the death of Lieutenant Emily J. T. Perez, a platoon leader who was killed by a roadside bomb in Baghdad on September 12, 2006, Alvarez noted, "Despite longstanding predictions that America would shudder to see its women coming home in coffins, Lieutenant Perez's death, and those of other women . . . have stirred no less—and no more—reaction at home than the nearly 2,900 male dead." Alvarez cites military sociologist Charles Moskos's rationale for the apparent lack of public response: "The public doesn't seem concerned they are dying. . . . They would rather have someone else's daughter die than their son."[22] Just as the general public seems to be unsurprised by women's participation in torture, it is also inured to the death of servicewomen. While I am not suggesting that there *should* be more outrage over women's deaths than men's, I am highlighting these moments as a turning point in larger cultural narratives about women's vulnerability and traditional status as victims. More importantly, this shift in public sentiment signals the ethical failure of militarized liberal feminism's short-sighted push for gender equity. By arguing that "women belong, as much as men do, in combat," this kind of promilitary feminism avoids a larger critique of U.S. war policy and neoliberal militarism's corrosive effects on citizenship, rights, and democracy.[23]

We have largely moved away from Woolf's essentialist biological views on violence to a political, if not social, embrace of militarized liberal feminism. Now, more than ever, we must draw on critical Chicana feminist imaginaries that offer a nonviolent future. In *Bodies at War*, I have assembled a partial genealogy of Chicana authors, activists, and artists who have challenged neoliberal militarism and have dared to reimagine the meaning and value of nationalism. In what remains, I incorporate Latina and Chicana artists Favianna Rodriguez and Nao Bustamante, whose work recuperates the soldadera figure as part of a Chicana feminist antiwar ethic and aesthetic. Their work reveals the contradictions encoded in the soldadera icon and points toward a tactics of resistance that can help us collectively undermine the project of neoliberal militarism.

Afro-Peruvian American printmaker, visual artist, and activist Favianna Rodriguez creates work that is largely inspired by the tradition of Chicano protest art from the sixties and seventies, in its mode and internationalist appeal to anti-imperialist solidarity. Her 2007 print *Resist U.S. Imperialism* (figure 10) reflects the aesthetic and political influence of earlier Chicana/o artists, including Rupert García.[24] Like García's *¡Fuera de Indochina!*, Rodriguez's work implies an internationalist appeal for anti-imperialist solidarity, as it boldly compares the Chicano homeland to the Iraq battlefield. The statement that "Iraq is Aztlan" wills into existence a solidarity between never-before-paired collectivities whose primary basis for unity is the shared experience of and resistance to U.S. imperialism. By establishing this connection, the soldadera implicitly calls for an ethical identification with Iraqi victims of the U.S. war machine—a call that is both a mandate and an obligation to defy wartime nationalism. In simple imperative statements, the viewer is commanded to act, in addition to feel, against neoliberal militarism. Rodriguez's strategic focus on a nameless soldadera—the everywoman of the Mexican Revolution—instead of the more recognizable Emiliano Zapata highlights women's marginalized history of agency while also summoning a Chicana viewership to identify with the soldadera. Thus, the piece is a specific gendered appeal to Chicanas to oppose U.S. war policy. Just as Chicana activists from the sixties and seventies reinterpreted the soldadera icon to construct what Blackwell calls "an alternative genealogy" of Chicana agency, Rodriguez has done the same for a new generation by reframing her soldadera as an antiwar figure opposed to U.S. imperialism in the Middle East.[25]

Rodriguez's soldadera is an incredibly complex figure because she is not only an antiwar symbol but also a warrior. The soldadera's cartridge belts and saber also remind us of the subject-making potential of violence. The soldadera figures

FIGURE 10. *Resist U.S. Imperialism*, screen print by Favianna Rodriguez, 2007. Used with permission.

in *Peacetime* and *Erased Faces*, as well as Chicana Iraq War veteran Mickiela Montoya, demonstrate how weaponry signifies agency and power for women who are trained in specialized forms of violence. The soldadera in Rodriguez's work is called upon to be a "warrior for [her] people" and thus to partake in Chicano nationalism's masculinist protectionism—a form of defense that, as we have seen, often leads to the sociospatial subordination of women and a warrior mentality that justifies male dominance. The weaponry and the warrior rhetoric visually and discursively privilege violence as the primary and most effective means of opposition. While Rodriguez is not calling for Chicanas/os to literally take up arms, the symbols of violence unintentionally replicate the violent rhetorics that states and subaltern militants use to perpetuate war. As bell hooks argues, to fight militarism, "we must resist the socialization . . . that tells us violence can be eliminated with violence."[26] Rodriguez's soldadera reminds us how difficult it is—yet vitally necessary—to disassociate from prevailing notions of resistance. Chicana authors and activists have shown that violence only further perpetuates injustice, oppression, and more violence. In addition to promoting our ethical detachment from others, violence undercuts any sense of liberation and autonomy it might produce.

Like the Zapatistas, we are obligated to rethink militarism as a model of opposition. The Latina antiwar activist-in-trenzas from Lorna Dee Cervantes's poem "Coffee" has shown us how we can deploy different modes—like the pen, the video, and the computer—to challenge state power rather than reflexively resort to the use of resistant violence. If we are to move beyond war, we need to unlearn, defamiliarize, and denaturalize the symbols of violence that normalize war and militarism and instead create new feminist antiwar imaginaries that draw on symbolic repertoires of nonviolent resistance. Because Rodriguez's soldadera is encoded with contradictory stances on violence, she makes the ideal starting point for imagining a way out of war's paradigm. For these reasons, I consider Rodriguez's *Resist U.S. Imperialism* to be a bold, compelling, yet initial gesture toward a nonviolent, peace-affirming Chicana antiwar activism and aesthetics.

Chicana performance artist Nao Bustamante has also translated the early twentieth-century soldadera's experience into a feminist antiwar message for a new audience. Her 2015 multimedia exhibit *Soldadera* mixes historical artifact with video reenactments and modern re-creations of outfits worn by soldaderas. The installation includes a group of five headless mannequins wearing Edwardian-style dresses that were designed based on photos of soldaderas from the Mexican Revolution. Each of the dresses, along with a rebozo or shawl, which hangs draped on a wall, is made of Kevlar, a synthetic fiber used in bulletproof vests. In contrast to Rodriguez's cross-dressing soldadera in sombrero and bandoleers, Bustamante offers us the other garb more typically worn by soldaderas: floor-sweeping cotton dresses as well as the versatile and utilitarian rebozo, which was perfect for carrying food, supplies, and babies slung onto one's back. This difference in uniform highlights the roles and gender expectations of the time, which included modesty and refinement. Bustamante's historically accurate combat dresses also highlight the inappropriateness of the soldadera's garments. We can surmise how the constrictive dresses were ill suited for the long slogs in harsh Mexican terrain and probably increased women's exposure to harm by hindering mobility. In one sense, the out-of-placeness of the Edwardian combat dresses signals the Mexicana's and Chicana's long struggle of trying to accommodate to the sartorial demands of war and the notion of inclusion and citizenship that military uniforms represent. Both Rodriguez's bandoliered soldadera and Bustamante's Edwardian combat dresses depict antecedents of the Chicana body that struggle to achieve full legibility as representatives of nationalism or cultural nationalism. Whether it is the menstruating Chicana body in boot camp, who learns how to apply military cosmetics; the huipil-wearing Zapatista insurgent, who wears boots for the first time; the Chicana mother air force pilot in her green flight suit; or the Chicana/Latina bodies in military recruitment ads who wear the blood stripe of U.S. imperialism on their dress uniforms, we have seen how the Chicana/Mexicana/Latina body accommodates itself to military garb with varying levels of success and failure.

Part of Bustamante's exhibit includes "Test Shoot for 'Tierra y Libertad'" (2012), a short video that features Bustamante and a gun expert shooting one of the combat dresses with period weapons and calibers somewhere in the snowy environs of upstate New York (figure 11). The video begins with the following question in white letters against a black screen: "How would a woman fighting in the Mexican Revolution stand up to the weaponry of 1910 . . . If she were clad in an Edwardian combat dress made of bullet resistant Kevlar®?"[27] The answer is: not very well. While the dress successfully stops the lead bullets of a six-shot .45 Colt revolver, it does not repel the seven-millimeter bullet of a Remington Rolling Block rifle. The bullet easily penetrates the Kevlar chest bib and remains lodged in the bodice. After Bustamante shoots and metaphorically kills the soldadera with a variety of different guns, the dress is left riddled with holes, gunpowder, and embedded lead bullets. For Bustamante, the test shoot is not merely

FIGURE 11. "Test Shoot for *Tierra y Libertad*," mannequin in soldadera dress made of Kevlar, before the test shoot, 2012. Courtesy of the artist, Nao Bustamante.

an exercise to verify Kevlar's repellant capabilities. Rather, her point is to illustrate the precariousness of the real women who endured the brutal conditions of the war.[28] For example, *Soldadera* also includes a mixed-media stereoscopic video that features Bustamante's interview with Leandra Becerra Lumbreras, a 127-year-old woman who is described as the last survivor of the revolution. Lumbreras recounts her experience of the war and thus helps us imagine the kind of women who would have benefited from a Kevlar combat dress.

Vulnerability is at the heart of Bustamante's project. Both the bodiless dresses and the target practice emphasize the vulnerability of women's bodies without resorting to visual references to blood and injured limbs. Ironically, the absent or invisible soldadera body is even more illustrative and evocative than a representation of an actual body, because it requires viewers to rely on our imaginative powers to place real women's bodies into the uninhabited garments. It is also important to note that the ingeniously designed and executed Kevlar dresses are, after all, combat dresses and thus refer to women's role in participating in or enabling combat in some form. In this way, Bustamante's disembodied soldaderas are similar to Rodriguez's anti-imperialist soldadera in their depiction of the complicated ways in which the soldadera icon is enmeshed in a legacy of violence. Yet, Bustamante's use of the soldadera as target practice emphasizes women's exposure to violence and enables us to associate the Kevlar soldadera with other instances when Mexicanas and Chicanas serve as targets of violence, including the pregnant body of the "illegal" border-crossing Mexican woman featured in racist video games (discussed in chapter 4).

Bustamante's project is motivated by an attempt to protect vulnerable soldadera bodies. In an interview with Bitch Media, Bustamante explains, "I thought maybe I could make a dress for them as a kind of memorial piece, or time travel to protect these women."[29] Bustamante's *Soldadera* reflects a profound concern with corporeal vulnerability that stems from the compassionate and protective impulse to shield others from harm. Thus, I read Bustamante's Kevlar combat dresses as emanating from an ethical and humanist belief and respect for the value of life and, in this case, the value and dignity of Mexican women's lives and bodies. Indeed, both Rodriguez's and Bustamante's soldadera pieces are invested in a humanist protective impulse, which I consider a powerful challenge to neoliberal militarism's ethic of self-care and its violent biopolitical disregard for life. Their artistic acts of protection are also devoid of patriarchal territorialism predicated on women's spatial immobility and gender oppression. Rather, both pieces encourage us to exercise and mobilize our agency to protect the lives of those who are framed as being outside the purview of what the state deems to be a grievable life.

Like many of the texts discussed in *Bodies at War*, Rodriguez's and Bustamante's soldaderas challenge the uncritical celebrations of the soldadera and the romanticization of La Adelita that disempower what is actually a complex and radical icon of Mexicana/Chicana agency. Both artists leverage the historical legacy of the anti-imperial, decolonial, and historically grounded soldadera icon to imagine a future of transnational solidarities. In this regard, we should follow Blackwell's contention that Chicana depictions of soldaderas are often "visual negotiations of political subjectivity, [and] forms of political participation," that can expose "the way spaces of belonging [are] articulated."[30]

I have insisted on the soldadera's polysemicity throughout *Bodies at War* because I want to further place it as a viable and productive icon for a Chicana feminist antiwar practice, ethic, and aesthetic.[31] I end *Bodies at War* with Rodriguez's and Bustamante's work because their depictions present the soldadera as a threshold figure who marks the transition from an antiwar resistance to a nonwar existence. In other words, I am in search of symbols of hope, courage, and resilience that can inform our attempts to boldly imagine a future without war. The soldadera is an ideal figure for thinking about the past and the future, for, as Bustamante explains, "there's a part of the Mexican Revolution that we still carry with us and will carry with us into the future."[32] The Chicana feminist future that awaits us includes not only the demilitarization of Aztlán, but also the end to war and other forms of violence. While some might disregard this vision as being hopelessly naïve, Ellie Hernández cautions us to "not be so quick to dismiss the power of imaginary visions, for without a prospectus for the future, we have no true sense of continuity for our goals." She argues, "To act as visionaries is more than wish fulfillment. It is also a way of honoring the imagination and our political imaginings as women."[33] The activists, authors, and artists discussed in *Bodies at War* have provided the inspiration and models for constructing the kind of idealist feminist antiwar imaginary needed to challenge neoliberal militarism's dominance. Part of this imaginary includes the soldadera, a figure that holds contradictions within as it spins toward a new yet unknown and unchartered future where soldiers become obsolete. Because this future is admittedly hard to see from our current vantage point, we must rely on the radical imaginations and the dreamwork of Chicana feminists and others who heroically envision a world sans war.

NOTES

INTRODUCTION

1. Oropeza, *¡Raza Sí! ¡Guerra No!*, 24.
2. "Dress Blues."
3. Anzaldúa, *Borderlands/La Frontera*, 216.
4. Ibid., 3, 11.
5. Ibid.,7–8.
6. Mendible, "Embodying Latinidad," 7.
7. Castañeda, "Chicanas/Latinas," 97. I use the term "uncanny" in Freud's sense of the word to describe the sensation of encountering something that is both threatening yet familiar.
8. Ibid., 97–98. *Garras* has two meanings in Spanish and Chicana/o slang. Castañeda emphasizes both meanings: (1) talons or claws, and (2) "clothes, or more specifically, tattered filthy rags" (96).
9. Cooke, *Women and the War Story*, 29.
10. Elshtain, *Women and War*, 167.
11. Ibid., 48.
12. Enloe, *Maneuvers*, 3.
13. Butler, "Bodies that Matter," 240.
14. Ibid., 236.
15. Mendible, "Embodying Latinidad," 1.

16. Ibid., 5.
17. Ibid.
18. Two important works that seek to challenge this scholarly omission are Pérez's *Citizen, Student, Soldier* and Fusco's *Field Guide for Female Interrogators*. I address both works in the concluding chapter.
19. Ong, *Neoliberalism as Exception*, 4.
20. Ibid., 6.
21. MacLeavy and Peoples, "Workfare-Warfare," 910.
22. Here, again, Ong's work on neoliberalism is helpful. She cautions against relying on definitions of what she calls Neoliberalism with a capital *N*, which is defined as a set of economic policies that have the power to transform any new situation in predetermined ways regardless of local or national specificities. In contrast to this totalizing and simplified view, Ong describes neoliberalism with a small *n* as being a more flexible mode of governing that "coexists with other political rationalities" (*Neoliberalism as Exception*, 4). For Ong, neoliberalism's features include "extreme dynamism, mobility of practice, responsiveness to contingencies and strategic entanglements with politics" (3). Her view of neoliberalism as an "assemblage" (5) enables us to appreciate its mutable qualities rather than perceive it as a rigidly defined economic rationality incapable of change and with predetermined outcomes in all contexts. The contradictions between neoliberalism and militarism are easily managed if we consider neoliberalism's shape-shifting nature and its ability to adapt to contingencies.
23. Hardt and Negri, *Multitude*, 17.
24. Enloe, *Curious Feminist*, 219.
25. Žižek, *Sublime Object of Ideology*, 49.
26. Mariscal, *Aztlán and Viet Nam*, 203.
27. Jeffords, *Remasculinization of America*, xv.
28. Ibid., 182.
29. Enloe, *Curious Feminist*, 219.
30. Lutz, "Making War at Home," 723.
31. Ferguson and Turnbull, *Oh, Say, Can You See?*, 3.
32. Ibid., xiii.
33. Butler, *Frames of War*, 168, 7.
34. Gilmore, "Globalisation and U.S. Prison Growth," 178–81.
35. Ibid., 179.
36. Ibid., 178.
37. Cowen and Siciliano, "Surplus Masculinities," 1517.

38. See Mittelstadt, *Rise of the Military Welfare State*. See also MacLeavy and Peoples, "Workfare-Warfare."
39. Segal, *Recruiting for Uncle Sam*, 38.
40. Hillman, "Female Shape of the All-Volunteer Force," 151. Hillman notes that at the time the draft ended, in 1973, women accounted for less than 2 percent of the U.S. military. By 2005, their number had increased to 16 percent (ibid.).
41. Sutton and Novkov, "Rethinking Security, Confronting Inequality," 18–19.
42. McKenna, *U.S. Military Logistics Management*, 2–4. Former secretary of defense Donald Rumsfeld ushered in new neoliberal approaches to strengthening national defense during his tenure. His program of "defense transformation" called for increased partnerships with private industries to develop and manufacture high-tech weapons systems (MacLeavy and Peoples, "Workfare-Warfare," 899). Speaking at the National Defense University in 2002, Rumsfeld took a page out of the neoliberal handbook to describe his vision for a reformed national defense: "We must promote a more entrepreneurial approach to developing military capabilities, one that encourages people, all people, to be proactive and not reactive, to behave somewhat less like bureaucrats and more like venture capitalists" (quoted in MacLeavy and Peoples, "Workfare-Warfare," 900).
43. Cypher, "From Military Keynesianism."
44. Young, "Logic of Masculinist Protection," 21.
45. Harvey, *Brief History of Neoliberalism*, 2.
46. Stephen, "*Los Nuevos Desaparecidos y Muertos*," 83.
47. Ross, *Rebellion from the Roots*, 41.
48. Marcos and CCRI-CG, Sixth Declaration.
49. Sassen, "Women's Burden," 505–11.
50. Ibid., 506.
51. Olivera and Furio, "Violencia Femicida," 107.
52. Enloe, *Maneuvers*, xiii.
53. Enloe, *Maneuvers*, xvi.
54. James, *Freedom Bought with Blood*, 9.
55. Vigil, *War Echoes*, 14.
56. Mariscal, *Aztlán and Viet Nam*, 26.
57. Olguín, "From Counter to Hegemonic," 183.
58. Ibid., 181.
59. Ibid., 181–83.
60. Delgadillo, "Criticality of Latino/a Fiction," 600.

61. Vigil, *War Echoes*, 5.
62. Nguyen, "Remembering War, Dreaming Peace," 152.
63. Mariscal, *Aztlán and Viet Nam*, 24.
64. Rodríguez, "Cross-Genealogies," 46.
65. For Rodríguez's discussion of subaltern counterpoetics, see "Cross-Genealogies," 48–52.
66. Scarry, *Body in Pain*, 81.
67. For specific work on the discursive constructions of Latina bodies, see Mendible, *From Bananas to Buttocks*; Molina-Guzmán, *Dangerous Curves*; Negrón-Muntaner, *Boricua Pop*; Ramírez, *Woman in the Zoot Suit*; and Gutiérrez, *Fertile Matters*. For a more general look at the Latina/o body politic, see Lima, *Latino Body*.
68. Mendible, "Embodying Latinidad," 5.
69. Molina-Guzmán, *Dangerous Curves*, 12.
70. Mendible, "Embodying Latinidad," 6.
71. Olguín, "Sangre Mexicana," 89, italics in original.
72. Ibid.
73. Sutton, *Bodies in Crisis*, 62.
74. The bodies of soldiers and their families are also subject to the enervating effects of economic insecurity. For example, in 2013 military families redeemed approximately $103.6 million in food stamps at military commissaries. Analysts attribute the steady rise in redemption rates to the economic recession of 2007–2009 and to the 30 percent unemployment rate of active-duty military spouses. Another factor for the increasing use of food stamps may be the low base pay of junior soldiers with spouses and children, who receive, on average, an income of $20,000 a year, which places them slightly above the national poverty line (Liberto, "Food Stamp Use Among Military Rises Again").
75. Sutton, *Bodies in Crisis*, 47.
76. Scarry, *Body in Pain*, 133.
77. Ibid., 14.
78. Butler, *Frames of War*, 25.
79. For an excellent analysis on the formation of social value and its relationship to state violence, see Cacho's *Social Death*.
80. Foucault, *Foucault Reader*, 181. It may be obvious why and how militaries practice what Foucault calls the "mechanics of power," but his notion of disciplining "docile" bodies is not without predecessors if we consult the long history of feminist writing on embodiment. Susan Bordo traces antecedent versions of

the concept to writers as early as Mary Wollstonecraft, who in 1792 described the corporeal microcontrol of the "domesticated woman of privilege" (Bordo, "Feminism, Foucault," 248–49). While Foucault's theorization adds new vocabulary and dimensions to the study of embodiment and power, it is important to remember a prior history of feminist theorizing, because Foucault's description of disciplinary regimes of power disregards the role that gender plays in the production of docility, an issue that prompted Sandra Lee Bartky to ask, "Where is the account of the disciplinary practices that engender the 'docile bodies' of women, bodies more docile than the bodies of men?" ("Foucault, Femininity," 95). Bartky argues that women's bodies are subjected to "larger disciplines that construct a 'feminine' body out of a female one" through "perpetual and exhaustive" disciplinary regimes that regulate "the body's size and contours, its appetite, posture, gestures, and general comportment in space and the appearance of each of its visible parts" (101, 107).

81. Foucault, *Foucault Reader*, 181. From the perspective of institutional power, such disciplinary methods were a cost-effective way of dominating and utilizing bodies that replaced earlier forms of discipline (slavery, vassalage, service, asceticism, etc.).
82. Ibid., 182.
83. Ibid., 174.
84. Furumoto, "No Poor Child Left Unrecruited"; Hay, "Designing Homes"; Kaplan, "Precision Targets"; Turse, *The Complex*; Stahl, *Militainment, Inc.*; Dunn, *Militarization of the U.S.-Mexico Border*; Levario, *Militarizing the Border*; González, *Militarizing Culture*; and MacLeavy and Peoples, "Workfare-Warfare."
85. Office of the Under Secretary of Defense, Personnel and Readiness, *Population Representation*, 29. The report notes that in FY 1978, 6.1 percent of accessions were Hispanic (men and women), a number that mirrored their civilian cohort of comparable age range. (I use the term "Hispanic" here to reflect the word choice in this and other military reports.)
86. Segal and Segal, *America's Military Population*, 30. The percentages include enlisted women and female officers.
87. See appendix B, table B-3, "Non-Prior Service (NPS) Active Component Enlisted Accessions, FY 13: by Service, Gender, and Race/Ethnicity with Civilian Comparison Group," in Office of the Under Secretary of Defense, Personnel and Readiness, *Population Representation*, 9. In FY 2010, Hispanic active-duty enlisted women represented 13 percent of enlisted women, and Hispanic

active-duty enlisted men were 12 percent of all enlisted men (Patten and Parker, *Women in the U.S. Military*, 5).

88. Smith, "U.S. Army Told to Advertise."
89. Quoted ibid.
90. Quoted ibid.
91. Cone, "Soldier 2020," 29.
92. The original photo of Corporal Tejeda can be seen in Smith's article "U.S. Army Told to Advertise."
93. Cone, "Soldier 2020," 29.
94. Not all branches have welcomed the new policy of gender integration. Portions of a leaked internal report conducted by the Marines found that "women are injured more frequently and shoot less accurately than men" (Lamothe, "As Marines Take Heat"). Based on these findings and the Marine Corps' general reluctance to change its patriarchal culture and structure (for example, the Marines are the only branch that maintains segregated boot camps for men and women), military observers believe that the Marines will petition to keep some infantry and reconnaissance units closed to women.
95. Molina-Guzmán, *Dangerous Curves*, 7.
96. Ibid., 13.
97. Enloe, *Maneuvers*, 34.
98. Grewal, "Security Moms," 28.
99. Ibid., 29.
100. See hooks, "Feminism and Militarism," 63.
101. Ibid.
102. Sutton, "Poner el Cuerpo," 150.
103. Ibid., 130.
104. Valdés, "Hearts on Fire," 225.
105. Ibid., 226.
106. Ibid., 225.
107. Butler, *Precarious Life*, xii.
108. Ibid., xiii.
109. Butler, *Frames of War*, 12.
110. Ibid., 24.
111. Arrizón, "*Soldaderas* and the Staging of the Mexican Revolution," 90.
112. Mariscal, "Las Adelitas 2003."
113. Ibid.

114. Latorre, "Re-Mapping the National Consciousness," 97; emphasis in original.
115. Mignolo, *Idea of Latin America*, 8.

CHAPTER 1

1. Herrera-Sobek, "Untitled," 234.
2. Ibid., 234–35.
3. Herrera-Sobek, "Vietnam," 232.
4. Herrera-Sobek, "Vietnam—A Four-Letter Word," 235.
5. Sutton, "Poner el Cuerpo," 130.
6. For more on the Chicano Moratorium and the aftermath of the shootings, see Oropeza, *¡Raza Sí! ¡Guerra No!*, 172–82.
7. Herrera-Sobek, "Chicana Vietnam Blues," 233.
8. Young, "Logic of Masculinist Protection," 9.
9. Butler, *Precarious Life*, xix.
10. Herrera-Sobek, "Chicana Vietnam Blues," 233.
11. Herrera-Sobek, "Untitled," 234; emphasis in original.
12. Rodríguez, *Next of Kin*, 1–2.
13. Bebout, *Mythohistorical Interventions*, 113.
14. Roth, "Dialogical View," 722.
15. Blackwell, *¡Chicana Power!*, 112.
16. Zaretsky, *No Direction Home*, 7.
17. Enloe, *Morning After*, 166, italics in original.
18. Rodríguez, *Next of Kin*, 7.
19. Correa, "Targeting of the East Los Angeles Brown Berets," 83–101.
20. Ibid., 84. The FBI's interest in monitoring the Brown Berets and other protest groups was far from benign. In 1975 the *New York Times* broke the news that, according to an ACLU report released that year, the FBI had recruited a group of "right-wing terrorists and supplied them with money and weapons to attack young anti-war demonstrators." The FBI had created and sponsored, from 1971 to 1972, a group of paramilitary extremists known as the Secret Army Organization as part of Richard Nixon's broader agenda to "intimidate and silence domestic critics." The "army" was established to head off potential disruptions during the upcoming 1972 Republican Convention, to be held in California. The ACLU alleged that Peter Bohmer, an economics professor at San Diego

State University, and "Linco Bueno, a member of the Brown Berets, a left-wing Chicano organization, were to be lured across the Mexican border to a desolate area near Tijuana. There, they were to be killed by the Mexican Federal police for possession of a cache of smuggled weapons. The plot was abandoned . . . presumably when the Republican convention was moved to Miami Beach" (Holles, "A.C.L.U. Says F.B.I. Funded 'Army'").

21. Blackwell, *¡Chicana Power!*, 98.
22. Holst-Warhaft, *Cue for Passion*, 1–2.
23. Ibid., 6.
24. According to Gail Holst-Warhaft, Greek authorities recognized the destructive potential of unchecked grief as early as the sixth century BCE, when blood feuds between rival clans imperiled the newly established state of Athens (Holst-Warhaft, *Cue for Passion*, 7).
25. Ibid., 4.
26. Cheng, *Melancholy of Race*, 174; italics in original.
27. Ibid., 174.
28. Ibid., 174–75.
29. Eng and Kazanjian, *Loss*, 4.
30. Ibid., ix.
31. Ibid., 5.
32. Muñoz, "Feeling Brown," 69.
33. Deborah Paredez's work on the memorialization of Selena, the Tejana singer who was murdered in 1995, provides a powerful example of how Latinas/os "do" citizenship by using performances of mourning to expose histories of marginalization and struggles for political inclusion. By mourning Selena, Latinas/os "create[d] visions for a future change of state in light of shifting and renewed assertions of *latinidad*." See Paredez, "Remembering Selena, Re-membering Latinidad," 69, italics in original.
34. Deborah Cowen points out, "The general timing of the termination of conscription in the early 1970s . . . is also the moment that neoliberalism emerged publicly as a force to contend with" (Cowen, "Fighting for 'Freedom,'" 169).
35. Segal, *Recruiting for Uncle Sam*, 36. John Singleton explains how Friedman's theory of the AVF may have influenced Nixon even before he became president. In 1966, Martin Anderson, a finance professor at Columbia University, joined Nixon's presidential advisory team and suggested that Nixon embrace the AVF. Anderson then sent Nixon a detailed memo that drew heavily from Friedman's work. In 1967, Nixon publicly announced his support for the AVF,

a popular position that may have led to his victory. See Singleton, "Slaves or Mercenaries," 21–23.

36. Gates, *Report of the President's Commission on an All-Volunteer Armed Force*, 38. Hereafter cited as the Gates Commission report.
37. Flynn, *The Draft*, 266.
38. According to Singleton, Friedman's early interest in ending the draft was likely influenced by his son David, a student at Harvard, needing to apply for annual college deferments to avoid service (Singleton, "Slaves or Mercenaries," 8).
39. One hidden cost is the opportunity cost that a draftee pays when he is forced to give up the potential for greater economic gain by not pursuing alternatives. The report provides the following example: "Thus, suppose a draftee or draft-induced volunteer is compelled to enter the service who would do so voluntarily only if he were offered $8,000 per year. If there exists a true volunteer who would be equally productive in the military, prepared to enlist for $6,000 per year, the difference of $2,000 is an additional real cost imposed by the draft. The $2,000 can reflect either a difference in the productivity of the two persons in the civilian economy, or differences in taste for military life. Whichever it is, the loss is a real cost (and a waste) in precisely the same sense as is any other cost," Gates Commission report, 31.
40. Ibid., 25.
41. Cowen, "Fighting for 'Freedom,'" 172; Gates Commission report, 23–24.
42. Gates Commission report, 13.
43. Ibid., 10, 12.
44. Ibid., 14.
45. Cowen argues that Friedman favored a form of radical individualism that "prioritized individual economic rights over national duty," a position that exceeded classical liberalism's view of the relationship between the individual and the state. See Cowen, "Fighting for 'Freedom,'" 171.
46. Gates Commission report, 31.
47. Segal, *Recruiting for Uncle Sam*, 71.
48. Ong, *Neoliberalism as Exception*, 9.
49. Segal, *Recruiting for Uncle Sam*, 69.
50. Snyder, *Citizen-Soldiers and Manly Warriors*, 1.
51. Ibid., 1–2.
52. Civic republican militarists often emphasize the need for a form of national service, which may or may not include military service. Quester explains that advocates such as Charles Moskos believe that national mandatory service

would be "healthy for the nation" and would serve "as the embodiment and renewal of a concept of duty" ("Demographic Trends and Military Recruitment," 34). At the center of many civic republican arguments is the idea of equal representation. "Just as the elected Congress must be representative of the nation as a whole," the military should also reflect the national polity. By mandating national service, the military would be representative of the entire population, thereby altering the current reliance on enlistees from working-class backgrounds and theoretically democratizing the institution: "Critics point to several problems with the unrepresentativeness of the current military, including, most prominently, that economic and political elites are shielded from the realities of war. Because the elites who make the decision to go to war are shielded from its direct effects, making the decision is that much easier" (Feldman, "Citizen-Soldier as a Substitute Soldier," 204). The civic republican militarist position is a cautionary position since mandatory all-inclusive civilian participation would "encourage civilian control of the military" and would hold officials accountable for making war policies that affect all citizens in equal ways, thus potentially "induc[ing] a more cautious approach to the use of military force" (ibid., 203–4).

53. For more on the generational differences, see Oropeza's *¡Raza Sí! ¡Guerra No!*
54. Ibid., 67–68.
55. Ibid., 68–69.
56. Greenberg, *Project 100,000*, 7. Defense Secretary Robert McNamara initiated the program in 1966. It ended in 1971, when the government abolished the use of quotas. The program was specifically designed to accept men who had previously been rejected from the military because of failure to meet mental standards or because of certain physical disabilities. One of the goals of the program was to increase the pool of men subject to the draft.
57. Ibid.
58. Oropeza, *¡Raza Sí! ¡Guerra No!*, 104.
59. Ibid., 104–5.
60. Ibid., 105.
61. Ibid., 82.
62. Ibid., 92–93.
63. Ybarra and Genera, *La batalla*, inside cover, italics in original; my translation.
64. In a subsequent article on Chicano Viet Nam veterans, Ybarra explains that the phrase "la batalla está aquí" was "a rallying cry in the 1960s and 1970s for those within the Chicano community who opposed the U.S. war in Viet Nam. They held that the real battle was in the United States, not in Viet Nam, and

that the billions of dollars that were being spent on the war abroad were needed for the war against poverty at home" ("Perceptions of Race," 69). I argue that the phrase also helped reaffirm gendered notions of war and masculinist protectionism.

65. Ybarra and Genera, *La batalla*, 2.
66. Ibid.
67. Ibid. Ybarra later wrote that Guzman's bleak report "served as a manifesto for the growing antiwar movement in the Chicano community" ("Perceptions of Race," 71). Oropeza explains that a later study of the Latino casualty rate during the war estimated a much lower yet still significant rate of casualties. See *¡Raza Sí! ¡Guerra No!*, 216.
68. Ybarra and Genera, *La batalla*, 4.
69. Ibid. Genera and Ybarra, along with Maria Elena Ramirez, transformed the ballad into an antiwar *acto* (skit), which they then performed "at high schools, community centers, and even in people's homes throughout the Bay area and beyond" (Oropeza, *¡Raza Sí! ¡Guerra No!*, 106). *La batalla* includes a photo of the three performing the acto.
70. E-mail to author, November 3, 2016. García explains that his airbase "formed part of Operation Rolling Thunder, a [*sic*] aerial bombardment campaign conducted against North Vietnam from March 2nd, 1965[,] until November 1st, 1968, during the Vietnam War. My airbase mainly bombed the Ho Chi Minh Trail."
71. García, "Rupert García—In His Own Words."
72. E-mail to author, December 7, 2016.
73. Levinas, *Totality and Infinity*, 50.
74. Ibid., 51.
75. Ibid., 198.
76. Ibid., 200.
77. Butler, *Precarious Life*, 134.
78. Levinas, *Totality and Infinity*, 199. While Levinas uses the biblical commandment to express the face's imperative, the expression should not necessarily be taken literally. In other words, if we replace "murder" with other words that stand in for myriad forms of violence (hatred, racism, oppression, dehumanization, etc.), we can see that the face's edict calls for a kind of respect for and responsibility to the Other.
79. Butler cites the following passage from Levinas and Kearney, "Dialogue": "The celebrated 'right to existence' that Spinoza called the *conatus essendi* and defined as the basic principle of all intelligibility is challenged by the relation to the face.

Accordingly, my duty to respond to the other suspends my natural right to self-survival, *le droit vitale*. . . . To expose myself to the vulnerability of the face is to put my ontological right to existence into question. In ethics, the other's right to exist has primacy over my own, a primacy epitomized in the ethical edict: You shall not kill, you shall not jeopardize the life of the other" (23–24); quoted in Butler, *Precarious Life*, 132.

80. Burggraeve, "Violence and the Vulnerable Face of the Other," 31.
81. Foucault, "Ethics of the Concern of the Self," 285. Ong expands on this notion in her description of neoliberal ethics: "Techniques of economic globalization are invested with a moral calculus about more or less worthy subjects, practices, lifestyles, and visions of the good. *Ethics* is used here in the ancient Greco-Roman sense of a practice of the self, or normative techniques in self-care for attaining a particular mode of being. An ethical regime can therefore be construed as a style of living guided by given values for constituting oneself in line with a particular ethical goal. Religions—and, I would argue, feminism, humanitarianism, and other schemes of virtue—are ethical regimes fostering particular forms of self-conduct and visions of the good life. Ethical notions of citizenship include the expression of national spirit, a style of being subjects who express the key values of a particular nation." (*Neoliberalism as Exception*, 22).
82. McNamara, "Interview."
83. Tyner, *War, Violence, and Population*, 59.
84. Quoted ibid., 59–60.
85. Ibid., 60.
86. Boggs, "Vietnam, McNamara," 462.
87. Robert McNamara's deposition, undated, folder 15, box 11, Larry Berman Collection (*Westmoreland v. CBS*), the Vietnam Center and Archive, Texas Tech University, accessed November 23, 2013, http://www.vietnam.ttu.edu/virtual archive/items.php?item=0251115005.
88. According to Raymond Tanter, "The strategy of attrition tries to locate the enemy's main force units and seeks to destroy them. . . . Primary indicators of progress in such a strategy are the body count of enemy casualties and the so-called kill ratio—a ratio of friendly to enemy casualties" (Tanter, "Relative Impact of U.S. Military Action," 24).
89. Young, "Counting the Bodies," 232.
90. According to one survey of military personnel conducted in 1968, many officers "reported various kinds of pressures from their headquarters to turn in high body counts," a pressure so intense that it "led to 'grave-digging' by some units to get numbers" (Tanter, "Relative Impact of U.S. Military Actions," 17).

91. McNamara deposition.
92. Hallin, *Uncensored War*, 175. Interestingly, Hallin argues that while journalists and broadcasters showed sympathy for U.S. soldiers killed, the coverage of civilian casualties dropped after the Tet Offensive: "And the tone, if anything, became more matter-of-fact. Rarely does one find after Tet either the shock expressed by [Morley] Safer when he first saw a village being burned or the defensiveness other reporters had expressed about similar events" (176).
93. Scarry, *Body in Pain*, 136.
94. Elaine Scarry asserts that it is not enough that the "instrumental language of strategy and alliance . . . brings the wounded into being"; it also enables the "disappearance of the injuries themselves from all spheres of language" (Scarry, *Body in Pain*, 134, 136).
95. Carbonella, "Home Front," 126.
96. Scarry, *Body in Pain*, 121; emphasis in original.
97. Ibid., 124.
98. Associated Press photojournalist Eddie Adams captured his iconic image in February 1968. Often called *Saigon Execution*, the photograph depicts South Vietnamese general Nguyen Ngoc Loan executing captured Vietcong prisoner Nguyen Van Lem. One month later, Sgt. Ron Haeberle accompanied soldiers from Charlie Company as they entered a hamlet called My Lai suspected of housing Vietcong troops. Under the orders of Mexican American captain Ernest Medina, the members of Charlie Company opened fire on and murdered 504 men, women, and children. Haeberle's color and black-and-white photographs captured the massacre and were later published in the final months of 1969 in *Life* and *Time* magazines. In June 1972, Nick Ut photographed a group of Vietnamese civilians fleeing the village of Trang Bang in South Viet Nam, which had just been hit by an aerial napalm attack. Among the people fleeing was nine-year-old Kim Phuc, whose burned body was exposed after the napalm had seared away her clothes.
99. Sontag, *Regarding the Pain of Others*, 18.
100. Oropeza, *¡Raza Sí, Guerra No!*, 107–8.
101. Ibid., 108. Other Chicana activists apparently used photographs to make similar ethical appeals. Oropeza describes, for example, the antiwar writings of Valentina Valdez, a young Chicana activist who wrote articles for *El Grito del Norte*, a New Mexico newspaper affiliated with the land-grant group Alianza Federal de Pueblos Libres. Oropeza writes, "Valdez lamented the death and destruction rained down by U.S. bombs. Her articles included several graphic photographs that highlighted the devastation. Horrified by the carnage inflicted by

the American war machine, Chicano activists like Valdez demanded an immediate end to the war" (Oropeza, *¡Raza Sí! ¡Guerra No!*, 92–93).

102. Ybarra and Genera, *La batalla*, 1.
103. Sontag, *Regarding the Pain of Others*, 75.
104. Sontag, *On Photography*, 24.
105. Sontag, *Regarding the Pain of Others*, 63.
106. Ibid., 65. Throughout this passage, Sontag's use of pronouns reveals her assumptions about who constitutes the American viewers of war photography. By stating that the "exotic" or racialized subject is "not someone (like us)," she assumes that her reader is nonexotic or, in other words, white. My analysis of the atrocity photos in *La batalla* suggests that Ybarra and Genera presumed and therefore addressed a Chicana/o readership whose own experience of racialization would inform their reaction to the photos.
107. Sontag, *Regarding the Pain of Others*, 40.
108. Ibid., 91.
109. Ibid., 91–92.
110. Ybarra and Genera, *La batalla*, 4.
111. Ibid., 6.
112. Ibid., 7.
113. Ibid., 8.
114. Photos need narrative framing because they can be interpreted in oppositional ways. In other words, the unreliability of photos is partly attributed to the viewers who respond differently to what they see. For some, atrocity photos elicit a kind of fascination akin to pornography. There can be a kind of pleasure in being horrified (Sontag, *Regarding the Pain of Others*, 36–37). Some people are voyeuristically fascinated by the gruesome and objectify the images in a process that revictimizes those who suffer. For other viewers, the photos of bodies made unrecognizable by violence actually dehumanize victims, thereby contributing to a process of Othering that prevents or discourages identification. In other cases, photos lose their power or fail to motivate action as people become inured to violence—a kind of fatigue threatens to set in as viewers are continuously exposed to photos of war. Viewers can also feel shame in looking at photos, as if only those who can stop the suffering should be looking at the suffering. This invokes a double sense of helplessness and impotence within the viewer: *I cannot stop the violence, and I feel like an inappropriate spectator.*
115. Butler, *Frames of War*, 10.
116. Zaretsky, "Private Suffering," 206.

117. Ibid.
118. Hunt, *Melvin Laird and Nixon's Quest*, 12.
119. Zaretsky, *No Direction Home*, 27.
120. Ibid., 31.
121. James O. Clifford, "Captured U.S. Pilot's Family Question the Waste of War," August 7, 1972, folder 2, box 22, Douglas Pike Collection: Unit 03—POW/MIA Issues, the Vietnam Center and Archive, Texas Tech University.
122. "POW Will Face Change."
123. Alvarez and Pitch, *Chained Eagle*, 153.
124. Ibid., 154.
125. Ibid., 153.
126. Roberts, "Sister of P.O.W."
127. Alvarez and Pitch, *Chained Eagle*, 156.
128. Ibid., 155.
129. Ibid., 207–8, 210.
130. "Prisoners' Families in Rift," 63. The league focused on petitioning the North Vietnamese government to follow the Geneva Conventions and allow international inspectors into the POW camps to ensure humane living conditions. This, the league argued, was a "humanitarian, non-controversial goal" that was divorced from the war itself. Their position seemed to be orchestrated by or at least neatly aligned with U.S. strategy on the POW issue. For example, after meeting with a group of POW wives and mothers, Richard Nixon reiterated the government's attempt to frame the POW release as a nonpolitical issue: "What I have assured these very courageous women is that . . . clearly apart from reaching an overall settlement of the war[,] that this Government will do everything that it possibly can to separate out the prisoner issue and have it handled as it should be, as a separate issue on a humane basis" (Nixon, "Remarks"). Delia formed her own group, called the POW-MIA Families for Immediate Release, which criticized the limited and short-sighted approach of the league and the Nixon administration in a statement that read, in part, "It is appalling to us that at this late date the government would want to focus attention away from the real goal, which is to end the war and bring the men home, and on to a goal that would at best let American prisoners rot in comfort" ("Prisoners' Families in Rift," 63).
131. Delia Alvarez appeared with Jane Fonda at a two-day event held at the Jewish Cultural Center in Miami Beach in August 1972, sponsored by the Miami Convention Coalition and the Youth International Party. Referred to as a

"Nixon investigation," the event featured Fonda, Alvarez, and George Smith, a former Army Green Beret and POW, held captive for two years. See Burnside, "Jane Fonda Hits Bombing of Dikes."

132. Quoted in Zaretsky, "Private Suffering," 210.
133. Roberts, "Sister of P.O.W."
134. Ibid.
135. Clifford, "Captured U.S. Pilot's Family Question the Waste of War."
136. Zaretsky, "Private Suffering," 211.
137. Burnside, "Jane Fonda Hits Bombing of Dikes."
138. Muñoz, "Feeling Brown," 68–69.
139. See Zaretsky's excellent analysis of Delia Alvarez's POW activism, including examples of moments when Delia portrayed stoicism rather than the despondent female relative, in "Private Suffering," 218–19.
140. Muñoz, "Feeling Brown," 69.
141. "Alvarez Critical of Anti-war Efforts," 2.
142. Alvarez and Schreiner, *Code of Conduct*, 15.
143. Quoted in Zaretsky, "Private Suffering," 221.
144. Burgin, "Understanding Antiwar Activism," 29.
145. Ibid., 20.
146. Armstrong and Prashad, "Solidarity," 220.
147. Ibid.
148. John Alba Cutler argues, "Much of the movement's antiwar rhetoric depended on imaging the Mexican male warrior as protestor rather than soldier, setting up an opposition between authentic Chicano identity and war participation" (Alba Cutler, "Disappeared Men," 587).
149. Espinoza, "Revolutionary Sisters," 36. My discussion of Las Adelitas de Aztlán is indebted to Espinoza's thorough analysis of the Adelitas' cultural, political, and feminist intervention in Chicano movement activism.
150. Ibid., 37.
151. Burgin discusses of how some feminists within the mainstream antiwar movement opposed the reliance on what they viewed as "traditional" forms of femininity to protest the war. See especially Shulamith Firestone's critique of the Jeannette Rankin Brigade, an antiwar organization that sponsored a convention and march to appeal to congressional members to end the war: "The Brigade was playing upon the traditional female role in the classic manner. They came as wives, mothers and mourners; that is, tearful and passive reactors to the actions of men rather than organizing as women to change that definition

of femininity into something other than a synonym for weakness, political impotence, and tears" (quoted in Burgin, "Understanding Antiwar Activity," 22). My reading of Chicanas' mourning practices differs from Firestone's view of mourning. Whereas she regards "tears" as a sign of "weakness" and "political impotence," I argue that public mourning, in the instances I have identified, is a performance that makes political and ethical demands on the state and the public.

152. Sutton, "Poner el Cuerpo," 130.
153. Ibid., 140.
154. Hong, "Fun with Death," 243–44.
155. Ibid., 243.
156. For a firsthand account of the conference, see Vidal, *Chicanas Speak Out.*
157. Hong, "Fun with Death," 248.
158. Ruiz, *From Out of the Shadows*, 111. Quoted in Vidal, *Chicanas Speak Out*, 5.
159. Hong, "Fun with Death," 248.
160. Ibid., 249.
161. Ibid.
162. Burgin, "Understanding Antiwar Activism," 29.
163. Blackwell, *¡Chicana Power!*, 114.
164. Cantú, "Women, Then and Now," 9. This misperception of soldaderas has long-lasting implications for Chicanas even beyond the movement. Cantú argues that the lack of Chicana writers represented in Chicano studies programs is attributable to what she called the "Adelita complex," the belief that Chicanas are ancillary figures who follow men because, like soldaderas, they "are perceived as followers, not leaders, or thinkers" (9).
165. Latorre, "Re-Mapping the National Consciousness," 97.
166. Ibid.
167. Espinoza, "Revolutionary Sisters," 39.
168. Ibid., 40.
169. Sutton, "Poner el Cuerpo," 152.
170. Espinoza, "Revolutionary Sisters," 40.
171. Duarte's novel is one of several contemporary Chicana novels that refer to or take place during the U.S. war in Viet Nam. These include Lucha Corpi's *Eulogy for a Brown Angel* (2002), Norma Cantú's *Canícula: Snapshots of a Girlhood en la Frontera* (1997), Helena María Viramontes's *Their Dogs Came with Them* (2008), and Patricia Santana's *Motorcycle Ride on the Sea of Tranquility* (2004). Significantly, the latter three texts focus on the sisters of Chicano soldiers who

have either died in the war or who return but with posttraumatic stress syndrome. John Alba Cutler provides an excellent analysis of *Motorcycle* and *Their Dogs* in *Ends of Assimilation*.

172. Alvarez and Schreiner, *Code of Conduct*, xi–xvi.
173. Berlant, *Queen of America*, 31–32.
174. Ibid., 30.
175. Anderson, *Imagined Communities*, 11.
176. Duarte, *Let Their Spirits Dance*, 32, 35.
177. Ibid., 165.
178. White, "¿Darles Voz?," 7.
179. Ibid., 8.
180. Ruddick, "Women of Peace," 215.
181. Bayard de Volo, "Drafting Motherhood," 244.
182. Duarte, *Let Their Spirits Dance*, 216, 248.
183. Ibid., 79.
184. Ibid., 290, 99.
185. Ibid., 288.
186. Ibid., 52.
187. Ibid., 252.
188. Mariscal, "Reading Chicana/o Writing," 32, 38.
189. Tal, "Mind at War," 84.
190. Ibid., 77.
191. White, "¿Darles voz?" 16, 9, 13.
192. Duarte, *Let Their Spirits Dance*, 308. George Mariscal writes that the surnames Johnson and Rodriguez "appear most often" on the Wall (Mariscal, *Aztlán and Viet Nam*, 3). While "'Johnson' combines the Caucasian and African American sacrifices, . . . 'Rodriguez' stands for the Latino experience during the war. . . . Histories of the war and cultural representations of the war have yet to hear the voice of 'Rodriguez.'"
193. Griswold and Griswold, "Vietnam Veterans Memorial," 691.
194. Correll, "Rem(a)inders of G(l)ory," 168.
195. Ibid., 161–62. Indeed, symbolic valuation is critical to the state religion of nationalism. Through the monument, the state can grant immortality and regeneration, a power that the state is anxious to demonstrate, as in the case of the Tomb of the Unknown Soldier. In 1971, Richard Nixon had anticipated using the remains of an unknown soldier from the Viet Nam War as a symbolic

call for national unity once the war had ended. To this end, he ordered that a crypt be constructed to hold the remains of a U.S. serviceman alongside the unidentified remains of servicemen from WWI, WWII, and the Korean War (Allen, "Sacrilege of a Strange, Contemporary Kind," 94–95). Nixon's plans were dashed when it was determined that no unidentified remains could be found because of advancements in forensic testing. The Viet Nam crypt was left empty until 1984, when Ronald Reagan held a ceremony to inter the remains of a soldier whose identity was supposedly undetermined. In 1998, through private investigations and investigative reporting, the remains of the "unknown" were identified as belonging to air force lieutenant Michael J. Blassie, who had been shot down in 1972. The discovery, disinterment, and reburial of Lt. Blassie's remains led to charges that the Reagan administration had "known the identity of the remains . . . but had concealed that information in order to enact a ritual of national reunion in an election year" (Allen, "Sacrilege of a Strange, Contemporary Kind," 91).

196. In another example of the monument's failure, Teresa describes how the military ceremony held in honor of the caravan's arrival at the Wall is a disingenuous show of political expediency: "Ricky tells me the ceremony is media propaganda to give the Clinton Administration credit for recognizing the 191,000 men of Latin descent who served during the Vietnam War, and that's not counting all the others with Latino roots who don't carry Spanish surnames. He tells me we don't have to acknowledge any of it, but I tell him the more publicity, the better" (Duarte, *Let Their Spirits Dance*, 304).

CHAPTER 2

1. Rodriguez, *Peacetime*, 123.
2. Enloe, *Morning After*, 178.
3. Ibid., 223.
4. Ibid., 196.
5. Burke, *Camp All-American*, 103.
6. Eisenstein, "Resexing Militarism," 30.
7. Feinman, *Citizenship Rites*, 72.
8. MacLeavy and Peoples, "Workfare-Warfare," 895.
9. Ibid., 897.

10. Ibid.
11. The range of cash and in-kind benefits that military personnel receive in today's military, which Brian Gifford calls the "military welfare state," is truly remarkable (Gifford, "Camouflaged Safety Net," 379). The benefits for active-duty service members with families include in-kind and nontaxable housing allowances, universal participation in the military's health insurance plan (which does not require monthly premiums or co-pays), additional stipends known as the family separation allowance and the basic allowance for subsistence, consumer subsidies in the form of "tax-free department stores and gas stations," and access to subsidized childcare (when and where available). Despite the military's efforts to compete with the labor market by touting its benefits programs, it "nonetheless recognizes the inadequacy of service members' base pay to support a family" (ibid., 379–82). The irony is that a higher, competitive salary would make these benefits redundant.
12. Segal, *Recruiting for Uncle Sam*, 8–9.
13. Ibid., 85–86.
14. Alexander, *Pedagogies of Crossing*, 223.
15. Interestingly, MacLeavy and Peoples suggest that military workfare is a "possible way to combat male unemployment in particular (as a complement to programs instituted through TANF [Temporary Aid to Needy Families], which attempt to reconnect welfare mothers to the workforce)"; "Workfare-Warfare," 906.
16. Cowen and Siciliano, "Surplus Masculinities," 1520.
17. Ibid., 1521
18. Alexander, *Pedagogies of Crossing*, 233.
19. Rodriguez, *Peacetime*, 4–5.
20. Ibid., 126.
21. Burke, *Camp All-American*, 13.
22. Rodriguez, *Peacetime*, 12–13.
23. Burke, *Camp All-American*, 13.
24. Rodriguez, *Peacetime*, 98–99, 103.
25. Ibid., 102.
26. Ibid., 138, 104.
27. Ibid., 165–66.
28. Ibid., 104.
29. Ibid., 1.

30. Ibid., 181. Kelly Oliver describes how women physically accommodate to male soldiering by taking certain kinds of birth control to minimize or stop their menstruation, or by using "a portable urination device," colloquially called a "weenus," during long trips (*Women as Weapons of War*, 1).
31. Ironically, Rodriguez used the notion of female physical limitations to her advantage to get out of her military contract. According to Olguín's personal interview with Rodriguez, she "received a medical discharge after boot camp by strategically invoking her male drill sergeant's sexist views that women were too feeble for military service" (Olguín, "Sangre Mexicana," 94).
32. Höpfl, "Becoming a (Virile) Member," 26–27.
33. Rodriguez, *Peacetime*, 158.
34. Oliver, *Women as Weapons of War*, 5.
35. Ibid., 27.
36. Rodriguez, *Peacetime*, 104–6.
37. Department of the Army, "Uniforms and Insignia," 5. The army's manual also reflects a wider and historical military perspective on military women's embodiment. Elizabeth Hillman cites the Naval Academy's 1976 guidelines on women's appearance: "Conservative cosmetics may be worn by women midshipmen. . . . Moderate make up and lipstick, faint eyeshadow, and light rouge are appropriate if generally unnoticeable in appearance" (quoted in Hillman, "Dressed to Kill?," 71). Hillman reveals how such policies not only allayed the anxiety of male military officials but were presumably in the best interest of servicewomen. She cites a 1976 planning memo from the Air Force Academy in which military officials insist that "women's standards must promote an attractive, feminine image," and that a change in women's uniforms "would help the women cadets present themselves in a more feminine manner, helping them identify more easily as a woman" (Hillman, "Dressed to Kill?," 70).
38. Enloe, *Maneuvers*, 270; Hillman, "Dressed to Kill?," 71.
39. Enloe, *Maneuvers*, 271.
40. Hillman, "Dressed to Kill?," 71.
41. Ibid., 69.
42. Butler, "Bodies that Matter," 236.
43. Enloe, *Maneuvers*, 236.
44. Butler, "Bodies that Matter," 236.
45. Ibid.
46. Rodriguez, *Peacetime*, 224–25.

47. Ibid.
48. Brown, *Edgework*, 42.
49. Rodriguez, *Peacetime*, 124.
50. Brown, *Edgework*, 42.
51. Ibid.
52. Olguín, "Sangre Mexicana," 93–94.
53. Ibid., 94.
54. Rodriguez, *Peacetime*, 152–53. Adela's tragic background story helps us understand her critique of the military and, more significantly, of voluntary enlistment. She tells Medrano that after her family moved to Los Angeles, both her parents died in an elevator at their place of employment. Despite repeated complaints about the faulty elevator before their accident, the factory owner neglected to fix it. After her parents' death, Adela broke the windows of the factory out of anger. Consequently, she was arrested for damaging property and only enlisted after being given an ultimatum by the court: "The judge told me either I'd join the military or go to jail. You can guess which I picked" (153).
55. The quotation in the heading ("I'm a soldier, not a gender") is from Benedict, *Lonely Soldier*, 174. Mickiela Montoya is one of the five female soldiers featured in Helen Benedict's *Lonely Soldier*. Benedict interviewed Montoya over several years and provides a comprehensive interview that covers Montoya's life before, during, and shortly after her service in Iraq. As a result of being featured in Benedict's book, Montoya has given numerous interviews, appeared on programs such as the *Oprah Winfrey Show*, and participated in various forums discussing servicewomen's experiences in the U.S. military. I draw primarily from Benedict's text but also cite other interviews and news articles that feature Montoya.
56. Ibid., 18.
57. According to Benedict, the army increased its training to ten weeks in 2007. Incidentally, the Marines train for twelve weeks; ibid., 41.
58. Ibid., 41–42.
59. Ibid., 44–45.
60. Ibid., 45.
61. Ibid., 46.
62. Ibid.
63. Ibid., 51.
64. Ibid.
65. Myrttinen, "Pack Your Heat," 31.

66. Benedict, *Lonely Soldier*, 5. The refrain is apparently common across all services. In Jennifer Silva's study of female ROTC cadets, she cites one respondent who describes a similar experience: "In the Navy the joke is that a woman in the Navy is either a bitch, a slut or a lesbian, and *none of them are good categories to fall into*, and if you are stern with your people then you are a bitch, but if you're a guy and stern people are like, wow, I respect him for being a good leader, and it's frustrating but it makes it even more self-fulfilling when you do earn that respect" (Silva, "A New Generation of Women?," 950; emphasis in original). Kayla Williams, a former military intelligence officer who served in Iraq, adds that she was part of "that whole 15 percent [of women in the military] trying to get past an old joke. 'What's the difference between a bitch and a slut? A slut will fuck anyone, a bitch will fuck anyone but you.' So if she's nice or friendly, outgoing or chatty—she's a slut. If she's distant or reserved or professional—she's a bitch" (*Love My Rifle More than You*, 13).
67. Montoya, "Sexual Abuse Allegations Persist."
68. Williams, *Love My Rifle More than You*, 13; emphasis in original.
69. Benedict, *Lonely Soldier*, 47.
70. Williams, *Love My Rifle More than You*, 12–13.
71. Montoya, "Sexual Abuse Allegations Persist."
72. Benedict, *Lonely Soldier*, 48.
73. Höpfl, "Becoming a (Virile) Member," 24.
74. Ibid., 26, 24.
75. Quoted in Silva, "A New Generation of Women?," 944; emphasis in original.
76. Ibid., 945.
77. Höpfl, "Becoming a (Virile) Member," 28.
78. Benedict, *Lonely Soldier*, 167.
79. Montoya, "Private War of Women Soldiers."
80. Zucchino, "Family Disputes Army's Suicide Finding."
81. Lavandera and Associated Press, "Adult, Fetus Found."
82. Benedict, *Lonely Soldier*, 50.
83. Foucault, *Docile Bodies*, 186.
84. Ibid., 181.
85. Duggan, *Twilight of Equality?*,14.
86. Ibid., xii.
87. Quoted in Fletcher and Biberica, "For Female Vets, a New Fight at Home."
88. ibid.
89. Quoted ibid.

CHAPTER 3

1. This capacity to integrate multiple worldviews and practices is best exemplified in the group's syncretic namesake Votán Zapata. In the Zapatistas' April 16, 1995, communiqué to *La Jornada*, they invoked the figure of Votán Zapata as a spiritual guide. As José Rabasa explains, Votán is a "pre-Columbian Tzeltal and Tzotzil god" who is also revered as the "guardian and heart of the people" ("Of Zapatismo," 400). The group was also inspired by the modern figure of Emiliano Zapata, an insurgent leader of the Mexican Revolution, who represents the people's struggle against the state and the fight to retain land rights. In a 1995 interview, Subcomandante Marcos described the symbolic value of Votán Zapata: "In us, in our arms, in our covered face, in our true word, Zapata united the wisdom and the struggle of our most ancient ancestors. Joined with Votán, the Guardian and Heart of the People, Zapata rose up again to struggle for democracy, liberty and justice for all Mexicans. Although he has Indian blood, Votán Zapata does not struggle only for the indigenous, he also struggles for those who are not indigenous but who live in the same misery" (quoted in Benjamin, "Time of Reconquest," 447).
2. Others in the press criticized the Zapatistas for their use of violence, their purported financing by drug cartels, their ties to Bishop Samuel Ruiz and liberation theology, and, of course, the claim that Subcomandante Marcos was the *real* leader of the organization (Rabasa, "Of Zapatismo," 412).
3. Ibid., 418.
4. Ibid., 401.
5. In addition to works discussed in this chapter, the genre includes Chicano poet Juan Felipe Herrera's *Mayan Drifter: Chicano Poet in the Lowlands of America* (1997). Latina/o writers and poets inspired by the Zapatistas include Puerto Rican poet and essayist Martín Espada. See his poem "Sing Zapatista," in *Alabanza: New and Selected Poems* (2004). Subcomandante Marcos has also turned to literature with his crime novel *Muertos incómodos* (2004; Inconvenient dead), co-authored with Paco Ignacio Taibo II, and his children's book *La historia de los colores/The Story of Colors: A Bilingual Storybook from the Jungles of Chiapas* (1996).
6. Ignacio López-Calvo reads *Erased Faces* as "a dialogue between Chicanismo and Zapatismo," wherein the feminist, egalitarian, and transnational nature of Zapatismo is an important influence on "Chicana/o cultural production and leadership" (López-Calvo, "Chicanismo Meets Zapatismo," 65).

7. Cummins Muñoz, "Postnational Bodies," 49.
8. Sandoval, "Mestizaje as Method," 354–55. Inspired by nineteenth- and twentieth-century decolonization struggles worldwide and by the Third World liberation movement of the sixties, U.S. feminists of color developed a global perspective to coalition building. "Third world liberation," Sandoval explains, "signified solidarity among new masses of peoples differentiated by nation, ethnicity, language, race, class, culture, sex, and gender demarcations but who were allied nevertheless by virtue of their similar sociohistorical, racial, and colonial relationships to dominant powers" (ibid., 355–56). Additionally, U.S. Third World feminists broke with the rigid fidelity to singular oppositional strategies and ideologies—such as the exclusive focus on gender oppression—and instead developed what Sandoval calls a differential mode of consciousness, one that allows for movement between ideological positions based on the contingencies of the power being opposed (*Methodology of the Oppressed*, 59).
9. Quotation in heading ("An armed woman commands them") from Marcos, "Twelve Women," 7; Marcos, "Flowers, Like Hope," 173.
10. It was at that time that the Mexican government adopted a series of neoliberal policies: "Neoliberal policies have forced the end of government investment in the economy; they have also led to trade liberalization aimed at boosting nonoil exports, the privatization of most public enterprises, the reduction of import tariffs to increase domestic competitiveness, the withdrawal of subsidies and price guarantees for agricultural products, and opening the agricultural sector to foreign investors to increase productivity" (Jung, "Politics of Indigenous Identity," 438).
11. In addition to neoliberal reforms, communities in Chiapas were further devastated when, in the late eighties, "the price of coffee on the world market dropped by half" (ibid.).
12. Courtney Jung further explains that ejidos are "an area comprised of individual plots and communal property that could not be sold, rented, or used as collateral" ("Politics of Indigenous Identity," 440). Furthermore, "ejidos account for almost one-half of all the land in Mexico, although most of it is of poor quality and under-capitalized. In Chiapas, ejidos and comunidades agrarias [indigenous lands] make up 57 percent of all exploitable land—the highest percentage in a Mexican state" (440).
13. Marcos and CCRI-CG, Sixth Declaration. Porfirio Díaz was the Mexican president from 1876 to 1911.
14. Marcos, "Sea of My Insomnia," 139.
15. Marcos, "Importance of Diverse Voices."

16. In Nicole Guidotti-Hernández's study of the Yaqui Indians of Northern Mexico in the late nineteenth and early twentieth centuries, she theorizes the effects of state violence and its role in producing subjectivities. As the Yaquis resisted state domination, they were "inaugurated as subjects in the historical record when they inflict violence against the nation-state and when the nation-state documents the violence it inflicted upon them" (Guidotti-Hernández, *Unspeakable Violence*, 240). In other words, subjectivity becomes possible through state recognition and historical documentation, an interpellation that requires the wounding of bodies. This process also occurs when the Zapatistas cross the state's radar and become legible subjects by taking up arms.
17. Marcos, "Twelve Women," 8.
18. Quoted in Millán Moncayo, "Indigenous Women and Zapatismo," 84.
19. Quoted ibid., 82.
20. Marcos, "Twelve Women," 5.
21. The LRM includes the following ten demands: women have the right (1) to "participate in the revolutionary struggle in a way determined by their desire and capacity"; (2) to receive a just salary; (3) to determine the number of children they will bear; (4) to "hold positions of authority if they are freely and democratically elected"; (5) to receive primary medical attention for themselves and their children; (6) to have an education; (7) to "choose their romantic partner, and . . . not to be forced into marriage"; (8) to not be beaten by family members; (9) to hold leadership positions within the EZLN and "hold military ranks in the revolutionary armed forces"; and (10) to "have all the rights and obligations elaborated in the Revolutionary Laws and regulations" (Women's Revolutionary Law). Comandante Susana, head of the women's commission of the CCRI, the top organizing body for the EZLN, compiled the list of demands after speaking with women in various communities about their major concerns. In March 1993, she presented the LRM to the CCRI assembly for ratification. In an interview, Subcomandante Marcos described the crowd's response to Susana's provocative demands: "The Women's Revolutionary Law that Susana had just read meant a real revolution for indigenous communities. The men looked to one another, nervous, restless. . . . The women were singing; men were scratching their heads. I prudently called for a recess. . . . That is the truth: the first Zapatista uprising was in March 1993 and was led by Zapatista women. There were no losses, and they won" (quoted in Millán Moncayo, "Indigenous Women and Zapatismo," 85–86).
22. Millán Moncayo, "Indigenous Women and Zapatismo," 86. The LRM also exemplifies how women construct their own spaces of enunciation, similar to

the Mexican feminists who struggled to be heard in the years following the Mexican Revolution. Because "women's politics may have been subordinated under a nationalist paradigm," women practiced what Emma Pérez calls a third space feminism "within and between dominant male discourses," where "women and men became each other's doubles, 'doubling' or even repeating each other's rhetoric" (*Decolonial Imaginary*, 32). Using the vocabulary of rights and equality that male nationalist discourse appropriated as its own, Mexican feminists in the Yucatán spoke the "doubled" language of feminism-in-nationalism. The same can be said for Zapatista women, who define themselves as rights-bearing subjects and who use the Zapatistas' rhetoric of liberation.

23. Mora, "Zapatismo," 175.
24. Women are involved in all levels from the CCRI to the descending organizational levels of the EZLN's military structure. Violeta Zylberberg Panebianco describes the EZLN structure as follows: "Below the CCRI is the military and regular structure of the EZLN, composed of men and women who live in the military camps in the region's mountains. At the third level are the women's militias, composed of women who live in their communities but who have had military training; they form irregular troops that are called into action at specific times. Finally, there are the women who are part of the support bases" ("We Can No Longer Be Like Hens," 222–23).
25. Roy, "Ethical Ambivalence," 145.
26. Hutchings, "Feminist Ethics," 101.
27. Carrigan, "Afterword: Chiapas," 435.
28. Marcos and CCRI-CG, Sixth Declaration.
29. Marcos, "For Those Who Protest," 132–33. Even before the Acteal massacre, the Zapatistas struggled with their ambivalence about warfare and armed insurrection, especially when they considered that the soldier they would face in battle was a "brother" sent to kill "in other clothing": "He came to kill. To die. Again, we did not want to raise our hand to confront the one sent to kill and die among the same brothers and sisters" (Marcos, "Come, Brothers and Sisters," 73). Instead, they heeded the counsel of "different brothers and sisters" and that of their antecedents, embodied in "a big voice that came with the wind," which said, "War must not walk," as it implored the Zapatistas to follow another path toward justice (72–74).
30. Marcos and CCRI-CG, Second Declaration, 116. In "Professionals of Hope," Subcomandante Marcos responds to the letter of a thirteen-year-old Mexican boy, who describes how he believed that the Zapatistas were justified in

using violence because "there was no alternative to rising up in arms, since the government did not listen to the needs of the Indians." In Marcos's reply to the young man, he contends that the Zapatistas are not "professionals of violence," a label given to them by their earliest critics, but are professionals of hope: "But our profession is hope. We decided one fine day to make ourselves soldiers so that one day soldiers would not be needed. That is, we picked a suicidal profession because it is a profession whose objective is to disappear: Soldiers who are soldiers so that one day nobody will need to be a soldier. . . . But it turns out that in order for soldiers to no longer be necessary, one has to become a soldier and prescribe a discrete quantity of lead, hot lead writing freedom and justice for all, not for one or for a few, but for all, everyone, the dead of before and of tomorrow, the living of today and always, all of those who we call people and country, those without anything, the losers of always before tomorrow, the nameless, the faceless" (254–55).

31. Marcos, "Twelve Women," 11.
32. Ibid., 12.
33. A former professor of Chicana/o studies, Limón is the author of six novels to date. Her earliest novel, *In Search of Bernabé* (1993), about the civil war in El Salvador, was inspired by her activism in the sanctuary movement. Most of her literary oeuvre focuses on a feminist interpretation of colonial histories in Mexico (*Song of the Hummingbird*, 1996); significant events in Mexican history, such as the Battle of Puebla (*The Madness of Mamá Carlota*, 2012); struggles against cultural institutions (*The Memories of Ana Calderon*, 2001); migration (*The River Flows North*, 2009); class, race, and patriarchy (*The Day of the Moon*, 1999); and violence and loss (*Left Alive*, 2005).
34. In his review of the novel, Michael Harris seems to miss this point: "The contemporary context of the revolt—Mexican economics and politics, the military odds, sources of support for the rebel movement and conflicts within it—is as murky here as the historical justification is clear"("In Chiapas").
35. Limón, *Erased Faces*, 206; italics in original.
36. Ibid., 113.
37. Ibid., 90–91.
38. Ibid., 79, 91.
39. Ibid., 102.
40. Ibid.
41. Ibid., 103.
42. Ibid., 104.

43. Ibid., 109.
44. Ibid., 104.
45. Ibid., 110.
46. Ibid., 219.
47. Ibid., 213–14.
48. Hutchings, "Feminist Ethics," 100.
49. Limón, *Erased Faces*, 111.
50. Anderson, *Imagined Communities*, 24–26.
51. Marcos, interview by Carlos Loret de Mola, May 9, 2006.
52. Bhabha, *Location of Culture*, 212.
53. Rabasa, *Without History*, 3.
54. Ibid., 2–3.
55. Freeman, "Time Binds, or, Erotohistoriography," 57–58.
56. Freeman, *Time Binds*, 4.
57. Ibid., xii.
58. Limón, *Erased Faces*, 3.
59. The incident Limón describes here may be "the battle of Sumidero in 1532, when, according to legend, Chiapaneca rebels in an act of heroic defiance threw themselves into the steep Sumidero Canyon rather than accept Spanish conquest and slavery" (Benjamin, "Time of Reconquest," 431).
60. Limón, *Erased Faces*, 21.
61. The Zapatistas' preoccupation with time helps dispel the commonplace misperceptions of Native peoples' primordialism. Thomas Benjamin describes how Indians in Mexico are often perceived as "people without history," a condition that is both historiographical and philosophical ("Time of Reconquest," 418). In the historiographical sense, before the Indian revitalization movement that began in the seventies, "Indians of this region since the Conquest have not produced written chronicles and histories of their own" (418). Consequently, Spanish and Mexican historians have often depicted Indians as "passive victims and inert obstacles to progress (that is, 'to the course of history')" (418). In the philosophical sense, "people without history" refers to the notion that the Mayan sense of the past is confined to mythologies distinct from traditional historical consciousness (420). In fact, as Benjamin explains, the Maya do not lack a historical consciousness, but their conception of the past is markedly different from Western notions of history: "Most scholars have reported a cyclical rather than linear temporal order in the abundant sacred narratives and secular stories that make up the oral tradition of the native peoples of the

region. . . . Narratives were of mythic origins, epic events, and futures foretold. The remote past was telescoped into the present, while events were related in a distorted temporal fashion or presented outside of time altogether" (420).

62. Limón, *Erased Faces*, 58–59.
63. Ibid., 95.
64. Mignolo, *Idea of Latin America*, 53; emphasis in original.
65. Ibid., 8; emphasis in original.
66. Ibid., 53.
67. Limón, *Erased Faces*, 23.
68. Ibid., 71.
69. Guidotti-Hernández, *Unspeakable Violence*, 240.
70. Mignolo, *Idea of Latin America*, 98.
71. In a 2003 lecture, Limón discussed her colleague Roberto Flores's description of the Acteal massacre as based on hatred for women. Limón went on to explain why she thinks women were targeted: "Why women? Well, for many reasons, you can answer that. But one of them is because the women in Chiapas, in the Chiapas revolution[,] took key roles. This is another magnificent thing. They were avant-garde. Seven cities capitulated to the [Zapatistas, and] of those seven, four of them were commandeered by women, indigenous women. So in a land of huge macho, of huge military ego, to surrender to a five-foot, four-foot-eight indigenous woman, you can imagine. Don't you wish you could have been a fly right there? To see it all, to see a bemedaled colonel handing over his weapon to a four-foot-seven woman, masked?" See "Zapatistas, Literature."
72. Limón, *Erased Faces*, 241–42.
73. Ibid., 100.
74. Alexander, *Pedagogies of Crossing*, 196–98.
75. Ibid., 197.
76. Limón, *Erased Faces*, 253–54.
77. Ibid., 256; emphasis in original.
78. Hutchings, "Simone de Beauvoir," 120–21.
79. Muñoz, *Cruising Utopia*, 27.
80. Muñoz argues that in the context of heteronormative straight time, the "only futurity promised is that of reproductive majoritarian heterosexuality, the spectacle of the state refurbishing its ranks through overt and subsidized acts of reproduction" (ibid., 22). Instead of promoting straight time's imperative to reproduce, Muñoz argues that the future can be reconceived in more liberatory terms by drawing on the affective worlds of the past to reimagine queer uto-

pian futurity. Muñoz argues that futurity promises a queer utopianism that remains undefined and therefore open to infinite possibilities.

81. Ibid., 7.
82. Pérez, *Decolonial Imaginary*, 76.
83. Rodríguez y Gibson, "Poetry of Improbability," 137.
84. Cervantes, "Coffee," 9.
85. Ibid.
86. Ibid., 10–11.
87. Ibid., 9.
88. Roett, "Mexico-Political Update."
89. Cervantes, "Coffee," 10. Although the Mexican government denied involvement in the massacre, recently obtained cables from the U.S. Defense Intelligence Agency recount the Mexican army's direct support of paramilitaries as part of their counterinsurgency campaign against the Zapatistas.
90. Ibid., 11.
91. Ibid., 10.
92. Ibid., 11.
93. Butler, *Precarious Life*, 36–37.
94. Cervantes, "Coffee," 12. Guadalupe Vázquez Luna, who was thirteen years old at the time, recounts losing her parents and five sisters during the massacre: "We were in the chapel praying for peace when about 90 men burst in and started shooting at everybody, even babies. Then they went through the village shooting. The assassins ran after me and my father. When my father was hit by a bullet, he shouted, 'Run, Lupita, run,' but I couldn't. Again he told me, 'Run, run,' and I ran faster than the bullets until I couldn't run anymore" (quoted in Kennis, "Ten Years Later").
95. Vásquez, "Poetry as Survival," 293.
96. Rodríguez y Gibson, "Poetry of Improbability," 140.
97. Cervantes, "Coffee," 14.
98. Ibid., 15.
99. Ibid., 14.
100. Alexander, *Pedagogies of Crossing*, 190.
101. In a footnote, Hernández Castillo explains that the account in *The Other Word* "is a literary essay that does not attempt to reproduce the testimony of the women of Acteal word-for-word. All the events described below, however, are true. This is a collective piece of work based on testimonies collected by Ana María Garza, Juana María Ruiz, R. Aída Hernández, Martha Figueroa and

Mercedes Olivera from survivors of Acteal and inhabitants of the neighboring communities. . . . [N]ames have been changed to protect the interviewed" (37).

102. Cervantes, "Coffee," 17.

103. Ibid. The following passage includes a description of Mícaela's experience on the day of the massacre. She recounts how her mother decided to leave the church and flee with her children to safety. Her mother carried her two youngest children in her arms and held Mícaela by the hand as they attempted to run up a steep embankment. The paramilitaries followed them to a stream and then executed Mícaela's mother and siblings: "The bullet hit her mother in the back; the children's crying gave her away. First they shot her mother and then the two little ones. She lay under their bodies, which is what saved her; she kept quiet, she could feel the weight of her mother's warm body; she did not know if she was dead. . . . From where she lay, Mícaela saw them, recognized Diego, Antonio, Pedro: 'There were many of them, more than fifty, from los Chorros, Pequichiquil, la Esperanza, and from Acteal as well. They came dressed in black, with balaclavas, they were real paramilitaries; the others, the leaders, were dressed like soldiers, . . .' she would say later in her testimony to the human rights people. She saw them killing the catechist and shooting women and children in the back. When the men left, Mícaela went to hide on the bank of the stream. From there she saw how they came back with machetes in their hands" (Hernández Castillo, *The Other Word*, 33).

104. Ibid.

105. Rodríguez, "Fiction of Solidarity," 218.

106. Cervantes, "Coffee," 18. The activist in Cervantes's poem reenacts the marches of solidarity that took place around the globe, as protesters rallied in five continents to condemn the Mexican government's brutal attack on Acteal and to demand justice for the slain. News of the global protest reached the Zapatistas, who encouraged the global scrutiny of state violence: "As for the demonstrations in the twenty-seven other countries, the Mexican government and that racket called the PRI are rather annoyed at the 'internationalization' of the conflict these demonstrations signify. It seems what they sneeringly call 'an Internet war' has given their embassies and consulates many headaches. Takeovers, protests in central squares and in the streets, and thousands of letters demanding peace and justice are keeping the Mexican government from its sleep" (Marcos, "For Those Who Protest," 134).

107. Ibid.

108. Mohanty, "Under Western Eyes," 65.

109. "Indians in Chiapas Protest Massacre"; "Violence Flares at Chiapas Massacre Protest."
110. In Marcos's letter entitled "From Vietnam to Chiapas," he describes the U.S. government's support of the Mexican government as being based on the manipulation of fear. He also implies that U.S. taxpayers should be more discerning about their government's actions: "So much money to finance deceit can only be explained by fear. But what does the U.S. government fear? The truth? That the North American people realize that their money is helping to back the oldest dictatorship in the modern world? That the North American people realize that their taxes pay for the persecution and death of the Mexican indigenous population?" (176). Instead, Marcos asks, "Shouldn't they fear the violence that the lack of freedom, democracy, and justice irrevocably brings about?"
111. Cervantes, "Coffee," 18.
112. Enloe, *Maneuvers*, 295.
113. Cervantes, "Coffee," 19.
114. Ibid., 18.
115. Marcos, "A Storm and a Prophecy," 23.
116. Marcos and CCRI-CG, Sixth Declaration; emphasis added.
117. Mohanty, *Feminism without Borders*, 4.
118. Importantly, Cervantes's turn to the consumer coincides with an important shift in the rise of the Latina/o consumer. As Arlene Dávila writes, Latinas/os in particular are being targeted as pliable shoppers open to manipulation: "At precisely a time when the state has withdrawn most directly from providing its citizens the basics for social welfare, security, and mobility, groups are increasingly being measured and valued with regard to their marketability, that is, for their value as consumers, and for their ability to become a targetable 'niche' constituency for marketers, politicians, and privatization pundits" (*Latino Spin*, 4). In this conception, Latina/o consumers have gained visibility as a self-sufficient, politically disengaged market that fulfills "dominant society's longing for docile, unthreatening consumers" (89).
119. Cervantes, "Coffee," 19.
120. Here, I refer to the work of César Chávez, Dolores Huerta, and the United Farm Workers who led nationwide boycotts against table grapes grown in central California in the sixties and seventies. Although boycotts are seemingly small gestures of protest, such acts of politically informed consumption are the basis for larger alliances between consumers and the laborers who produce goods and

can make important differences in the living and working conditions of workers (Wright, *Disposable Women*).

121. Cervantes, *Drive*, 45.
122. Jameson, "End of Temporality," 702.
123. Ibid., 704.
124. Marcos, "Sea of My Insomnia," 139.
125. Alexander, *Pedagogies of Crossing*, 191.
126. Cervantes, "Coffee," 19.
127. Ibid.; Marcos, "Twelve Women," 11.
128. Mohanty, "U.S. Empire," 17.
129. Rabasa, "Of Zapatismo," 421; emphasis in original.
130. Marcos, "Twelve Women," 8–9.
131. Feldman, *Formations of Violence*, 7.

CHAPTER 4

1. "Your daughter wants to enlist," Armed Forces advertisement, "The Latinas Issue," *Hispanic*, June/July 2008, 9.
2. Enloe, *Maneuvers*, 254.
3. Because the military advertisements and recruitment data I examine in this chapter do not specify ethnicities, I use *Latina* instead of *Chicana* in most sections, except when the texts refer to or suggest Chicana experiences.
4. Smith, "Contours of a Spatialized Politics," 63–64.
5. The notion of republican motherhood arose in the United States in the late eighteenth century, when educators such as Judith Sargent Murray argued that mothers had a powerful moral influence over their sons and thus played an important role in shaping future leaders of the Republic. In *Home Fronts*, Lora Romero identifies this notion of republican motherhood as a precursor to the nineteenth century's culture of domesticity. There is a large body of scholarship on this topic, but Jane Tompkins's work on Harriet Beecher Stowe's *Uncle Tom's Cabin* and the domestic novel is one place to start (see Tompkins, "Sentimental Power"). See also Amy Kaplan's analysis of nineteenth-century domestic novels, which helps undermine the presumed boundaries between home and public spheres, and, more specifically, between the domestic and the foreign. Kaplan shows how such texts often imagined the home as the mother's

"empire" ("Manifest Domesticity," 586). As the territorial metaphor suggests, the domestic space relied on notions of guarded borders, expansion, and protectionism. This kind of "imperial domesticity" undermined the separation between the domestic home and foreign policy.

6. Brady, *Extinct Lands*, 9.
7. Ibid., 172–73.
8. Smith, "Contours of a Spatialized Politics," 67.
9. Brady, *Extinct Lands*, 174.
10. Pulido, "Rethinking Environmental Racism," 20.
11. Young, "Logic of Masculinist Protection," 4.
12. Ibid., 3.
13. Ibid., 8.
14. Graham, *Cities Under Siege*, 31.
15. Malkin, "Candidates Ignore 'Security Moms.'"
16. Rodino, "War Mothering," 382.
17. Ruddick, "Women of Peace," 215.
18. Chavez, *Latino Threat*, 72.
19. Ibid., 75.
20. For a brief discussion of this video game, see Daniels and LaLone, "Racism in Video Gaming," 90–91. They explain that the game appears on Tom Metzger's white supremacist website *The Insurgent* along with other racist video games. Metzger is a former Ku Klux Klan leader who continues to operate an Aryan newsletter, website, and radio broadcast. Daniels and Lalone do not credit Metzger with creating the low-quality game, however, which also appears on various other websites, including www.flashrolls.com and www.dailyfreegames.com.
21. Terry, "Significant Injury," 212.
22. Enloe, *Maneuvers*, 11.
23. Bayard de Volo, "Drafting Motherhood," 241–42.
24. Ibid., 188.
25. Miller and Rose, "Governing Economic Life," 7.
26. Matthews, "Introduction: Primer," 1.
27. Ibid., 7.
28. Hattiangadi, Lee, and Quester, *Recruiting Hispanics*, iii.
29. Ibid., 1–2, 5, 9.
30. Jones, "Diversity in the 21st Century Army," 57.

31. Sackett and Mavor, *Attitudes, Aptitudes, and Aspirations*, 3.
32. Quester, "Demographic Trends and Military Recruitment," 27.
33. Hattiangadi, Lee, and Quester, *Recruiting Hispanics*, 20
34. JAMRS is the creation of the corporate advertising firm Mullen, which was contracted to serve the DoD's advertising needs in 2002. Mullen's $161 million contract was renewed in 2012. Mullen provides marketing, corporate branding, and communication services, which include "wire releases, broadcast clippings, media training and Factiva searches" (Dickson, "Mullen Wins"). The initial JAMRS Youth Polls uncovered disturbing trends for military planners, including the finding that despite general support for combating terrorism, youth "stated that the situation related to the 'War on Terrorism' made them less likely to join the military" and that their favorable opinion of the military had dropped since its peak in October 2001 (JAMRS, *October 2002 Youth Poll*, iii). From this annual data trove, analysts determined that Latinas and Latinos had, on average, higher service propensities, meaning that they were more likely to say that they would "definitely" or "probably" enlist in the military (20). For example, the disaggregated data showed that for "female high school seniors, propensities were 24 percent for Hispanics, 28 percent for blacks, and 10 percent for whites" (20).
35. Sackett and Mavor further categorize parents as "role-incumbent significant others" because they "have power and authority over a young person, who, for that reason[,] is beholden to them" (*Attitudes, Aptitudes, and Aspirations*, 184). Sackett and Mavor also cite sociological youth surveys showing that "youth choose to follow their parents' career advice not because they have to but because they want to. The implication for military recruitment is that enlisting parental support may yield enlistment dividends" (ibid., 188).
36. JAMRS, *August 2003 Influencer Poll*, 4.
37. Ibid., 11.
38. Ibid., 22.
39. Sackett and Mavor, *Attitudes, Aptitudes, and Aspirations*, 186. They also explain that the findings were consistent across race, but they only refer to black and white respondents. It is not clear if data exist on Latina/o youth respondents or if Sackett and Mavor omitted or overlooked them.
40. Ibid., 188.
41. Ibid.; emphasis added.
42. JAMRS, *August 2003 Influencer Poll*, 36.

43. JAMRS, *Influencer Poll Report and Crosstabulations*, 5.
44. Sackett and Mavor, *Attitudes, Aptitudes, and Aspirations*, 255. They further explain that average levels of maternal education will continue to increase in the next two decades, and as a result, "the majority of youth will [be] raised by mothers who have completed at least some college" (ibid.).
45. Bicksler and Nolan, *Recruiting an All-Volunteer Force*, 11.
46. Dept. of the Navy, *Annual Report on Diversity*, 10.
47. Hattiangadi, Lee, and Quester, *Recruiting Hispanics*, 37.
48. Moving away from an exclusive focus on juridical and disciplinary forms of power, modern states in the eighteenth century began to take an interest in their citizens as a species, a population whose collective biological capacities became the objects of new forms of power and regulation.
49. Gutiérrez, *Fertile Matters*, 36. Doctors, nurses, and residents pressured women into coercive sterilizations by intimidating them into signing consent forms while in active labor, threatening them with deportation, taking advantage of their limited English fluency, and lying to them by implying that their lives were at risk, among other tactics (ibid., 35).
50. Tajima-Peña, "Más Bebés?"
51. Shuit, "Prenatal Care Cut."
52. Inda, "Value of Immigrant Life," 153.
53. Foucault, *Security, Territory, Population*, 48.
54. Ibid., 48–49.
55. Ibid., 45. This other dimension of biopower perhaps accounts for the military's support of immigration reform and its refusal to mimic the anti-immigrant and xenophobic sentiment that circulate in popular and political discourse. For example, the Pentagon has been one of the earliest and strongest supporters of the Development, Relief, and Education for Alien Minors (DREAM) Act since its inception. The act would provide a path toward legalization for qualified undocumented youth who complete either two years of college or two years of military service. Citing a 2005 report from the Center of Naval Analyses, Margaret Stock notes that "much of the growth in the recruitment-eligible population will come from immigration" (*Essential to the Fight*, 7). The report also describes how "immigrants add valuable diversity to the armed forces and perform extremely well, often having significantly lower attrition rates than other recruits" (7). Stock argues that passage of the DREAM Act would enable the military to "tap into an overlooked pool of home-grown talent" (8).

Without immigrants, Stock argues, "the military could not meet its recruiting goals and could not fill the need for foreign-language translators, interpreters, and cultural experts" (8).

56. "Su entrenamiento empezó en casa," U.S. Marines advertisement, *Hispanic* magazine, September 2007. The full Spanish-language text appears below, followed with my English translation: "Ustedes se esmeraron en su crianza para que fuera un joven bien educado, respetuoso y cortés. Le enseñaron a caminar derecho, a hacer siempre el bien y a respetar a los ancianos. Pero sobre todo, le enseñaron que nada en la vida es fácil. En resumen, le enseñaron los valores que buscamos en un Marine. Denle la oportunidad de servir a su país con honor mientras desarrolla su carácter con auto-disciplina y liderazgo. Así él completará lo que ustedes empezaron en casa." (With great effort, you raised him so that he could be well behaved, respectful, and courteous. You taught him to walk straight, to always do things well, and to respect his elders. But above all, you taught him that nothing in life is easy. In short, you taught him the values that we look for in a Marine. Give him the opportunity to serve his country with honor while he develops his character with self-discipline and leadership. That way he will complete what you began at home.)
57. Lipsitz, *Possessive Investment in Whiteness*, 76.
58. Dávila, *Latinos Inc*, 9.
59. Ibid., 14–15.
60. Dávila, *Latino Spin*, 9.
61. Ibid., 67.
62. Ibid., 88.
63. Ibid.
64. Elshtain, *Women and War*, 144.
65. Ibid., 9–10.
66. Malkin, "Candidates Ignore 'Security Moms.'"
67. Kaplan, "Homeland Insecurities," 90.
68. Grewal, "Security Moms," 30–31.
69. Treviño, "Latina Mother Realizes Childhood Dream."
70. Fulton, "Mom, Son Complete BCT Family Tree."
71. It is difficult to ascertain the actual number of Latina servicewomen who are mothers. I have not been able to find sources that document this trend.
72. Throughout my discussion of *Captain Mama*, I use the term *soldier-mother* rather than the more accurate *airman-mother* because I am using *soldier* as a generic descriptor for servicewomen in general. Each military branch uses its

own specific terms: army and National Guard members are *soldiers*; navy members are *sailors*; Marines are *Marines*; and air force members are *airmen*. My use of *soldier* as a generic term will undoubtedly offend some readers. I thank Graciela Tiscareño-Sato for explaining the distinction in terminology.

73. The idea for the book came when Tiscareño-Sato was preparing for an event at her son's preschool. While wearing her flight suit the night before the event, her son began asking about her uniform. She then began to think about representations of Latina servicewomen and asked herself, Do women who serve write children's books? Appalled, though not necessarily shocked, by the lack of representation, Tiscareño-Sato wrote *Captain Mama* in order to present positive depictions of Latina servicewomen and veterans and to expose children to the kind of advanced technical careers made possible through and paid by the military (phone interview with author, November 28, 2016). Tiscareño-Sato captured the spontaneous conversation with her son on video. To watch the exchange, see the *Good Night Captain Mama* home page: http://www.captainmama.com/index.php?page=home.
74. Elshtain, *Women and War*, 165.
75. *Captain Mama* also facilitates the militarization of the children who read it by providing a template at the back of the book and inviting them to design and decorate their own military patches. In our phone conversation, Tiscareño-Sato pointed out that *Captain Mama* is not necessarily encouraging Marco to enlist but merely answering his questions. She explained that through *Captain Mama* and her public speaking engagements at schools, she does not encourage young people to enlist. As she put it, she "wants to get ahead of recruiters." (Interestingly, she noted that when she was younger, she avoided the military recruiters in her high school cafeteria because she wanted to attend college.) Tiscareño-Sato explained that her goal is to encourage young people to go to college first and then consider military service. She further encourages youth to enroll in college ROTC programs so that the military can pay for their tuition. While I appreciate this clarification, my reading of the text argues that the positive depiction of the military is an endorsement, even if it is unintentional. As I have shown through the military's own research, mothers have significant influence on their children's career choices and educational attainment. Hence, Captain Mama's military service would make her the ideal maternal influencer for military recruiters.
76. Villa, *Barrio-Logos*, 5. See Cota-Cárdenas's "Faith of Activists" for a survey of early Chicana urban literature.

77. Brady, *Extinct Lands*, 9.
78. Kaplan, "Homeland Insecurities," 88.
79. Graham, *Cities Under Siege*, 44.
80. See Marine Corps, *Military Operations*, 1–3.
81. Davis, *Planet of Slums*, 203. According to the Marine Corps' *Military Operations*, MOUT "is defined as *all military actions planned and conducted on a topographical complex and its adjacent terrain where manmade construction is the dominant feature. It includes combat in cities, which is that portion of MOUT involving house-to-house and street-by-street fighting in towns and cities*" (1–3; italics in original).
82. Quoted in Davis, *Planet of Slums*, 203.
83. Cowen, "National Soldiers," par. 14. The *Military Operations* manual describes the "more than 200 miles of storm sewers" located under Los Angeles streets to exemplify the importance of assessing subterranean systems (1–3).
84. For a thorough overview of the history of racialization in Los Angeles, start with Pulido's "Rethinking Environmental Racism."
85. Quoted in Davis, *Planet of Slums*, 204.
86. Graham, *Cities Under Siege*, 80.
87. In an interview, Grise describes the ambiguous setting of her play: "It is set in the barrio in the United States of America. People from Tejas think its San Antonio, people from California think it's Los Angeles. There are specific references to both places throughout the script. I was interested in the elements of similarity between the places and how the State, institutional violence, war, poverty, and desire manifest themselves in the barrio" (Grise, "Virginia Grise Looking Up").
88. Pulido, "Rethinking Environmental Racism," 26. Pulido also notes the role that defense industries played in shaping the landscape because military industries initially settled in urban centers, bringing employment and sparking a housing boom, before moving to the suburbs in the fifties in search of more space and drawing more white workers with them (ibid., 30).
89. Gilmore, "Globalisation and U.S. Prison Growth," 176.
90. James Cypher describes National Security Document 68 (NSC-68) as one of the most important government articulations of military Keynesianism. Written and submitted to President Truman in 1950 (but not publicly released until 1975), the NSC-68 "made the then novel argument that the U.S. economy had excess capacity and that high levels of military spending on a permanent basis would act as a stimulant to the economy—creating multiplier

effects on employment and spending by absorbing the unemployed and the untapped production capabilities of U.S. industry" (Cypher, "From Military Keynesianism").

91. The rise of the New Right, which included the election of Ronald Reagan as governor of California in 1966 and Richard Nixon as president in 1968, propagated new policies to dismantle what New Right proponents viewed as the government's runaway spending on social programs. In their view, "it was the welfare state, military Keynesianism's *social* face, rather than capitalism's surplus-generated crisis, that bore popular political blame for economic turmoil" (Gilmore, "Fatal Couplings," 19; emphasis in original). The "*social* face" was racialized and gendered in political discourse as the "welfare queen" (Gilmore, "Globalisation and U.S. Prison Growth," 177).
92. Loyd, "Peace Is Our Only Shelter," 864.
93. Jenna Loyd argues that the "apparent autonomy of the white home stood in inverse relation to the dependency of the black home, an ideological relation that obscured how the privilege of the white home was in fact a racial entitlement backed by the state" (ibid., 856).
94. Gilmore, "Globalisation and U.S. Prison Growth," 175.
95. While Gilmore notes that state repression is not new, she argues, "What's new is the scale of militarism being directed at people inside the United States, and the scope of what comes into the crosshairs of the prison industrial complex rather than some helping agency" ("Behind the Power").
96. Gilmore, "Globalisation and U.S. Prison Growth," 174.
97. Grise, *blu*, 24.
98. Ibid., 23.
99. In the author's note, Grise provides the following stage directions: "There are moments when characters speak the same lines and have the same memory. At other times, characters interrupt and take over each other's monologues because they live a shared experience. These voices should not be in unison but should overlap, unless otherwise noted" (ibid., 4).
100. Rodríguez, "(Non)Scenes of Captivity," 26.
101. Ibid., 11.
102. Ibid., 14.
103. The helicopter not only surveils bodies but invades psyches, fomenting anxiety and inciting micro acts of violence. It is when Eme becomes overwhelmed by the "metal birds . . . huntin [*sic*] people like vultures" that he hits Soledad (Grise, *blu*, 31).

104. Gilmore, *Golden Gulag*, 274.
105. Marine Corps, *Military Operations*, 1–8.
106. Kaplan, "Homeland Insecurities," 89.
107. Ibid.
108. Anzaldúa, *Borderlands/La Frontera*, 30.
109. Brady, *Extinct Lands*, 146.
110. El Plan, 402.
111. Ibid., 405.
112. Brady, *Extinct Lands*, 146.
113. Young, "The Logic of Masculinist Protection," 4.
114. Ibid.
115. We can look to Cherríe Moraga's description of the Chicano patriarchal constriction of the public and private spheres of discourse for an example of the kind of protection bargain Young is alluding to. Moraga argues that the movement promoted an antiquated model of the family: "In the name of this 'culturally correct' familia, certain topics were censored both in cultural and political spheres as not 'socially relevant' to Chicanos and typically not sanctioned in the Mexican household. These issues included female sexuality generally and male homosexuality and lesbianism specifically, as well as incest and violence against women—all of which are still relevant between the sheets and within the walls of many Chicano families" (*Last Generation*, 146).
116. Young, "Logic of Masculinist Protection," 6. Cherríe Moraga also critiques how certain Chicano nationalists used Aztec myth and history to reaffirm their own gender dominance: "In reaction against Anglo-America's emasculation of Chicano men, the male-dominated Chicano Movement embraced the most patriarchal aspects of its Mexican heritage. . . . At times, they took the worst of Mexican machismo and Aztec warrior bravado, combined it with some of the most oppressive male-conceived idealizations of 'traditional' Mexican womanhood and called that cultural integrity" (*Last Generation*, 146). Elizabeth Martínez described the Chicano nationalist embrace of Aztlán in even more withering terms: "Not surprisingly, the concept of Aztlán has always been set forth in ferociously macho imagery. The average Chicano today hardly takes Aztlán seriously as a goal, but he might secretly imagine himself garbed in an Aztec warrior outfit gazing on the naked breasts of some red-lipped princess. If you note the whiff of sexual possession there, it's no accident. Merely as symbol, the concept of Aztlán encourages the association of machismo with domination" ("Chingón Politics," 127).

117. Anzaldúa, *Borderlands/La Frontera*, 54–55. Huitzilopochtli, speaking through shamans who transmit his divine prophecies, commanded the Aztecs to aspire to the full control of the human race: "We shall proceed to establish ourselves and settle down, and we shall conquer all peoples of the universe; and I tell you in all truth that I will make you lords and kings of all that is in the world; and when you become rulers, you shall have countless and infinite numbers of vassals, who will pay tribute to you" (Carrasco, *Aztecs*, 20). Under Huitzilopochtli's divine rule, the Aztecs established an imperial regime that mandated perpetual and preemptive war and thus glorified the role of the warrior.
118. Grise, *blu*, 33–34.
119. Ibid., 45.
120. Fregoso, *MeXicana Encounters*, 92.
121. Grise, *blu*, 22.
122. Ibid., 51.
123. Ibid., 51–52.
124. Ibid., 34.
125. Fregoso, *MeXicana Encounters*, 94.
126. Ibid.
127. Ibid.
128. See Ben Olguín's *La Pinta* for a discussion of how Raul Sanchez's poetry depicts pachucos as defenders of the barrio from invading gringos (101).
129. Martínez, "Chingón Politics," 128.
130. Hernandez, "Exploratory Study of Hispanic Officer Recruiting," 27.
131. Ibid., 43.
132. Ibid., 94.
133. Ibid., 99.
134. Kaplan, "Precision Targets," 694. For Caren Kaplan, the prevalence of target marketing signals the widespread militarization of the population. She argues that consumers and citizens "come together as militarized subjects through target marketing that seeks to identify their tastes, desires, and interests" (708). Citizens and consumers have become "the 'targets' of two seemingly distinct contexts and practices: the target of a weapon and the target of a marketing campaign. In both cases, something or somebody has to be identified, coordinates have to be determined with available technologies, and the target has to be clearly marked or recognized in time and space" (696).
135. Mariscal, "Homeland Security," 46. Cowen further describes how class and racial composition shape military labor geographies: "Today recruitment in the

U.S. follows two dominant and distinct geographies of poverty: rural whites who still make up the vast majority of recruits, and inner city blacks and increasingly Latinos" ("National Soldiers," par. 26).

136. Cowen, "National Soldiers," par. 5.
137. Grise, *blu*, 43.
138. Ibid., 38.
139. Ibid., 43–44.
140. Ibid., 44.
141. Ibid., 43.
142. Leal, "In Search of Aztlán," 8.
143. Gonzales, "I am Joaquín," 16.
144. Ibid., 26.
145. Anaya, "Aztlán," 233.
146. Ibid., 236.
147. Gonzales, "I am Joaquín," 27.
148. Korte, *Nosotros*, 179.
149. Ibid. In Ben Olguín's analysis of Raul Sanchez's poetry, he elaborates on the meaning of *desmadre* and notes that it also means "to fuck." He goes on to explain how "this valence is historically and culturally grounded in Mexican and Chicana/o myth—specifically, the sense of consummate subordination associated with Malintzin, or La Malinche, the archetypal Mesoamerican mother whose 'violation' by the 'enemy' leads to the birth of the 'mixed-race,' or mestizo, peoples of the Americas" (*La Pinta*, 101).
150. El Plan, 405; emphasis added.
151. Grise, *blu*, 17–18, 35.
152. Ibid., 31–32.
153. Brady, *Extinct Lands*, 128.
154. Fregoso, *MeXicana Encounters*, 73.
155. Cowen and Gilbert, "Citizenship in the 'Homeland,'" 274.
156. Brady, *Extinct Lands*, 128.
157. Grewal, "Security Moms," 36–37.
158. Caputi, "Afterword: Goddess Murder," 280.
159. Carrasco, *Aztecs*, 73.
160. León-Portilla and Shorris, *In the Language of Kings*, 206.
161. Carrasco, *Aztecs*, 73.
162. Grise, *blu*, 47.
163. Ibid., 52.
164. Ibid., 46.

165. Pérez, "Spirit Glyphs," 47.
166. Grise, *blu*, 55.
167. According to the divine song, upon emerging from Coatlicue's womb, Huitzilopochtli adorned himself in plumage and painted his arms and legs blue (León-Portilla and Shorris, *In the Language of Kings*, 206).
168. Carrasco, *Aztecs*, 64.
169. Carrasco explains how Aztec temple architecture depicts the "daily drama of the sun (Huitzilopochtli) rising out of the earth (Coatepec-Coatlicue) and then battling with its light the stars (the four hundred siblings) and the moon (Coyolxauhqui), which it dismembered and absorbed into its own brilliance" (Carrasco, *Aztecs*, 74).
170. Moraga, *Last Generation*, 190.
171. Flores, "Creating Discursive Space," 145–46.
172. Ibid., 146.
173. Malkin, "Candidates Ignore 'Security Moms.'"
174. Collins, *Black Feminist Thought*, 118.

CONCLUSION

1. Castillo, *Massacre of the Dreamers*, 21; emphasis in original.
2. Before Woolf concedes to donate one of her three guineas to the gentleman, she writes a book-length rebuke of the state's marginalization of women and its imperial violence.
3. Ibid., 126.
4. Ibid., 127–29.
5. Pérez, *Citizen, Student, Soldier*, 8.
6. Mohanty, "U.S. Empire," 10.
7. Ibid.
8. Woolf, *Three Guineas*, 9.
9. Ibid.
10. Fusco, *Field Guide for Female Interrogators*, 18.
11. Ibid., 20, 48.
12. Fusco provides an example based on descriptions from a Yemeni detainee: "A detainee claimed that when he refused to talk in an interrogation, a female interrogator was dispatched to his booth in a tight t-shirt; she asked him what his sexual needs were, showed off her breasts, and simply stated, 'Are you going to talk, or are we going to do this for six hours?'" (*Field Guide for Female Interrogators*, 46).

13. Ibid., 54.
14. Ibid., 50, 54.
15. Hillman, "Dressed to Kill?," 78.
16. Quoted in Terkel, "Ban on Women in Combat."
17. American Civil Liberties Union, "Combat Exclusion Policy for Women."
18. Ibid.
19. According to the Selective Service System website, the specific penalties for men who fail to register before the age of twenty-six include ineligibility for federal and, in some cases, state student financial aid, most federal employment, security clearances for contractors, and for immigrant men, U.S. citizenship. Failure to register is also a "felony punishable by a fine of up to $250,000 or a prison term of up to five years, or a combination of both." See Selective Service System, "Benefits and Penalties."
20. Barry, *Unmaking War, Remaking Men*. I want to emphasize here that this expendability will not be a new condition for women but will merely be a different state-sanctioned form of it. In other words, I recognize that women, particularly women of color, already face conditions that diminish and threaten their lives in their homes and in public places—including the battlespace of war. Nonetheless, the forced registration into the Selective Service will add to their exposure to violence and their role as combatants in committing violence.
21. Ibid., 15. Barry argues that fear often manifests in acts of violence toward others, particularly women. Throughout her work, Barry directly addresses her male readers to prompt self-reflection on a practice that has become socially normalized. For example, she asks, "Men, is being expendable and knowing that you may have to fight and die in war too much for you to know consciously? After all, being expendable is contrary to your life force. It goes against your own growth and development. If you were imagining your own mortality, fully aware of being expendable, you would not be able to go on with your daily life. There would be little point in planning a future, developing projects, making plans. Why bother if your life is without value and likely to be sacrificed in a war?" (18). These are precisely the questions that women will also have to ask themselves in the future.
22. Alvarez, "Jane, We Hardly Knew Ye Died."
23. O'Neill, quoted in Terkel, "Ban on Women in Combat."
24. Rodriguez talks about García's influence in her blog post "Event Honoring Artist, Elizabeth Catlett.".
25. Blackwell, *¡Chicana Power!*, 188.

26. See hooks, *Feminist Theory*, 130.
27. Bustamante, "Test Shoot."
28. In an interview, Bustamante explains that the idea to work with Kevlar came from her own experience of dealing with the negative and hurtful online comments she received about her appearance on *Work of Art*, a show on the Bravo channel that aired in 2010. She writes, "I imagined making a Kevlar gown that went all the way up to my head and all the way down to my feet and all the way down to the floor—a kind of talisman to protect me" (Johnson, "Bulletproof," 35). When she was asked to contribute to an exhibition on the Mexican Revolution, she began to assert a link between different forms of female vulnerability: "The women in these battalions were actually wearing the same kind of dress that I had imagined" (34–37).
29. Quoted ibid., 34.
30. Blackwell, *¡Chicana Power!*, 187.
31. My position is inspired by Elizabeth Salas's description of how Chicanas turn time and again to the power of the soldadera figure: "Because the soldadera image was largely about assertive or passive women, Chicanas more than other groups have felt challenged or offended by the symbol. It is Chicanas who persistently debate the consequences of the image on their own developing ideas of cultural integrity and women's rights to pursue individual goals" (Salas, *Soldaderas in the Mexican Military*, 119). I would add that the soldadera is an important symbol that informs how many Chicanas view warfare and our role in either participating in or opposing it.
32. Johnson, "Bulletproof," 6.
33. Hernández, "Future Perfect," 88. I subscribe to Hernández's view on the power of futurity and the relationship between the future and hope: "Without the tenet that the future holds a better way of life, better social equity, and less racism, homophobia, and sexism, we are left without hope, without prospect. Instead, the visionary moment is a dynamic way of enlisting the place of power in our lives" (88).

BIBLIOGRAPHY

Alba Cutler, John. "Disappeared Men: Chicana/o Authenticity and the American War in Viet Nam." *American Literature* 81, no. 3 (September 2009): 583–611.

———. *Ends of Assimilation: The Formation of Chicano Literature*. New York: Oxford University Press, 2015.

Alexander, M. Jacqui. *Pedagogies of Crossing: Meditations on Feminism, Sexual Politics, Memory, and the Sacred*. Durham, N.C.: Duke University Press, 2006.

Allen, Michael J. "'Sacrilege of a Strange, Contemporary Kind': The Unknown Soldier and the Imagined Community after the Vietnam War." *History and Memory* 23, no. 2 (Fall/Winter 2011): 90–131.

"Alvarez Critical of Anti-war Efforts." *Los Angeles Times*. Reprinted in the *Geneva Times*, March 2, 1973, 2.

Alvarez, Everett, Jr., and Anthony S. Pitch. *Chained Eagle: The Heroic Story of the First American Shot Down over North Vietnam*. Washington, D.C.: Potomac Books, 2005.

Alvarez, Everett, Jr., and Samuel A. Schreiner. *Code of Conduct*. New York: Donald I. Fine, 1991.

Alvarez, Lizette. "Jane, We Hardly Knew Ye Died." *New York Times*, September 24, 2006.

American Civil Liberties Union. "Combat Exclusion Policy for Women." ACLU. November 28, 2016. https://www.aclu.org/feature/combat-exclusion-policy-women.

Anaya, Rudolfo A. "Aztlán: A Homeland without Boundaries." In *Aztlán: Essays on the Chicano Homeland*, edited by Rudolfo A. Anaya and Francisco A. Lomelí, 230–41. Albuquerque, N.Mex.: Academia/El Norte Publications, 1989.

Anderson, Benedict. *Imagined Communities: Reflections on the Origin and Spread of Nationalism*. New York: Verso, 1991.

Anzaldúa, Gloria. *Borderlands/La Frontera: The New Mestiza*. 1987. 3rd ed. San Francisco: Aunt Lute Books, 2007. Page references are to the 2007 edition.

Armstrong, Elizabeth, and Vijay Prashad. "Solidarity: War Rites and Women's Rights." *CR: The New Centennial Review* 5, no. 1 (Spring 2005): 213–53.

Arrizón, Alicia. "*Soldaderas* and the Staging of the Mexican Revolution." *Drama Review* 42, no. 1 (Spring 1998): 90–112.

Astor, Avi. "Unauthorized Immigration, Securitization and the Making of Operation Wetback." *Latino Studies* 7, no. 1 (2009): 5–29.

Barry, Kathleen. *Unmaking War, Remaking Men: How Empathy Can Reshape Our Politics, Our Soldiers and Ourselves*. Santa Rosa, Calif.: Phoenix Rising Press of Santa Rosa, 2011.

Bartky, Sandra Lee. "Foucault, Femininity, and the Modernization of Patriarchal Power." In *Feminism and Foucault: Reflections on Resistance*, edited by Lee Quinby and Irene Diamond, 61–86. Boston: Northeastern University Press, 1988.

Bayard de Volo, Lorraine. "Drafting Motherhood: Maternal Imagery and Organizations in the United States and Nicaragua." In Lorentzen and Turpin, *The Women and War Reader*, 240–53.

Bebout, Lee. *Mythohistorical Interventions: The Chicano Movement and Its Legacies*. Minneapolis: University of Minnesota Press, 2011.

Benedict, Helen. *The Lonely Soldier: The Private War of Women Serving in Iraq*. Boston: Beacon Press, 2009.

Benjamin, Thomas. "A Time of Reconquest: History, the Maya Revival, and the Zapatista Rebellion in Chiapas." *American Historical Review* 105, no. 2 (April 2000): 417–50.

Berlant, Lauren. *The Queen of America Goes to Washington City: Essays on Sex and Citizenship*. Durham, N.C.: Duke University Press, 1997.

Bhabha, Homi K. *The Location of Culture*. New York: Routledge, 1994.

Bicksler, Barbara A., and Lisa G. Nolan. *Recruiting an All-Volunteer Force: The Need for Sustained Investment in Recruiting Resources—An Update*. Arlington, Va.: Strategic Analysis, December 2009.

Blackwell, Maylei. *¡Chicana Power! Contested Histories of Feminism in the Chicano Movement*. Austin: University of Texas Press, 2011.

Boggs, Carl. "Vietnam, McNamara, and the Fog of History." *New Political Science* 26, no. 3 (September 2004): 459–72.

Bordo, Susan. "Feminism, Foucault and the Politics of the Body." In *Feminist Theory and the Body: A Reader*, edited by Janet Price and Margrit Shildrick, 246–57. New York: Routledge, 1999.

Bost, Suzanne. *Encarnación: Illness and Body Politics in Chicana Feminist Literature*. New York: Fordham University Press, 2010.

Brady, Mary Pat. *Extinct Lands, Temporal Geographies: Chicana Literature and the Urgency of Space*. Durham, N.C.: Duke University Press, 2002.

Brown, Wendy. *Edgework: Critical Essays on Knowledge and Politics*. Princeton, N.J.: Princeton University Press, 2005.

Burggraeve, Roger. "Violence and the Vulnerable Face of the Other: The Vision of Emmanuel Levinas on Moral Evil and Our Responsibility." *Journal of Social Philosophy* 30, no. 1 (Spring 1999): 29–45.

Burgin, Say. "Understanding Antiwar Activism as a Gendering Activity: A Look at the U.S.'s Anti–Vietnam War Movement." *Journal of International Women's Studies* 13, no. 6 (December 2012): 18–31.

Burke, Carol. *Camp All-American, Hanoi Jane, and the High-and-Tight: Gender, Folklore, and Changing Military Culture*. Boston: Beacon Press, 2004.

Burnside, Susan. "Jane Fonda Hits Bombing of Dikes." *Miami Herald*, August 22, 1972.

Bustamante, Nao. "Test Shoot for 'Tierra y Libertad.'" Vimeo video, November 24, 2012. https://vimeo.com/54191803.

Butler, Judith. "Bodies that Matter." In *Feminist Theory and the Body: A Reader*, edited by Janet Price and Margrit Shildrick, 235–45. New York: Routledge, 1999.

———. *Frames of War: When Is Life Grievable?* New York: Verso, 2009.

———. *Precarious Life: The Powers of Mourning and Violence*. New York: Verso, 2006.

Cacho, Lisa Marie. *Social Death: Racialized Rightlessness and the Criminalization of the Unprotected*. New York: New York University Press, 2012.

Cantú, Norma. "Women, Then and Now: An Analysis of the Adelita Image versus the Chicana as Political Writer and Philosopher." In *Chicana Voices: Intersections of Class, Race, and Gender*, edited by Teresa Córdova, Norma Cantú, Gilberto Cardenas, Juan García, and Christine M. Sierra, 8–10. Austin: University of Texas Press and the Center for Mexican American Studies, 1986.

Caputi, Jane. "Afterword: Goddess Murder and Gynocide in Ciudad Juárez." In *Making a Killing: Femicide, Free Trade, and La Frontera*, edited by Alicia Gaspar de Alba, with Georgina Guzmán, 279–94. Austin: University of Texas Press, 2010.

Carbonella, August. "Home Front: The Culture of U.S. Imperialism from Vietnam to Iraq." In *Rethinking America: The Imperial Homeland in the 21st Century*, edited by Jeff Maskovsky and Ida Susser, 122–47. Boulder, Colo.: Paradigm, 2009.

Carrasco, David. *The Aztecs: A Very Short Introduction*. New York: Oxford University Press, 2011.

Carrigan, Ana. "Afterword: Chiapas, the First Postmodern Revolution." In Marcos, *Our Word Is Our Weapon: Selected Writings*, 417–43.

Castañeda, Antonia. "Chicanas/Latinas y la nuevas garras del imperialism." *Chicana/Latina Studies* 4, no. 1 (Fall 2004): 97–98.

Castillo, Ana. *Massacre of the Dreamers: Essays on Xicanisma*. New York: Plume, 1995.

Cervantes, Lorna Dee. "Coffee." *Drive: The First Quartet*. San Antonio, Tex.: Wings Press, 2006. An earlier version of the poem was originally published in *Dark Nights: Field Notes* by Dark Night Press in 1998. Page references refer to the 2006 edition.

Chavez, Leo R. *The Latino Threat: Constructing Immigrants, Citizens, and the Nation*. Stanford, Calif.: Stanford University Press, 2008.

Cheng, Anne Anlin. *The Melancholy of Race: Psychoanalysis, Assimilation, and Hidden Grief*. New York: Oxford University Press, 2000.

Collins, Patricia Hill. *Black Feminist Thought: Knowledge, Consciousness, and the Politics of Empowerment*. New York: Routledge, 1991.

Cone, Robert W. "Soldier 2020." *Army*, November 2013. https://www.ausa.org/sites/default/files/Cone_Nov2013.pdf.

Cooke, Miriam. *Women and the War Story*. Berkeley: University of California Press, 1996.

Correa, Jennifer. "The Targeting of the East Los Angeles Brown Berets by a Racial Patriarchal Capitalist State: Merging Intersectionality and Social Movement Research." *Critical Sociology* 37, no. 1 (2010): 83–101.

Correll, Barbara. "Rem(a)inders of G(l)ory: Monuments and Bodies in 'Glory' and 'In the Year of the Pig.'" *Cultural Critique* 19 (Autumn 1991): 141–77.

Cota-Cárdenas, Margarita. "The Faith of Activists: Barrios, Cities, and the Chicana Feminist Response." *Frontiers* 14, no. 2 (1994): 51–80.

Cowen, Deborah E. "Fighting for 'Freedom': The End of Conscription in the United States and the Neoliberal Project of Citizenship." *Citizenship Studies* 10, no. 2 (May 2006): 167–83.

———. "National Soldiers and the War on Cities." *Theory and Event* 10, no. 2 (2007): n. p.

Cowen, Deborah, and Emily Gilbert. "Citizenship in the 'Homeland': Families at War." In *War, Citizenship, Territory*, edited by Deborah Cowen and Emily Gilbert, 261–79. New York: Routledge, 2008.

Cowen, Deborah, and Amy Siciliano. "Surplus Masculinities and Security." *Antipode* 43, no. 5 (2011): 1516–41.

Cummins Muñoz, Elizabeth. "Postnational Bodies: Chicana Community in Alicia Gaspar de Alba and Graciela Limón." *Letras Femeninas* 33, no. 1 (Summer 2007): 43–71.

Cypher, James M. "From Military Keynesianism to Global-Neoliberal Militarism." *Monthly Review* 59, no. 2 (2007). https://monthlyreview.org/2007/06/01/from-military-keynesianism-to-global-neoliberal-militarism.

Daniels, Jessie, and Nick LaLone. "Racism in Video Gaming: Connecting Extremist and Mainstream Expressions of White Supremacy." In *Social Exclusion, Power, and Video Game Play: New Research in Digital Media and Technology*, edited by David G. Embrick, J. Talmadge Wright, and Andras Lukacs, 85–100. Lanham, Md.: Lexington Books, 2012.

Dávila, Arlene. *Latino Spin: Public Image and the Whitewashing of Race*. New York: New York University Press, 2008.

———. *Latinos Inc.: The Marketing and Making of a People*. Berkeley: University of California Press, 2012.

Davis, Mike. *Planet of Slums*. New York: Verso, 2006.

Delgadillo, Theresa. "The Criticality of Latino/a Fiction in the Twenty-First Century." *American Literary History* 23, no. 3 (2011): 600–624.

Department of the Army. *Uniforms and Insignia: Wear and Appearance of Army Uniforms and Insignia*. Army Regulation 670-1. Washington, D.C.: Headquarters, Dept. of the Army, February 2005/RAR May 11, 2012.

Department of the Navy, Force Management Oversight Council. *Annual Report on Diversity*. Office of the Assistant Secretary of the Navy for Manpower and Reserve Affairs. Washington, D.C.: Dept. of the Navy, 2009.

Dickson, Virgil. "Mullen Wins U.S. Armed Forces Recruitment Contract." *PR Week*, January 2, 2013. http://www.prweek.com/article/1277118/mullen-wins-us-armed-forces-recruitment-contract.

"Dress Blues." U.S. Marine Corps. Accessed May 21, 2008. http://www.marines.com/page/usmc.jsp?flashRedirect=true.

Duarte, Stella Pope. *Let Their Spirits Dance: A Novel.* New York: Rayo, 2002.

Duggan, Lisa. *The Twilight of Equality?: Neoliberalism, Cultural Politics, and the Attack on Democracy.* Boston: Beacon Press, 2003.

Dunn, Timothy J. *The Militarization of the U.S.-Mexico Border, 1978–1992: Low-Intensity Conflict Doctrine Comes Home.* Austin: University of Texas Press, 1997.

Eisenstein, Zillah. "Resexing Militarism for the Globe." In *Feminism and War: Confronting U.S. Imperialism*, edited by Chandra Talpade Mohanty, Minnie Bruce Pratt, and Robin L. Riley, 27–46. New York: Zed Books, 2008.

El Plan Espiritual de Aztlán. *Aztlán: An Anthology of Mexican American Literature*, edited by Luis Valdez and Stan Steiner, 402–6. New York: Vintage Books, 1972.

El Vez and the Memphis Mariachis. "Misery Tren." *G.I. Ay, Ay! Blues.* Nürnberg: Semaphore, 1996. CD.

Elshtain, Jean Bethke. *Women and War.* Chicago: University of Chicago Press, 1987.

Eng, David L., and David Kazanjian, eds. *Loss: The Politics of Mourning.* Berkeley: University of California Press, 2002.

Enloe, Cynthia. *The Curious Feminist: Searching for Women in a New Age of Empire.* Berkeley: University of California Press, 2004.

———. *Maneuvers: The International Politics of Militarizing Women's Lives.* Berkeley: University of California Press, 2000.

———. *The Morning After: Sexual Politics at the End of the Cold War.* Berkeley: University of California Press, 1993.

Espinoza, Dionne. "'Revolutionary Sisters': Women's Solidarity and Collective Identification among Chicana Brown Berets in East Los Angeles, 1967–1970." *Aztlán* 26, no. 1 (Spring 2001): 17–58.

Feinman, Ilene Rose. *Citizenship Rites: Feminist Soldiers and Feminist Antimilitarists.* New York: New York University Press, 2000.

Feldman, Allen. *Formations of Violence: The Narrative of the Body and Political Terror in Northern Ireland.* Chicago: University of Chicago Press, 1991.

Feldman, Leonard C. "The Citizen-Soldier as a Substitute Soldier: Militarism at the Intersection of Neoliberalism and Neoconservatism." In Sutton, Morgen, and Novkov, *Security Disarmed*, 198–212.

Ferguson, Kathy E., and Phyllis Turnbull. *Oh, Say, Can You See?: The Semiotics of the Military in Hawai'i.* Minneapolis: University of Minnesota Press, 1999.

Fletcher, Lisa, and Felicia Biberica. "For Female Vets, a New Fight at Home." *ABC News*, March 14, 2010. http://abcnews.go.com/WN/homeless-female-veterans-americas-streets/story?id=10099653.

Flores, Linda A. "Creating Discursive Space through a Rhetoric of Difference: Chicana Feminists Craft a Homeland." *Quarterly Journal of Speech* 82 (1996): 142–56.

Flynn, George Q. *The Draft, 1940–1973*. Lawrence: University Press of Kansas, 1993.

Foster, David William. "Out of the Barrio: Stella Pope Duarte's *Let Their Spirits Dance*." *Bilingual Review* 27, no. 2 (May–August 2003): 171–79.

Foucault, Michel. "7 January 1976." In *"Society Must Be Defended": Lectures at the Collège de France, 1975–1976*, edited by Mauro Bertani and Alessandro Fontana, 1–22. New York: Picador, 2003.

———. *Docile Bodies*. In *The Foucault Reader*, edited by Paul Rabinow, 179–87. New York: Pantheon Books, 1984.

———. "The Ethics of the Concern of the Self as a Practice of Freedom." In *Ethics: Subjectivity and Truth*, vol. 1, edited by Paul Rabinow, 281–302. New York: New Press, 1994.

———. *The Foucault Reader*. Edited by Paul Rabinow. New York: Pantheon Books, 1984.

———. *Security, Territory, Population: Lectures at the Collège de France, 1977–1978*. Edited by Michel Senellart. New York: Palgrave, 2007.

Freeman, Elizabeth. "Time Binds, or, Erotohistoriography." *Social Text* 23, nos. 3–4. (Fall–Winter 2005): 57–68.

———. *Time Binds: Queer Temporalities, Queer Histories*. Durham, N.C.: Duke University Press, 2010.

Fregoso, Rosa Linda. *MeXicana Encounters: The Making of Social Identities on the Borderlands*. Berkeley: University of California Press, 2003.

Fulton, Delawese. "Mom, Son Complete BCT Family Tree." U.S. Army, September 24, 2009. https://www.army.mil/article/27785/mom-son-complete-bct-family-tree.

Furumoto, Rosa. "No Poor Child Left Unrecruited: How NCLB Codifies and Perpetuates Urban School Militarism." *Equity and Excellence in Education* 38, no. 3 (2005): 200–210.

Fusco, Coco. *A Field Guide for Female Interrogators*. New York: Seven Stories Press, 2008.

García, Rupert. "Rupert García—In His Own Words." *Latinopia*, March 6, 2010. http://latinopia.com/latino-art/rupert-garcia.

Gates, Thomas S., Jr. *The Report of the President's Commission on an All-Volunteer Armed Force*. Washington, D.C.: Government Printing Office, February 1970.

Gifford, Brian. "The Camouflaged Safety Net: The U.S. Armed Forces as Welfare State Institution." *Social Politics* 13, no. 3 (August 2006): 372–99.

Gilmore, Ruth Wilson. "Behind the Power of 41 Bullets: An Interview with Ruth Wilson Gilmore; What Is Domestic Militarization and How Did It Come About?" *Colorlines*, January 31, 2000. https://www.highbeam.com/doc/1P3-494722431.html.

———. "Fatal Couplings of Power and Difference: Notes on Racism and Geography." *Professional Geographer* 54, no. 1 (2002): 15–24.

———. "Globalisation and U.S. Prison Growth: From Military Keynesianism to post-Keynesian Militarism." *Race and Class* 40, nos. 2–3 (1998): 171–88.

———. *Golden Gulag: Prisons, Surplus, Crisis, and Opposition in Globalizing California*. Berkeley: University of California Press, 2007.

Gonzales, Rodolfo. "I am Joaquín: an Epic Poem, 1967." In *Message to Aztlán: Selected Writings*, edited by Antonio Esquibel, 16–29. Houston, Tex.: Arte Público Press, 2001.

González, Roberto J. *Militarizing Culture: Essays on the Warfare State*. Walnut Creek, Calif.: Left Coast Press, 2010.

Graham, Stephen. *Cities Under Siege: The New Military Urbanism*. New York: Verso, 2011.

Greenberg, I. M. *Project 100,000: New Standards Program*. Washington, D.C.: U.S. Department of Defense, 1972.

Grewal, Inderpal. "'Security Moms' in the Early Twentieth-Century United States: The Gender of Security in Neoliberalism." *Women's Studies Quarterly* 34, nos. 1–2 (Summer 2006): 25–39.

Grise, Virginia. *blu*. New Haven, Conn.: Yale University Press, 2011.

———. "Virginia Grise Looking Up at the Sky: *blu*." Interview by Tatiana de la Tierra. *La Bloga*, October 23, 2011. http://labloga.blogspot.com/2011/10/virginia-grise-looking-up-at-sky-blu.html.

Griswold, Charles L., and Stephen S. Griswold. "The Vietnam Veterans Memorial and the Washington Mall: Philosophical Thoughts on Political Iconography." *Critical Inquiry* 12, no. 4 (Summer 1986): 688–719.

Guidotti-Hernández, Nicole. *Unspeakable Violence: Remapping U.S. and Mexican National Imaginaries*. Durham, N.C.: Duke University Press, 2011.

Gutiérrez, Elena R. *Fertile Matters: The Politics of Mexican-Origin Women's Reproduction*. Austin: University of Texas Press, 2008.

Guzman, Ralph. *Mexican American Casualties in Vietnam*. Santa Cruz: University of California at Santa Cruz, 1969.

Hallin, Daniel C. *The "Uncensored War": The Media and Vietnam*. Berkeley: University of California Press, 1986.

Hardt, Michael, and Antonio Negri. *Multitude: War and Democracy in the Age of Empire*. New York: Penguin, 2004.

Harris, Michael. "In Chiapas, Death and Defeat Are Never Final." *Los Angeles Times*, November 26, 2001. http://articles.latimes.com/2001/nov/26/news/cl-8399.

Harvey, David. *A Brief History of Neoliberalism*. New York: Oxford University Press, 2005.

Hattiangadi, Anita U., Gary Lee, and Aline O. Quester. *Recruiting Hispanics: The Marine Corps Experience Final Report*. Alexandria, Va.: Center for Naval Analyses, 2004.

Hay, James. "Designing Homes to Be the First Line of Defense: Safe Households, Mobilization, and the New Mobile Privatization." *Cultural Studies* 20, nos. 4–5 (July–September 2006): 349–77.

Hernández, Ellie D. "The Future Perfect: Chicana Feminist Critical Analysis in the Twenty-first Century." *Chicana/Latina Studies* 5, no. 2 (Spring 2006): 60–91.

Hernandez, Javier. "An Exploratory Study of Hispanic Officer Recruiting in the Mexican-American Community of South-Central Los Angeles: Implications for the Officer Corps of the Future." Master's thesis, Naval Postgraduate School, 2003.

Hernández Castillo, Rosalva Aída, ed. *The Other Word: Women and Violence in Chiapas Before and After Acteal*. Copenhagen: International Work Group for Indigenous Affairs, 2001.

Herrera-Sobek, María. "Chicana Vietnam Blues." In Mariscal, *Aztlán and Viet Nam*, 233.

———. "Untitled." In Mariscal, *Aztlán and Viet Nam*, 234–35.

———. "Vietnam." In Mariscal, *Aztlán and Viet Nam*, 232.

———. "Vietnam—A Four-Letter Word." In Mariscal, *Aztlán and Viet Nam*, 235.

Hillman, Elizabeth L. "Dressed to Kill? The Paradox of Women in Military Uniforms." In *Beyond Zero Tolerance: Discrimination in Military Culture*, edited by Mary Fainsod Katzenstein and Judith Reppy, 65–80. Lanham, Md.: Rowman and Littlefield, 1999.

———. "The Female Shape of the All-Volunteer Force." In *Iraq and the Lessons of Vietnam: Or, How Not to Learn from the Past*, edited by Lloyd C. Gardner and Marilyn B. Young, 150–61. New York: New Press, 2007.

"Hispanic Families Instill Important Values." U.S. Marines. Accessed July 20, 2011. http://www.mca-marines.org/leatherneck/photo/hispanic-families-instill-important-values-our-marines-embody-them-everyday.

Holles, Everett R. "A.C.L.U. Says F.B.I. Funded 'Army' to Terrorize Antiwar Protesters." *New York Times*, June 27, 1975.

Holst-Warhaft, Gail. *The Cue for Passion: Grief and Its Political Uses*. Cambridge, Mass.: Harvard University Press, 2000.

Hong, Grace Kyungwon. "Fun with Death and Dismemberment: Irony, Farce, and the Limits of Nationalism in Oscar Zeta Acosta's *The Revolt of the Cockroach People* and Ana Castillo's *So Far from God*." In *Strange Affinities: The Gender and Sexual Politics of Comparative Racialization*, edited by Grace Kyungwon Hong and Roderick A. Ferguson, 241–69. Durham, N.C.: Duke University Press, 2011.

hooks, bell. "Feminism and Militarism: A Comment." *Women's Studies Quarterly* 23, nos. 3–4 (1995): 58–64.

———. *Feminist Theory: From Margin to Center*. Boston: South End Press, 1984.

Höpfl, Heather J. "Becoming a (Virile) Member: Women and the Military Body." *Body and Society* 9, no. 4 (2003): 13–30.

Hunt, Richard A. *Melvin Laird and Nixon's Quest for a Post-Vietnam Foreign Policy, 1969–1973*. Cold War Foreign Policy Series, Special Study 6. Washington, D.C.: Historical Office of the Office of the Secretary of Defense, 2014.

Hutchings, Kimberly. "Feminist Ethics and Political Violence." *International Politics* 44 (2007): 90–106.

———. "Simone de Beauvoir and the Ambiguous Ethics of Political Violence." *Hypatia* 22, no. 3 (2007): 111–32.

Inda, Jonathan Xavier. "The Value of Immigrant Life." In *Women and Migration in the U.S.-Mexico Borderlands: A Reader*, edited by Denise A. Segura and Patricia Zavella, 134–57. Durham, N.C.: Duke University Press, 2007.

"Indians in Chiapas Protest Massacre, Police Killing." *CNN*, January 15, 1998. http://www.cnn.com/WORLD/9801/14/mexico.chiapas.

James, Jennifer C. *A Freedom Bought with Blood: African American War Literature from the Civil War to World War II*. Chapel Hill: University of North Carolina Press, 2007.

Jameson, Fredric. "The End of Temporality." *Critical Inquiry* 29, no. 4 (Summer 2003): 695–718.

Jeffords, Susan. *The Remasculinization of America: Gender and the Vietnam War*. Bloomington: Indiana University Press, 1989.

Johnson, Kjerstin. "Bulletproof: Artist Nao Bustamante Bridges Past and Present in *Soldadera*." *Bitch* 68 (Fall 2015): 34–37.

Joint Advertising, Market Research and Studies (JAMRS). *August 2003 Influencer Poll 1 Overview Report*. JAMRS Report No. 2004-001. Arlington, Va.: Defense Human Resources Activity, Department of Defense, March 2004.

———. *Influencer Poll Report and Crosstabulations, May 2004.* JAMRS Report No. 2004-005. Arlington, Va.: Defense Human Resources Activity, Department of Defense, November 2004.

———. *October 2002 Youth Poll Overview Report.* JAMRS Report No. 2003-002. Arlington, Va.: Defense Human Resources Activity, Department of Defense, April 2003.

Jones, Joseph C. "Diversity in the 21st Century Army: Leadership Issues." In *Population Diversity and the U.S. Army*, edited by Lloyd J. Matthews and Tinaz Pavri, 57–68. Carlisle Barracks, Pa.: Strategic Studies Institute, 1999.

Jung, Courtney. "The Politics of Indigenous Identity: Neoliberalism, Cultural Rights, and the Mexican Zapatistas." *Social Research* 70, no. 2 (Summer 2003): 433–62.

Kaplan, Amy. "Homeland Insecurities: Some Reflections on Language and Space." *Radical History Review* 85 (2003): 82–93.

———. "Manifest Domesticity." *American Literature* 70, no. 3 (September 1998): 581–606.

Kaplan, Caren. "Precision Targets: GPS and the Militarization of U.S. Consumer Identity." *American Quarterly* 58, no. 3 (September 2006): 693–714.

Kennis, Andrew. "Ten Years Later, It's Time to Recognize the U.S. Government's Responsibility for Acteal." *Narco News Bulletin*, December 30, 2007. http://www.narconews.com/Issue48/article2948.html.

Korte, Alvin O. *Nosotros: A Study of Everyday Meanings in Hispano New Mexico.* East Lansing: Michigan State University Press, 2012.

"POW Will Face Change." *Lakeland Ledger*, February 9, 1973.

Lamothe, Dan. "As Marines Take Heat for Handling of Gender Integration, Army Stays Quiet on Plan." *Washington Post*, September 23, 2015. https://www.washingtonpost.com/news/checkpoint/wp/2015/09/23/as-marines-take-heat-for-handling-of-gender-integration-army-stays-quiet-on-plan.

Latorre, Guisela. "Re-Mapping the National Consciousness: Agustín Victor Casasola and the Chicana/Chicano Artist." In *Mapping Latina/o Studies: An Interdisciplinary Reader*, edited by Angharad N. Valdivia and Matthew Garcia, 83–102. New York: Lang, 2012.

Lavandera, Ed, and Associated Press. "Adult, Fetus Found in Shallow Grave May Be Missing Marine." *CNN*, January 12, 2008. http://www.cnn.com/2008/CRIME/01/12/missing.marine.

Leal, Luis. "In Search of Aztlán." In *Aztlán: Essays on the Chicano Homeland*, edited by Rudolfo A. Anaya and Francisco Lomelí, 6–13. Albuquerque, N.Mex.: Academia/El Norte Publications, 1989.

León-Portilla, Miguel, and Earl Shorris, eds. *In the Language of Kings: An Anthology of Mesoamerican Literature—Pre-Columbian to the Present*. New York: Norton, 2001.

Levario, Miguel Antonio. *Militarizing the Border: When Mexicans Became the Enemy*. College Station: Texas A&M University Press, 2012.

Levinas, Emmanuel. *Totality and Infinity: An Essay on Exteriority*. Translated by Alphonso Lingis. Pittsburgh, Pa.: Duquesne University Press, 1969.

Levinas, Emmanuel, and Richard Kearney. "Dialogue with Emmanuel Levinas." In *Face to Face with Levinas*, edited by Richard A. Cohen, 13–34. Albany: State University of New York Press, 1986.

Liberto, Jennifer. "Food Stamp Use Among Military Rises Again." *CNNMoney*, February 17, 2014. http://money.cnn.com/2014/02/17/news/economy/military-food-stamps.

Lima, Lázaro. *The Latino Body: Crisis Identities in American Literary and Cultural Memory*. New York: New York University Press, 2007.

Limón, Graciela. *Erased Faces*. Houston, Tex.: Arte Público Press, 2001.

———. "Zapatistas, Literature, and the Chicano Experience." Symposium video. UCTV Voices series, edited and directed by Todd Gillespie, 89 min. University of California, Santa Barbara, February 14, 2003. http://www.uctv.tv/shows/Zapatista-Literature-and-the-Chicano-Experience-7852.

Lipsitz, George. *The Possessive Investment in Whiteness: How White People Profit from Identity Politics*. Philadelphia, Pa.: Temple University Press, 1998.

López-Calvo, Ignacio. "Chicanismo Meets Zapatismo: U.S. Third World Feminism and Transnational Activism in Graciela Limón's *Erased Faces*." *Chasqui* 33, no. 2 (November 2004): 64–74.

Lorentzen, Lois Ann, and Jennifer Turpin, eds. *The Women and War Reader*. New York: New York University Press, 1998.

Loyd, Jenna M. "'Peace Is Our Only Shelter': Questioning Domesticities of Militarization and White Privilege." *Antipode* 43, no. 3 (2011): 845–73.

Lutz, Catherine. "Making War at Home in the United States: Militarization and the Current Crisis." *American Anthropologist* 104, no. 3 (September 2002): 723–35.

MacLeavy, Julie, and Columba Peoples. "Workfare-Warfare: Neoliberalism, 'Active' Welfare and the New American Way of War." *Antipode* 41, no. 5 (2009): 890–915.

Malkin, Michelle. "Candidates Ignore 'Security Moms,' at Their Peril." *USA Today*, July 20, 2004. http://usatoday30.usatoday.com/news/opinion/editorials/2004-07-20-malkin_x.htm.

Marcos, Subcomandante. "Come, Brothers and Sisters, March 12, 1995." In *Our Word Is Our Weapon*, 72–74.

———. "Flowers, Like Hope, Are Harvested, September 1995." In *Our Word Is Our Weapon*, 173–74.

———. "For Those Who Protest with Us after Acteal, January 21, 1998, Planet Earth." In *Our Word Is Our Weapon*, 132–36.

———. "From Vietnam to Chiapas, Twenty Years Before, September 13, 1995." In *Our Word Is Our Weapon*, 175–77.

———. Interview by Carlos Loret de Mola. *Primero Noticias de Televisa Chapultepec*, Televisa Chapultepec, May 9, 2006.

———. "On the Importance of Diverse Voices, January 20, 1994." In *Zapatistas! Documents of the New Mexican Revolution*, edited by Editorial Collective, 102–3. New York: Autonomedia, 1994. http://lanic.utexas.edu/project/Zapatistas/Zapatistas_book.pdf.

———. *Our Word Is Our Weapon: Selected Writings*. Edited by Juana Ponce de León. New York: Seven Stories Press, 2001.

———. "Professionals in Hope, March 5, 1994." In *Zapatistas! Documents of the New Mexican Revolution*, edited by Editorial Collective, 254–56. New York: Autonomedia, 1994. http://lanic.utexas.edu/project/Zapatistas/Zapatistas_book.pdf.

———. "The Sea of My Insomnia: The Table at San Andres, March 1998." In *Our Word Is Our Weapon*, 137–42.

———. "A Storm and a Prophecy—Chiapas: The Southeast in Two Winds, August 1992." In *Our Word Is Our Weapon*, 22–37.

———. "Twelve Women in the Twelfth Year: The Moment of War, March 11, 1996." In *Our Word Is Our Weapon*, 5–12.

Marcos, Subcomandante, and the Clandestine Revolutionary Committee-General Command (CCRI-CG). Second Declaration of La Realidad for Humanity and against Neoliberalism, August 1996. In Marcos, *Our Word Is Our Weapon*, 116–19.

———. Sixth Declaration of the Selva Lacandona. Enlace Zapatista, June 2005. http://enlacezapatista.ezln.org.mx/sdsl-en.

Marine Corps Combat Development Center. *Military Operations on Urbanized Terrain (MOUT)*. Marine Corps Warfighting Publication (MCWP) 3-35.3. Washington, D.C.: Headquarters USMC, 1998.

Mariscal, George, ed. *Aztlán and Viet Nam: Chicano and Chicana Experiences of the War*. Berkeley: University of California Press, 1999.

———. "In the Wake of the Gulf War: Untying the Yellow Ribbon." *Cultural Critique* 19 (Autumn 1991): 97–117.

———. Introduction to *Aztlán and Viet Nam: Chicano and Chicana Experiences of the War*. Berkeley: University of California Press, 1999.

Mariscal, Jorge. "Homeland Security, Militarism, and the Future of Latinos and Latinas in the United States." *Radical History Review* 93 (Fall 2005): 39–52.

———. "Las Adelitas 2003, Mexican-American Women in Iraq." *Counterpunch*, November 13, 2003. http://www.counterpunch.org/2003/11/13/las-adelitas-2003-mexican-american-women-in-iraq.

———. "Reading Chicana/o Writing about the American War in Viet Nam." *Aztlán* 25, no. 2 (Fall 2000): 13–49.

Martínez, Elizabeth. "'Chingón Politics' Die Hard: Reflections on the First Chicano Activist Reunion." In *Living Chicana Theory*, edited by Carla Trujillo, 123–27. Berkeley, Calif.: Third Woman Press, 1998.

Matthews, Lloyd J. "Introduction: Primer on Future Recruit Diversity." In *Population Diversity and the U.S. Army*, edited by Lloyd J. Matthews and Tinaz Pavri, 1–16. Carlisle Barracks, Pa.: Strategic Studies Institute, 1999.

McAlister, Melani. *Epic Encounters: Culture, Media, and U.S. Interests in the Middle East, 1945–2000*. Berkeley: University of California Press, 2001.

McClancy, Kathleen. "The Iconography of Violence: Television, Vietnam, and the Soldier Hero." *Film and History* 43, no. 2 (Fall 2013): 50–66.

McKenna, Dave. *U.S. Military Logistics Management, Privatization, and Contractors on the Battlefield. What Does This All Mean?* USAWC Strategy Research Project. Carlisle Barracks, Pa.: U.S. Army War College, 2002.

McNamara, Robert. "Interview with Robert McNamara." Episode 11: Vietnam, December 6, 1998. Online transcript. National Security Archives, George Washington University. http://www2.gwu.edu/~nsarchiv/coldwar/interviews/episode-11/mcnamara1.html.

Mendible, Myra, ed. *From Bananas to Buttocks: The Latina Body in Popular Film and Culture*. Austin: University of Texas Press, 2007.

———. "Introduction: Embodying Latinidad—An Overview." In *From Bananas to Buttocks*, 1–28.

Mignolo, Walter. *The Idea of Latin America*. Malden, Mass.: Blackwell Publishing, 2005.

Millán Moncayo, Márgara. "Indigenous Women and Zapatismo: New Horizons of Visibility." In Speed, Hernández Castillo, and Stephen, *Dissident Women*, 75–96.

Miller, Peter, and Nikolas Rose. "Governing Economic Life." *Economy and Society* 19, no. 1 (1990): 1–31.

Mittelstadt, Jennifer. *The Rise of the Military Welfare State*. Cambridge, Mass.: Harvard University Press, 2015.

Mohanty, Chandra Talpade. *Feminism without Borders: Decolonizing Theory, Practicing Solidarity*. Durham, NC: Duke University Press, 2003.

———. "Under Western Eyes: Feminist Scholarship and Colonial Discourses." *Feminist Review* 30 (1988): 61–88.

———. "U.S. Empire and the Project of Women's Studies: Stories of Citizenship, Complicity and Dissent." *Gender, Place and Culture* 13, no. 1 (2006): 7–20.

Molina-Guzmán, Isabel. *Dangerous Curves: Latina Bodies in the Media.* New York: New York University Press, 2010.

Montoya, Mickiela. "The Private War of Women Soldiers: Female Vet, Soldier Speak Out on Rising Sexual Assault Within U.S. Military." Interview by Amy Goodman. *Democracy Now*, March 8, 2007. https://www.democracynow.org/2007/3/8/the_private_war_of_women_soldiers.

———. "Sexual Abuse Allegations Persist in U.S. Military." Interview by Madeleine Brand and Luke Burbank. *Day to Day.* National Public Radio, March 16, 2007. http://www.npr.org/templates/story/story.php?storyId=8955260.

Mora, Mariana. "Zapatismo: Gender, Power, and Social Transformation." In Lorentzen and Turpin, *The Women and War Reader*, 164–76.

Moraga, Cherríe. *The Hungry Woman.* Albuquerque, N.Mex.: West End Press, 2001.

———. *The Last Generation: Prose and Poetry.* Boston: South End Press, 1983.

Muñoz, José Esteban. *Cruising Utopia: The Then and There of Queer Futurity.* New York: New York University Press, 2009.

———. "Feeling Brown: Ethnicity and Affect in Ricardo Bracho's 'The Sweetest Hangover (And Other STDs).'" *Theatre Journal* 52, no. 1 (March 2000): 67–79.

Myrttinen, Henri. "'Pack Your Heat and Work the Streets'—Weapons and the Active Construction of Violent Masculinities." *Women and Language* 27, no. 2 (Fall 2004): 29–34.

Negrón-Muntaner, Frances. *Boricua Pop: Puerto Ricans and the Latinization of American Culture.* New York: New York University Press, 2005.

Nguyen, Viet Thanh. "Remembering War, Dreaming Peace: On Cosmopolitanism, Compassion, and Literature." *Japanese Journal of American Studies* 20 (2009): 149–74.

Nixon, Richard. "Remarks Following a Meeting With Wives and Mothers of Prisoners of War and Servicemen Missing in Action in Vietnam." December 12, 1969. *The American Presidency Project*, Gerhard Peters and John T. Woolley. http://www.presidency.ucsb.edu/ws/?pid=2368.

Office of the Under Secretary of Defense, Personnel and Readiness. *Population Representation in the Military Services: Fiscal Year 2013 Summary Report.* Arlington, Va.: CNA, 2014. https://www.cna.org/pop-rep/2013/summary/summary.pdf.

Olguín, Ben V. "From Counter to Hegemonic: Re-Mapping Ideology in Latina/o Life Writing from the War on Terror." *Biography* 36, no. 1 (Winter 2013): 179–210.

———. *La Pinta: Chicana/o Prisoner Literature, Culture, and Politics*. Austin: University of Texas Press, 2010.

———. "Sangre Mexicana/Corazón Americano: Identity, Ambiguity, and Critique in Mexican-American War Narratives." *American Literary History* 14, no. 1 (Spring 2002): 83–130.

Oliver, Kelly. *Women as Weapons of War: Iraq, Sex, and the Media*. New York: Columbia University Press, 2007.

Olivera, Mercedes, and Victoria J. Furio, "Violencia Femicida: Violence Against Women and Mexico's Structural Crisis." *Latin American Perspectives* 33, no. 2 (2006): 104–14.

Ong, Aihwa. *Neoliberalism as Exception: Mutations in Citizenship and Sovereignty*. Durham, N.C.: Duke University Press, 2006.

———. "Neoliberalism as a Mobile Technology." *Transactions of the Institute of British Geographers* 32, no. 1 (2007): 3–8.

Oropeza, Lorena. *¡Raza Sí! ¡Guerra No!: Chicano Protest and Patriotism during the Viet Nam War Era*. Berkeley: University of California Press, 2005.

Paredez, Deborah. "Remembering Selena, Re-membering Latinidad." *Theatre Journal* 54, no. 1 (March 2002): 63–83.

Patten, Eileen, and Kim Parker. *Women in the U.S. Military: Growing Share, Distinctive Profile*. Washington, D.C.: Pew Research Center, December 2011. http://www.pewsocialtrends.org/2011/12/22/women-in-the-u-s-military-growing-share-distinctive-profile.

Pérez, Emma. *The Decolonial Imaginary: Writing Chicanas into History*. Bloomington: Indiana University Press, 1999.

Pérez, Gina. *Citizen, Student, Soldier: Latina/o Youth, JROTC, and the American Dream*. New York: New York University Press, 2015.

Pérez, Laura E. "Spirit Glyphs: Reimagining Art and Artist in the Work of Chicana *Tlamatinime*." *Modern Fiction Studies* 44, no. 1 (1998): 36–76.

"Prisoners' Families in Rift." *Reading Eagle*, December 9, 1971, 63.

Pulido, Laura. "Rethinking Environmental Racism: White Privilege and Urban Development in Southern California." *Annals of the Association of American Geographers* 90, no. 1 (2000): 12–40.

Quester, George H. "Demographic Trends and Military Recruitment: Surprising Possibilities." *Parameters* 35, no. 1 (Spring 2005): 27–40.

Rabasa, José. "Of Zapatismo: Reflections on the Folkloric and the Impossible in a Subaltern Insurrection." In *The Politics of Culture in the Shadow of Capital*, edited by Lisa Lowe and David Lloyd, 399–431. Durham, N.C.: Duke University Press, 1997.

———. *Without History: Subaltern Studies, the Zapatista Insurgency, and the Specter of History*. Pittsburgh, Pa.: University of Pittsburgh Press, 2010.

Ramírez, Catherine S. *The Woman in the Zoot Suit: Gender, Nationalism, and the Cultural Politics of Memory*. Durham, N.C.: Duke University Press, 2008.

Roberts, Steven V. "Sister of P.O.W. thinks He Will Face a 'Shock.'" *New York Times*, February 8, 1973.

Rodino, Michelle. "War Mothering." *Feminist Media Studies* 5, no. 3 (2005): 380.

Rodríguez, Ana Patricia. "The Fiction of Solidarity: Transfronterista Feminisms and Anti-Imperialist Struggles in Central American Transnational Narratives." *Feminist Studies* 34, nos. 1–2 (2008): 199–226.

Rodríguez, Dylan. "(Non)Scenes of Captivity: The Common Sense of Punishment and Death." *Radical History Review* 96 (Fall 2006): 9–32.

Rodriguez, Elena. *Peacetime: Spirit of the Eagle*. San Jose, Calif.: Chusma, 1997.

Rodriguez, Favianna. "Event Honoring Artist, Elizabeth Catlett." Favianna.com (blog), September 29, 2007. http://favianna.typepad.com/faviannacom_art_activism/2007/09/just-returned-h.html.

Rodríguez, Ileana. "Cross-Genealogies in Latin American and South Asian Subaltern Studies." *Nepantla: Views from South* 1, no. 1 (2000): 45–58.

Rodríguez, Richard T. *Next of Kin: The Family in Chicano/a Cultural Politics*. Durham, N.C.: Duke University Press, 2009.

Rodríguez y Gibson, Eliza. "'The Poetry of Improbability': Lorna Dee Cervantes's Global Chicana Feminism." In *Stunned into Being: Essays on the Poetry of Lorna Dee Cervantes*, edited by Eliza Rodríguez y Gibson, 136–54. San Antonio, Tex.: Wings Press, 2012.

Roett, Riordan. "Mexico-Political Update: Chase Manhattan's Emerging Markets Group Memo." Real History Archives. January 13, 1995. http://www.realhistoryarchives.com/collections/hidden/chase-memo.htm.

Romero, Lora. *Home Fronts: Domesticity and Its Critics in the Antebellum United States*. Durham, N.C.: Duke University Press, 1997.

Rose, Nikolas, and Peter Miller. "Political Power beyond the State: Problematics of Government." *British Journal of Sociology* 43, no. 2 (June 1992): 173–205.

Ross, John. *Rebellion from the Roots: Indian Uprising in Chiapas*. New York: Common Courage Press, 1995.

Roth, Benita. "A Dialogical View of the Emergence of Chicana Feminist Discourse." *Critical Sociology* 33 (2007): 709–30.

Roy, Srila. "The Ethical Ambivalence of Resistant Violence: Notes from Postcolonial South Asia." *Feminist Review* 91 (2009): 135–53.

Ruddick, Sara. "'Women of Peace': A Feminist Construction." In Lorentzen and Turpin, *The Women and War Reader*, 213–26.

Ruiz, Vicki L. *From Out of the Shadows: Mexican Women in Twentieth-Century America*. New York: Oxford University Press, 2008.

Sackett, Paul R., and Anne S. Mavor, eds. *Attitudes, Aptitudes, and Aspirations of American Youth: Implications for Military Recruitment*. National Research Council Committee on the Youth Population and Military Recruitment. Washington, D.C.: National Academies Press, 2003.

Salas, Elizabeth. *Soldaderas in the Mexican Military: Myth and History*. Austin: University of Texas Press, 1990.

Sandoval, Chela. "Mestizaje as Method: Feminists-of-Color Challenge the Canon." In *Living Chicana Theory*, edited by Carla Trujillo, 352–70. Berkeley, Calif.: Third Woman Press, 1998.

———. *Methodology of the Oppressed*. Minneapolis: University of Minnesota Press, 2000.

Sassen, Saskia. "Women's Burden: Counter-geographies of Globalization and the Feminization of Survival." *Journal of International Affairs* 53, no. 2 (2000): 503–24.

Scarry, Elaine. *The Body in Pain: The Making and Unmaking of the World*. New York: Oxford University Press, 1985.

Segal, David R. *Recruiting for Uncle Sam: Citizenship and Military Manpower Policy*. Lawrence: University Press of Kansas, 1989.

Segal, David R., and Mady Wechsler Segal. *America's Military Population*. Population Bulletin vol. 59, no. 4. Washington, D.C.: Population Reference Bureau, December 2004.

Selective Service System. "Benefits and Penalties." U.S. Selective Service System. Accessed November 15, 2016. https://www.sss.gov/Registration/Why-Register/Benefits-and-Penalties.

Shapiro, Michael J. *Violent Cartographies: Mapping Cultures of War*. Minneapolis: University of Minnesota Press, 1997.

Shuit, Douglas P. "Prenatal Care Cut Urged for Illegal Immigrants." *Los Angeles Times*, January 8, 1994.

Silva, Jennifer M. "A New Generation of Women? How Female ROTC Cadets Negotiate the Tension between Masculine Military Culture and Traditional Femininity." *Social Forces* 87, no. 2 (December 2008): 937–60.

Singleton, John D. "Slaves or Mercenaries: Milton Friedman and the Institution of the All-Volunteer Military." Center for the History of Political Economy Working Paper No. 2014–07, Duke University, Durham, North Carolina, February 2014.

Smith, Jennifer. "U.S. Army Told to Advertise for Recruits Using 'Average Looking Women' Because They Are Perceived as More Competent than Prettier Soldiers." *Daily Mail*, November 20, 2013. http://www.dailymail.co.uk/news/article-2510492/U-S-Army-told-advertise-recruits-using-average-looking-women.html.

Smith, Neil. "Contours of a Spatialized Politics: Homeless Vehicles and the Production of Geographical Scale." *Social Text* 33 (1992): 54–81.

Snyder, R. Claire. *Citizen-Soldiers and Manly Warriors: Military Service and Gender in the Civic Republic Tradition*. Lanham, Md.: Rowman and Littlefield, 1999.

Sontag, Susan. *On Photography*. New York: Picador, 1977.

———. *Regarding the Pain of Others*. New York: Picador, 2003.

Speed, Shannon, R. Aída Hernández Castillo, and Lynn M. Stephen, eds. *Dissident Women: Gender and Cultural Politics in Chiapas*. Austin: University of Texas Press, 2006.

Stahl, Roger. *Militainment, Inc.: War, Media, and Popular Culture*. New York: Taylor and Francis, 2009.

Stephen, Lynn. "*Los Nuevos Desaparecidos y Muertos*: Immigration, Militarization, Death, and Disappearance on Mexico's Borders." In Sutton, Morgen, and Novkov, *Security Disarmed*, 79–100.

Stock, Margaret D. *Essential to the Fight: Immigrants in the Military Eight Years after 9/11*. Special Report, Immigration Policy Center. Washington, D.C.: American Immigration Council, November 2009.

Sutton, Barbara. *Bodies in Crisis: Culture, Violence, and Women's Resistance in Neoliberal Argentina*. New Brunswick, N.J.: Rutgers University Press, 2010.

———. "Poner el Cuerpo: Women's Embodiment and Political Resistance in Argentina." *Latin American Politics and Society* 49, no. 3 (Fall 2007): 129–62.

Sutton, Barbara, Sandra Morgen, and Julie Novkov, eds. *Security Disarmed: Critical Perspectives on Gender, Race, and Militarization*. New Brunswick, N.J.: Rutgers University Press, 2008.

Sutton, Barbara, and Julie Novkov. "Rethinking Security, Confronting Inequality: An Introduction." In Sutton, Morgen, and Novkov, *Security Disarmed*, 3–29.

Tajima-Peña, Renee. "'Más Bebés?': An Investigation of the Sterilization of Mexican-American Women at Los Angeles County-USC Medical Center during the 1960s and 70s." *S&F Online* 11, no. 3 (Summer 2013). http://sfonline.barnard.edu/life-un-ltd-feminism-bioscience-race/mas-bebes-an-investigation-of-the-sterilization

-of-mexican-american-women-at-los-angeles-county-usc-medical-center-during-the-1960s-and-70s.

Tal, Kalí. "The Mind at War: Images of Women in Vietnam Novels by Combat Veterans." *Contemporary Literature* 31, no. 1 (Spring 1990): 76–96.

Tanter, Raymond. "The Relative Impact of U.S. Military Actions on Viet Cong / North Vietnamese Attacks in South Vietnam." D-20150-1-ARPA, Rand Corporation, Santa Monica, California, June 17, 1970.

Terkel, Amanda. "Ban on Women in Combat Is Discriminatory, High-Level Military Panel States." *Huffington Post*. January 14, 2011. http://www.huffingtonpost.com/2011/01/14/women-military-commission-combat_n_809241.html.

Terry, Jennifer. "Significant Injury: War, Medicine, and Empire in Claudia's Case." *Women's Studies Quarterly* 37, nos. 1–2 (Spring/Summer 2009): 200–225.

Tiscareño-Sato, Graciela. *Good Night Captain Mama/Buenas Noches Capitán Mamá*. Hayward, Calif.: Gracefully Global Group, 2013.

Tompkins, Jane P. "Sentimental Power: *Uncle Tom's Cabin* and the Politics of Literary History." In *The New Feminist Criticism: Essays on Women, Literature, and Theory*, edited by Elaine Showalter, 81–104. New York: Pantheon, 1985.

Treviño, Marisa. "Latina Mother Realizes Childhood Dream of Serving Her Country." *Latina Lista*, July 2, 2012. http://latinalista.com/general/marilyn.

Turse, Nick. *The Complex: How the Military Invades Our Everyday Lives*. New York: Metropolitan Books, 2008.

Tyner, James A. *War, Violence, and Population: Making the Body Count*. New York: Guilford Press, 2009.

Valdés, Gina. "Hearts on Fire." In Mariscal, *Aztlán and Viet Nam*, 225–26.

Vásquez, Edith. "Poetry as Survival of and Resistance to Genocide in Lorna Dee Cervantes's *Drive: The Last Quartet*." *Journal of International Women's Studies* 10, no. 4 (May 2009): 290–300.

Vidal, Mirta. *Chicanas Speak Out*. New York: Pathfinder Press, 1971.

Vigil, Ariana E. *War Echoes: Gender and Militarization in U.S. Latina/o Cultural Production*. New Brunswick, N.J.: Rutgers University Press, 2014.

Villa, Raúl Homero. *Barrio-Logos: Space and Place in Urban Chicano Literature and Culture*. Austin: University of Texas Press, 2000.

"Violence Flares at Chiapas Massacre Protest." *BBC News*, January 13, 1998. http://news.bbc.co.uk/2/hi/americas/46599.stm.

White, Katrina. "¿Darles voz?: Chicana Narrative as Reaffirming National Belonging in Stella Pope Duarte's *Let Their Spirits Dance*." Paper 18. National Association for

Chicana and Chicano Studies Annual Conference, Chicago, Illinois, March 15–17, 2012. http://scholarworks.sjsu.edu/naccs/2012/Proceedings/18.

Williams, Kayla, with Michael E. Staub. *Love My Rifle More than You: Young and Female in the U.S. Army*. New York: Norton, 2005.

Woolf, Virginia. *Three Guineas*. 1938. Annotated and with an introduction by Jane Marcus. Orlando, Fla.: Harcourt, 2006. Page references are to the annotated edition.

Women's Revolutionary Law. In Speed, Hernández Castillo, and Stephen, *Dissident Women*, 3–4.

Wright, Melissa W. *Disposable Women and Other Myths of Global Capitalism*. New York: Routledge, 2006.

Ybarra, Lea. "Perceptions of Race and Class Among Chicano Vietnam Veterans." *Vietnam Generation* 1, no. 2 (1989): article 7.

Ybarra, Lea, and Nina Genera. *La batalla está aquí: Chicanos and the War*. Revised ed. El Cerrito, Calif.: Chicano Draft Help, 1972.

Young, Iris Marion. "The Logic of Masculinist Protection: Reflections on the Current Security State." *Signs* 29, no. 1 (2003): 1–25.

Young, Marilyn B. "Counting the Bodies in Vietnam." In *Body and Nation: The Global Realm of U.S. Body Politics in the Twentieth Century*, edited by Emily S. Rosenberg and Shanon Fitzpatrick, 230–40. Durham, N.C.: Duke University Press, 2014.

Zaretsky, Natasha. *No Direction Home: The American Family and the Fear of National Decline, 1968–1980*. Chapel Hill: University of North Carolina Press, 2007.

———. "Private Suffering and Public Strife: Delia Alvarez's War with the Nixon Administration's POW Publicity Campaign, 1968–1973." In *Race, Nation, and Empire in American History*, edited by James T. Campbell, Matthew Pratt Guterl, and Robert G. Lee, 201–28. Chapel Hill: University of North Carolina Press, 2007.

Žižek, Slavoj. *The Sublime Object of Ideology*. 2nd ed. New York: Verso, 2009.

Zucchino, David. "Family Disputes Army's Suicide Finding in Daughter's Death." *Los Angeles Times*, March 8, 2009. http://articles.latimes.com/2009/mar/08/nation/na-women-soldier-suicides8.

Zylberberg Panebianco, Violeta. "'We Can No Longer Be Like Hens with Our Heads Bowed, We Must Raise Our Heads and Look Ahead': A Consideration of the Daily Life of Zapatista Women." In Speed, Hernández Castillo, and Stephen, *Dissident Women*, 222–38.

INDEX

Abu Ghraib prison, 187, 208
Acteal, Chiapas, massacre, 121, 141, 142, 143, 145, 146, 147, 148, 150, 151–52, 248n71, 249n89, 250n106; survivor accounts, 249n94, 249n101, 250n103
Adelita, 35–36, 80, 83–84, 117, 120, 217; "Adelita complex" 235n164
Adelitas de Aztlán, 37, 79–84, 234n149
All-Volunteer Force (AVF), 13, 37, 51–54, 93, 109, 119, 170, 226n35
Alvarez, Delia, 36–37, 73, 75–79, 83, 85, 233n130, 233n131, 234n139
Alvarez, Everett, Jr., 73–76, 78–79, 85
Alvarez, Soledad, 75, 77, 78
antidraft activism, 44, 51, 55, 56, 62, 71, 79–80 93, 211
antiwar aesthetics, 44, 48, 69, 71
Arellanes, Gloria, 80
Aztecs, 138, 161, 188, 190; Aztec warrior myth, 192–93, 199, 260n116
Aztlán, 39, 56, 87, 161, 182–83, 188–90, 195, 197–98, 203–4, 212, 218, 260n116

battlespace, 164, 184
Beautiful Soul, 176, 177, 179, 180
Brown Berets, 80, 225n20
Bustamante, Nao, xv, 39, 212, 214–18, 265n28

Chicana/o Zapatista literature, 15, 17, 121, 123, 242n5
Chicano Moratorium, 37, 42, 59, 80, 84, 225n6
Coatlicue, 200, 201, 263n169
Coyolxauhqui, 200, 201, 202, 203, 263n169

desmadre, 182, 196, 197, 198, 199, 262n149
discipline, processes of, 22, 25–26, 104–6, 112, 116–18, 175, 222n80, 223n81
domestic militarization, 186
draft, 13, 14, 37, 43, 47, 49, 51, 54, 226n34, 227n39, 228n56. *See also* Selective Service

El Plan Espiritual de Aztlán, 56, 188, 189, 196, 197

Friedman, Milton, 13, 51, 54, 58, 92, 93, 226n35, 227n38, 227n45

García, Rupert, xv, 59, 60, 61, 212, 229n70, 264n24
Gates Commission Report, 13, 51, 52, 53, 227n39
Genera, Nina, 36–37, 55–58, 61, 65, 67–69, 73, 78, 83, 229n69, 232n106

Huitzilopotchli, 87, 188, 190, 200, 201, 202, 261n117, 263n167, 263n169

"I am Joaquin: An Epic Poem, 1967," 195–96

Joint Advertising Market Research and Studies (JAMRS), 169, 170, 254n34
Junior Reserve Officer Training Corps (JROTC), 206–7

Latina fertility, 165, 166, 171, 173
Latina soldier-mother, 178, 179, 180, 181

Marcos, Subcomandante, 123, 124, 125, 126, 128, 129, 136, 154, 156, 242n1–2, 251n110
masculinist protectionism, 15, 164, 180, 187, 189, 190, 193, 196, 197, 199, 203–4, 214, 228n64
mater dolorosa, 87, 88, 89, 165
maternal protectionism, 161, 180
McNamara, Robert, 25, 62–64, 76, 228n56
Mexican Revolution, 35–36, 71, 123, 124, 127, 212, 215, 218, 244n22
militarism: definition of, 10–12; 17, 128. *See also* neoliberal militarism; Zapatista feminist militarism
militarization, 3, 12
militarized liberal feminism, 39, 109, 208–12
military advertising, 3, 26, 30, 161, 175; focus on mothers, 167, 168, 170, 176, 177; women in, 4, 27–30, 39, 159–60, 166, 173–75, 176–77
military enlistment, women, 14, 95, 96, 119, 221n40; Latina enlistment, 27
Military Operations on Urbanized Terrain (MOUT), 184, 187, 258n81, 258n83
military recruitment: economic recession 14; use of demographic data, 168–69, 171–73, 193, 261n135
military uniforms, 3, 99, 104–6, 179–81, 215, 239n37
Montoya, Mickiela, 26, 38, 95, 110–19, 214, 240n55

neoliberal ethics, 61–62, 93, 108, 230n81
neoliberalism, 9, 96, 107, 108, 118, 123, 124, 185, 220n22; in Mexico 243n10
neoliberal militarism: 118, 119, 154, 161; 210; definition of, 6, 11, 15; impact on bodies, 23, 26, 95, 110, 152; spatial logic of, 39, 160, 162–63, 183, 203,

204; historical consciousness, 155–56; social disorder, cause of, 199; in Mexico, 15–16. *See also* militarism; Zapatista feminist militarism
neoliberal military, 14, 53, 118, 221n42
Nixon, Richard, 13, 51, 74,77,78, 225n20, 226n35, 233n130, 236n195, 259n91
North American Free Trade Agreement (NAFTA), 16, 120, 123–24

prisoners of war (POWs), 36, 56, 73–78, 233n130; "Go Public" campaign, 74, 77–78; policies toward "quiet diplomacy," 74

Rodriguez, Favianna, xv, 39, 212–14, 215, 216, 217, 218, 265n28

security moms, 165, 177, 178, 179, 204
Selective Service, 209, 210, 264n19. *See also* draft
sexual assault, in the military, 95, 115, 116, 118, 209; depicted in *Peacetime*, 101–2
soldadera, 35–36, 39, 81, 83–84, 127, 133, 235n164, 265n31; depicted in *Peacetime*, 94–95, 101, 108–10, depicted in *Erased Faces*, 123, 158; as antiwar icon, 212, 214–18,

Tiscareño-Sato, Graciela, xv, 39, 161, 179, 256n72, 257n73, 257n75

Woolf, Virginia: *Three Guineas*, 206–8, 210, 212, 263n2

Ybarra, Lea, xv, 36–37, 55–58, 61, 65, 67–69, 73, 78, 83, 228n64, 229n67, 229n69, 232n106

Zapatista feminist militarism, 38, 121, 126–27, 129, 132–35. *See also* militarism; neoliberal militarism
Zapatistas, 16, 38, 120–21, 123–24, 146, 157; namesake, 242n1; women, 124, 125, 126, 127, 128, 129, 130, 245n24; Women's Revolutionary Law, 127, 244n21; views on nonviolence, 245n29–30

ABOUT THE AUTHOR

Belinda Linn Rincón is an assistant professor of Latin American and Latina/o studies and English at John Jay College of Criminal Justice, at the City University of New York. Her work appears in *Latino Studies*, *Women's Studies Quarterly*, and *Modern Fiction Studies*. She is the co-founder and co-organizer of the Biennial U.S. Latina/o Literary Theory and Criticism Conference.